By Mildred Savage

A GREAT FALL

IN VIVO

PARRISH

A GREAT FALL

by Mildred Savage

Simon and Schuster   /   New York

*To my Father
and to Charles Suisman
who was his devoted
attorney and friend*

Contents

Foreword

The largest part of this book is concerned with two trials for murder, both of which I attended as a member of the press. The court proceedings are taken from the official transcripts, with background material from my own notes. In any trial, there is repetition—and some of this repetitious material has been cut or summarized. All courtroom dialogue (except for three identified short speeches) is taken from the official transcript. It has not been altered except for some polishing and cutting, for the sake of comprehension and readability, of repetitious phrases or statements which inevitably occur in extemporaneous speech. Two of the three speeches taken from my own notes occurred at moments of excitement when it was apparently impossible for the court stenographer to record several simultaneous utterances. Out-of-court comments of attorneys, judges, reporters and spectators are taken from my notes.

I wish to acknowledge my debt to several of the principal figures in these trials.

I am grateful to Superior Court Judges, the Honorable Herbert S. MacDonald and the Honorable Douglass B. Wright, for illuminating discussions (after the trials were over) of controversial points and rapidly changing law, and for permission to quote. I owe a debt to Defense Attorneys William B. Shew and John McKeon for information and for permission to quote, and to Mrs. June Shew for extensive reference to notes and documents that she collected while assisting her husband in the preparation of his case. All disclosures of private conversations between the defendant and his lawyers are revealed with his express consent.

I wish to express my gratitude and acknowledge my debt to State's Attorney Thomas F. Wall, who, after the trials were over, permitted me to listen to the tapes of those police interrogations that were in his possession and, in order that I might do so, extended the hospitality of his office for several days. Mr. Wall made these tapes available to me even though he was aware that by the end of the trials he and I had arrived at different conclusions on several points.

I wish to thank Harry Solberg for making available material which was of a confidential nature.

For background information I am grateful to Gerald Demeusy of the Hartford Courant *and to Joseph Crowley, formerly of the Hartford* Times *and presently with WTIC-Radio and TV.*

Events from the day of the murder to the beginning of the first trial were reconstructed from courtroom testimony, official transcripts of the Coroner's Hearings, interviews with attorneys, newspaper articles (especially from the Hartford Courant), *visits to the area and the scene of the crime, and from many interviews with eyewitnesses. Among the latter I am especially grateful to the victim's closest neighbors, the Stadler family, including Dr. and Mrs. Robert Stadler, Mr. and Mrs. Robert Stadler, Jr., Paul Stadler, and the late Mrs. Sadie Mann, mother of Mrs. Robert Stadler, Sr.*

A final word about my own occasional comments on court proceedings. They represent one layman's view of justice. I am aware that many lawyers will take exception to some of my opinions. In private conversation some (happily, not all) have already done so. Their position has been, "This is the Law. These are the rules of the game." In many of these debates, it seemed to come down, in the end, to a question of Justice vs. Jurisprudence and my comments have been on the side of what appeared to me to be justice. And where there are no pat answers, I have tried at least to ask the questions.

M.S.

"A criminal trial is not a game in which the State's function is to outwit and entrap its quarry. The State's pursuit is justice, not a victim. . . ."

James V. Giles *et al.* *v.* State of Maryland (Supreme Court of the United States) 386 US 66. February 20, 1967

PART
ONE

THE
CRIME

I

Litchfield County lies in the northwest corner of Connecticut, a ragged-edged square on the map. It is an untouched part of the state, dotted with forests, lakes, and large reservoirs, with small towns and smaller villages, with acres of open land—stretching flat for miles, rising into the famed Litchfield Hills, falling away again to flatlands and forests and lakes.

In Litchfield there are no large urban centers as in Hartford County to the east, no clusters of commuters as in Fairfield County to the south, no transient population as in coastal New London County. Litchfield remains intact, traditional, tucked into its hills. Four-lane highways do not intrude. Large defense industries have not come here, bringing strangers with new attitudes and new ideas. In many towns supermarkets have not replaced the general store. A county of little towns—little clusters of towns—tight-knit little groups. There is good fishing, good hunting in the woods, skiing in the hills. When it snows the men turn out to hunt wildcat. In June the black flies are fierce.

The political allegiance is Republican, and men with long memories will tell you that a generation ago Litchfield County ran the state. "We used to say you should get a passport to cross over into Litchfield County," they will tell you. And, "During Prohibition you could always get a drink in Litchfield. 'Have a drink,' they'd say. And if you said, 'Do we go downstairs?' they'd say, 'Have it right here. Hell, you're in Litchfield!'"

The political power is gone, but shades of the attitude linger.

The town of Barkhamsted, at the eastern edge of Litchfield County, and the town of Hartland, at the western edge of Hartford County, are part of the same little town-cluster, in spite of the county line that separates them, and socially the one spills over into the other.

To get there you turn off Interstate Route 91 north of Hartford at the Bradley Field exit (the Hartford Air Terminal). Driving west on Route 20, after a few miles you leave the airport behind and with it the flavor of modern industry and commerce. The road narrows to two lanes, you move into Connecticut tobacco country with its tented fields and slatted sheds, and then on through the town of Granby (carefully preserved old colonial homes, the land between them filling in with newer houses, small, neat) and out to farm country again. On one side the land falls away to a narrow river. On the other, white birches lean out of the woods. In the distance the hills begin and you are nearing Litchfield County.

Then you are in the village of East Hartland. You know you are there when you reach Hayes' General Store, a neat red-brick and white-clapboard building with a gasoline pump in front. This is the Center. The other public structure at the Center is the Community Church (Congregational), white, spired, a faithful example of the white, spired Congregational Church found in every old New England town.

The only other church in East Hartland is the Bethany Lutheran Church—the Norwegian Church—a strict fundamentalist sect that prohibits smoking, drinking, dancing. The two churches represent the population of the town. The Yankees have been there longer; the Norwegians outnumber them. The two groups do not mix much, not so much from snobbery as from a lack of common interests and mores. For the Yankees the social center is the firehouse. For the Norwegians, a thrifty hard-working people engaged mostly in the building trades, it is the Bethany Lutheran Church.

The center of communication between the two groups is Hayes' Store, where, without much coaxing, a visitor can learn who is quality and who is trash, who is legitimate and who is not, who is playing with whom, and why. In small towns there are no secrets.

Leave Hayes' Store and turn south onto Route 179 and you pass, in quick succession, the small brick-and-board post office, the firehouse, the school, and a row of small neat houses. That is all of East Hartland and the last of Hartford County.

A mile or so down the road (you are not sure when) you cross into the town of Barkhamsted and you are in Litchfield County. Route 179 goes on—the traffic is light—the fields and woods go on, a house shows up every few hundred yards, perhaps every quarter of a mile. This is quiet, peaceful country, the pace is slow, the pattern of life is uncomplicated.

About two miles from the Center, on the west side of Route 179, is the home of Robert Stadler, Jr., and his wife, Carole. Directly across the road is the house owned by Arnfin Thompsen. On Tuesday morning, June 15, 1965, at 9:30, Randy Stadler, aged three and a half, went across the street to play with Christa Thompsen, aged two and a half. Dorothy Thompsen, Christa's mother, opened the front door to admit him, and the children played indoors until 11:45, when Randy went home. Except for Christa, and except for the murderer, the little boy was probably the last person to see Dorothy Thompsen alive. Sometime around midday, she was murdered. Nobody, not even Carole Stadler, who was home all day, saw a disturbance. Nobody heard a sound.

But the silent death of this ordinary young housewife in this sleepy village, far removed from the mainstream of politics and of power, was to prove to be a time bomb. The delayed explosion reached far from Barkhamsted, touching the careers of men in high places who had never heard of Dorothy Thompsen, and stirring up angry issues that had probably never been discussed at the firehouse or the Bethany Church or Hayes' Store.

◆

For Arnfin Thompsen, aged thirty-two, a slender man of medium height with pale complexion and black hair, that Tuesday morning began much as any other weekday began for him. An accountant and bookkeeper at the Carpenter Brick Company in South Windsor, about thirty miles away, Arnfin was due at work at 8:30. When he arose at seven o'clock, Dottie and Christa were already up and coffee was ready. Arnfin took his usual breakfast of toast and coffee and settled down with it in the living room. Outside a gray, overcast day was getting started.

This was a small house—a white-board and gray-brick Cape Cod cottage with the living room on the right, running front to back, the kitchen rear-center, and a bedroom wing on the left—two bedrooms and a bath. Upstairs another two rooms and bath, occupied at that time by his widowed mother, Agnes. No stranger to construction (the Norwegians in this area are famous as specialists in laying wood floors, and Arnfin had worked at this trade prior to studying bookkeeping and accounting), Arnfin had done most of the work on the house himself—was, in fact, still building it. There were a few more kitchen cabinets to hang; the steps to the second floor had not been varnished. Only this past weekend he had worked on the back porch.

When Arnfin and Dottie were first married they had rented a small cottage from Thorbjorn "Tobey" Solberg, the local plumbing and heating contractor. The cottage was behind Tobey's own house, and the Solbergs and the Thompsens became close friends. When Arnfin built his own home, Tobey installed the heating and plumbing, and Arnfin hired Tobey's son, Harry, a high-school student, to help with the framing. The rest he had done alone.

From his living room, if Arnfin looked that morning, he could see, through the sliding glass doors of the dining area, the unfinished back porch. He had laid the floor and set posts for a rail, which on this porch was essential. The land behind the house sloped down so that the porch, although level with the dining area, was eight feet off the ground. Over part of the porch, the second floor overhang formed a roof, and in a sheltered corner were Arnfin's tools where he had left them on Sunday—a claw hammer, a sledgehammer, a screwdriver, a nail set (shaped like a steel spike) for driving nails into the floor without marring the surface. Although it stayed light late these days, Arnfin had not worked on the porch last evening. He had not returned home until after eleven o'clock.

After a few minutes Dottie joined Arnfin for coffee—a quiet, nervous girl, tall and very thin (5 feet 6 inches, 115 pounds) with black hair and red-framed eyeglasses. Dorothy Burdick had grown up in New Hartford, the next town south of Barkhamsted, where her family ran an orchard. When she was graduated from high school—the Gilbert School in Winsted, which serves several small towns in the area—Dorothy was a quiet, pretty girl with black curly hair and a vivacious smile. After high school she worked in the bank in New Hartford, the Riverside Trust Company, and played the organ at the local Lutheran Church. When she married Arnfin in 1959 she continued to work in the bank until a few months before Christa was born on Christmas Eve, 1962.

Now, at thirty, Dorothy was still a quiet girl, devoted to Christa and unusually close to her own mother, whom she telephoned three times a day. Although she had a car she rarely went anywhere except to Hayes' Store or to visit her mother. To her neighbor, Carole Stadler, Dorothy talked mostly about Christa, a bright pretty child with brown eyes and light-brown hair, the image of Arnfin. To other neighbors she seemed friendly but nervous, "apprehensive— as though she had a reason to look back over her shoulder." There are those who believe the reason may have been Agnes.

Agnes Thompsen had had a disturbing history. She was a woman who had worked hard all her life, who had raised her two sons, Arnfin and Theodore, alone, who had always done heavy jobs around her own home, and she was still a very strong woman physically. The same could not be said of Agnes's mental condition. She had come to Arnfin's house the past December after having spent ten months at the Connecticut Valley Hospital in Middletown, a state institution for the mentally ill. Even now she was only home on probation to determine whether she could adjust to the outside world—a world in which Agnes's prime interest was religion.

The Bethany Lutheran Church in East Hartland is a strict fundamentalist church that emphasizes the Word of God and preaches the dominance of the Will of God over everything on Heaven and Earth. "We must hear God speaking if we are to worship. . . . The Bible is inspired and free from error, and is therefore the final and authoritative guide for faith and conduct." In church literature there are references to Man falling into sin through the temptation of Satan, and to the struggle between Salvation and Corruption in the souls of men. It speaks of the casting out of Demons and of the establishment of the Kingdom of Heaven. Agnes Thompsen was more than a devout and faithful member of this church. She was a religious fanatic.

As her mind failed, she experienced religious hallucinations and delusions, and a parallel can be found between them and church teachings, which she seems to have accepted absolutely literally.

She believed that God spoke to her. She spoke of a pressure in her head which she attributed to the presence of the Devil. She believed that God and the Devil were waging a battle in her head. One day, to let the Devil out, she took a knife to her own legs. In February, 1964, it had become necessary to commit Agnes to the Connecticut Valley Hospital.

The hospital report of February, 1964, attests to her extreme religious beliefs: "She talks about spirits touching her fingers and head. She said, 'Satan will be thrown to the lake, then the revelation will come and the world will end.' She talks about ghosts and experiences tactile hallucinations." In the hospital Agnes was agitated, restless, and demanding. Her one thought was to get out. For hours she would stare at the door through which she might leave the ward and the hospital and go home.

For several months Agnes Thompsen's condition does not appear to have changed a great deal. Then, gradually, she began to improve and she was allowed to go home on visits, which were reported to be increasingly successful. "Her son claimed she was greatly improved," a hospital doctor said later, "and expressed a desire to have her return home, feeling that she could make a satisfactory adjustment." On December 22, when seen by her doctor, she was overexcited and talkative, but there was no evidence of delusions or hallucinations. It was decided that she might try an extended visit home.

But she could not be permitted to live alone, and Arnfin, again with the help of Tobey and Harry Solberg, converted the upper floor of his house into a separate apartment—two rooms, a bath, a prefabricated kitchen. On December 26, 1964, Agnes came home.

For a few months she was fine. She took care of herself and her apartment and even found employment three days a week doing housework. But in late spring Agnes began to fail again. She became increasingly nervous. Two of her daywork employers let her go. The third persevered a little longer and then, a day or two before that Tuesday morning of June 15, laid her off for a month. Agnes complained again of the pressure in her head.

And so, besides his house and certain financial problems, Arnfin probably had his mother on his mind that Tuesday morning. And—it was to turn out—still more.

He finished his coffee, went to the bedroom to dress, came back for another cup of coffee, engaged in ordinary family conversation. Christa asked if he would be home after work that night, and Arnfin said that he would. Dorothy asked him not to be late—she was planning to cook a roast. Arnfin agreed. He left for work, walking through the small front hall past the steps to Agnes's apartment, and went out the front door—the only possible exit. (The other doors were the glass sliding doors leading to the back porch, eight feet above the ground, and, underneath the porch, a walk-in cellar door.)

He backed out his car, a white '62 Corvair, and drove north on Route 179 to East Hartland Center. At Hayes' Store he turned and drove east to Interstate 91 and then south to the Carpenter Brick Company.

◆

By queer twists of fate the paths of certain lives seem to cross again and again, neither by desire nor by design of either party, but in a way that suggests a strange predestination. Carole Stadler and Dorothy Thompsen did not have a great deal in common. Carole, a small, healthy-looking girl with brownish blonde hair, was more of an extrovert. Dorothy was thin, nervous, withdrawn. When they got together, as they did two or three afternoons a week, they didn't actually have a great deal to talk about. Mostly, Carole recalls, Dottie talked about Christa. And sometimes about Agnes. As girls, they had lived in different towns—Carole in East Hartland, Dorothy in New Hartford. At the Gilbert High School they were classmates but not close friends. Probably Carole never felt so much involved with Dorothy Thompsen while she lived as she has felt since Dorothy died. And yet it was Carole who introduced her to Arnfin.

"It was in 1956," Carole recalled later. "In the Pizza House in Avon. Arnfin was there with a bowling team, and Dorothy and a girl friend came in and I introduced them around. That's how Arnfin met Dottie."

Then, only two months before that day in June, Bob and Carole Stadler moved into this house, just up the road from Bob's parents,

Dr. Robert Stadler, a veterinarian, and Eunice, an executive at G. Fox & Company in Hartford.

Now Carole was the first to hear from Arnfin that Dorothy was dead.

Carole Stadler worked that entire day in her front yard. Her older son was in school, and she came out at 9:30, when Randy crossed the road to play with Christa. "It was cold that day—overcast," she said later. "I remember I had a jacket on outside." She worked on the lawn and planted petunias and marigolds.

At quarter to twelve Randy came home because Christa and her mother were about to eat lunch. This was a regular arrangement. Randy played with Christa in the morning, and when they were ready to eat—always at quarter to twelve—Dorothy would send him home. That day Randy stayed home for a few minutes and then walked down the road a few hundred yards south to his grandfather's house. Carole watched him go and continued planting.

At 1:05 she went into the house for a sandwich. From her kitchen it is possible to see the Thompsen house through the front windows and through a large dining room window on the south side of the house. Depending on what she was doing, Carole might—or might not—have noticed a caller across the street.

At 1:25 she came outside again and walked down the road to collect Randy, who by now had trotted off to play with the little boy who lived directly across the street from his grandfather. At the Dr. Stadler home, only Eunice Stadler's mother, Mrs. Mann, was home and Carole sat down for a cup of coffee with her. Through a window she saw the patrolman for the Metropolitan Water District drive past, headed south, and she remarked, just to make conversation, "There goes the water board cop." At 2:30, after spending an hour with Mrs. Mann, she collected Randy and walked home. As she passed the Thompsen house, Carole glanced over. Through the bay window she could see through the living room to the sliding glass doors at the rear. She saw no one.

She went into her own house to prepare dinner (corned beef hash), then decided to grind some vegetables and walked back to her mother-in-law's at 2:45 to use the vegetable grinder, returning home at 3:00. Preparations for dinner behind her, Carole worked outdoors for the rest of the afternoon. Late in the day a breeze pushed off the low clouds and the sun shone. No sound came from the Thompsen home. No one went in or came out.

At about five o'clock Bob Stadler, a quick wiry young man, came home and they went inside, and at a little before six, the family sat down to dinner, Carole facing the highway, Bob with his back to it. Carole was hurrying tonight—she was going out—and when she finished her own dinner she carried her dishes into the kitchen. "I looked at the clock," she recalled later, "and saw that it was six ten and I said, 'I've got to be going.' I put down the dishes, looked up and there was Arnfin, running up our driveway. When I first saw him I thought the house was on fire. He burst through the kitchen door—he was pale, ashen green—just something you never see. His voice was shaking so he could hardly talk."

When he did speak, the words ran together so that Carole could hardly understand him. He mumbled, "Where is Christa? I can't find Christa . . . Dottie is in the back . . . off the back porch . . . I think she is dead . . . I can't find the baby."

Bob hurried into the kitchen. Carole asked whether Arnfin had called the police, said she would do it, and Bob and Arnfin rushed back to the Thompsen house. Hastily Carole sent her two sons to Dr. Stadler's house, watching them walk down the road while she telephoned the Canaan Barracks of the State Police. She telephoned Mrs. Mann to keep the boys with her and made a third telephone call—to Arnfin's brother, Ted. Then she went across the street.

• • •

"I didn't hear him say she was dead," Bob Stadler said later. "I thought the baby was missing and Dottie was in the back yard looking for her."

Even in ordinary conversation Arnfin Thompsen speaks in a very soft voice. Later Carole said, "He speaks very unplainly, he speaks low. You really have to listen hard when he talks. That night his words seemed to run together." Carole, standing very close, had barely heard him. Bob, several feet away in the dining room, had caught only snatches.

"I rushed back with him. He ran into the house, still looking for Christa. And I rushed around to the back of the house."

Thus, totally unprepared for what he found, Bob Stadler came upon Dorothy Thompsen, lying on the ground under the edge of the back porch, dead.

"Her body was lying right at the back porch," Bob testified later. "Where the back porch ends there is about, maybe, a ten-foot drop to the ground, and she was lying directly under that edge of the porch."

Frozen with shock, Bob Stadler stared down at the almost unrecognizable face of the woman he had expected to find alive, searching for her lost child. Dorothy was lying on her back, one arm flung out, the other crooked across her chest. One look told him that she had been the victim of a vicious, frenzied attack. Her face and head were crushed, the jaw appeared to be broken, the left temple was smashed in. Her face was heavily caked with blood, especially above the mouth, all the way into her hair. There were stab marks at her throat. Knotted around her neck was an electric cord pulled tight enough to strangle.

For at least a full minute, possibly longer, Bob Stadler stood there, unable to move. "I've seen quite a few dead people," he said later. "This was the first time I was really upset. It bothered me for about a year." Then a sudden irrational reaction swept over him. "I took a look at her—I took a look around, and I thought, 'This is no place for me!'"

He raced back to the front door and found Arnfin in the entrance hall, standing at the foot of the stairs to Agnes's apartment. Arnfin offered the information that he had found Christa, giving no details. Then suddenly, upstairs the door opened and Agnes Thompsen stood at the top of the steps and said, "Is she dead yet?"

Although he felt the question was directed to him, Bob made no reply and Agnes closed the door. Arnfin, mumbling that he needed a drink—"a shot"—headed for the kitchen, and Bob, a step behind him, stopped abruptly in the doorway. The kitchen was covered with blood. There was blood spilled across the floor, blood spattered on the walls, blood smeared on the cabinets.

Arnfin took a glass from a cabinet next to the sink, wandered across the bloody floor to get a bottle from another cabinet next to the refrigerator, poured himself a stiff drink and went into the living room.

For another minute, Bob Stadler lingered inside and then, drawn by that which he had fled, he returned to the back yard. Again he saw the details of the injuries. He saw a pile of rocks just under the porch beside the body. He saw that Dorothy's clothing—blue slacks and black and white fishnet-design blouse—appeared to be undisturbed. "Then I saw Arnfin carrying what looked like a red blanket," he said later. "I saw it through the sliding door in the dining room. So I went back into the house and asked if he was going to cover her up, and he said, 'Yes,' and I told him I would do it for him."

When Bob returned again to the living room, Carole had arrived and the three of them—Arnfin, Carole, and Bob—sat and waited for the police. "While I was sitting there," Bob went on, "I noticed the blood on the curtain by the sliding doors, so I went into the dining room to look and Arnfin came with me. It looked like she had been murdered in the kitchen and dragged through the dining room and out onto the porch. On the kitchen floor there was a big pool of blood, and then there was a single path of blood—maybe ten or twelve inches wide—like something had been dragged from the kitchen out through the dining room and across the porch."

In the middle of the pool of blood on the kitchen floor was an ordinary table fork, bent out of shape; on the floor in front of the stove, a two-pronged meat fork. Just at the entrance to the dining room lay Dorothy's red-rimmed eyeglasses. In a corner of the dining area the ironing board stood in the place where Dottie usually ironed; on it a partially pressed white shirt, spattered with blood. The trail of blood angled past it to the sliding glass doors which were open, one behind the other, and continued across the porch, ending near the middle rail post in another pool of blood. At the very edge of the porch just above Dorothy's body was a steel nail set, upright, struck into the floor. Knotted around it was a short stub of electric cord that resembled the cord around Dorothy's neck.

Arnfin and the Stadlers returned to the living room and sat down. A few minutes later the first State Police officer arrived.

•   •   •

Trooper Enrico Soliani, a stocky, dark-haired young man, was about five miles away when the call came over his radio. Beacon flashing, he made his way to the Thompsen house, the first officer to arrive at the scene.

Concerning his first actions there is a small and unimportant discrepancy in testimony—one of many before the case was over.

Soliani testified that he went directly into the house, found Arnfin sitting on the living room sofa with a glass in his hand, followed the trail of blood to the back porch and looked down at the covered body. Bob Stadler testified that he took him around back to the body and Soliani lifted the red blanket and looked at it.

At any rate, after determining that there was a body, Soliani had to report. He picked up the telephone to call the barracks, remembered he shouldn't touch anything, put it down, took out his handkerchief and picked it up again. He reported the murder, returned to the living room and ordered everyone out of the house. On the front step, Carole turned back to tell Soliani that there were two more people in the house. She had learned from Arnfin that Christa was with his mother which, considering Agnes's condition, did not seem wise. Soliani told Carole to go up and get them. Carole refused. (Paul Stadler, Bob's brother, a student at Springfield College, who had arrived by now, quoted Carole as saying, "You're kidding me!")

"For a minute Carole and Soliani just looked at each other," Paul said later. "Then Soliani went upstairs and told Agnes to bring down the baby. When Agnes came down she was talking incessantly, squeezing the baby. She talked about a green car, a black car, a man in work clothes, about having to take care of her flowers in the front yard. I was standing in a patch of shrubs under the bay window trying to look inside, and she told me not to walk on her flowers."

Carole, speaking later of Agnes and of that night, said, "She was a short stocky woman with a very nice complexion and big, round baby-blue eyes. I always thought she was a very sweet person—I told Dottie that—even though I felt a little funny having an insane person living next door. I used to talk to her. But that night she didn't know me! She seemed very nervous. She said she had heard a couple of knocks and had seen a man in a big green car."

Downstairs Christa remained in her grandmother's arms, but when she saw Carole Stadler, she cried out, "She killed—she killed—"

After a moment, Arnfin took Christa from his mother, and Carole took the baby across the street to her own home, leaving Arnfin sitting on the front stoop, a drink in his hand, his mother beside him. He was still sitting there when other police officers began to arrive. First, Sergeant Joseph Riley of the Canaan Barracks; then, in rapid succession, three men who were to play important roles in the case—Trooper Gerald Pennington, a tall lean man who lived nearby, at 7:05; Detective Fred Rebillard of the Canaan Barracks at 7:13; Lieutenant Cleveland Fuessenich, Commanding Officer at Canaan, at 7:17. Then more men from Canaan and more still from the Detective Division in Hartford. Reporters raced to the scene. Neighbors, relatives, friends, passersby—the concerned and the curious—began to fill the yard, the street, the house across the street. They came and they stayed for a long, confused chaotic night.

2

"Every investigation is different," a veteran detective has said of murder cases, "but some procedures are standard. You get to the scene, the body is there, you have many things to do. You get to the hottest information first. At the start you ask, 'What do we have? Who found the body?' You talk first to the person who found the body. You start with him. In the back of your mind everyone is a suspect—they have to be eliminated.

"Every cop is tense—he doesn't want to make a mistake. Especially in this, the worst kind of crime, the killing of a human being. Every cop is alert—the murderer might still be on the premises. Every cop is suspicious—he doesn't want to let anyone slip through. You wait for the specialists—the photographers, medical examiner, fingerprint men. Meanwhile everyone pours men in to help you. You have to stop them at the perimeter so they don't hurt you, trample on the evidence, disturb things.

"You start from the center to find the evidence, and you go where this leads you. You send your men out and you call them back. At first you don't know what you're looking for. You just keep looking. You keep going as long as you have to, but there is a certain stage at which you stop. Certain things will keep well. You put it to bed. Your mind will be clear in the morning."

• • •

"You start from the center to find the evidence, and you go where this leads you."

In the kitchen the blood told part of the story. The heaviest concentration of blood was the pool on the floor near the counter next to the sink. At the center, the blood was still moist; around the

County. Then I asked if they wanted me to carry on and
Go ahead.'"

ck yard the house blocked a long shadow over Dorothy's
. Murphy bent down to examine it. "The body was lying
t black hair, very mussed up, blood all over the scalp
ck mass of blood that had taken quite a while to cake,
ven or eight hours. The right eye was semi-open—the lid
there was a lot of hemorrhage-clotted blood over it. I
pe it off—it just caked over, that heavy blood. There was
around the neck and on just the upper part of the blouse.
breast down there was very little, if any—I couldn't see

ft temple, there were two ragged deep lacerations about
wide. Dr. Murphy explored them with his hand. "I felt
l fragments of bone in that area. That is, when you feel
like a lot of sand, rough stone. That's what we call
l—where the bone is broken many times. It gives you a
ravel at the end of your fingers. There was only a small
hickened blood around the wound. Over the top of the
ck of the head there was considerable blood in the hair."
hy forced open the right eye. "The eye was drawn way
head; there was no hemorrhage on the white of the eye."
pen the other eye and found it the same.

e around her neck had been twisted many times. It
ough it had been garroted to choke. An ordinary fork—
le fork—lay nearby on the ground, about ten inches
this twisted wire around her neck. I assume that during
force of the body hitting the ground—it disentangled
it stayed about ten inches away.

as blood all over her face and a lot of blood in her
Dorothy's throat were stab marks from a four-pronged
n her back, two sets of deeper wounds made by the two-
k. "On the left hand there was a trickle of caked blood.
stwatch was still running and showed the correct time.
watch was smeared with blackened blood—old blood."
hy concluded that Dorothy had actually been killed by
vs on the head—at least two—that she had died of
ctures of the skull. "The impressions made by these

edges it had dried. Hours had passed since this blood had been spilled—enough hours for it to cake where it had run thin; not enough for it to dry where it had spilled out, thick, onto the floor. Clearly etched in this heavy pool was a mesh print that matched the fishnet design of Dorothy's blouse. And also in the blood, even at the narrowest points, were shoeprints—in the pool of blood and in the trail that traced as clearly as a map the course the murderer had followed, from kitchen to dining room to porch. There was blood on the cabinet, blood on the telephone and on the table next to the telephone, blood spattered on the refrigerator and on the stove across the room.

On the floor were the two forks—the four-pronged table fork and the larger two-pronged meat fork—both bent out of shape. In the dish drain beside the sink there were dishes. Had Dorothy then been killed after lunch? On the ironing board, beside Arnfin's shirt, the iron was standing on end. Somebody touched it and found that it was hot. Then she had been ironing and had been interrupted. Unpressed clothing was piled on a chair nearby. No pressed articles —she had not been ironing long.

And so a picture began to form of Dorothy finishing lunch, washing the dishes, starting to iron—and then interrupted and killed.

Lieutenant Cleveland Fuessenich is a medium-tall, husky man in his forties, whose voice can be deceptively mild one minute and clipped and driving the next. When he entered the house he was directed to the kitchen and then out to the porch.

A police officer does not see a body as a doctor does, nor as a friend does. "She had a lot of blood on her head," he testified. "Her arms had dried blood on them. There was dry blood on an Ace-type bandage wrapped around her waist. Her blouse had been pulled up revealing this bandage. Her slacks were heavily coated with blood on the front. She had shoes on, no stockings, and there was some blood on the toes of her shoes. The zipper on her slacks had been pulled down so that the slacks were open but they were still buttoned at the top. She had underpants on which did not appear to have been disturbed."

Lieutenant Fuessenich saw the cord around the neck, "very tightly drawn, two half-hitches," saw that it matched the cord attached to the nail set and that it also matched a bit of cord still attached to a pink toaster lying on the ground, six feet from the body. Near the body was a six-foot aluminum stepladder, standing upright, just at the edge of the porch. Had the murderer used it—to climb up to enter the house? To go down again?

Underneath the porch was a pile of small rocks. Beside the body was a single rock, cone-shaped, about eight inches in diameter and ten inches high. Under the rock was a pink kitchen sponge, soaked with blood. There was blood on the rock.

A short time later, Captain Thomas O'Brien, a ruddy-faced man with graying hair, field captain of the western division of the Connecticut State Police, arrived. From this point on it is uncertain who, for the next six days, was technically in charge of the investigation, Fuessenich or O'Brien.

"You talk first to the person who found the body. You start with him."

Detective Fred Rebillard is of medium height, about five feet seven, with dark hair and eyes, a serious, good-looking man who speaks in a low monotone. He arrived at the scene early, remained throughout the entire evening, and participated in the investigation, although at the trial he gave few details. He did acknowledge that he is the man who interviewed Arnfin.

Meanwhile, upstairs, Trooper Gerald Pennington was having his troubles trying to talk to Agnes Thompsen. Soon after his arrival, he was told to take Agnes upstairs to question her, but Agnes was nervous and jumpy, speaking rapidly, with a heavy Norwegian accent. Pennington was having difficulty simply getting the names of the people who lived in the house.

During the evening, Agnes talked to several officers—to Pennington, to Captain O'Brien, to Policewoman Virginia Butler, who was summoned to sit with her. By the end of the long night, Agnes had told this story: That she heard two hard bangs in the kitchen. In the kitchen and out on the porch. That she looked out the rear window

of her bedroom (which forms porch) and saw a man on the p ing something down to the gro downstairs to investigate the I Dorothy's brother. She also sa because Dottie had company, crocheting, and that, from the s had seen a car in the driveway— car.

But in spite of her condition man lowering something off the something to think about. *"Every to let anyone slip through."*

Late in the evening an officer i Agnes's apartment appeared to Questioned about this, Agnes to sanded the stairs to remove a coming. These stairs were unfini harmful. She had gone downsta o'clock. But otherwise she had rei

• • •

Dr. Owen Murphy has been pract and for thirty-three of them he h towns in Hartford County—Sims Hartland. He is a spry, energetic and bright blue eyes behind round he sits, he leans forward and a Something of a legend around Si Rockwell painting of the old family his patients, and part of every day throughout the area. He was at a when a call came from the State murder on Route 179.

Arriving at the Thompsen house ized that he had crossed over into must have been called in error becau county line. "There were six or s arrived," he recalls. "They were c

Litchfield they said, In the body as 1 face up. area, a b probably open—an couldn't some bla From th any bloc On th two inc commin down, i commin feeling amount skull an Dr. N back in He fore "The looked a silve away f the fal the for "Th mouth table : prong A sm: Most Dr. terrifi multi blows seemed to be uniform. They were made by a rounded, blunt instrument probably one-and-a-half to two inches wide."

From the Stadler home Dr. Murphy telephoned the Hartford Hospital to order an autopsy and then returned to the Thompsen house where he spent a few minutes downstairs observing the bloody scene. Then he turned his thoughts to Agnes Thompsen.

About two years had passed since Dr. Murphy had been summoned one Sunday afternoon to Agnes Thompsen's home in East Hartland. At that time Agnes was already failing mentally, experiencing auditory hallucinations. "All at once she'd say, 'Do you hear that?' Well, I went along with her and I said, 'Yes, I do. I hear it, Mrs. Thompsen. Plain.' She said God ordered her to do this and that—and God everything—and she lived with God. Then she said, 'You know, last night I killed the devil with a butcher knife.'"

Because her sons were reluctant to send her to a mental institution, Dr. Murphy suggested that Sunday afternoon that they take her first to a hospital in Hartford and then, if necessary, have her transferred from there to a mental hospital, which in the end they did.

Now, in Arnfin's house, Dr. Murphy climbed the stairs to see Agnes Thompsen once again. "When I came into the room she was very pleased to see me," he testified later. "She was very effusive, full of joy and happiness—really ebullient with joy—and she said, 'Dr. Murphy, I am awful glad to see you.' I think she was in a grandiose state of mind, stimulated by some action of religious origin between her and her Maker, and she was kind of subconsciously looking for a reward—she had rendered some service. That's the attitude I felt. Her condition was of a manic type—rapid thinking, rapid flow of words—but she was quite confused.

"I said, 'Have you seen the body?' She said, 'Yes.' I said, 'Have you been downstairs?' She said, 'Yes, I know all about it.' Then she said that she heard two noises downstairs and a big man drove away. I said, 'Was it a big man, little man? Thin man, fat man? Was he dark?' She said, 'Yes, yes' to everything."

Dr. Murphy stayed with Agnes for about fifteen minutes. When he reached home he telephoned the Hartford Hospital to confirm his autopsy order and was told that it had been cancelled. Someone in authority had decided that the body would be sent to the Charlotte Hungerford Hospital in Torrington.

• • •

Dusk began to settle over the hills and thread into the nearby woods. By now Arnfin's brother, Ted, had arrived and Dorothy's brother, Paul Burdick. Ted's wife, Karen, came and left, taking Christa with her, and Carole Stadler came back across the street. Eunice Stadler, Bob's mother, found a white shoelace in the driveway with blood on it, "a short shoelace—it could have been a child's." Paul Stadler counted fifteen police cars, fifteen detectives in plain clothes and five or six police in uniform.

Although robbery did not appear to be the motive—the house had not been ransacked, money in Dorothy's purse had not been touched—Arnfin was asked to go into his house to see if anything was missing. He did so. And at that hour, just as it was growing dark, he introduced into the case what was to become the single most troublesome detail. Christa's pink plastic piggy bank was gone.

◆

At eight o'clock the photographers, Sergeant Riley from Canaan and Sergeant Richard Chapman from the Detective Division in Hartford, began the task of recording on film the details of the scene and of the body.

Inside—in the kitchen. The pool of blood with the fishnet print in it and the footprints and the two forks. And the blood on the walls and cabinet and counter and on the telephone and the refrigerator and the stove. And, too, the ordinary signs of daily life—a can of Chase and Sanborn coffee, the dish drain with dishes on edge and a saucepan. On the windowsill two pairs of baby shoes. A washer, a dryer.

The dining room. A baby's high chair, a small round rug, the edge caught up and turned back. The ironing board with the blood-spotted shirt and the iron standing on end. In the background, the glass doors and the blood-spotted curtains. Clothes draped over a laundry rack. The pile of unpressed clothes on the chair. And a cabinet with a plant.

On the back porch—with its posts and no rail and Arnfin's tools in a corner. The trail of blood across it. At the center post, where the nail set was hammered into the floor, another pool of blood, and in it another print of Dorothy's fishnet blouse.

Outside—the body. Photographed as it was discovered, with the cord around the neck. Then turned on a side to reveal the back. The pile of rocks under the porch, the single rock on the other side of the body, the ladder, the toaster, the silver table fork. And a garden hose nearby. And a chair in which Dorothy might have sat in the sun.

• • •

Hayes' General Store is a large, attractive store, well-run and well-stocked. Included on its shelves is a special section of Norwegian delicacies—reindeer meatballs, *Fiskekaker* (fish cakes), Norwegian fruit desserts, *Frukt kompott* (fruit compote), and *Sviske kompott* (apricot-prune).

Russ Hayes' father ran the store before him and lived, too, in the white rambling house next to it. Russ, a stocky cheerful man with a bald head and a belly, opens the store at 7:30 in the morning and doesn't close until 8:00 at night. It is generally conceded in East Hartland that if you want to know anything, you go to the store and ask Polly Hayes. A peppy, wiry woman with eyes bright as a sparrow's, a cigarette-smoking, beer-drinking, slacks-wearing woman, Polly Hayes hears all, knows all, and expresses her opinions in succinct language laced with mild profanity.

On the evening of June 15, Polly Hayes had the misfortune to go bowling, which kept her from hearing the news until at least a full hour later than she might have. Russ was in Hartford and when Polly returned from bowling, the store was full of people, asking what all the cars were doing in front of the Thompsens'. Polly didn't know. At eight o'clock she went home and the telephone rang and a friend, Shirley Williams, told her the news. At once Polly thought of Agnes. "Everyone thought of Agnes," Polly said later. But Shirley Williams had a problem. Near the Thompsen house that day she had seen a car that she thought belonged to the son of a friend. Should she give this information to the police?

It was late before Russ and Polly joined the still-swelling crowd outside the Thompsen house. Cars filled the driveway and hemmed the road and crowded into the Stadlers' driveway across the street, spilling over onto their freshly seeded lawn. Inside the Thompsen house all the lights were on, upstairs and downstairs. Outside, people who, like Polly, had thought of Agnes, were saying, "He never should have had her there. She should go back to the hospital. That's where she belongs."

But Polly knew they hadn't always said that. "Those Norwegians are a tight clan," Polly said later. "There were so many on that poor guy and girl's back. 'Bring her home, bring her home,' they kept saying. As though it was their business. But they kept saying it. 'Bring her home.' "

• • •

Tobey Solberg is a shy, gentle man who has won the affection and respect of his adopted community in his adopted country. As a young man Tobey came to the United States from Norway and gravitated to a community of his compatriots in Brooklyn, New York, where he married his wife, Solveig, an American-born Danish girl. When their oldest child, Harry, was two years old, they moved to East Hartland, joining a small Norwegian community already established there. Now the Norwegian community had mushroomed, Harry was nineteen and about to be graduated from Gilbert High School, and Tobey had prospered modestly as a heating and plumbing contractor. A quiet, patient man, Tobey would take his sons fishing, and in the summers they would help him with his work, but on the whole he left the rearing of the two boys and three girls to Solveig, a strict and careful mother. Overcareful, some thought. The Solbergs are a deeply religious family, and the Bethany Church plays a dominant role in their lives.

Tobey was at a church meeting when he heard the news about Dottie Thompsen. In a stunned community, probably no one was more shocked than Tobey Solberg. He had been Dottie's and Arnfin's landlord and close friend. Solveig had taken care of Christa the first night Dottie came home from the hospital. After that Dottie, nervous and depressed, had gone to live with her mother, and Arnfin had remained in the little cottage behind the Solbergs while he built his own house two miles down the road. Tobey went home from the church meeting and told his family the news. A little later they heard it over the radio on the eleven o'clock news broadcast.

On the same broadcast was an appeal from the police. Had any passersby noticed anything unusual that day around the Thompsen home—had anyone seen a strange car in the vicinity?

．　．　．

It was nearly midnight when the body of Dorothy Thompsen was moved at last to the Charlotte Hungerford Hospital in Torrington for an autopsy. And still the crowd stayed. Inside the house the police worked on, labeling bloodstained articles and turning them over to Trooper Allan Yuknat of the CSBI (Connecticut State Bureau of Identification) to be delivered to the laboratory in Hartford for testing. Other officers searched the house, looking for anything that might be important. Looking especially for a pink plastic piggy bank.

At 1:30 there was another flurry of excitement when Agnes Thompsen, neatly dressed but talkative and excited, came out of the house accompanied by two policemen and the policewoman and entered a police car, to be driven to the Connecticut Valley Hospital in Middletown, her probationary leave ended.

A few minutes later the police prepared to go home, leaving an officer on guard at the house; the crowd dispersed and the long night came to an end. It was after two o'clock when Bob and Carole Stadler locked their doors. "This house swarmed the whole night with police," Carole recalls. "It was so full of smoke you couldn't breathe. I made coffee all night—the last time at two A.M. I never even got a thank you." And Bob Stadler: "It was a madhouse. About midnight somebody called and accused me of breaking into Hayes' Store. Or if not, what had I done? What were all the police cars doing in front of my house?"

．　．　．

By the end of that night some of the pieces fit together. The bloody kitchen and the trail of blood told part of the story; the nail set and the pieces of electric cord told another part. The forks on the kitchen floor matched the stab wounds. But where was the weapon that had dealt the crushing blows to the head—that had left its impression clearly visible in the skull—blunt, round, nearly two inches in diameter? And why was the stepladder standing in that spot? For what purpose?

And what had become of the piggy bank?

◆

"At first you don't know what you're looking for. You just keep looking."

On Wednesday morning the men who had worked late into the night met at the Thompsen home at nine o'clock—Captain O'Brien, Lieutenant Fuessenich, men from the Detective Division, men from Canaan. A fingerprint expert arrived from CSBI.

The first important development came at ten o'clock. Soliani and another officer were searching the woods to the south (diagonally to the right as one faces the back yard from the porch), an area of medium-sized trees and stubby bushes. Suddenly, a few feet in from the yard, Soliani stopped. In front of him, nestled in the underbrush, he had spotted a sledgehammer.

It had a wooden handle and a round iron head, and it was stained with blood. The head measured about two inches in diameter.

•   •   •

A second development that morning occurred several miles away. Mr. William Flagg of Winsted, a patrolman for the Metropolitan Water District, telephoned police headquarters. On the late news the night before, he had heard the police appeal asking whether any passersby had noticed a car or any unusual activity at the Thompsen house that afternoon. The news was of concern to William Flagg for two reasons. First, he had dated Dorothy before she married Arnfin. Second, Route 179 is on his patrol route around the reservoir, and that afternoon Mr. Flagg *had* seen something.

"It was about one thirty in the afternoon and I was on routine patrol. I was headed south." As he passed the Thompsen house, Flagg reported, a car was just coming to a stop in front of it, heading north, toward East Hartland. "It was a black '59 Ford."

Mr. Flagg had a particular reason to look carefully at this car and at its occupant. "About two weeks previous we had a case of indecent exposure at one of the beaches, and the fellow in question had

a 1959 Ford and that is why I happened to notice it." Through his
rearview mirror Flagg saw a man walking around the front of the
car. "Five foot ten or eleven inches, fairly well built. He had on a
pink shirt and I would say gray pants. Light hair." He guessed the
man's age at about thirty.

Having satisfied himself that this was not the man who had been
involved in the incident at the beach, Flagg drove on. He did not
note the license number—he had no reason to do so. Nor did he
look closely enough to be able to identify the man again. He knew
only that it was a black 1959 Ford and that the time was about one
thirty.

•   •   •

In the hectic closing hours of the previous night, only the most
obvious pieces of evidence had been taken—the fork, the telephone,
the rock, the toaster, the porch board removed with the nail set still
embedded in it. The short piece of cord stayed on the nail set. The
long piece of cord stayed with the body.

Now, teams of men combed the house, taking tools, kitchen
utensils, clothing, towels, dishcloths. They emptied the contents of
wastebaskets and garbage pails into plastic bags. They probed into
plumbing fixtures and took water from sink traps and then took the
traps themselves. Around noon Captain O'Brien found a white,
bloodstained dress in the clothes dryer in Dorothy's kitchen.

In the afternoon Dr. Abraham Stolman, chief toxicologist for the
State of Connecticut, arrived to do on-the-spot testing. Samples
were taken of the blood on the kitchen floor, on the dining room
rug, on the porch, on the ground below. On Dr. Stolman's orders,
the third step going up to Agnes's apartment, which had been
sanded but still showed an obvious brown stain, was removed and
taken to his laboratory.

To the laboratory from the hospital came Dorothy's clothing,
along with her wristwatch and the Ace bandage. And a sample of
her blood and a sample of her hair.

Then, from Dr. Lincoln Opper, the pathologist, came another
piece of information. In addition to the stab wounds and the blows
to the head, in addition to the evidence of strangulation from the
electrical cord, Dr. Opper had found still another type of injury.
With some unknown instrument there had been a firm blow to the

stomach. The skin was not broken, not even discolored. But internally, after making an incision at the navel, he found considerable hemorrhage and torn tissue, indicating a heavy blow.

All that day the search continued, upstairs and downstairs, inside and outside, turning up a mountain of evidence. But at the end of the day, the one item that every man was looking for was conspicuously missing—the pink, plastic piggy bank.

•   •   •

The morning newspaper with the largest circulation in this area is the old and responsible Hartford *Courant*. In Wednesday morning's edition, the murder was the lead story, although details were still scant at press time. The story was accompanied by a photograph showing Dr. Murphy and two state troopers standing over the body, with the ladder to one side and the unfinished back porch in the background.

By Thursday morning, June 17, details were overflowing. The *Courant* headlined: HAMMER IS FOUND. The story, by Joseph A. O'Brien, reported that the red-stained hammer had been found in the woods. It went on to say that Mrs. Thompsen had been stabbed in the back and elsewhere with forks, beaten about the head with a blunt instrument, and hung with an electrical cord off the back porch from which her body fell ten feet to the dirt below.

". . . State Police found a large, red-stained, steel-headed hammer in woods at the rear of the house. . . . The shape of a small sledgehammer, it was described as a 'stone hammer' by Captain O'Brien. It has an 18-inch handle and such hammers usually weigh from three to five pounds."

Captain O'Brien appears to have been generous with the press. He is quoted [a summary]:

"Captain O'Brien said [Mrs. Thompsen] had been stabbed first in the back with a large fork with two tines, the type used for meat roasts. There were other, less severe, stab wounds caused by a four-tine table fork and at least one such fork was found at the scene, he said. O'Brien said a blood-stained telephone was found near the murder scene. 'It was still on the hook.' A telephone book nearby was opened to a page that included the phone number of the Carpenter Brick Co.

"A large pool of blood was on the kitchen floor where it is believed the major attack occurred. A trail of blood, about 18 inches wide led from the kitchen through an adjoining room. It went past an ironing board draped with a freshly ironed shirt spattered with blood. 'It would appear she had been dragged out,' O'Brien said. . . . The track led out a rear French-type door, onto the rear floor of the sunporch and across the porch to a point above where the body was found ten feet below. The body was found face-up in dirt beside a pile of small rocks.

"Captain O'Brien said the electrical cord was around the woman's neck and attached to a nail-punch driven in the edge of the porch. 'The cord was attached and broke when she dropped,' he said."

The article describes Dorothy's clothing, and reports, "Police believe that [she] was killed 'in the early afternoon.' The autopsy Wednesday showed that she had eaten lunch, they said." Also, "Two passing motorists said they had seen a black Ford in the area between 1:15 and 1:30 P.M. Tuesday and one described it as a 1959 model."

This is full, detailed reporting. As of Thursday, June 17, from the articles and the photograph, a total stranger could give a good description of the house, the porch, the yard, the victim and the weapons—and an accurate step-by-step and blow-by-blow reconstruction of the crime. But if it is true that every complicated murder case attracts its share of false confessions, then the task for any deranged individual wishing to do so had been made simpler, and the task of distinguishing the false from the true had been made immeasurably harder.

If there were holes in the picture, most of them were filled in the following morning (Friday) when the results of the autopsy were reported. Dr. Opper, the pathologist, described the exact location of the wounds and the probable sequence in which they were administered.

Hartford *Courant*, Friday, June 18: "The killer probably stabbed Mrs. Thompsen first with a small fork, 'chiefly over the front of the left side of the neck,' the pathologist said, 'but it bent and wasn't usable after very many blows.' . . . The killer then twice plunged a large carving fork into the back, penetrating both lungs. . . . She probably fell to the floor after she was stabbed and there she was hit on the head by 'sledge-hammer type' blows. 'Very likely she was down when the blow over the temple was struck' the doctor said. . . . The killer also crashed the hammer into the left side of the woman's face over her eye. . . . Then she was struck in the abdomen. It was 'a heavy blow,' the autopsy showed, and 'could have been [caused by] the flat side of the sledge hammer' . . . 'My guess,' he said, 'is that the cord was wrapped around her neck in order to extinguish the last bit of life.' "

Also on Friday, the black Ford was mentioned again, and for the first time, the piggy bank. Police "disclosed that . . . a child's piggy bank was discovered missing. . . . Neighbors said the bank is about a foot long, made of pink opaque plastic and was kept in the Thompsen living room on a table by a window."

•   •   •

On Friday, June 18, at two o'clock, Dorothy Thompsen was buried. Funeral services were held at St. Paul's Lutheran Church in New Hartford where, as a girl, Dorothy had played the organ.

•   •   •

On Saturday the piggy bank reached the headline. The *Courant*, June 19: POLICE SEARCH CENTERS ON CHILD'S PIGGY BANK. The story reported that state police detectives were continuing to look for the bank and also to check leads to the identity of the driver of a black 1959 Ford.

This was the last piece covering the murder for several days. By the weekend the furore had quieted down. No arrest had been made.

•   •   •

On Saturday, for the first time since Dorothy died, Arnfin Thompsen stopped to pick up his mail at the East Hartland Post Office and found a letter in his box, postmarked June 17, Winsted, Connecticut. The letter, printed in capital letters, read:

I KILLED YOUR WIFE. SHE WORKED WITH ME AT THE BANK. I TOLD HER IF I COULDNT HAVE HER NO-ONE WOULD. SHE DIDNT BELIVE ME. IT TOOK A LONG TIME BUT I SUCCEEDED IN WHAT I PLANED. SOON I WILL KILL

THE BABY SO NO SIGN OF HER WILL REMAIN IN MY MIND. I STABED HER WITH A MEAT FORK. I STAMPED ON HER FACE. I STABED HER WITH A FORK. I DRAGED HER THROUGH THE HOUSE WITH AN ELECTRIC CORD. I USED A HAMMER TO POUND IN THE SKIKE TO HANG HER. SHE FELL TO THE GROUND. I BASHED HER HEAD IN SEVERAL TIMES WITH A LARGE ROCK. I USED A NABORS CAR, A DARK BLUE 58 FORD HARD TOP CON. I WANTED TO TAKE HER WITH ME AWAY FROM HERE BUT SHE WOULDN'T GO. MY CAR WAS TO OLD AND RAN VERY POORLY SO I STOLD SOMEONS ON THE WAY TO HER HOUSE. PRETTY SMOOTH EXCEPT SHE WOULDNT GO WITH ME. I'LL KILL THE BABY SOMEDAY SOON. I'LL KILL THE BABY TOO, AND MY WIFE.

3

"This person is not the killer. He doesn't have the facts."

The speaker was Major Samuel S. Rome, chief of the Detective Division of the Connecticut State Police. In his Spartan office on the third floor of State Police Headquarters in Hartford, Major Rome studied the letter along with the mass of reports that had been brought to his desk.

"The letter is from a crank," he said, when he had read it. "He's written everything that was printed in the newspapers. And when he goes beyond what was in the papers, the facts are wrong. He's sick—he needs help. But he's not the murderer." Eventually he returned the letter to the Canaan Barracks with instructions to try to find the writer, who should be apprehended as a psychopathic individual who had threatened the child and who needed treatment.

Rome was picking up the case late. During the week of June 15 he had been on vacation, and although he was available at his home in Bloomfield, a suburb of Hartford, he had not been summoned. In Connecticut, a case does not go automatically to the Chief Detective. Commissioner Leo J. Mulcahy has established the rule that Rome must wait to be assigned, even in a case of murder.

Rome's first hint of trouble in the Thompsen case came when he returned to work. On Monday morning, as he walked into his office one of his men greeted him with, "Thank God you're back!" Within State Police ranks, it is safe to assume, the feeling was not unanimous. Local barracks do not like to have Detective Division men step into a case, even though they are specialists. Pride, ambition, professional jealousy, whatever the reason, the local people feel it reflects on their ability to handle the matter themselves. In Con-

necticut it is no secret that they particularly do not welcome Sam
Rome.

Connecticut's Chief Detective is a tall, solid man of fifty-nine, with
keen blue eyes, white hair thinning on top, and the quick firm step
of a man half his age—a police officer for twenty-nine years and a
detective for most of them. He is one of the most controversial
figures in the state.

Ask around about Sam Rome and you will hear: "A fantastic
investigator, the finest the state has ever had. Possibly without peer
in the country. He has integrity, character, brilliance."

Ask again and you will hear: "He's the most hated man in the
State Police. A tough cop."

"He's completely honest."

"He's a liar."

"Dedicated."

"Arrogant."

"He has the absolute devotion of the men who work for him."

"There are men who have worked for him who would never go
back."

"A touch of genius."

"Psycho!"

Ask around about Sam Rome and you will hear that he is a
moralist who passionately hates crime. And you will hear, "He's a
hard-nosed cop just out for a pinch. The toughest man I know."
Rome is called, both affectionately and disdainfully, "The Major."
Officially there are three State Police Majors, but "The Major"
means Rome.

People speak of his guts and his "gut sense."

He is articulate and uncompromising.

Defense lawyers hate him.

The Mafia has a price on his head.

He is the man who caught the Boston Strangler.

He is an Orthodox Jew.

This complex man never moves without a gun. "I hate the things,
but I'd never go out anymore without one. There are too many old
scores." In his house there is no point, including attic and basement,
at which he can be surprised out of arm's reach of a gun. But at
night he reads, unworried, in front of a wide window.

You cannot ask around about Sam Rome and get no opinion at all. He is the stuff of which legendary heroes were fashioned in other, more flamboyant times—colorful, courageous, unconventional —a maverick.

Rome's investigation began the morning he returned from vacation when Commissioner Mulcahy assigned him to the case. Picking up the scent six days late, he began by meeting with the men who had been on the scene and worked on the case—Captain O'Brien, Lieutenant Fuessenich, the officers from his own Detective Division, and the men from Canaan. He examined the police photographs, he read the investigators' reports and the laboratory reports. He studied the autopsy report. Having briefed himself, he headed for Barkhamsted.

With him that day was his right-hand man, Sergeant Orlando Ragazzi. Ragazzi had worked on the case from the start, but with Rome's entry into it, his role assumed greater importance. When Rome interviews a witness or a suspect, he concentrates on the subject, watching for any revealing gesture, any flicker of change in the eyes, in attitude, in reaction. A man at his side takes notes. When Rome examines a scene he concentrates on details, looking for any scrap that will tell him something, and the man at his side takes notes. Until recently, that man was Ragazzi, a solidly built, dark-haired man with a warm Italian face—an efficient, intelligent hard-working cop.

Rome went through the Thompsen house to get oriented, to see for himself the way things were, the way they had to be, when the crime took place. He examined the kitchen, the living room, the porch, the yard. He stood in the entrance hall at the open arch to the living room, where there was no door, and looked up the steps. He went upstairs and studied Agnes's apartment. He looked out the rear window. With the details fixed in his mind, he drove to the hospital in Middletown to talk to Agnes if she was able to talk to him.

"With Agnes, at the beginning, the big thing in my mind was availability," Rome said later, discussing the case with one of the lawyers. "She was there all afternoon. If anyone had come in she just had to peek down those stairs. I had to consider that."

Lieutenant Fuessenich did not agree, and the reason for the

immediate sharp difference in opinion was a single piece of evidence. By now, the police had decided that the unknown weapon used to deal that heavy blow to the stomach had been a rock—the large, cone-shaped, bloodstained rock that had been found some distance away from the pile of rocks, beside the body. According to Fuessenich, this rock weighed nineteen pounds. To Major Rome, Agnes Thompsen was a strong suspect, to be carefully investigated. To Lieutenant Fuessenich, head of the Canaan Barracks, she was not. Agnes was a little old lady, barely five feet tall, a hundred and fifteen pounds, sixty-four years old. Fuessenich didn't believe she could have lifted the nineteen-pound rock.

•   •   •

That Monday afternoon, June 21, Major Rome spoke with Agnes Thompsen for the first time. Accompanying him that day were Lieutenant Fuessenich, Sergeant Ragazzi, and Arnfin Thompsen. "I wanted to have a talk with her—to make her acquaintance—to review what she'd told the others," he told the attorney later. "I'd been told that she wouldn't talk. I wanted to try to determine, for my own satisfaction, whether there was something there you could work with, or whether it was truly a closed mind that couldn't be reached."

At the hospital he met first with a doctor and inquired whether Agnes was able to be interviewed. Physically, he was told, she was well enough to see him, and he waited while a nurse brought her to a reception room. The nurse remained in the room, as did Ragazzi, Arnfin, and Fuessenich. A doctor came and went; when he was not actually in the room he could listen over a microphone in an adjacent office.

The interview went better than Rome had expected. "At first we just sat and talked. I studied her gait, her carriage, her appearance. From the way she got up and sat and walked I saw that she was physically able-bodied. Later I learned that she was exceptionally strong for her age and sex.

"We talked about all kinds of things. Her personal history. She told me that her husband died when her children were young, that Arnfin was a sickly kid. I felt that, if she had memory, and if she could speak coherently from time to time, even if not always, I could extract enough. She would stop and smile as she remembered these things. Her memory was good.

"We'd stop while they brought her a glass of milk. She loved milk. When I commented that she was unusually strong, she said, 'Well, I lived on fish foods my whole life.' She was a neat, clean personality. She had a hard life."

But during the interview, when Rome guided the conversation around to the day of the murder, her attitude would change. At the mention of Dorothy she would get up and walk away or make no reply at all. She repeated all the statements she had made to other police officers. When Rome challenged them, she became upset and said, "That's a lie. I want to leave." Rome asked another question but now Agnes had become unresponsive. She went down on her knees to pray. The interview was over.

For Rome's part, he had not gained any new information—he had not expected to—but he came away with the feeling that he should meet with Agnes Thompsen again. Several points nagged him, among them a statement Agnes had made to police that she had heard two blows, "like heavier than a hammer." It was too close to a description of the sledgehammer. And he had sensed throughout the interview that Agnes was on the defensive. "I felt that I just had to be there at the right time—and ask in the right way—to get what I was seeking."

•   •   •

That night, in Groton, Connecticut, a town about seventy miles southeast of Barkhamsted, a young man from East Hartland, distraught and full of liquor, was arrested after a motorist reported that he was lying down on a dark road and then flinging himself at approaching cars. Shouting abuses when local police arrested him, the man was reported in the Hartford *Courant* to have screamed, "I couldn't have murdered that woman!" The *Courant* reported that he was committed to the Norwich State Hospital, another state mental institution, and that he was being questioned for any possible connection with the Thompsen murder.

•   •   •

Good investigation is an art and a science and legwork—and the legwork continued. Rome and Ragazzi called on Dorothy's parents,

Mr. and Mrs. Asa Burdick in New Hartford. They visited Christa at Ted Thompsen's house; the baby remembered nothing.

Even though dozens of men had already swarmed over the house like locusts, Rome ordered another complete search of it, including the unfinished attic space under the eaves alongside Agnes's apartment. He came with his men at night and turned an ultraviolet light on clothing in Agnes's closet, looking for washed-out bloodstains which would not be visible in ordinary light. In ultraviolet light such stains would be seen clearly. And still more items went to Dr. Stolman. At first they were looking for anything—any instrument, any bloodstains, any information. But before long the prime object of the continuing and frustrating search was one specific object—an inexpensive, dime-store, thin plastic, pink piggy bank.

On the possibility that the bank had been buried, they dug up the ground wherever it appeared to have been freshly patched. Then Rome brought in a mine detector and, after testing to see whether it reacted to coins, he went over the entire yard with it. "What we picked up was a lot of beer cans. They had been grading the lawn, drinking while they worked and tossing off their empties."

He took a more drastic step. On the possibility that the bank had been broken up and flushed down the toilet, he turned off the water and pumped out the septic tank.

And still no piggy bank. Whole or in pieces.

•   •   •

The first *Courant* story that week about the Thompsen case did not appear until Thursday, June 24. No longer front-page news, it was a small piece on page 21, about the young man who had been arrested in Groton and was being questioned in connection with the slaying.

The next day—Friday, the twenty-fifth—there was a follow-up piece which contained the first press reference to Major Rome since he entered the case. The article reported: "Rome said that the foremost line of investigation is not tied to a 32-year-old East Hartland man, now a patient at the Norwich State Hospital." Concerning the letter received by Arnfin, it quoted him as saying, " 'I am satisfied it's definitely the work of a psychotic individual, a sick person. He should have treatment.' He said that State Police would continue their efforts to find the writer of the letter. 'We are very much interested in him as a mentally disturbed person who has threatened the child.' "

But in this interview he said, too, that he was confident of a successful solution in the case. By now Rome's mind was making itself up. Reconstructing the crime, he had concluded that (1) it was the work of a woman, (2) it was the act of an insane person, and (3) it was done by someone who had *time*, who was not in a hurry to get away. Moreover, from Dorothy's family and from her neighbors, he had learned that the relationship between Agnes and her daughter-in-law had not been entirely cordial. Dorothy would not let Christa go upstairs, would not let Agnes take care of her, and Agnes resented this as well as other things about Dorothy. Considering Agnes's mental illness, he felt this resentment could have exploded into the motive. "The more you searched, the more you dug, the more satisfied you became that it was Agnes."

"I don't think she planned to kill her," he said later. "She just got mad at her. It started in a fit of anger. Then she saw what she'd done and she thought she'd better finish the job. Then she had another fit of thought—to make it look like a suicide. Then another fit—to make it look like robbery. It's the work of a confused person—someone who couldn't carry an idea around the corner."

Apparently by the end of the week Commissioner Mulcahy was convinced, too. The *Courant*, Saturday, June 26, headlined: MURDER PROBE ENDING. POLICE KNOW SUSPECT. The article reported:

"State Police said Friday night they have a suspect in the brutal slaying last week of Mrs. Dorothy Thompsen. . . . State Police Commissioner Leo J. Mulcahy said he wanted to reassure residents of the Barkhamsted area that the killer is not at large. . . . Commissioner Mulcahy did not elaborate but said he will ask for a Coroner's Inquest. . . ."

The solution of the crime appeared to be at hand.

•   •   •

The Coroner's Inquest was held, but not concluded, on July 16 in the town of Litchfield, the county seat. Coroner H. Gibson Guion issued a tentative finding that there was reason to conclude that Agnes Thompsen was "criminally *suspect*," and asked the police to further clarify certain points of evidence.

The newspaper reports included the fact that the piggy bank still had not been found.

Three more times Major Rome interviewed Agnes Thompsen. Then, in early August he announced that more evidence had been obtained and that in his mind the case was solved. The new evidence, which he did not divulge at the time, was an alleged confession which he had obtained from Agnes at the hospital.

On October 11 the Inquest was concluded. Coroner Guion found that there was "reasonable cause to believe that Agnes Thompsen was criminally *responsible.*" During the hearing the Coroner had listened to the tapes of Major Rome's interviews with Agnes Thompsen which included the alleged confession, and had ruled them inadmissible as evidence. In his statement he said, "I have not considered them in reaching my decision. . . . On the basis of evidence . . . other than any statements or declarations of Agnes Thompsen, I conclude that motive, opportunity, the time element and physical evidence at the scene, compel the conclusion that Agnes Thompsen was responsible. . . ."

In reply to questions about the piggy bank, he said, "I think I can say that question is not resolved."

A warrant was issued against Agnes Thompsen and lodged at the Connecticut Valley Hospital—a technicality to permit her arrest if she were ever released from the hospital. Earlier, Coroner Guion had been quoted as saying, "As I understand it, there is no expectation of her release in the immediate future." Nobody—neither Major Rome nor anyone else—expected that the warrant would ever be used.

Major Rome closed the case of the murder of Dorothy Thompsen.

• • •

On December 31 the five grandchildren of Mrs. Cora Clark, a long-time resident of East Hartland, were playing in an uncultivated field next to her home in which small trees and brush had taken root.

During the afternoon Mrs. Clark called to the children from the road, asking where they were, and they called back, indicating that they were coming out of the field by way of a seldom-used path, overgrown with brush, that ended at a crumbling old stone wall.

As Mrs. Clark came up to the wall, one of the children stopped short, staring down at something. "Granny," the child said, "—a piggy bank!"

The field is located on the corner of Martin Road (a right turn a half-mile south of the Center, off Route 179) and Westwoods Road (a right turn a quarter-mile down Martin Road). The bank was just behind the crumbling stone wall, about ten feet back from West-woods Road.

It was dirty, with matted leaves stuck to it, and it looked as though it had been there a long time. A two-inch hole had been cut in the top, very carefully, back from the slot. The bank was empty.

At the New Year's Eve party at the East Hartland firehouse that night, they talked of nothing else. How did the pink piggy bank, said to have been in the Thompsen house when Dorothy was murdered, get to a spot behind a stone wall in a wooded field two and a half miles away?

The newspapers called it the missing link, hinted that the police were renewing their investigation of the killing. They pointed out that Agnes Thompsen did not drive a car. The suggestion that the field was a spot that had been used at times for dumping rubbish did little to quiet the speculation that erupted.

When Major Rome examined the bank he said that it only convinced him all the more that the guilty person was Agnes. He called attention to the way the bank had been emptied, by "very carefully enlarging the slot with a sharp instrument. It doesn't appear to be the work of someone who tried to get the proceeds of a robbery, but the work of someone who was not normal. A child or a demented person."

He said that police were interested in how the bank got to that spot, but that it did not warrant reopening the case.

There were no further reports to Major Rome's office about the Thompsen case.

•   •   •

On Tuesday, March 15, 1966, nine months after the crime, Sam Rome heard over the radio that Harry Solberg of East Hartland had been arrested by State Police and charged with the murder of Dorothy Thompsen.

PART
TWO

THE
TRIAL

The Beginning

4

On Thursday morning, September 22, 1966, as Attorney William D. Shew prepared to leave for court in Litchfield, he was, by his own admission, a puzzled man. In the forty years that he had been practicing law he had never gone into a trial with more questions and fewer facts. Harry Solberg had told him almost nothing except, "I can't remember."

Shew is a tall, slender, attractive man in his early sixties, who was on the boxing team and the varsity crew at Yale—an easygoing man, as young in spirit as his beautiful and straightforward wife, June, who is half his age. He practices law in Hartford, lives in East Hartland, on Martin Road in a handsome two-hundred-year-old house, with an adjacent kennel where he and June raise prize-winning St. Bernard dogs. In the basement of the house, the pipes, on the word of Tobey Solberg, are "a nightmare." It is Tobey who keeps the heating and plumbing in working order.

Over his coffee that morning, Shew read the lead article in the Hartford *Courant,* written by Gerald Demeusy, an old friend and the *Courant's* star courtroom reporter. Headlined: "Pink Piggybank" Murder Trial to Start Today, the article began:

"Connecticut's bizarre pink piggybank murder case will be in the spotlight in Superior Court at Litchfield this morning as a 20-year-old aircraft worker goes on trial for his life. Harry A. Solberg of East Hartland is accused of the brutal slaying of 30-year-old Dorothy Thompsen in her Barkhamsted home 15 months ago. If State's Attorney Thomas F. Wall convicts him of first degree murder, Solberg could go to the electric chair. Defense Attorney William D. Shew—a neighbor of Solberg—said he found his client 'unconcerned and in good spirits' when he conferred with him at Litchfield State Jail on the eve of the trial Wednesday."

" 'Unconcerned and in good spirits,' " Shew said to June, who has served as his secretary since they were married. "Sometimes I think he's enjoying it! He likes all this attention. I don't believe Harry's ever considered the possibility that he could be found guilty and go to the chair." In high school, after six years, the boy had stood 130th in a class of 139. "I don't think he fully understands what's happening."

Yesterday Shew had come away from the Litchfield jail knowing little more than on the day, six months ago, when he took the case—March 15—the day after Harry Solberg was arrested.

•   •   •

Shew was at his broker's when he learned of the arrest. "We left early that morning—too early for anyone to have called with the news. At breakfast we saw the early edition of the *Courant* and there was nothing in it. Later at Fahnstock I picked up a later edition and read that Harry Solberg had been arrested for the murder. I phoned June to ask if that was Tobey Solberg's boy, and she called Hayes' Store and called me back to say it was." For the rest of the day Shew had expected a call from Tobey—he had handled small legal matters for him before. By evening he was puzzled that it had not come.

"We got home about seven o'clock," June remembers, "and a minute later the phone rang. It was a neighbor who'd been watching for us. Mrs. Solberg had asked her to speak to Bill. At the moment, Bill's first thought was that a whole day had passed without a lawyer." (This turned out to be an understatement. Several days had passed without a lawyer.)

"Why didn't she call me at the office?" he said.

"She didn't dare bother you there!" the neighbor said.

In the Solberg living room they were waiting for him—Tobey, a small shy man, with pale complexion and pale blue eyes; Solveig, a small thin woman, brown hair, blue eyes, more outspoken than Tobey; and Sharon, Harry's wife, whom he had married exactly two months before, at a large wedding at the Bethany Lutheran Church.

Only eighteen years old, Sharon was a round pretty girl with heavy light-brown hair framing a face that still had a baby look about it. One of ten children, Sharon Provencher had turned, with a remarkable intensity in one so young, to seek strength in religion. Born a Catholic, at twelve she rejected Catholicism, "because I couldn't understand it," and went in search of a church, first trying the Congregational Church and then the Bethany Lutheran Church, where in the simple, strict God-fearing faith, she found what she was looking for and where she met and married Harry Solberg.

Waiting that night with Harry's parents and his wife were two elders of the Bethany Church.

In bits and pieces Shew learned that Harry had been picked up by the police on Sunday morning (it was then Tuesday night) and taken first to the Canaan Barracks for questioning, and then, in the afternoon, to headquarters in Hartford for a polygraph test. On Sunday evening he went home with his parents who had gone to Hartford headquarters to be with him. He promised to return on Monday, after work, to repeat the lie detector test—and did so. On Monday he was given another test and booked for murder.

The following day at the Litchfield jail, Shew learned that he had a client who couldn't tell him very much. In a conference room he sat across from a pale, full-lipped young man, about 5 feet 10 inches, 185 pounds, with light-brown wavy hair and pale-blue eyes, who kept putting on and taking off his heavy tortoise-shell eyeglasses. He was a quiet boy and there was something a little soft about him—perhaps it was just that he was young and had been handicapped all his life with severe asthma. Among the things he had taken with him to jail were his asthma pills and his Bible.

In response to Shew's questions, Harry Solberg told him: "I stopped at the Thompsen house that day for some information I needed for an economics paper. I parked in front of the house and went to the door and knocked, but no one came. The door was half-open and I could hear the baby crying. I walked in and called for Dottie but there was no answer. I walked through the hall into the kitchen and saw all the blood and the mess. There was a trail of blood leading to the dining room and I followed it out onto the porch and found her in the back yard. And that's all I remember. Except for the ladder. I don't remember getting down to the ground but I remember climbing up the ladder—back up to the porch. And then I was in my car and driving around and around—I don't know

why. And then I went to work with my father. And that's all. I don't
remember anything else."

Shew studied his client carefully. "How did you know she was
dead when you left her?"

"I didn't."

"You mean to say you left a woman dying when you might have
helped her!"

"I don't know," Harry murmured. "I was scared. I don't remember."

During the months to follow that was to be Harry Solberg's
answer to nearly every question his attorney put to him: "I don't
remember!"

"What did you tell the police?" Shew asked.

"The same as I told you now."

A month later, at the Coroner's Hearing, Shew learned that Harry
had apparently told the police considerably more than he told him
that day—that he had actually given them some sort of confession.
Lieutenant Fuessenich, the chief witness at this Inquest, testified
that Solberg said he killed Mrs. Thompsen and that he gave details
of the crime. Confronted with this testimony, Harry told his lawyer
that they told him what to say, "And I guess I said it."

And that was all the information Shew had ever had from Harry
Solberg, right up to this morning when the boy would go on trial for
his life.

•   •   •

Shew finished reading the article in the Hartford *Courant*. Since the
arrest the newspapers had published, not once but many times, the
details of the case against Harry, including the facts that he drove a
black '59 Ford and that the piggy bank was found a half-mile from
his house. And, in the final paragraph in the *Courant* this morning:
"One of the most damaging pieces of evidence . . . against Solberg
is a letter he allegedly sent Thompsen stating he had killed Mrs.
Thompsen. . . . Handwriting experts say Solberg wrote the letter."

Shew finished his coffee and picked up his briefcase. What had
appeared in the press was just about the sum and substance of what
he knew, too. Harry was at the Thompsen house that day. He wrote
the letter saying he killed her. The bank was found near his home

And he claimed a complete lapse of memory. Bill Shew was far from certain that his client was not guilty.

On the other hand, Sam Rome still said the kid didn't do it.

◆

The town of Litchfield is an official historic landmark with fine old homes and pre-Revolutionary buildings that are protected against change. The center of town is one block long with a dozen or so small stores on one side of the street only, facing the green. Near the head of the street is the courthouse—a late-nineteenth-century gray stone building; across the green from it, resembling the old houses among which it stands, is the jail.

On the second floor of the courthouse, in a high-ceilinged, oak-paneled room that looks like the town—sturdy, old and unchanging —is Superior Court.

◆

"Do you have any strong feelings about capital punishment?"

"To be honest, I wouldn't want to make a decision like that."

The voir dire (the selection of the jury) began around mid-morning, and this one short question was becoming an ominous motif, reminding one that the charge was murder in the first degree. On the bench the Judge, black-robed, listened attentively—Judge Herbert S. MacDonald, a tall, solid man, ruddy face, gray hair parted in the middle—a patient, courteous man with a way of hunching forward when the interrogation turned in a direction that would require his decision. Below the bench, the court reporter sat at a small stand, taking down the proceedings on a noiseless transcriber.

The State's Attorney, who was questioning the prospective juror, stood several feet away, near the low barrier that separated principals from spectators. Mr. Thomas F. Wall—a short, stocky man with an oval face, round blue eyes, a thin mouth. Mr. Wall is from an old Torrington family; his father was a lawyer before him, his brother is a Superior Court Judge. In a rather droning monotone he posed his questions: "You couldn't bring yourself to find someone guilty?"

"No—not murder."
"No matter how convinced?"
"No."
Excused by the Court.

To the left, at two long tables, lined up side by side, the principal participants faced the empty jury box across the room. At the State table—nearer the bench—Trooper Gerald Pennington, tall, thin, gray-haired, was working with the State's Attorney, assigned to him as an assistant for the trial. On the evening of the murder, Pennington was one of the first men to reach the Thompsen home.

At the Defense table Harry Solberg, wearing a blue sweater and a sport shirt, sat beside Mr. Shew. Prison-pale, brown wavy hair carefully combed, he toyed with his glasses, picked absently at his full lower lip, let his eyes go over to his parents in the spectator section, blew frequent kisses to his wife. Harry seemed relaxed and unconcerned. Sharon was eight months pregnant. Pregnancy had given her a bovine look, and the dreary months had traced lines of harassment and unhappiness on the childlike countenance.

"Have you read about this case in the newspapers?"
"Well—some—"
"And has what you have read caused you to form an opinion?"
"No, sir."
"Are you aware that the Defendant is the second person to be charged with this crime?"
"Oh, yes—"
"And nothing that you have read has caused you to form an opinion?"
"No, sir." The gentleman shifted about. "But to tell you the truth—I don't see how that old lady could have done it!"

A decision must be unanimous and both attorneys were questioning carefully. The State had to get twelve votes if Harry Solberg was to be found guilty; the Defense twelve if he was to walk out a free man. Even one deep-rooted preconceived opinion, either way—one juror who refused to budge—would mean a hung jury. And a retrial.

"Do you have strong feelings about capital punishment?"

"I'm not really opposed—but I'm not too much in favor of it."
"Even if the law told you that the brutality of the crime required capital punishment?"
"I'd prefer life imprisonment."
Excused by the Court.

This is a small courtroom. The spectator section seats about seventy-two persons. In front of the dividing barrier a single row of chairs is reserved for witnesses and for the press. During the morning half a dozen reporters straggled in, exchanged a few words to explore what the other fellow knew, chatted with court officials, establishing possible sources of information. Comments in the press row are a blend of gossip, conjecture, and real knowledge. Ordinarily the members of the press are peripheral figures, faceless except to each other, rarely drawn into the trial proceedings. In this case, over-loaded before it was through with strange developments and hotly debated issues, the role of the press was to become one more point of contention, with the storm centering on the work of the most experienced and knowledgeable of the reporters, Gerald Demeusy of the Hartford *Courant*.

Demeusy, a tall, thin, dark-haired man who has been covering the courts for twenty-five years, is a real aficionado. He knows as much trial law as many lawyers; he knows the courtroom strategy of criminal cases better than many whose work has been in civil law. He knows the judges, the defense lawyers, the State's Attorneys, the police. He reminisces about other cases, lovingly, remembering every detail, quoting testimony verbatim. He has known murderers —has visited them in prison, in death row, has ghostwritten their memoirs. Inside the courtroom he is very serious. Outside, he is a Peck's Bad Boy.

"Do you have any strong feelings about capital punishment?"
"I could never agree to it. I have to live with myself afterwards."
A pattern was becoming apparent; one could recognize the points most troublesome to either side. Mr. Wall, in addition to his close examination on capital punishment, was questioning as carefully as Mr. Shew about prior knowledge about the case. He too seemed to be concerned about the effect of the information that someone else was first accused of this crime. (It could not be avoided—everyone

knew it. What effect *would* it have? Would a juror think: "It can't be a cut-and-dried case, then"? Or: "If the police *admitted* they made a mistake the first time, then this time they must be very sure"?)

With twenty-five peremptory challenges for each side, no explanations of rejections were necessary. The reason could be anything from an obvious prejudice to the merest intuition—a suspicion by Mr. Wall of sentimental sympathy for the defendant, because of his youth, his parents, his pregnant wife—or, on Mr. Shew's part, a wish to avoid those who might identify with the person who was not on trial here, but whose presence already loomed over the courtroom, Agnes Thompsen. Mr. Shew was wary of older people—although the panel was weighted with older people—especially those living with a son and daughter-in-law.

And Mr. Shew revealed another concern. Several months ago he had heard from an old friend who was close to the Canaan Barracks that there was ill feeling there against Major Rome. Then, just after Solberg was indicted, Shew had met a Litchfield County official who had said to him, "They've really got this kid cold." And Shew, curious, had asked, "Where does this leave Sam Rome?" The answer, with a certain relish, was, "This leaves Sam Rome way out in left field."

Where there is contention, people tend to take sides. This morning, Lieutenant Fuessenich and Detective Rebillard, the men who apprehended Harry Solberg, were sitting in the front row. They had put a lot into this case—their commitment showed in their faces. This was their home base, some of these people were from their home towns. Mr. Shew pointed them out, along with Trooper Pennington, who also worked out of the Canaan Barracks, and asked each prospective juror whether he knew them.

"Do you have any strong feelings about capital punishment?"
"Yes, sir. It's against my religion."

One o'clock. Luncheon adjournment until two. A sheriff slipped handcuffs on Harry Solberg to take him across the green to the jail. Then there was a small flurry as Sharon rushed through the gate to her husband and Harry slipped his locked wrists over her head and drew her to him. Spectators paused a moment and then continued on out of the courtroom.

A striking feature of the morning session had been the number of people, in these violent times when life has become cheap, who said in effect, "I will not be responsible for taking a life—even if I should be convinced that it is that of a man who deliberately took another." One had a sense of nature evening things up; as more people have moved toward violence, more people have moved the other way, against it. Going down the stairs a reporter said, "The bill against capital punishment is going to have to pass soon in the legislature."

•   •   •

Outside, small groups lingered a moment on the courthouse steps. Among the reporters the talk was not about the voir dire:

"Is it true that Rome is coming here?"

"What's *he* coming for?"

"Canaan is here in force."

"What's Rome mixing in for *now?*"

"They never closed this case in Canaan. Even after the warrant against Agnes, we knew there was more coming. We heard things."

"They say that in twenty-nine years Sam Rome never made a mistake. Well, now he made one."

Just a few words—the brief interchange lasted only a minute. But suddenly in that minute, it had become clear that there was a foreign ingredient here. For some, there were feelings in this case that had nothing to do with Harry Solberg.

On Rome there is no middle ground, and two of his strongest supporters are Demeusy of the *Courant* and Joe Crowley of the evening paper, the Hartford *Times.* Both men cover State Police Headquarters. Crowley, a quiet, even-tempered man, is a former policeman who says, unblushingly, "I'm strong for the cop." In one of the three restaurants in the one-block center of town they sat with other reporters at lunch and discussed Sam Rome.

"It's true that he has a flawless record," Demeusy said. "He's never made a wrong arrest. Ninety-nine percent of the defendants have pleaded guilty. The other one percent have gotten off on technicalities."

"He's the most hated man by lawyers in the State Police," Joe Crowley said. "They can't get the best of him on the stand."

"Since Sam has led the Detective Department, damn few cases have gone unsolved. And many were solved only with unusual sleuthing. The day they caught Taborsky and Culombe, Sam Rome could have run for governor and gotten elected."

When it turned out that at least one reporter did not know about Taborsky and Culombe, Demeusy, the aficionado, supplied the story of Rome's most famous case—with a name that sounds like the title of a bad movie—"The Mad-Dog Killers." Culombe was an illiterate; Joe Taborsky a convicted murderer whose conviction had been reversed on a technicality. On December 15, 1956, these two joined forces and went on a rampage of murder across Connecticut that lasted for nearly two months. Fourteen victims were attributed to the killers—six people killed at an average gain of thirty-seven dollars a killing, another four pistol-whipped, and still another four shot and left for dead.

"This state was in terror. People were afraid to open their doors. They screamed for the police to capture the killers, and the killers left no witnesses and no clues. Sam broke that case when he learned that one of the killers wore a size twelve shoe. He had them picked up for questioning on a Saturday afternoon. He couldn't get a warrant and he arrested them that night under a Connecticut statute permitting arrest without a warrant where an officer had reason to believe that the person had committed a felony. Sam was so sure they were the killers he'd have kept them in his own home for the weekend if he had to, until he could present them in court. On Monday morning he still didn't have a confession—and Sam is one of the great interrogators of our day. They were booked on Monday at New Britain police headquarters for breach of the peace.

"The next morning—Tuesday—when Sam presented them in Court, they didn't even leave the cage—they were afraid they'd be lynched. The courtroom was packed with people hollering, 'Kill 'em! Hang 'em now! Lynch 'em!' When Sam took them out again, there was a sea of people—he had a time keeping everyone at arm's length.

"They were tried specifically for the double murder of two gas station attendants in New Britain and were found guilty and given the death sentence. Taborsky chose not to appeal and he died in the

electric chair. Culombe went to the United States Supreme Court—"
Demeusy smiled—"and there his conviction was set aside on the
grounds that his confession was involuntary and should not have
been admitted at his trial. Rome had questioned him—although
intermittently—over a period of five days.

"A week later Culombe pleaded guilty to second degree murder
and he was sentenced to a life term."

Now ten years had gone by since people were afraid to open their
doors and screamed for the police to stop the "Mad-Dog Killings."
"People forget," Demeusy said. "All they remember now is that Sam
Rome was reversed in the Supreme Court—they don't recall what
the case was all about. They talk as though Rome was the villain."

"Sam Rome is the best cop in the country," Joe Crowley said,
flatly.

5

At two o'clock that day, the State offered to let Harry Solberg plead guilty to manslaughter. When Mr. Shew returned from lunch he was asked to step into Chambers, where Mr. Wall and the Judge were waiting, and at that hour, on the first day of court, the offer was made. To Mr. Shew it was not totally unexpected.

"I can't say exactly when I knew a manslaughter plea was available," he said later. "From the time the grand jury brought in the indictment I deliberately stayed away from Wall. I felt that the best I could have gotten at that time was second degree. Then gradually I became aware that a manslaughter plea was a possibility. At the opening of the criminal term, Tom Wall and I met in his office and we discussed it very guardedly. He didn't say he would go for it—and I didn't say I would take it. It was more that if I indicated that I wanted to take a plea he would strongly consider it."

Now in the Judge's Chambers the implied offer became explicit. The fact that it was not unexpected did not make the decision less agonizing. "At that time I wasn't at all sure what to think about Harry," Shew says frankly. "He hadn't given me any lucid account of what happened that day while he was at the Thompsen house. When I tried to talk to him I always ran into the same stone wall. Just vagueness—or 'I don't remember.' I had to present the offer to him. If he went to trial and lost, it could mean the chair. On the other hand, I didn't want to tell an innocent man to plead guilty. I felt that Wall wanted me to take the offer—and Judge MacDonald, too. I could only say that I would make the boy and his parents aware of it."

Shew took Harry and his family into a back room and explained the offer. "If you are guilty, you'd better take it," he said to Harry. "It's a pretty easy way out—if you actually committed this bloody crime."

Harry took off his glasses and sighed. "All right, maybe we'd better take it."

"First you'll have to tell me how you did it," Shew said. "Or the Judge won't accept it."

And there was the same stone wall: "I can't remember."

Hoping to jog him, Shew went through it again. When he finished, Harry said, "All right, I'll take it. That's what you want me to do, isn't it?"

"That's *not* what I want you to do!"

In his files Shew had a letter that shed some light on Harry's mental processes and also added to the dilemma. It was a letter that Harry had written to his mother from the Litchfield jail. It read:

Hi Mom.

    I dont really feel like writing anybody a letter tonight. But I thought I'd better tell you this. I talked to the laywer once and Im going to talk to him again tomorrow, I think. I talked to Pastor Bugga today, the Lutenant also. Tomorrow Im gonna ask if I can talk to the Sheriff, and I'm not going to ask Shew if I shold do that or not. I dont feel that theres anybody that bleives in my being not guilty anymore. So I'm going to figure it this way from now on. If I go into court and plead not guilty, and they find me guilty, the least I can get is 20 years, and thats on proll and good conduct. I could be sentanced to death. If I plead gulity to mansloter I could get a bid of 5 to 7. On the other hand I could get 12 to 17 max. There not much differec in 17 and 20 years. Im going to talk to the people who know the judge or prosetur good and see if they can help me. I dont mean put in a good word for me, but to find out what kind of bid they would expect to give me. By the time you get this letter you will probly herd from Shew already as to tomorrows meeting. I cant promis anything and I wouldn't blame you if you didn't see me on Sautrday. If I plead guilty there won't be any reason I can give, I won't be able to give the police any motive. Im going to take the shortest way out and only pray its short enough for Sharon to wate.

                                       Love
                                       Harry

Say hi to dad.

At three o'clock Sam Rome showed up in court. Shew and the Solbergs were still in conference in the back room, and Rome guessed at once what was going on. He rapped on the door and said to Shew, "I just want you to know I'm here." Shew acknowledged his presence and Rome remained outside. Later Shew said of this episode: "Sam knew what was up and he was terribly afraid I would accept it. I'd subpoenaed him and he was reporting to me under the subpoena. But he was concerned and he wanted me to know he was there."

Gerry Demeusy, who knows both Rome and Shew well, comments: "At the start, Shew honestly didn't know. His feeling was that Harry probably did it and it was his job to get him the best deal. He went to talk to Rome, and Rome said, 'If you let your man plead guilty to manslaughter, you are derelict in your duty. He didn't do it.' At the start, anyway, Sam gave Shew backbone."

In the back room Shew continued to press Harry either to refuse to plead or to tell him how he did it. After two fruitless hours, Tobey Solberg and Shew made the decision: "Forget it—we'll go ahead with the trial."

"I came out of the back room and said to Wall, 'Nothing doing,'" Shew recalls. "And I moved away to report to Judge MacDonald. Then I saw that Wall was furious. He jerked his head toward Rome and said, 'He was hanging around outside the door the whole time—listening to everything you said.' I felt that Wall was disappointed—that he thought I would plead before I was through—and that he felt I would have, if not for Rome. But that's not true. I wouldn't let Harry take a plea if he couldn't tell me what happened."

As a result of the two-hour meeting Shew reached another decision. This had been a most intensive effort—under pressure of an impending trial—to persuade Harry to talk, and Harry still offered nothing except, "I can't remember." Shew made a motion to have his client examined by a psychiatrist.

"I didn't have an insanity plea in mind," he says. "But I was about convinced that Harry had no clear recollection of what happened at the Thompsen house that day. I wanted to know why and how he had gone as far as he had, writing letters and confessing to the police, when he didn't seem to know what had happened. I sensed that something was wrong with the boy and didn't know what it was."

Mr. Wall agreed and joined in the motion, and Judge MacDonald ordered that Harry Solberg be taken to the office of Dr. Charles F. Von Salzen in Hartford on Saturday morning.

When the voir dire was resumed at last, late in the day, there was a new ingredient in the room. Sometimes sitting in the press row, sometimes standing at the back—a straight, solid, white-haired figure—Major Rome watched and listened with total attention. At the other end of the press row Lieutenant Fuessenich and Detective Rebillard—younger, less imposing figures—also listened and watched. There was no confrontation, no overt gesture, not even the lack of a gesture, but the sense of conflict was there.

At the end of the day five jurors had been chosen.

• • •

The following morning a four-column headline in the Hartford *Courant* told the story: ROME WILL TESTIFY IN SOLBERG DEFENSE. The article read: "Connecticut's best known sleuth is scheduled to be star witness for the defense at the 'pink piggybank' murder trial. . . . State Police Major Samuel Rome lodged a murder charge against Mrs. Agnes Thompsen. . . . But the State is putting Harry Solberg of East Hartland on trial for the murder. Rome, it is believed, still stands by his original conclusions."

All across the state the story touched off comment among lawyers.

"It's unheard of! . . . Absolutely unprecedented! . . . Never in the history of jurisprudence has the Chief Detective of a State Police Department come forward as a witness for the defense. . . . It's something that just doesn't happen!"

But it *was* happening. Major Rome, who had never spoken to Harry Solberg—nor even seen him before the first day of court— had come forward as a witness for the defense.

• • •

On Friday a certain tension, the kind more sensed than seen, pervaded the courtroom (What gives it away? A certain coolness, a quicker turn, a tighter mouth? You cannot define it; it is there), more apparent in Mr. Wall, who is a much more nervous man, than in Mr. Shew. In a mildly strained atmosphere, the voir dire continued until one o'clock when the original jury panel was exhausted, and Court adjourned for the weekend. Four more jurors had been selected.

• • •

On Tuesday morning Mr. Wall and Mr. Shew disappeared into Chambers as soon as they arrived in Court, and there was a long delay in the start of the day's proceedings. The court attendants, elderly gentlemen in black jackets, chatted near the jury room door. Fuessenich, Rebillard, and Pennington were present and standing by. A few reporters lounged about; Major Rome came in. The door to Chambers remained closed.

When at last the day began, it was not with the voir dire.

"If Your Honor please, may I interrupt with a matter which I consider to be pertinent to the conduct of this trial." Obviously upset, Mr. Wall came forward to address the Court. Within a few minutes he had recited a broad-based complaint—against the press treatment of this trial, against the Hartford *Courant* in particular and its reporter, Mr. Demeusy, against Mr. Shew's relationship with the press, and against Major Rome.

"On Friday morning an article appeared in the Hartford *Courant*," he said, "in which an opinion of someone relating to this case, that would not be possibly admissible in evidence, was the subject of the lead article with the largest headline." (The headline: "ROME WILL TESTIFY IN SOLBERG DEFENSE." The opinion: "Rome, it is believed, still stands by his original conclusions.") Had that been the end of it, Mr. Wall informed the Court, he had intended to ignore it, in spite of the fact that it was "a highly prejudicial article." But that was not the end of it.

Criticism of press coverage of a trial—and of pretrial publicity—is hardly new. The "Free Press, Fair Trial" issue has been the subject of heated public debate. It was Mr. Wall's manner that in a short time had everyone sitting up, feeling rather uncomfortable.

After introducing a copy of the *Courant* article, he followed with copies of three other area newspapers, the Waterbury *Republican*, the Torrington *Register*, the Winsted *Evening Citizen*. In these papers, he charged, Mr. Shew was quoted as "repeating the same opinion and repeating that this opinion was held by a person whose name was quoted [Major Rome]. The person happens to be in the courtroom at the moment, Your Honor." Accusation crept into Mr. Wall's voice, even while he noted that it was not "the person" who gave the statement to the newspapers.

Along the press row all eyes went to Major Rome and then to Mr. Shew. Mr. Wall continued his attack. "I don't say whether Counsel has said this or not—but if true, it is in complete violation of Canon 20 [Canons of Professional Ethics], and a very serious breach. . . . I ask that no action be taken at this time," he said, "as far as disciplining anyone [is concerned], because we are in a trial and should continue with the trial. But there might very well be a warning by Your Honor that this case should be tried in the courtroom and not in the newspapers." Abruptly Mr. Wall turned away.

As nearly as could be determined, through quick consultation along the press row, after the *Courant* story another reporter allegedly asked Mr. Shew if this was correct, received some sort of an affirmative reply, and other papers published that Mr. Shew said Major Rome believes the wrong person is on trial. But could not the matter between Counsel have been discussed privately in Chambers? Someone muttered that perhaps they *did* discuss it in Chambers—they had been in there a long time this morning. Then why this public airing now?

Coming forward to answer, Mr. Shew shrugged off the personal attack. "I certainly have no control over what the papers say." He then went on to point out that the press had not been especially favorable to his client, citing first the *Courant* article on the opening day of court.

Immediately Mr. Wall put in, "I have not seen it, Your Honor." He came forward to take the article and suddenly both lawyers were speaking at once, Mr. Shew trying to make his point, Mr. Wall again pursuing his own grievance.

Mr. Wall: "I trust then that what Counsel feels is that action should be taken against the Hartford *Courant* and the author of all these articles."

Mr. Shew: "So I certainly think—"

Mr. Wall [snapping] "I agree with him!"

Mr. Shew: "—if one was prejudicial, the other was just as prejudicial."

Persisting, Mr. Shew spoke of earlier articles that had appeared since the Coroner's Hearing, giving details of the evidence against Solberg, which, he said, were most prejudicial. Mr. Wall replied that the earlier articles had not appeared during the trial. His objection was to the timing of these articles and to the statements attributed to Mr. Shew. "If there is any possibility of anything like that in the future, I think Counsel should be warned and the papers warned about prejudicial matters that haven't come out in evidence."

For a moment it appeared that Mr. Shew was willing to let him have this last word and that the little flurry was over. Then, almost before one realized it was happening, Mr. Shew brought up another matter.

"While we are at it, Mr. Wall"—his casual voice gave no warning of the explosion he was touching off—"Major Rome came to me Friday, very much upset. He said that you told him he had no right to talk to me, and that if he continued to do it, you were going to make a complaint to the Commissioner—"

Instantly Mr. Wall was back around the table. "I never said any such thing!"

"Maybe I misunderstood Major Rome—"

Now Major Rome, standing at his seat, spoke up. "May I be heard?"

Judge MacDonald nodded. "Certainly."

Mr. Wall [again, heatedly] "I never said any such thing!"

The Judge: "Major Rome, you can explain your position."

Mr. Wall [very caustic] "May he be sworn, Your Honor!"

The Judge agreed. Mr. Wall plunged on. "I have several witnesses present—"

The Judge interrupted to ask that this matter be kept in absolute order and then took a moment to add that he had read the newspaper articles and had noted that all of them reported that Major Rome, when questioned, simply stated that he was under subpoena and would not say anything more on the subject. Turning to Major Rome, he said, "The Court is aware that, as far as any statements or opinions went, you did not make them."

Now, under oath, Major Rome told his story. "I asked Mr. Shew on Friday whether I had a right to discuss the case with him; and he said, 'You most certainly do.' I said, 'I was instructed by State's Attorney Wall not to discuss the case with the Defense attorney. I was told that I was subpoenaed as a witness and I was merely to answer questions when I took the stand.' I asked Mr. Shew to take this up at the next court session so that I would know my stand. I was told twice that I was a State Policeman—that if I had any information, I was to give it to Mr. Wall; and I told Mr. Wall that he most certainly could have anything I had, if he would subpoena me.

"I was also told by Mr. Wall that he was going to write a letter to Headquarters—I don't know what for—that I was to understand that I was not to discuss this case with the Defense attorney—any part of it. I told Mr. Wall that I have never been placed in this position before and I asked him to make it an order as a State's Attorney to a State Policeman—to order me not to discuss this with the Defense attorney so that I would know where I stood."

When Major Rome had finished, Judge MacDonald asked Mr. Wall if he wished to comment. "Major Rome is in a sort of tough spot," the Judge pointed out, in an obvious effort to contain an explosive situation. "As a State Policeman, of course, he is to co-operate with the State's Attorney—and he obviously realizes that. He wanted an order if an order was necessary. On the other hand, he has been subpoenaed as a witness. He's under obligation to testify with respect to any evidence that's properly admissible, that might be inquired of him by the defense. Now let's clarify his position."

But Mr. Wall was not to be contained. "His position was completely clarified to him, Your Honor," he said sharply, "—when I told him in the presence of several State Policemen that I had no objection whatsoever to his testifying, that he had every right to tell all the *facts* that he wanted to, but that he was to express no opinions on the subject and certainly not to *blurt out* any opinions. [Acid voice] The very next day his opinion was stated in the newspapers. He was here for two days. I never, at any time, told him that he was not to confer with Mr. Shew. *That is a complete and downright lie!*"

Major Rome [instant protest] "I'm sorry, Mr. Wall—"

"It is. It is a lie. I never said any such thing, Your Honor."

Major Rome: "Your Honor, I would like to have Mr. Wall put on the stand and placed under oath and have him repeat this."

Mr. Wall [very cutting] "I don't know who Counsel is—I will be glad if Counsel wants me, but not somebody who tells a lie!"

Major Rome: "Mr. Wall is referring to another incident—the first time that I met him—he had some men there. He told me that I was not to blurt out and I was not to state any opinion. This part is true. [Firmly, looking directly at Mr. Wall] I am talking about something that took place in this courthouse Friday afternoon when you and I were alone."

Mr. Wall [denying everything] "We were alone at another time and that is a lie!"

Major Rome [exploding] "Don't tell me that is a lie! I want you to take the stand and say that's a lie!"

"I don't mind saying it at all!"

"Just a minute—" the Judge broke in. "Just a minute—just a minute—just a minute—!"

With a tenuous order restored—all parties quiet on orders, but poised to strike—the Judge began to speak, slowly and with deliberate calm: There may have been a misunderstanding. . . . Major Rome has a long history of cooperation with the State's Attorneys as a very conscientious law officer. . . . Major Rome did *not* make the statements to the newspapers. . . . Some of the statements in the press have been upsetting to the Court, too. . . . In Hartford yesterday several lawyers referred to this case as "The Sheppard Case in reverse." . . . But the statements were not quoting Major Rome, and Major Rome cannot be blamed for them. The statements, whether accurately or not, were quoting Mr. Shew. . . . Major Rome has a duty to the accused person as well as to the State to testify. . . . As to his presence in the courtroom, there have been State Policemen here who are going to testify, presumably, for the State. Major Rome has been here and he is, presumably, going to testify for the Defendant. What's fair for one is fair for the other.

When he concluded this long and reasonable monologue, the Judge turned again to Mr. Wall. "Is there any question, Mr. Wall, about Major Rome's right to confer with Mr. Shew?"

[Testily] "None whatever, Your Honor."

"All right. That's clarified. Is there any other comment you wish to make about his presence here—or his conduct here?"

Mr. Wall [The ten-minute monologue has done nothing for his

temper] "No. I think his presence here is all right. There is no objection to it, from the point of view of a right as a citizen. As a member of the State Police Department, that might be something that he and his superior would have something to do with. As a citizen, he is entitled to come to this courtroom as much as anybody else."

The Judge nodded, and now Major Rome, who all this while had been on the stand, turned to the bench. "May I say something now, Your Honor?"

"If it adds anything to this and does not add fuel to the fire."

"I am here in the courtroom this morning," Major Rome said evenly, "only because I asked Mr. Shew to bring up this question to the Court. I wanted an answer from the Court. Mr. Shew told me that he felt I had a perfect right to confer with him [quicker, firmer] and I resent, for the record, being called a liar by the State's Attorney."

"Let's say there was a misunderstanding," the Judge said hastily. "Now let's not—"

But the fire had flared up again. "There was no misunderstanding," Mr. Wall cut in. "It was a direct lie. There isn't any question about it. I talked to him the day previous and told him this. Why would I come, the next day, and say something entirely different? I said in the presence of three other—five other people, the day previous, that he had every right—"

Again, quickly, the Judge doused the flames. "Let's not have a trial here on what was said. I am glad the question was raised. It is just as well to get the atmosphere cleared."

Major Rome stepped off the witness stand. No word passed between him and the State's Attorney. Not for a moment did anyone believe that the atmosphere had been cleared.

• • •

At recess Major Rome streaked into Chambers and asked that both he and Mr. Wall be given polygraph tests and that there be a hearing before a panel of three judges to determine who was lying—*before Solberg went on trial.* "You talk about a person's constitutional rights! Solberg's rights are not protected when I go to the stand branded a liar."

"Sam—there's a trial on," the Judge said. "We can't stop for that!"

(Later Judge MacDonald commented, still puzzled: "Sam Rome isn't a liar—he's a dedicated cop and he's honest. And Tom Wall swears he never said it." And Mr. Shew said: "Sam came out to my house that afternoon in a rage—boiling mad. I can't believe he could have dreamed it up. He had no reason to.")

Over coffee that morning, Joe Crowley commented: "Lawyers are always saying Sam Rome is a liar. But it's *not true*. Sam sticks very close to the truth. Otherwise he'd need too good a memory. He runs more than a hundred cases at a time."

And Demeusy said: "Lawyers primarily have painted this image. They don't like Rome. He provides them with work but he's a big stumbling block to them. They lose a lot of cases because of him. Sam's got the brass on the witness stand to overcome the advantage a lawyer has in cross-examination. Wall told him twice not to blurt things out. Sam's clever. If he has something to say, he gets it in."

Few people believed it began that morning. No one believed it had ended there.

The Case for the State

6

"Ladies and Gentlemen of the Jury—" The clerk, Mr. Thomas McDermott, read the indictment: "The Grand Jurors of the County of Litchfield accuse Harry A. Solberg . . . of the crime of Murder in the first degree and charge that on the 15th day of June, 1965 . . . the said Harry A. Solberg did willfully, deliberately, and with premeditation and malice aforethought kill Dorothy B. Thompsen . . . by lying in wait and stabbing, beating and strangling her, in violation of Section 53-9 General Statutes of Connecticut. . . ."

Dutifully the jurors listened, sitting rather stiffly, still unaccustomed to their places in the jury box. Interestingly, after three days' screening, they appeared to be truly a cross section—eight women and four men, ranging in age from about thirty to sixty-five, representing a variety of ethnic and social groups. Twelve individuals selected out of many times that number, who even now were being instructed:

"To this indictment, Ladies and Gentlemen of the Jury, the accused has pleaded not guilty. It is your duty, therefore, to inquire whether he is guilty or not guilty—and if you find him guilty or if you find him not guilty, you will say so by your foreman and say no more. Kindly attend to the evidence."

The *evidence*. Never has there been a more deceptive word. It sounds so exact, so definite; in fact, it is so nebulous, so relative, so subject to interpretation. The evidence, in a trial, is like a football— it is displayed, manipulated, kicked around, clutched tight, passed forward and backward and sideways, and by the end of the game it can be quite dirty. But it is the thing the game is played with, from start to finish—the only thing with which one side or the other can score.

"Mr. Arnfin Thompsen." The State called its first witness—and the trial was under way. A rustle of interest as Arnfin, pale, extremely nervous, made his way to the stand. Here was the person who was closest to the victim. Here was her husband. But Arnfin was more than nervous—he appeared to be absolutely wretched—and with his first words it was apparent that if he had a story to tell, we were not likely to hear much of it. His voice was a swallowed whisper, a mumble behind a hand propping his face. Immediately the Judge urged him, "Please keep your voice up, Mr. Thompsen, so you can be heard by the Court Reporter, heard by Mr. Shew and Mr. Wall, heard by the Jury, and heard by me."

Straining to catch his words we learned that there had been changes in Arnfin's life. He had moved out of the Barkhamsted house and was living in Massachusetts. Mr. Shew, working alone, without an assistant, interrupted, "Would you speak up, please?"—a request echoed by the Judge, and on the next question by Mr. Wall: "Perhaps just a little louder so we can all hear, Mr. Thompsen."

Every lawyer has a courtroom personality—voice, mannerisms, a certain way of putting his questions. Mr. Wall was very slow and deliberate. Speaking in a monotone, he gave every question—important or trivial—equal weight, and every word equal measure, sometimes repeating part of the question within itself, so that the effect with routine questions was one of tedium. But tedium was not the case this morning because everyone was working very hard to hear even snatches of what the witness had to say.

With a series of questions Mr. Wall had Arnfin paint in the background material in broad strokes: the unfinished home in Barkhamsted; the family—himself, Dorothy and Christa; the former residence, located behind the Solberg home. Losing no time, Mr. Wall introduced the Defendant into the picture. "And was the accused, Harry Solberg, also living in the front house?"

"Yes."

"And did you know the Solberg family very well?"

A mumbled answer. The Judge urged Arnfin to speak up. But this was a story of people who were once close neighbors, and Arnfin's voice trailed off as he spoke of their former friendship.

In the jury box the twelve men and women were leaning forward, craning to hear. For many it was their first trial. They were primed for their responsibility. A man's life was in their hands. The man was just across the courtroom, fifteen feet away, his mother and father twenty feet away in another direction, beside them his pregnant wife, still only a child, about to give birth any day now. And the father of the victim was here, too—Asa Burdick, a small, forlorn-looking old man alone in the back row near the door. And directly in front of them the husband of the young woman whose life was brutally cut off at thirty, who had a tale to tell. The jurors wanted to hear it—everyone wanted to hear it—and they could not.

And yet, bit by bit, Arnfin's story did come out. Accounting for his own time on June 15, 1965, he said that he spent the entire day at work at the Carpenter Brick Company, leaving only to go to lunch with the shop superintendent. That night, he testified, he left the office at five thirty, stopped briefly at the East Hartland Post Office at about ten minutes past six, then went directly home. He entered the house by the front door, walked through the hall and into the kitchen.

Mr. Wall [slow, neutral voice] "And as you entered the kitchen was there anything that you observed?"

[Whisper] "A pool of blood. It was bloody all over."

"And when you say 'all over,' was it on the floor or on the walls or on the furniture?"

"On the floor—and on the counter."

"And approximately what was the size of the pool of blood?"

The answer was inaudible. Arnfin was asked to repeat. When the answer still could not be heard, the Judge instructed the Court Reporter, who sat directly in front of the witness stand, to read it. "Three and a half feet."

The picture was being painted in finer strokes now, although with so much difficulty that one felt that each new fact clearly stated and heard was an achievement. Reporters glanced at each other's notes. Spectators murmured, "Can you hear him *at all?*" Rome, Fuessenich, and Rebillard sat quietly. They had already heard everything Arnfin had to say.

Mr. Wall continued. "Upon seeing this pool of blood, what did you do?"

"I went upstairs to ask my mother if she knew what had happened."

"And what did your mother say?"

"She said she thought Dottie had gone with her brother."

"Was that all the conversation that you had with your mother at that particular time?"

Again the answer had to be read by the Court Reporter: "Well, she said it was too bad she wasn't home to make supper for me. That was about it."

Arnfin's story continued: "I went downstairs to call Dottie's mother—Annie Burdick. . . . They had a regular procedure that they'd call three times a day. . . . I asked her where Dottie was and she said she didn't know. She hadn't heard from her since that morning. She was crying. . . . Then I took a good look at the room and I could see a trail of blood going out to the dining room. . . . It led out the glass doors onto the porch. The door was open. . . . The trail backtracked a little toward the north side and led off the edge. . . . I walked over to the edge of the porch. I looked down and saw her lying there—on the ground below the porch. . . . I ran back out the front door and around the house to her. . . . I touched her. She was cold. . . . She was dead."

The words fell on an absolutely silent audience. The twelve sober faces of the jurors were turned at one angle toward Arnfin. In the spectator section, Tobey Solberg, pale, stared at the floor; Solveig, face set, looked steadily at Arnfin. Sharon chewed her fingertips. At the Defense table Harry Solberg revealed little emotion, seeming throughout to be just another spectator.

Mr. Wall: "Upon making this discovery, what did you then do?"

"Well, I realized I hadn't seen my daughter and started calling for her." In a fading mumble Arnfin told of how he stood beside Dorothy's body, calling for Christa, receiving no response, and then ran across the street to Bob and Carole Stadler's house. Bob came back with him and rushed around to the back yard while Arnfin, himself, went into the house. "I hollered for Christa and I got an answer from her bedroom."

"And you had not previously gone to look in the bedroom?"

"No." Arnfin said that he found Christa standing up in her crib.

A logical time to clarify the location of the rooms, and for that

purpose Mr. Wall had on hand a large-scale plan of the first floor.
On it Arnfin identified the various areas of the house—the front hall,
with its stairs to the upstairs apartment and a passage leading to the
kitchen in the rear; the bedroom wing to the left (his own and
Dottie's bedroom in the back, Christa's in the front); the living
room on the right.

When Arnfin returned to the house that evening, did he observe any
changes that had occurred since morning?
"Well, the blood for one."
[Slow] "Did you make any observations to determine whether
anything was missing from the house?"
At once everyone was aware of what Mr. Wall was leading up to.
Not all the details of Arnfin's story were old hat, but this was one
item that *everyone* knew about—the object that is said to have
reopened the case, that, indeed, gave it its sobriquet: The Piggy
Bank Murder Trial.
"And what did you determine was missing?"
Arnfin introduced it into the trial. "A piggy bank."
Would Arnfin describe the piggy bank?
"It is made of pink plastic, about a foot long . . . six to eight
inches high."
"And when you left that morning, where was the piggy bank?"
"I think it was on the coffee table. Either one of two places—on
the coffee table or the raised hearth of the fireplace."
Now the bank was produced—a silly-looking pink pig with red
snout, ears, and feet—protected, because it was evidence, by a
plastic case. The famous hole, cut back from the slot, was an irregular circle, about an inch and a half in diameter. Gravely Mr. Wall
exhibited the pig. The witness identified it: "It is the missing piggy
bank." It was carried to the Judge, to the Defense table, where
Harry Solberg gave it only a quick glance, to the Jury. It was
marked and became an Exhibit. An important pig.
Mr. Wall: "Did you have knowledge as to approximately how
much money was in this piggy bank?"
"There is no real way of knowing, but I could guess—probably
about twenty to twenty-five dollars—"
"And that was all in coins or—?"

"It was all in coins."

So much for the piggy bank (one was rather glad to see it set aside), and Mr. Wall turned again to the subject of Christa. Where would Christa usually be when Arnfin came home evenings? "She would generally be in the window—in the picture window—in the living room and wave." And then? "My wife would open the door . . . to save me the trouble of unlocking it." Did his wife ordinarily keep the door locked? "Yes." Invariably? "Yes."

"And on June 15, 1965 was the door locked or unlocked?"

"It was unlocked."

In brief mumbled replies to question after question, Arnfin described his actions during the next half-hour, while he and the Stadlers waited for the police to arrive: "I got a blanket for Bob to cover Dottie's body. . . . I called Dottie's mother—I told her she was dead—guess I wasn't too tactful. . . . I poured myself a couple of good shots. . . . We waited in the living room for the police."

For a deliberate moment, Mr. Wall paused. He has a way of rocking a bit on his heels while he considers his words. Then he asked whether, during that half-hour, Arnfin moved anything or cleaned up any of the blood. Arnfin replied that he did not. But certain articles *were* out of their usual places that evening, and Mr. Wall began to question about them, introducing many of the articles at this time as State's Exhibits. "When you left in the morning had there been a ladder in any particular location?"

"It was under the porch—three or four feet under—standing upright."

"And when you returned at night . . . ?"

"It was off the edge of the porch. I had thought of using it to get down to the ground."

"And was there a carpenter's hammer on the back porch that morning?" There was. "And was it there when you returned, in the same position?" No, it was not in the same position.

"Now—was there a four-pound hammer also?" Yes. "And where had that been left in the morning?"

"It was on the porch also."

This hammer was produced and identified, and Arnfin testified that he did not see the four-pound hammer that night.

Next the nail set, still embedded in the section of the porch floor, with the short stub of cord still attached. Then the array of kitchen items presented for Arnfin to identify, the small ordinary possessions that had been part of the household he shared with Dorothy: the pink toaster, the electric cord, the three forks—the large bent two-pronged carving fork, the smaller bent four-pronged dinner fork, the other dinner fork, identical except that it was not bent. In rapid succession Mr. Wall had introduced eight pieces of evidence, all the tools and household items with which Dorothy had been stabbed, beaten and hanged.

In turn each article was carried to the Defense table for Mr. Shew's examination. Seated beside Mr. Shew, Harry Solberg would glance at it and look away, showing little emotion. But Harry had probably seen them all before—at the preliminary hearings—and, whether innocent or guilty, had lived with the idea of them for a long time now.

Arnfin had been on the stand for more than two hours when Mr. Wall directed his attention once again to Harry Solberg. "You said that you knew Harry Solberg as a neighbor and as a man who worked at your house. Did you have occasion to see him just prior to June 15, 1965, driving a vehicle?"

Arnfin acknowledged that he had, although he could not say how often.

"Did you know the kind of vehicle?"

And with his answer Arnfin brought in another of the incriminating facts against Harry Solberg. "A black '59 Ford."

Mr. Wall [slow, ponderous voice] "You have been describing what you observed and the events of June 15, 1965. Coming to June 19, 1965, [slight pause] did you have occasion to receive a letter?"

A silent group of spectators, hanging on, knowing very well what was coming as Arnfin described the famous Letter: It was addressed to him . . . printed . . . in ink. . . . He picked it up himself at the East Hartland Post Office.

Mr. Wall [slow, dramatic] "I show you this page of a letter—unsigned—and the envelope . . ." (The Letter and the envelope were encased, back to back, in a plastic cover.) "I ask you to look it over and tell me whether that is the letter you received on June 19, 1965, at the East Hartland Post Office?"

Arnfin: "That is the one."
"Are you certain that is the letter?"
"Yes."
Abrupt end of the morning session.

•   •   •

During the recesses all spectators are amateur sleuths.

"Why did he go flying upstairs to his mother *first?* They say you couldn't *miss* that trail of blood."

"He went across the street *before* he looked in the bedroom."

"The baby's bedroom was in the *front.* She'd have heard him come home."

"You mean to tell me the old lady was upstairs all day and didn't hear a thing?"

"It's not *normal,* mumbling like that."

And in a Litchfield restaurant Major Rome repeated to Mr. Shew what he had said when he first saw the very carefully cut hole in the bank—that it was a woman's job, or the work of an insane person. "If a normal person wanted the money he'd open it and take it. What were you going to do with the bank? Why, that boy would bash it in with his foot, take the money, and throw it away!"

•   •   •

There was no easing into the afternoon session as there had been in the morning. Arnfin was back on the stand, and Mr. Wall, the incriminating Letter in his hand, opened with a blast. He wished to read the Letter to the Jury. Before beginning he pointed out that the envelope was addressed to Mr. A. Thompsen, Barkhamsted, Connecticut, with East Hartland written in the lower corner. (The significance of this is that although Arnfin lived in Barkhamsted he received his mail at the East Hartland Post Office and that the writer knew this detail.) The Letter was postmarked, "Winsted, Connecticut, June 17" and then "New Hartford, June 18," having been missent, after all, before going to the East Hartland Post Office.

Very slowly, giving full weight to each damaging phrase (here the monotone was ominous and most effective), spelling out each misspelled word, Mr. Wall read the Letter: "I killed your wife. She worked with me at the bank. I told her if I couldn't have her no one would. She didn't *belive* me. . . ."

A trial does not necessarily proceed in chronological order, and after Mr. Wall finished reading the Letter he returned to the night of the murder for one final observation concerning the pile of stones in the back of the house. "On the day before June 15, will you describe the condition that that pile of stones was in?"

"Just a pile."

And that evening?

"There was one stone lying on the other side of Dottie."

Then a change in manner and in a casual, matter-of-fact tone, Mr. Wall asked Arnfin, "Are you now married?"

In the press row someone whispered, "He knows Shew will get to that. He's getting it in first." And now it came out that Arnfin had remarried.

"And how long have you been married?"

Arnfin's voice faded again, and Mr. Shew called out to ask for the answer. Crisply Mr. Wall gave it to him: "Ten months."

In the spectator section: "She's only been dead fifteen!"

•   •   •

A trial is bricklaying—to build a wall of proof. Each new brick is delivered, inspected, set into place. And then it is tested—tapped, thumped, examined in a strong light—to see whether it is sound and solid or full of holes and crumbling. By fitting brick on brick, the State hopes at the end to be able to say, "There's a wall you can't knock down." And the Defense, prodding and probing for weaknesses, hopes to be able to counter, "That's a wall that won't stand up."

Through Arnfin the State had delivered and set into place its first bricks, and now it was the Defense's turn to tap and thump and turn on the strong light. Mr. Shew began his Cross-Examination where Mr. Wall left off. In a conversational tone, he inquired about Arnfin's second marriage. How long had he known the girl?

Arnfin [mumbling] "Oh, possibly four years." Her name was Jean Griffin. She once worked with him in the same office.

"Whereabouts?"

But it was soon apparent that if Mr. Shew was going to learn about this matter, he was going to have to work at it. Under Cross-Examination, Arnfin's nervousness was even more acute. Mr. Shew did not hear the answer. The Judge did not hear it. Arnfin tried again. The Judge urged him to speak up—slowly and more distinctly. Another try. Sitting straight enough, Arnfin seemed to be shrinking into the chair. At last, with questions repeated and words spelled out, we had it: Rural Gas Service, Westfield, Massachusetts. (One had the feeling that not a single superfluous question ought to be asked—it required so much effort to get the answer.) Jean Griffin also did some bookkeeping for Arnfin at her home. He had a few part-time accounting jobs.

"And how long had she been helping you in your business?"

Clearly Mr. Shew was digging for something, and Mr. Wall was on his feet to cut it off. "Your Honor, I object to this line of questioning. I don't see any relevancy to it." The Judge ruled that Mr. Shew should have the opportunity to tie it in, and Mr. Shew continued: "And besides working for you, you saw her socially, did you not?"

A strong scent now of where this was going, and one could understand why the answer was inaudible. Another try—and another. "It developed that way."

"What do you mean by 'developed'?"

Answer unheard—read by the Reporter: "Well, I saw her socially."

"And when you saw her socially, what did you do?"

It had been quite a while since we had heard an answer, and we were not to hear this one. The Judge's patience was wearing thin. "Mr. Thompsen, I am sure you are tired of hearing me tell you, and I am getting tired of telling you. You will have to keep your voice up. Speak clearly."

Mr. Shew: "When and how often did you see her socially?"

"Oh, it started out possibly once a week."

"Couldn't it have been more often than once a week, Mr. Thompsen?"

"Yes, after a while."

Reluctantly—and naturally so—the story came out. After Christa was born, Dottie and the baby lived with Dottie's mother for eleven months, until they moved into the house in Barkhamsted, and Arnfin began to see the other girl.

"And after your wife came to live in Barkhamsted, was there any change in the social situation?" (So it was being termed in court.)

"Not too much, I guess."

Mr. Shew: "As a matter of fact, sometime previous to her death, you discussed divorce with your wife, did you not?"

"No, sir."

"Did she know about the social situation?"

[Deep sigh] "I don't believe so."

[Pressing] "Isn't it a fact, Mr. Thompsen, that she found a piece of evidence that made her aware of this situation?"

[Miserable, shaking his head] "Not that I know of."

[Very sharp] "Do you realize you are under oath, Mr. Thompsen?"

[Holding firm] "Yes."

(What evidence? What did she find—left about in a moment of carelessness? What did it precipitate? One wonders whether this was local gossip that Mr. Shew had heard or something more re-liable—from his only reliable source, Major Rome.) Rome was watching Arnfin closely, but Mr. Shew gave it up for now. He asked the last date, before June 15, on which Arnfin saw Jean.

Arnfin [unhappily] "I saw her the night before."

"And did your daughter meet you at the window when you came home that night?"

"I didn't get home until—probably eleven o'clock."

"So that was one night your daughter wasn't waiting at the window?"

"Not at that hour."

Questioned about the morning of the fifteenth, Arnfin said that he had coffee in the living room, dressed, and went to work. "So that when you said that you saw all those tools on the porch, you didn't go out and look for them, did you?"

"Not that morning. I left them there."

"When you told Mr. Wall that the tools were out there *that morning*, you were guessing, weren't you?"

[Insisting] "I know they were there. They were out there all summer long in the same place. I worked on the porch on Sunday."

Mr. Shew: "Did you *see* the piggy bank that morning?" Yes. "You *looked* at it?"

Arnfin: "It's right in the living room. I had coffee there. It was either on the hearth or on the coffee table."

"Do you know of *your own knowledge* whether the four-pound hammer was on the porch the morning of June 15?"

Arnfin admitted that he did not look that morning—but all the tools were out there all summer, so he assumed the hammer was there in the pile with the others that morning.

Now Mr. Shew turned his focus on the person whose name, inevitably, had to come into this trial, Agnes Thompsen. The Jury was given the bare facts—that Arnfin's mother had been a patient at the Connecticut Valley Hospital, that for five and a half months prior to June 15 she had lived in the upstairs apartment, that up until a week before, she had been employed doing housework.

"And was her health good?"

A twice-repeated answer: "No." But this subject was equally upsetting to Arnfin, and his voice trailed off again. Again the Judge ordered him to speak up. "Mr. Thompsen, I know it is disturbing to you and I sympathize with you, but your testimony has got to be heard."

Mr. Shew: "But she was able to work, doing housework?"

"She was failing. She was losing her few jobs."

"Do you know why she was losing them?"

"Just wasn't mentally capable of doing them, as far as I could see." Arnfin was mumbling behind a hand that seemed riveted to his face, and most of his answers were being read back by the Reporter.

In a trial it cannot be expected that important questions will be asked only once. The pertinent facts will be tapped again and again—for clarity, for emphasis, for a different emphasis—to uncover weaknesses in the story or facts omitted the last time around. Mr. Shew began a review of Arnfin's actions when he came home that evening, and Arnfin repeated his story that he went upstairs to ask his mother where Dottie was.

"Did you say anything else to your mother at that time?"

"I don't believe I did."

The three telephone calls a day to her mother—was that because Dottie was afraid to be alone in the house?

"I don't know—" But this was distasteful to Arnfin, his voice fell off, and the Court Reporter read back: "I don't think it really bothered her too much, if she had the door locked, but she wasn't overly fond of it." The answer was off the path that Mr. Shew was trying to follow because there was no door that Dorothy could have locked against Agnes—only against an outside intruder. Still, it is a fact that she always kept the doors locked.

Mr. Shew: "Hadn't she complained many times that she didn't want to be alone with your mother in that house? [Sharply] I want the truth, Mr. Thompsen."

An answer. Unheard. The Judge: "Speak up." Another try. Again: "Speak up." Mr. Shew turned away in disgust. "I give up!"

Now the Judge spoke quite sharply. "Mr. Thompsen, I am going to have to do something to make you understand that you have to speak up. Answer the question and keep your voice up from now on." Another try. Completely inaudible. The Court Reporter supplied the answer: "She didn't mind after my mother got there."

Mr. Shew: "Do you know whether she was afraid of your mother?"

"She was not afraid of my mother."

Had she ever told you she was afraid of your mother? "Before my mother got there, while she was still in the hospital and there was a chance of her getting out. I brought Dottie down to the hospital and talked to the doctor." Why did you do that? "To relieve her of any fears she might have had, which it did."

"And what were the fears she might have had?"

Answer inaudible. The Judge ordered Arnfin to answer again. Another try. The Judge's patience was nearing an end—the situation was simply impossible. A juror suggested that Arnfin sit directly in front of the jury box, and the Judge agreed. A chair was placed in front of the jury box and Mr. Shew came forward (one admired his stamina) to try again. "Do you know whether your mother did anything with regard to the clothing that Christa had on—while she had her up there?"

"I have no idea."

A change of direction. Before Agnes Thompsen was committed to the hospital, Mr. Shew brought out, she had owned her own home, which was then sold. Did Arnfin use that money to build his own house?

Arnfin: "Used it to build her upstairs apartment."

"So that your mother had to come to live with you, didn't she? She didn't have a house?"

A long answer that could not possibly be heard. Another try. The Court Reporter read it: "The house she was living in was not doing any good. Even if she got well enough to get out of the hospital, the authorities wouldn't permit her to go home to live alone, so I sold the house and she got better and lived in the apartment upstairs."

"What did your mother have to show for her equity in the house?" Mr. Shew persisted. "She had nothing on paper to show for her money, is that correct?"

"True."

"How many nights a week, on the average, do you think you didn't come home and meet your daughter at the picture window?" Perhaps three. "As a matter of fact, you very seldom came home to dinner during the year before your wife died, did you?"

"No—I think it averaged about three—two nights, probably." Arnfin was mumbling again. The Reporter read the answer. Arnfin scaled it down again. "Sometimes it was one and sometimes two."

"So it was nearer once a week that you saw Christa in the picture window, right?"

"Sometimes—I was coming home about two nights a week."

"And what reason did you give your wife for being away—business?"

[Unhappily] "Yes."

"You really lied to your wife, didn't you, Mr. Thompsen?"

"I didn't—I did have some business. But it wasn't all business."

"Will you answer my question?"

[A long pause, an audible sigh] "Yes."

Didn't she object to your being away all this time? "Every once in a while." What did she say? No response. Mr. Shew prodded. [Faint protest] "I am trying to think. She just asked if I couldn't get home earlier."

"And you didn't get home any earlier?"

"Guess not."

This painful subject done with, Mr. Shew returned to the other which seemed to be equally distressing to Arnfin. "Your mother was in pretty good shape, physically, wasn't she, Mr. Thompsen?" Arnfin might as well have been in another room, for all we could hear. He replied that she was failing, mumbled something about her planting something, and his voice faded completely.

Abruptly the Judge called a halt and excused the Jury for the afternoon recess. Then, sternly, he addressed Arnfin. "Mr. Thompsen, I realize that you are emotionally upset. I don't want to hold you in contempt for failing to answer questions. But this is a murder trial. A man's life is at stake. You have got to speak up and answer the questions. Now is there any explanation aside from the fact that I assume you are upset?"

Arnfin [unhappily] "I have been talking this way all my whole life—"

The Judge: "I want you, during this recess, to pull yourself together—and I want you to get out there determined to speak distinctly. We have got to get a record of this trial and it is impossible."

It had been only a little more than an hour since lunch. It seemed forever.

After the recess, Mr. Shew asked only a few more questions. How was his mother dressed? "A house dress." Did he see blood on her? "No."

"Was there blood on the telephone?"

"It was on the counter and it had to be on the phone, too."

"When did your mother first come downstairs?"

"When she brought the baby down after the police got there."

On Redirect, Mr. Wall made no attempt to repair the damage to Arnfin's character.

"When you first went upstairs to see your mother, did you then know your wife had died?" No. "Did you later talk to your mother about what had happened?" When I brought the baby up. "And what did you say to her then?"

"I told her Dottie was dead and please take care of the baby."

"And did you have time to have any conversation at that time or did you then go right out?"

"I went right out."

At last Arnfin was excused—subject to recall later, when it would be the Defense's turn to present its case.

◆

The next prosecution witness was Robert Stadler—a welcome relief, at least he could be heard—who corroborated that part of Arnfin's story that occurred after Arnfin rushed up his driveway. He told of how he went around to the Thompsens' back yard, not yet knowing that Dottie was dead, and came upon the body. He testified that he stayed there only a minute and then went back to the front door and into the house. "Arnfin told me that he found Christa. He was standing right by the stairs there—to go upstairs. He was just standing there. He told me he wanted a drink—a shot—and he went towards the kitchen."

"And you observed him taking a drink there?"

"He took the bottle and came back in the living room."

At this time, Bob Stadler said, he had not yet seen Christa himself. He returned a second time to the back yard, then saw Arnfin carrying the red blanket, and went back a third time to cover the body.

And so it went, a twice-told tale. The story was becoming more familiar and the setting, too. And this is essential. The important details must be repeated again and again if they are to stand out and be remembered.

After Officer Soliani arrived, Bob testified, he took him around back to the body. Then Soliani came inside, made a phone call, and ordered everybody out of the house. When he learned that Agnes and Christa were upstairs he went up for them, and Agnes came down the stairs.

Mr. Wall: "And was Christa there with her?"

"Yes, she was holding her."

Mr. Wall [with emphasis] "Mrs. Thompsen was holding her?"

"Yes."

Again Mr. Shew picked up the story at the point at which Mr. Wall had left it. "Did you hear the mother make any remark?"

"The first time—after I saw the body the first time—and I came back into the house." (When Agnes stood at the top of the stairs and Arnfin in the entrance hall.)

"What remark did the mother make?"

"She said to me, 'Is she dead yet?' "

"Did she say it to you or did she say it to Arnfin?"

"I really can't say because we were both close together."

"And she said, 'Is she dead yet?' "

"Yes."

A good place for Mr. Shew to stop and he did.

On Redirect, Mr. Wall asked where Christa was at this time, but Bob Stadler replied that he could not say because up to this time he had not seen Christa at all.

On Recross, Mr. Shew repeated his big point—the best he had had so far. "The grandmother said, 'Is she dead yet?' " Yes. "She volunteered that information?" Yes. "Right out of the clear sky?"

Bob Stadler: "Yes."

◆

The third prosecution witness—more experienced than the other two—stepped up briskly to take the stand for the short time remaining, but with him the prosecution managed to end the day on a dramatic note. In an even, authoritative voice, Lieutenant Fuessenich identified himself as a police officer of nineteen and a half years experience, five and a half years as Commanding Officer of the Canaan Barracks. He arrived at the Thompsen house that night, he said with great exactness, at 7:17. At the house at that time were "Trooper Soliani, Arnfin Thompsen, Sergeant Joseph Riley, Agnes Thompsen, Christa Thompsen—and there were several others that I didn't know."

"During the time that you were there," Mr. Wall asked, "did you have photographs taken under your direction?"

"Yes, sir." A practiced witness, Lieutenant Fuessenich answered the questions crisply, managing to sound efficient and informed without seeming overbearing. "The photographs were taken from— oh—about 7:30 to 8:30 or 9:00." Asked whether, before the photographs were taken, he had satisfied himself that nothing at the scene had been moved, changed, or cleaned up, Fuessenich again replied crisply, "Yes, sir." (How, one wonders, did he go about so satisfying himself? Perhaps he can be sure that nothing was changed after Soliani's arrival—or even after Bob Stadler's. But can he be sure that nothing had been changed since the time of the crime?)

But already Mr. Wall was moving ahead to his dramatic climax as he introduced the first of the police photographs—a shot of the kitchen showing the havoc and the large pool of Dorothy's blood spilled on the floor. The photograph was taken to the Defense table and then handed into the jury box. Altogether there were fifteen photographs—several of the kitchen and then, following the trail of blood, the dining area, the porch, the yard, and the bloody mutilated body. Long shots of the body and close-ups of the body. As the pictures were passed along, the jurors' faces revealed shock and revulsion. Several of them stared a long time at each photograph, not as though absorbing details but as though transfixed by the awfulness. More than one juror settled his eyes a long time on Harry Solberg as though reappraising him in the light of what he had seen, wondering whether this mild-appearing boy could have committed this vicious crime—not really expecting to find the answer in his face, just looking and wondering. Some were still staring straight ahead, as though reestablishing their own shaken composure, when the day ended.

•   •   •

That evening, before going back to East Hartland, Mr. Shew walked across the green to the jail. His aim today had not been solely to discredit Arnfin. Rome had told him that Agnes was resentful of the fact that her house had been sold. "She felt that this was her house. She was stuck upstairs in a little two-room attic in her own house. She was very unhappy." And as Shew saw it, "Arnfin moved her in upstairs and then he never came home. He knew her condition. He left her with Dottie without even a door that Dottie could lock between them." Considering how little Shew had to work with, the strength of his case was in direct ratio to the amount of suspicion that fell on Agnes Thompsen.

"Pretty good day, Harry," he said at the jail. "Don't you think?"

But Harry was disconsolate and reproving. "What'd you have to bring out all that about Arnfin for?" he said. "All that dirt."

7

Thursday, September 29

It was not expected that the jurors, even through careful examination of the police photographs, would single out the meaningful details. For that purpose, Lieutenant Fuessenich was provided as guide. "I ask you to point out certain items," Mr. Wall said to him, "which show in these photographs which are in evidence here." Beginning with a photograph of the kitchen, "Please point out any articles that appear on the floor."

Fuessenich turned first to the Judge. "This is the large two-pronged fork on the floor near the stove—and the bent four-pronged fork." Introduced yesterday, the innocuous-looking forks lay on the Exhibits table. The lieutenant continued, "Here is blood on the cabinet, where it was wiped on. Here are footprints, in the foreground, roughly equivalent to a man's shoe—"

A quick protest. Mr. Shew: "I object to that, Your Honor, and move that go out." Sustained. The characterization of the footprints should go out.

Mr. Shew [angrily] "I think the Jury should absolutely disregard that. I think the lieutenant knows better than to say it."

Mr. Wall [authoritative tone] "I think the lieutenant can—"

Mr. Shew [heatedly] "I don't care whether you do or not. I think he has enough experience to know better than that."

The Judge instructed the jurors to disregard the characterization, to simply note that there were footprints visible. (But can they? The words have been said. Later in the jury room when they look at this photograph, will they see only footprints? Or will they think: "A man's shoe—and the Defense objected to that description. Why?

What man's shoe?" Once heard, can a statement ever be completely removed from a juror's consciousness, simply by order of the Judge?)

Lieutenant Fuessenich, undisturbed by the little flurry, continued with his assignment, calling attention to significant details:

—On the kitchen floor, a pattern in the pool of blood that corresponded to the pattern of the blouse worn by the victim—an open mesh blouse . . . And two thin lines running along in the path of blood, from the center of the kitchen floor into the dining area . . . Also in the path of blood, a clear spot, "like an island in the pool of blood." (Another footprint?)

—Also in the kitchen, blood on the telephone and on the table near the telephone . . . Spots of blood on the refrigerator.

—The pair of eyeglasses on the floor between the dining room and the kitchen. In the dining area, the ironing board with the iron standing on end. Behind it, curtains spotted with blood.

"What was the condition of that iron?" Mr. Wall asked.

"The cord was plugged into the wall and the iron was still heating."

Continuing with a photograph of the back porch, Fuessenich pointed out Arnfin's tools to the right, the carpenter's claw hammer toward the center, and the trail of blood across the porch. "Directly in front of the center post is a larger pool of blood than the trail, and this pool of blood had the same open-mesh design as was on the kitchen floor. . . ."

Then the awful pictures of the body: The cord around the neck, the four-pronged table fork beside the head, the rock. Under the rock, a kitchen sponge. And under the porch, the pile of rocks.

"That rock that appears by itself," Mr. Wall said, "can you describe it?"

"It is about this large [indicating about eight inches across, ten inches high] and weighs about nineteen pounds, and when it was discovered it had blood on it."

To introduce the rock Mr. Wall picked it up off the table—and immediately strained under its weight, which was reported to be nineteen pounds. "Is this the rock?" It is.

(Knowing smiles in the press row as Mr. Wall continued to strain under the weight of the Exhibit. If the rock is too heavy for Mr. Wall, who appeared to be in his late fifties, it certainly would be too much for an old woman, five feet tall, sixty-four years old. Out goes Agnes Thompsen as a believable suspect.)

Observing Mr. Wall's difficulty, the Judge asked if he would like somebody to carry the rock for him.

Mr. Wall [gratefully] "I think so, Your Honor."

Mr. Shew: "I don't think it's that heavy!"

"Well, maybe you will carry it."

"Sure!" Coming forward, Mr. Shew, who is in his sixties, relieved Mr. Wall of his burden, which seemed miraculously to shed its weight. With one hand, buoyantly, he carried the rock around the room. (Back in goes Agnes Thompsen.) "If you have to move it again, Mr. Wall, I'll do it for you. I wouldn't want you to hurt yourself."

The lieutenant pointed out the bloodstain, still faintly visible on the side of the rock. Mr. Wall said he would show it to the Jury later.

"I will hold it for you," Mr. Shew promised.

"Just a young fellow." Then, all business again, Mr. Wall returned to the photographs and Fuessenich pointed out a few more details.

—Blood on the front of the victim's slacks. A rear view of the body. "An absence of any great amount of blood on the back side."

—The ladder. The toaster. And, on the edge of the porch, the nail set with a piece of cord attached.

Setting aside the photographs, Mr. Wall turned to questions about the police investigation. Was any clothing taken for examination from people in the house?

"Yes, sir. Arnfin Thompsen's shoes were taken to be examined for blood. And some clothes were taken from Agnes Thompsen."

Mr. Wall knew the information he was seeking, and the facts came out smoothly, as after a good dress rehearsal. "The four-pound hammer—was that located on the night of the fifteenth?"

"No, sir, it was not. It was located the following day, in the bushes to the southeast of the porch—about eighty feet from the porch."

"And when it was found, was there anything on it?"

"It had blood on it."

"And how many feet did you say that was away from the porch?"

"About eighty." About eighty? "Yes, sir." (The lieutenant was perfectly audible. This repetition was for emphasis, the implication being that the murderer *threw* the hammer from the porch into the woods. Could a little old lady heave a four-pound hammer eighty feet?)

In a crisp professional voice Fuessenich continued to reveal details of the investigation. The hammer—and all these other items—were examined for fingerprints. No pertinent fingerprints were found. The area where the hammer was found was examined—an area of bushes and small trees, no paths, no indication that anyone had been in there.

"During the evening," Mr. Wall asked, "were you with Agnes Thompsen at any time?"

"Yes, sir. I talked with her briefly as she was leaving the house to go to the Connecticut Valley Hospital at Middletown."

"What was her condition at the time?"

"I met her at the foot of the stairs as she came down. We spoke briefly—she seemed fairly composed. She was neatly dressed. There was nothing unusual about her that I noticed at the time."

Composed? Nothing unusual? Then why was she being rushed back in the middle of the night, to the mental hospital?

• • •

Mr. Shew began his Cross-Examination by asking for the names of the officers already on the scene when Fuessenich arrived. Fuessenich replied, "I don't remember all the names. Trooper Soliani. Sergeant Riley. Detective Rebillard and Trooper Pennington either were there or came shortly after." (One wonders why, if he does not remember, he does not consult notes or a report made at the time.)

Mr. Shew: "Were you in charge of the investigation?"

"I was under the direct supervision of my field captain, Captain Thomas O'Brien who happened to be at the scene."

[Zeroing in a bit] "Do you know who took particles of sanding from the stairs going up to Agnes Thompsen's apartment?" The next day Dr. Stolman tested spots on the stairs and ordered one of the steps removed and taken to his laboratory. "And was the step taken because of anything Agnes Thompsen said?"

"Yes. She said that she had sanded the steps in the afternoon of June 15."

"Did she give you any indication of what time she sanded the stairs?"

"She told officers who talked with her—the time varied—but it would be sometime between one and three o'clock."

(That seems to score one for the Defense—placing Agnes very close to the scene, at very close to the time of the murder.)

Mr. Shew [inquiring tone] "Officer, did you look over little Christa at all in connection with this matter?"

"No, sir."

"Actually was she there when you arrived or was she across the street?"

"I am not sure. I didn't see her at all that night."

(In the press row a quick flipping back of a notebook. Yesterday he testified that Christa was there when he arrived. An unimportant detail but he does not seem an exact witness. One has the uneasy feeling that all this happened fifteen months ago and he ought to use notes.)

"Did you inspect her bedroom or her bed?"

"The following day."

Did the lieutenant know whether any other officers inspected it that night? "No, I can't say." Did he inspect Agnes Thompsen's apartment that night? "No, sir, the following day." Did any officers inspect it that night? "Not aside from a cursory examination." (The lieutenant's answers were delivered in tones of authority but there was a certain vagueness.) If they had inspected it, would he have known about it? "I might not have. They were pretty busy there." It's possible that somebody did? "Yes, sir. It's possible." (Would O'Brien know? It does seem that somebody in charge should have known where the men were and what they were doing. In the spectator section a comment: "The neighbors said it was chaos that night—")

When they did search Agnes's apartment, did they take any articles for examination? "There were many articles taken that day and for three weeks after that. I don't recall now what they all were. . . . They were taken into Hartford for examination." Where could a list of those articles be found—he assumes the lieutenant kept track of them? "Yes, I believe I have a list." Is it in Court today? "Yes, sir."

Mr. Shew had arrived at his target. "May I see that list?"

Now Mr. Wall came forward. "I have something here that may refresh recollection, Your Honor." He handed the list to Fuessenich who examined it and acknowledged that it refreshed his memory, adding that it was not a complete list, and that some of the items were picked up under his supervision and some were not.

Gradually, during this Cross-Examination of Lieutenant Fuessenich, one had become aware of an obvious difference between the examinations by the two attorneys. Mr. Wall had posed his questions, knowing the answers in advance, his purpose to place fully anticipated information before the Jury. He had had access to the police files, presumably had studied them and discussed them with Lieutenant Fuessenich. Mr. Shew, on the other hand, was in the dark. With no access to the police files, with a client who could tell him nothing, Mr. Shew was on a fishing expedition. And the lieutenant was somewhat more reluctant and his memory somewhat less vivid than when he was questioned by the State's Attorney.

In a few minutes one became aware, too, that last Tuesday's clash was not an isolated incident, and that there was an undercurrent of animosity in this case, running close to the surface, ready to erupt.

Mr. Shew asked to look at the list, saying that he did not wish to use it for anything other than to question Fuessenich about it. The list was handed over, and with it Mr. Shew continued fishing to learn what he could. The first item was three partial prints found on the toaster. "Those produced no tangible results?"

"That is correct, sir."

"Do you have any prints of Dorothy Thompsen in your files?"

"We do."

Mr. Shew singled out another item—a white sleeveless dress found in the clothes dryer—Human Group O. "What does that mean?"

"Well, it could mean that the blood found on this dress was the same blood type as that of the victim."

Mr. Shew [summing up the information] "So there was a white sleeveless dress found in the clothes dryer with human blood on it, taken out by Captain O'Brien the following day—is that correct?"

Suddenly Mr. Wall, who had been silent until now, objected. "We expect to have this come out through Dr. Stolman, and I don't imagine this witness could tell what the blood type was." The Judge ruled that this should be limited to what Fuessenich knew of his own knowledge, and Mr. Shew agreed that that was all he wanted. But Mr. Wall was quite irate. "I handed it to Counsel to see—so he could examine it as to particular items, and there are other items on there that relate to what Dr. Stolman's testimony will be, and [snappy] I think he should hand me back this document if he is not carrying out what our agreement was—merely to ask—"

Mr. Shew [rather puzzled] "I didn't want to break any agreement. I still don't think I have; but if Mr. Wall will tell me what he thinks my agreement was—?"

The Judge interrupted to rule that Mr. Wall had questioned Fuessenich about articles found while he was in charge of the investigation and that Mr. Shew might do the same, but without going into technical descriptions. However, during the angry interchange, Mr. Wall had snatched away the list, and now Mr. Shew requested it again. "May I have my papers back?"

Mr. Wall [at once] "They are not your papers. You can have them for the purpose of refreshing the recollection of the witness." He handed them over, not to Mr. Shew, but to Lieutenant Fuessenich.

Mr. Shew: "What is the next item there, Lieutenant, under the sleeveless dress?"

Objection. ". . . If he wishes to have him list what he recalls himself—and if this does actually refresh his recollection—I have no objection."

The Judge's ruling appeared to concur. The lieutenant could mention any items that he actually remembered when he saw them listed. Mr. Shew's question appeared to follow the ruling. "What is the next item on there, Lieutenant, that you remember?"

Objection!

The situation was becoming increasingly muddled and no one, including the Judge, appeared to be certain any longer of the focus of Mr. Wall's objections or, for that matter, the reason for this sudden irritation. The Judge instructed Fuessenich to proceed down the list.

At last Fuessenich was permitted to speak and named another item. "Two white shoelaces found in the driveway . . . Short laces, more or less a child's size."

"All right. Let's have the next one, please."

"Arnfin Thompsen's shoes. . . . They were checked for blood on the soles."

"And did they have some?"

"According to the report they did." Another item: "Hair found in the hand of the victim."

"And what can you tell us about that?"

Mr. Wall: "I object."

The Judge: "The witness is stating that seeing that on the list refreshes his recollection that it was removed from the house while he was there."

Mr. Wall: "I have no objection to that, Your Honor. However when he is asked what significance was found at a later time, I question that—unless it is given by the person who did the work." (One doubts that Fuessenich did the work in testing the hammer for fingerprints, about which Mr. Wall asked him to testify.)

Mr. Shew asked what was done with the hair and learned that it was sent to the State Health Laboratory. Then: "Is there anything else on the list that refreshes your memory?"

"No, sir."

(Nothing else! There has been a great deal of smoke with this list, but the lieutenant remembered only four items, presumably in addition to the few already in evidence. And he was in charge of the investigation for the entire first week!)

◆

After recess it was learned that Dr. Murphy had arrived and Lieutenant Fuessenich's testimony was interrupted to permit the doctor to testify and leave. It was refreshing to hear that Dr. Murphy had asked to see his report. Blue eyes bright behind the round silver-rimmed spectacles, the thatch of gray hair falling where it would, he scanned the report. Thirty-three years a medical examiner, Dr. Murphy was an old hand on the stand. At Mr. Wall's request he went quickly into a description of the body as he found it, giving again the details of the heavy blood on the face and scalp (the description recalled the photographs), the deep lacerations in the region of the left temple, beneath them, the pulverized fragments of bone.

"A black mass of blood that had taken quite a while to cake—seven or eight hours. . . . Both eyes were drawn way back in the head. . . . A wire around the neck that had been twisted many times—" He looked up. "I felt that this was put on—can I give an opinion?—*after death* . . . because if she was alive, like so many hangings I've seen, the eyes bulge out by increased intercranial pressure. This was a case where the eyes were sunken, deflated, collapsed. It had to be put on after death. . . ." Dr. Murphy consulted his report and added, "There was no petechial hemorrhage on the bulbar conjunctiva. That means—the white part of the eye is called the conjunctiva—and where pressure like a rope around the neck causes compression, you will have little red spots—subconjunctival hemorrhages. There weren't any here."

Mr. Wall: "What significance do you attach to that fact?"

"If there was no hemorrhage, it shows that there was no increase of pressure in the brain. If there was increased pressure—like a hanging or garroting, as this seemed to be—simulated—there would be small hemorrhages in the conjunctiva and, very often, around the lips. There weren't any."

"And the significance that you attach to that, then, is that—?"

[Flatly] "Post mortem."

"At the time of the hanging, the woman was dead?"

"That's right." Dr. Murphy continued. "She wore dungarees, and although the pictures would make you believe that there was blood all down through, I didn't see any blood on the dungarees. Of course, it was by that time half past eight at night. It was quite dark. We were using flashlights before I got through. [Reading] A silver fork on the grass about ten inches lateral to the neck. I assumed that—during the fall, the force of the body hitting the ground disentangled the fork—I thought that was used to twist—tighten the cord. I believe that the garroting was done after actual death from a fracture of the skull. . . . A small wristwatch on the left wrist, still running and correct time, smeared with blackened blood." (No clue here to the exact hour of the crime.)

Mr. Wall: "Then your opinion is, doctor, that this deceased had died of a fracture of the skull, is that correct?"

"That is correct. Death must have been instantaneous, too."

"And was there one fracture or were there multiple fractures?"

"I would say multiple. It looked as though there were three direct blows—but I mention the two large ones."

Was he able to tell the type of instrument that caused these fractures?

"These impressions seemed to be uniform—and they were of a round blunt instrument—probably one and a half or two inches wide."

After death is there ever any more bleeding?

Dr. Murphy replied that there is not. This was a factor in his opinion that the garroting was an afterthought. "It was all done impulsively—and by a person who was thinking very rapidly and compulsively."

"Did you determine, Doctor, the source of such bleeding as did occur?"

"I determined that it came from the injuries in the head—and the mouth was full of blood, too. And that it was all done by terrific blows on the head and she died from the wounds of the fractured skull—not so much from the hemorrhage, but from a fracture, and the damage to the brain."

In Cross-Examination Mr. Shew was more interested in certain other observations that Dr. Murphy made that night, besides those for which he had been officially summoned. "Did you have a chance to observe Agnes Thompsen?"

In great detail! Dr. Murphy described Agnes Thompsen's warm greeting to him and the condition in which he found her. ". . . Full of joy and happiness—really ebullient with joy."

"And had you seen her before?"

Now Dr. Murphy gave details of Agnes Thompsen's condition on that day a few years earlier when she had begun to have auditory hallucinations. "She'd say, 'Do you hear that?' And I'd say, 'Yes, I do.' Then a few more times she said, 'Nobody hears that but I do.' Well, I said, 'I hear it, Mrs. Thompsen—plain.' And she turned around and said, 'You know, last night I killed the devil with a butcher knife.'"

Not surprisingly, Mr. Wall was on his feet to protest that Dr. Murphy was going "a little far afield," and Mr. Shew guided the testimony back to the night of the murder. "You say she was in a very joyful mood?"

Objection. "It's been stated. I don't see belaboring it." The Judge requested that Dr. Murphy give his observations, but without characterizations of other than appearance.

Mr. Shew: "Can you tell us what her physical condition was, as far as you could observe, Doctor?"

"She seemed to be in pretty good physical condition—very good."

After bringing out that Dr. Murphy had had two years of psychiatric training, Mr. Shew asked for his opinion on Agnes Thompsen's mental condition that night. And now came Dr. Murphy's vivid description: "I think she was in a grandiose state of mind, stimulated by some action of religious origin—something between her and her Maker—and she was subconsciously looking for a reward. She had rendered some service. That's the attitude I felt."

How would he describe her condition in psychiatric terms?

"Manic type—full of emotion—tense—rapid flow of words—she was quite confused. She would jump from one sentence to another, and often her sentences were choppy and not understandable."

"You say that you thought she was pleased and happy because she had done some service to the Lord. . . . Did she indicate to you what service she had performed?"

"No."

Mr. Shew turned to Dr. Murphy's other observations that night. "It appeared to you that the wounds were made rapidly and compulsively—those were your words, were they not, Doctor? Can you elaborate on what you meant by that?"

"Well, whoever did it struck first and thought afterwards. I had a feeling that the blow was done, and then the sense of crime came on—'My gosh, she is dead, she is down.'" Now Dr. Murphy volunteered a strange piece of information. "I didn't find too much blood on the floor. Your pictures show there is a great—a gallon there, but I only saw ounces. I don't think she lost much blood. She died suddenly."

(We are drifting into confusion. Three former witnesses have testified that there was a very large pool of blood. Is this a question of semantics or observation or of emotional reaction? Does a quantity of blood seem like a great deal to a layman, less to a doctor?) Dr. Murphy continued with his opinion: The camera can play tricks. It was a polished floor, there was no absorption—the blood had to spread out—it was summertime and blood would take longer to cake up, so it did spread. He believed there was not more than six or eight ounces of blood on the floor. "But when I saw this thing, it's like a lake." Then he told of looking up at the nail set in the porch with the bit of cord attached. " 'My God,' I said, 'a woman a hundred and fifteen pounds would never break that cord.' "

Mr. Shew was puzzled. "Do you mean that the body might have been hanging off the porch for a while before it broke?"

"No, I don't believe the body ever hung on it! It was done by somebody to make it simulate a hanging. They had a sense of, 'Something terrible has happened,' and tried to cover up. And then their ideas are all mixed up, back and forth—evil and good."

Along with his Medical Examiner's Report, Dr. Murphy was certainly contributing food for thought—much that would have to be weighed and sifted. Still, in thirty-three years, the doctor has been at the scene of a good many crimes.

"Doctor, in your opinion, was Agnes Thompsen strong enough to lift up the body of the deceased?" Yes. "Was she strong enough to lift the stone?" Mr. Shew pointed out the stone, told him it was reported to weigh about nineteen pounds.

"She could lift that, all right. She was an outdoor woman."

Mr. Shew handed Dr. Murphy the four-pound hammer. "Would she have any trouble lifting that?"

"No, she would not."

Now Mr. Shew attempted to ask whether Dr. Murphy thought that having a woman like Agnes Thompsen locked in a house with Dorothy would have been dangerous and whether Agnes was capable of taking such action as had been described here. Mr. Wall successfully blocked both answers, and Mr. Shew appeared to be satisfied not to pursue the subject further. (And in fact it did not seem necessary. One was well aware that Dr. Murphy believed Agnes Thompsen was physically capable of doing it, mentally capable of doing it, and, furthermore, one suspected that Dr. Murphy believed she did do it.)

•   •   •

After Dr. Murphy, Lieutenant Fuessenich returned to the stand.

Mr. Shew: "The white sleeveless dress found in the clothes dryer . . . Do you know which of the two women in the house the dress belonged to?" He does not. (It does seem that this could have been determined, if Dorothy was 5 feet 6 inches and slight, and Agnes is 5 feet and stocky—even allowing for the fact that an older woman might wear her dresses longer.)

"Had the dryer been operated with that in there or was it just there in rumpled condition?"

"There were other soiled clothes in the dryer. They had not been washed."

"Did you weigh the rock? Or is nineteen pounds . . . just a guess?"

"No, sir, I weighed it."

"You heard Dr. Murphy say that in his opinion the photographs do not give a correct picture of the condition of the floor. Can you account for that?"

[Crisply] "This is Dr. Murphy's opinion. The pictures were taken at eye level with a normal lens. [Defensively] We did our very best to portray the scene as it actually was."

On a very brief Redirect, Mr. Wall asked about the condition of the sponge that was underneath the rock.

"It was wet with blood."

◆

Today, in contrast to yesterday, there was a parade of witnesses. Just before lunch Carole Stadler took the stand and two important pieces of information were placed before the Jury. First, that her son, Randy, on the morning of Dorothy's death, played with Christa in the Thompsen house, from about 9:30 until 11:45. Second, that Carole herself worked outdoors most of that day, planting on the south side of her house—the side that would give her a view of the Thompsen house. She gave, within minutes, the exact times she was absent from this observation point:

1:05–1:25. She was inside her own house for lunch. She came out of her house at 1:25, walked down the road to the Dr. Stadler house, approximately six hundred feet away, about a five-minute walk.

1:30–2:30. Inside Dr. Stadler's house. At 2:30 she walked back to her own house and went inside.

2:30–2:45. Inside her own house, preparing dinner. At 2:45 she walked back to Dr. Stadler's house to use the vegetable grinder.

2:45–3:00. Inside Dr. Stadler's house. Returned to her own house at 3:00 and went inside for a few minutes.

From 3:00 until 5:00 she worked outside, until her husband came home.

Nobody underestimated the importance of Carole Stadler's testimony, so precisely limiting the hours during which a stranger could have entered the Thompsen house, and after the luncheon break, Mr. Wall reviewed it again.

"And otherwise, you had the Arnfin Thompsen property within your view where you would have seen anyone going in or coming out?" Yes. "And during that time, you did not observe anyone?" No. "Did you know the defendant, Solberg?" Not personally. She knew who he was.

Suddenly one realized that this was the first time today that Harry Solberg had been mentioned. Sitting beside Mr. Shew, he was busy with a pen (writing what?—taking notes?—doodling?), smiling occasionally, looking very much like a quiet-mannered school boy attending an assembly lecture. So far we had heard almost nothing about him. We had it now that if he was at the Thompsen house that day, it had to be between 1:05 and 1:25, 1:30 and 2:30, or 2:45 and 3:00. Twenty minutes, one hour, fifteen minutes. Total possibility: One hour and thirty-five minutes.

Then the questioning moved into familiar territory as Carole gave her version of the events of that evening, supplying further details of the episode involving Christa. "After the State Policeman made us get out of the house, I told him that Christa was upstairs with her grandmother and I didn't think that she should be. . . . He asked me to go upstairs and get her and I said no. So he went up and knocked on the door and she came right down with the little girl."

"And did you have any conversation with Christa as Christa came down?"

"Well, Christa said something—yes."

"And what did Christa say?"

"She said, 'She killed. She killed.'"

"And did you know from familiarity with her manner of speech what she intended to convey?"

Objection. She cannot know what was in the child's mind. Sustained. Mr. Wall [pressing for an interpretation of the remark] "What did you *understand* her to mean?" Objection. Sustained: She can testify only to what she *heard*. Mr. Wall: "Did Christa talk as an adult?" No—she spoke clearly, but not in sentences. [Doggedly] "And did you understand what that meant to you—what she said?" Objection. Sustained.

[Another try] "Was Christa in her conversation able to distinguish between the active voice and the passive voice?" She was not. And Mr. Wall would have to be satisfied with this. The child could have meant: She (Dorothy) had been killed. Or: She (Agnes) killed her. (Privately one wonders whether the child even knew the meaning of the word.)

Mr. Wall: "When Christa came down the stairs, did she go to you?"

Carole Stadler: "Not right away. . . . Her grandmother kept holding her."

"Was there any difficulty about her being transferred to your custody?"

"Yes. She didn't want to leave her grandmother."

[Emphatically] "She did not want to leave her grandmother?"

"No."

After that, Carole said, she took Christa across the street for about ten minutes until the child's aunt came and took her.

•   •   •

Mr. Shew's turn.

When the police officer asked Mrs. Stadler to go up and get Christa, why did she refuse? "Well, I didn't want to." Why? "Well, I knew Mrs. Thompsen wasn't mentally normal, and I didn't want to try to take the baby away from her." In other words, was she afraid to go up? "Not really afraid. I just didn't want to go up."

Mr. Shew: "You mean you weren't afraid because you had plenty of reinforcements around there?" (Smiles in the courtroom as Carole acknowledged that this was so.) "And if you had been alone in the house you would have been afraid?"

"I wouldn't have been in the house."

"Do you mean you would have been afraid to be in the house?"

At last. "I think I would have."

Having gained this, Mr. Shew continued. "Did Dorothy ever tell you whether she was afraid of her mother-in-law?" Yes. "*What* did she tell you?"

"She said that she was afraid of her."

"Did she ever elaborate on that?"

[Offhand] "No, just once she happened to mention it to me."

Mr. Shew [rather sharp] "I think you testified once before in a hearing in connection with this matter, didn't you, Mrs. Stadler? And at that time you were asked, 'And what was the occasion of her saying that she was afraid to live there?' And this is your answer—"

Mr. Shew was referring to the transcript of the Coroner's Hearing, and Mr. Wall interrupted to object to his reading it.

(At the Coroner's Hearing a witness's testimony, although given under oath and recorded by the court reporter, is not subject to cross-examination. For this reason, except to impeach present testimony, it cannot be read aloud in court.)

The Judge inquired whether the prior testimony was being offered to impeach the present testimony. Mr. Shew replied that it was to clarify it. Mr. Wall objected to clarification and was sustained.

Mr. Shew tried again. "What is your best recollection of what Dorothy Thompsen said about her relationship with her mother-in-law, Mrs. Stadler? Her exact words—if you can remember them."

Apparently, the altercation had its effect and this time Carole Stadler answered fully. "Well, after we moved there she told me that her mother-in-law lived upstairs and that she had been in Middletown—that she had been a mental case. I asked her wasn't she afraid to have her there. And she said, 'A lot of people ask me that. I am. I am petrified.'"

Dorothy made the remark in April, 1965—two months before the murder.

From the Coroner's Hearing Mr. Shew had learned that Christa was dry when Arnfin found her and when Carole Stadler took her across the street. To Major Rome, from the start, this detail had been important. Now Mr. Shew moved to bring it out in Court. Carole testified, "Well, while she was sitting there eating, she wet her pants all over my floor so I changed her to some of my son's clothes. . . . When I carried her over, she wasn't wet."

"Could you tell how long those pants had been on—just ten or fifteen minutes or maybe four or five hours?"

"I don't know. If she hadn't wet, I could have told whether she had wet before and they had dried."

"So that they had apparently been changed at some time or other?" The subject of child care was uncertain ground for Mr. Shew. "How long does a child go without wetting?" But Carole Stadler would not commit herself. Some children can go a long time. Others cannot. "They don't go three or four hours, do they?"

"They can."

A brief Redirect. Mr. Wall asked whether Carole Stadler knew the kind of car Harry Solberg drove.

"It was a black Ford. . . . Ages of cars I don't know."

Recross. "Did you see this particular car on June 15, 1965, in front of the Thompsen house or anywhere else?"

"No."

Redirect. "Did you see any car, other than Mrs. Thompsen's car, at the Thompsen house that day?"

"No."

◆

It was midafternoon when Dr. Lincoln Opper, the pathologist, a composed, scholarly-looking man, took the stand to discuss the autopsy report. Delivered partially at least in technical terms, these were the pertinent details, many of them familiar by now.

The wounds were the result of several different types of instruments. First, a torn *electrical cord* wound tightly around the neck, underneath which the grooved marking of strangulation was evident. Second, the *four-pronged instrument,* which made superficial wounds, two sets of wounds on the side of the neck and two on the front upper shoulder. The *two-pronged instrument*—deep wounds, at least two inches, in the right and left upper back. These wounds went through the soft tissues between the ribs and penetrated into the pleural cavities, producing considerable bleeding—about a half pint in each.

Dr. Opper went on to describe the condition of the face and head. The upper right side of the face had been dealt a crushing blow with a *blunt instrument*, the bones of the nose and cheek were broken, the eye was flaccid, apparently had ruptured. Later, after removing the brain, he found a sharply contoured fracture of the base of the skull corresponding to this blow. There were lacerations of the scalp on either side, at the temples; and under the left laceration was the same kind of sharply contoured fracture. But beneath this fracture, the brain was remarkably intact!

Mr. Wall brought out that it was the sledgehammer that caused these sharply contoured fractures.

Continuing, Dr. Opper said that the hyoid bone in the neck was fractured—"the type of injury seen in hanging and in strangulation—even with the bare hands. . . . The blood was quite fluid and dark . . . and this is usually interpreted as meaning asphyxia."

Concerning the final weapon: "There was very little discoloration of the skin surrounding the navel and the skin itself was not broken—but there was considerable hemorrhage in the fatty tissue under the skin. This was apparently a very heavy blow—there was tearing of tissues within the abdominal cavity, but no blood of any significance."

Mr. Wall: "Doctor, did you come to any conclusion as to whether any of the injuries occurred after death?"

Dr. Opper: "I have my own opinion . . . I would put it this way. Although the crushing injuries to the face and head were very severe, there was so little bleeding, relatively, associated with this, that I think that these blows occurred terminally—agonally—or possibly even after the victim was dead. The penetrating wounds in the back . . . obviously were early because there was sufficient collection of blood in each pleural cavity. . . . The lethal injury, without any question, I feel, is the strangulation injury with the fracture of the hyoid bone. The patient couldn't have survived this."

(One is immediately aware that this differs from Dr. Murphy's opinion. We are embarking on another voyage of confusion.)

"One other thing I might contribute," Dr. Opper continued. "In examining the gastrointestinal tract, I noted that there was a small amount of partially digested vegetable material in the stomach, none of which had passed on to the next segment of the tract—namely, the duodenum—indicating, to me at least, that death occurred shortly after the ingestion of food."

Mr. Wall returned to Dr. Opper's opinion that the cause of death was strangulation, asking him to explain his reasons.

Dr. Opper began by eliminating one possibility—exsanguination. The blood in the pleural cavities amounted to a total of about one pint—the quantity usually taken from a blood donor at one sitting—not enough to bleed to death. (It is not clear whether the blood on the kitchen floor, which may or may not have been a considerable quantity, was in addition to this one pint. It would seem that it is.)

Continuing, Dr. Opper said that because of the very sharp contours of the fractures, he felt that the head was immobilized when the blows to the face and head were struck. "I don't feel that the victim was standing up . . . but that the head was immobilized against the floor—or against the wall. . . . The lack of bleeding in these areas struck me as indicating that either the victim had ceased to live or was in an agonal state, without much blood being pushed by an active heart. It still narrows down to the fracture of the hyoid bone. . . . Without any other type of injury found in the body this in itself could mean death by strangulation."

Now Mr. Wall introduced the autopsy photographs—of all he had shown, the most shocking. There were photographs showing close-ups of the fork wounds, front and back, the cord around the neck, the crushed face and head. And one taken after the hair had been removed. The bared skull looked like a crushed eggshell.

Cross-Examination.

Referring to the two deep thrusts in the back, made with the meat fork, Mr. Shew asked, "What might be the effect of those two thrusts? Would it make the recipient unconscious?"

"From these she bled moderately into each pleural cavity."

"Would they render her unconscious? Would they render her helpless?"

"Not necessarily, but I do think it would vary from individual to individual. It might easily have to do with the emotional state of the individual—some people faint at the sight of blood. It's difficult to say whether in her case she was rendered unconscious."

"So it might have rendered her unconscious—or helpless?"

"It might have, yes."

"And those were in the back—so she had her back turned to whoever did them, presumably?"

"I would say so—yes."

"Knowing her size and build, would you say it was probable that these back wounds made her helpless?"

"Well, she was probably frightened. Now—the reason I say that is that she had no defense wounds of any kind as if she battled with her assailant. It would appear to me that she tried to run away— and this state of fright, combined with those two penetrating wounds might have caused her to faint or become unconscious."

Mr. Shew: "Would it be your opinion that the cord was put around the neck after these back wounds?"

Dr. Opper: "Well, in this matter of sequence, I can't be one hundred percent certain . . . but I feel that the first wounds were the fork wounds—made by both forks—and that then the cord was tied around her neck. . . ."

(One realizes suddenly that this is the first real effort to reconstruct the crime—and also how much we have already done this in our own minds and by comparing notes and deductions during the recesses. *Everyone* is his own do-it-yourself detective.)

And after the cord? Mr. Shew asked. Next, Dr. Opper believed, came the crushing injuries with the blunt instrument to the face and skull. And again, to back up his theory, "The brain itself was so intact and there was so little evidence of blood within the cranial cavity that it is my own opinion that the patient was either dying or dead."

"And presumably lying on her back?"

"Probably on her back. At any rate, with the head immobilized . . . because of the sharp contours of the fractures. A moving, weaving head would not show this. . . . And with immobilization of the head goes the thought that she was helpless, which would place it well along in the sequence."

How long does the doctor think it would take to inflict these injuries?

"From initial attack to death? . . . It would be hard to say." His guess would be five or ten minutes, but he would hate to be pinned down. (Some confusion here, since the doctor believes part of the attack continued after death.)

At Mr. Shew's request, Dr. Opper pointed out the hyoid bone (just beneath a man's Adam's apple). In most strangulations this hyoid bone cracks. "This can be done with the naked hand without too much effort, particularly in a fragilely built female."

Mr. Shew: "In other words, in a female of the type of the deceased, it wouldn't take a great deal more strength than the bare hands?"

"No, it doesn't take too much—no."

"So that, with any person with a great deal of strength in their hands, it wouldn't have had to be done in this way—with a cord and a fork to twist it? There is an easier way of doing it?"

Dr. Opper: "Yes. But not everybody is aware of the ease with which that can be done."

So there we are. Dr. Murphy, with the experience of three decades, says that Dorothy could not have died of strangulation. The usual signs—bulging eyes, hemorrhages in certain areas—were not present. He believes that she died of head injuries and that strangulation was post mortem. Dr. Opper, with an impressive scientific background, says that the head injuries occurred when she was dying or already dead—there was not enough blood surrounding them and the brain was intact. He believes that she died of strangulation. Both doctors offer sound reasons to support their opinions. But the opinions are diametrically opposite.

And how much does it matter, in determining the guilt or innocence of the accused, who is right?

◆

After nearly a whole day of gory testimony, the session ended on a more prosaic note, with two witnesses who were involved purely by chance, and we returned briefly to Harry Solberg.

First, Mr. William L. Flagg, the patrolman for the Metropolitan Water District, who had noticed and reported the black '59 Ford. Mr. Flagg, a stocky man in his mid-thirties, did not know Harry by sight, but he is a partner in a used-car garage and he knows a model of a car when he sees it. On June 15, 1965, he stated, on his regular patrol, alone in the police car, he went past the Thompsen house, traveling south, from East Hartland toward Barkhamsted. "It was roughly between one thirty and quarter to two. I noticed a real shiny '59 Ford pull up there when I went by. I looked in my mirror and I noticed the fellow getting out and walking around the front, and the reason I happened to notice this car was—about two or three weeks prior to this we had a suspect that we arrested on the reservoir beach for an indecent exposure case who was driving a car very similar to this one, and that is why this one attracted my attention." The car was heading north, toward East Hartland, and came to a stop just north of the Thompsen driveway—along the edge of the highway.

Mr. Wall: "Were you able to recognize the person who got out at that time?"

"No, I wasn't."

"Were you able to give any general description of him?"

"I gave a general description of him, but as soon as I saw the person had no connection with the person I thought he might be, I didn't pay too much attention. This man was fairly slim, but not skinny. Built very nice. Probably five foot eight. He had light hair—well-groomed, and had on a pink shirt and gray trousers. The car was definitely a 1959 Ford—definitely a two-door sedan." He did not note the license number.

In Cross-Examination Mr. Shew asked, "The man you saw get out of this car, you would not have any idea whether that was the man sitting beside me, would you?"

"Not positively."

"What do you mean, 'not positively'? You don't know, do you?"

"No, I don't."

• • •

The final witness of the day. Mr. Frederick P. Richards, a jeweler from Winsted, a small compact man, perhaps in his fifties. Mr. Wall devoted a few minutes to the exact location of Mr. Richards' store in Winsted and to the type of merchandise sold (a plug for Mr. Richards' establishment) and then proceeded to the information Mr. Richards had to offer, which was that Harry Solberg purchased an engagement ring and a wedding ring in his store. "I don't remember the exact date," Mr. Richards said, "but I do have it on sales slips." Mr. Wall handed him a sales slip and Mr. Richards said, "The date is June 17, 1965."

Then, explaining the transaction, "He came in to purchase an engagement ring and a wedding ring, which he did. The price is on here. He made arrangements to pay for it by time payments. I asked him if he was twenty-one years old and he said he wasn't. I said, 'You will have to have your mother or father sign for you.' He said he would do it, which he did. He didn't take the ring at that time. He came in later to get it."

"And did he make a payment on that day?"

"No, I guess he didn't. He agreed to pay ten dollars a week. He paid twenty-five dollars when he first took the ring."

"He did pay you twenty-five dollars?"

"The first payment was twenty-five dollars and he agreed to pay ten dollars a week after that."

Handing Mr. Richards the anonymous Letter, Mr. Wall directed his attention to the postmark. "I ask you whether that date is the same date as the one on which he came to make this payment to you?"

Mr. Richards: "Yes, the date on the envelope is June 17."

Now this is wrong! Mr. Richards testified that Harry came to the store on June 17, did *not* take the ring that day, did *not* make a payment that day, paid him twenty-five dollars *when he took the ring*. People do not listen—witnesses on the stand are often nervous and inexperienced. Mr. Richards' attention had been directed to the date on the Letter, and when asked if it was the same, he replied yes—not picking up the all-important word, the date he made *"payment,"* not the date he made the *"purchase."* But was this unintentional with Mr. Wall, or was it the trial technique of a skillful prosecutor? The suggestion is obvious: On June 15 Dorothy was murdered and a piggy bank stolen that Arnfin testified contained $20–$25. On June 17 Harry Solberg purchased a ring for which he agreed to make a down payment of $25. But Mr. Richards testified first that he did not make the payment that day. Later Mr. Wall suggested that he did pay $25 that day with a question to which Mr. Richards listened only in part and to which he replied yes.

To a layman this poses disquieting questions. Is it the function of the State to enter into a trial as though it were a contest—a football game—to win with anything, even with trick plays if necessary? If it is a fact that Harry Solberg did not pay $25 on June 17, should there be an effort to leave the impression with the Jury that he did?

But Mr. Shew did not pick this up, either. He had no questions for Mr. Richards—and the day was over, and the week, too. There was other business in this courtroom on Friday, and the Judge adjourned until the following Tuesday morning, with the usual warning to the jurors to avoid conversations, television and radio programs, and newspaper articles about the trial.

• • •

Even if they tried, one wondered if the jurors could remain insulated. Over the weekend the public as far as seventy miles away, and especially the lawyers who were watching this case, gossiped and argued. But not about the two days of testimony—not about the evidence—not about Harry Solberg. They played a medley of old tunes over again, both sides of the record, and added a few new ones.

"This is personal vindication. He's doing it to vindicate himself because they went over his head and arrested somebody else."

"Rome isn't certain about this case. He's never seen the evidence against Solberg. He's hearing it now—in court."

"He has a flawless record. Twenty-nine years without a mistake. Now he's made one. And he can't admit it."

And the other side.

"Oh, he's made arrests you could *object* to—he's detained more than one murderer to get a confession—but never a *wrong* arrest. Don't quote me. In court I'm always on the other side."

"You always see the side where the cop is out to get his man. Here's a police officer who came forward to take the part of a man he says is innocent."

"He didn't have to get mixed up in this. All he had to say was he hadn't seen the new evidence and couldn't comment."

The lawyers were a Greek chorus. They knew the leading characters and they understood the plot and they observed and commented and made predictions.

"The State Police are split wide open," they said. "This is more than a difference of opinion. This won't be the last of it."

In the end it always came full circle. Whatever the opinion of the case, whatever the opinion of Rome, his action was unprecedented, and because of that the trial was in the limelight. The offstage drama held the spotlight; the onstage drama played in its reflected glow. People who would never have noticed this trial questioned and argued about Harry Solberg's guilt because of Rome. Many people had already passed judgment on it based on their opinions of Rome. And the verdict on Harry Solberg would be a verdict on Rome.

8

Tuesday, October 4

After a four-day absence the setting was like a drama in
which the curtain rises on an empty stage and the stagehands walk
on and set up the props and then the minor players drift in and take
their places—everyone awaiting the arrival of the stars. The faces of
the bit players were becoming familiar—the Deputy Sheriffs, standing near the jury room door; the High Sheriff, an overseer at the
rear door; the County Detective, Sam Holden, mid-forties, tortoise-
shell glasses, medium build. Mr. Holden appeared to be a rather
nervous man; he would sit or stand awhile near the door, leave,
return, leave again. The High Sheriff's wife sat in the first row
where seats were reserved for her daily. A buxom lady—a bit of the
chatelaine of the village—she chatted with court officials, greeted
her friends, seemed to know everyone. Every day the visitors' section was filling up a little earlier, and once the seats were taken
people were turned away—no standing allowed. The "regulars"
were mostly women who lived in the area, "taking in the trial." Few
friends of the victim or of the defendant were present.

Today in a packed courtroom, one face was missing. On Saturday, in St. Francis Hospital in Hartford, Sharon gave birth to a
daughter.

The session began in a low key with the first part of the morning
devoted to establishing that Harry wrote the incriminating Letter.
On hand were two witnesses to identify known samples of his
handwriting; waiting in the wings, the State's handwriting expert,

Mr. Anthony Liberi. First, Mr. Robert Slattery, personnel investigator at Pratt-Whitney, identified the application form that Harry filled out when he was hired in February, 1966.

As this incriminating evidence against him unfolded, Harry, perfectly relaxed, wearing a neat brown suit, alternated between listening and writing in his notebook. One searched his face this morning for some sign of strain and found none. And yet this weekend must have been one of the great ordeals of his life. He had endured a four-day interruption in his trial, his wife was taken to the hospital, his daughter born while her father was in jail and on trial for his life. He had not seen his wife since the child arrived. He had not seen the child. As one looked at Harry, with that insulated look about him, one wondered whether he was as unworried, as unfeeling, as he seemed. What sustained him so that he showed no signs of agitation—even today? And what about Sharon? What reservoir of strength supported her through all this? Faith? Religion? Youth? Or was she simply numb? Or was it the unsolicited human instinct to survive—the astonishing capacity to absorb so many blows and still, somehow, to go on?

On the stand, Detective Frederick Keller of the Canaan Barracks was giving testimony about the second handwriting sample, which was more deliberately obtained. On Friday, March 11, 1966, Detective Keller went to Pratt-Whitney for the express purpose of having Harry write a certain paragraph, the text of which had been prepared by Mr. Liberi. (Two days later, on Sunday, March 13, Harry was picked up by the police.)

"Had he been arrested?" Mr. Wall asked. "Or was there at this time any claim about his responsibility in this connection?"

"He had not been arrested at that time. . . . A warrant had not been issued for his arrest."

There was a rather limp feeling about all this—it was generally accepted that Harry wrote the Letter. Nevertheless, when Mr. Wall sought to introduce this second sample, Mr. Shew asked to make an argument in the absence of the Jury. At this time, on this relatively minor point, Miranda—destined to be the second most explosive issue in this case—tiptoed into the trial.

Miranda is the bombshell decision that extended to the police station the Fifth Amendment privilege against self-incrimination. A cluster of four decisions that takes its name from the first, *Miranda v. Arizona*, it is defined among laymen as the decision that put an end to the right of the police to question a suspect. The decision itself reads, "We deal with the *admissibility* (*in court*) of statements obtained from an individual who is subjected to custodial police interrogation." *Miranda* was handed down on June 13, 1966. The Solberg trial, coming three months later, was one of the first in which it became a factor. On October 4, *Miranda* entered the case and drove through the day like a spike while snarled legal arguments wrapped and knotted themselves around it.

This was the first time the Jury had been sent from the courtroom. When the door closed, the Judge took a moment to discuss that other issue over which legal storm clouds have been gathering and which, in this trial, was already a sensitive subject—restrictions on the press. The present issue is this: In the event that testimony heard in the absence of the Jury is ruled inadmissible, can—and should—a Judge order the press not to report it? If it is published there is danger that jurors will learn of it and that their verdict will be influenced by inadmissible evidence. Under the banner of fair trial, one group argues that the press should be ordered not to publish such testimony under penalty of contempt. In the other camp, their opponents argue for freedom of the press and the right of the public to know.

On this issue, at this early stage, Judge MacDonald took a moderate, middle-of-the-road attitude. "I am making the very firm request—I won't say *order*—I'll say *request*. . . . If the evidence should be ruled inadmissible, I am requesting that no comment be made in the press. . . . If it is ruled admissible, it is free game for comment."

Then to Mr. Shew's argument, which was that this second sample was obtained by a police officer from Harry *after* the investigation had focused on him, without advising him of his rights under *Miranda*. (Both *Miranda* and its predecessor, *Escobedo*, use this term, "an investigation that had focused on the accused.")

Mr. Shew's argument was neither lengthy nor spirited. This entire episode proved to be more interesting for another reason. *Miranda*, brand new, explosive, a 5–4 decision, was the focus of raging controversy in law-enforcement circles everywhere. There is no judge, no attorney, no police officer who does not have an opinion on *Miranda*, and whether for or against, that opinion is clear and strong.

The objection was quickly overruled. "As I understand it, this was obtained during an investigation before he had been singled out as the person to be arrested or detained." Then, hunching forward a bit on the bench, the Judge offered additional comment. "This would be carrying *Miranda* one step further in the direction in which the Supreme Court has been going—that is, five of them have been going—but a direction in which I, personally—this particular Court—does not feel they should go. [Soberly, aware that this was not the end of *Miranda* in this trial] This is a point on which we have all done a great deal of soul-searching."

Clear enough where the Judge stands and he has plenty of company.

Then Mr. Liberi, the handwriting expert, to tie it all together. Hand up like a salute, quickly sworn, Mr. Liberi—gray-haired, articulate, an Italian accent—testified that the Letter was first submitted to him by Detective Rebillard, along with several handwriting specimens, on July 13, 1965. "We were able to eliminate several specimens, with the exception of one school registration card which was filed by Harry Solberg."

A startling piece of news! The police at the Canaan Barracks had this information in July, 1965—a month after the murder!

Mr. Wall stepped over this. "All I wish to bring out at this time, Mr. Liberi, is whether you did examine a large number of samples . . . and were able to eliminate a substantial number of those?" Yes, sir. "I believe you did start to mention a card. We won't go into that at the present time."

On March 3, 1966, Mr. Liberi received the Pratt-Whitney application form. "I was able to make an identification with this application." Then on March 11 Detective Keller brought him the second sample which he reported out the same day. His all-important conclusion: "My opinion is that whoever wrote the two samples is the same writer who wrote the letter."

With enlarged reproductions, Mr. Liberi demonstrated the similarities between the known samples and the Letter. Harry, interested now, leaned forward to watch, picking absently at his full lower lip.

Mr. Wall asked, "Mr. Liberi, are there any dissimilarities?"

"No, there are no fundamental dissimilarities."

"Is there any question in your mind that these were written by one and the same person?"

"There is no question, whatever, in my mind that they were written by one and the same person."

•   •   •

During the recess a flurry of comment: "They had his handwriting last July! If they thought he was the killer, why did they wait eight months? The person who did this shouldn't have been walking around."

"Did anyone tell Rome that Harry Solberg, friend of the family, had a black '59 Ford and might have written the Letter? Or was Canaan already running a separate investigation?"

"Did the Commissioner know?" (Commissioner Mulcahy was quoted on June 26 as saying that the killer was not at large.)

Supposedly it was the finding of the bank on December 31 that triggered the reopening of the investigation. Is it possible that the bank, found on a public road, carried more weight than his car and his handwriting? And why did the police wait until March? Why didn't they get another handwriting sample and have it analyzed within a week? (While they waited, Harry was married, on January 15, and his wife became pregnant. The child was born last Saturday.) What were the police doing between December 31 and March 11? For ten weeks, what was going on?

Returning from recess a lady stopped to speak to the Solbergs. "Who does the baby look like?"

Tobey gave an unexpected smile, and Solveig's face lit up as she said, "She looks like Harry."

•   •   •

After recess, three more routine witnesses. Two employees of the Carpenter Brick Company corroborated Arnfin's story that he was at work the entire day of the murder. Miss Patricia Bourez: "Arnfin didn't go out other than to lunch with the boss unless someone hit me over the head." The boss, Mr. Gordon Disley, echoed the story. Mr. Disley left the office at about 4:30 or 5:00, Miss Bourez at 5:00, leaving Arnfin alone. Arnfin testified that he left at 5:30.

Next Mrs. Cora Clark—a thin braid around her head, eyeglasses, a green print dress—whose grandchildren found the piggy bank just behind the broken-down stone wall. "I was startled just to see it there—I couldn't say anything for a minute." Mrs. Clark knew distances in East Hartland and confirmed that the spot was about two miles from the Thompsen house, about a half-mile from the Solberg house.

Then Lieutenant Fuessenich again, and abruptly the plodding pace was over as Mr. Wall turned to the arrest of Harry Solberg. We learned that Harry was picked up for questioning on Sunday morning, March 13, 1966, at 9:30 A.M. and that he was formally arrested at Hartford Headquarters by Fuessenich, himself, the next night, the fourteenth, at 9:30 P.M.

Mr. Wall began with the arrest on Monday night. "Had he come voluntarily to the Hartford Barracks on that day?"

"Yes, sir, he had." The answer slipped in a second ahead of Mr. Shew's objection. (A paragraph in *Miranda* states that "any statement given freely and voluntarily, without any compelling influence, is admissible. . . . The police are not required to stop a person who enters a police station and states that he wishes to confess to a crime.")

Mr. Shew: "This might be highly prejudicial. It should go no further in the presence of the Jury."

Another cautious step was permitted, however, and we heard that Harry was at the Hartford Barracks on Sunday and promised to return on Monday after work. On Monday night, after he was arrested, Fuessenich and Sergeant Victor Kielty took him to East Hartland. "He requested that he be allowed to speak with his wife and parents. He said he had a lot of things to tell."

Mr. Shew [immediately] "I object to anything he said from now on. He was in police custody."

Mr. Wall: "I claim it. This is a matter of what he wanted to talk to his mother and father about—"

But this was something he said *after* he was arrested. (*Miranda* reads: "By custodial interrogation we mean questioning initiated by law enforcement officers after a person had been taken into custody or otherwise deprived of his freedom of action in any significant way.")

There was a sense of extreme caution as *Miranda* hovered over the courtroom. Another careful step. Fuessenich said that he went into the house with Harry and told the family that he was under arrest. Mr. Wall said, "Will you relate what conversation took place between the accused and his father and mother at that time."

Objection!

Mr. Wall [flaring up] "*Miranda* has nothing to do with conversation between parent and child. It has as between an officer and the individual. Not between a father and mother . . . and son. *Miranda* is absolutely not any authority with relation to that, at all."

Mr. Shew: "Exception to the remark just made by Attorney Wall in the presence of the Jury."

Mr. Wall: "I resent any implication that there is anything improper in anything I said." (The fires in this trial flare quickly.)

"Mr. Wall, I can't help it. I object to remarks that are prejudicial in front of the Jury—" (In the official transcript this reads: "I resent your trying to bring this in—")

Taking no chances the Judge sent the Jury flying. "I think we should lean over backwards to see that nothing happens that could give rise to a mistrial or grounds for reversible error."

(In the press row: "These judges live in fear of being reversed. . . . *Miranda* is really slowing them down. . . . They're very nervous—")

What does *Miranda* say?

It directs: "The prosecution may not use statements stemming from custodial interrogation of the defendant unless it demonstrates the use of safeguards . . . to secure the privilege against self-incrimination." As guidelines to the warnings that must be given, it sets down six major points. The person must be clearly told at the outset:

(1) that he has the right to remain silent,

(2) that anything said can and will be used against him in court,

(3) that he has a right to consult with a lawyer and to have the lawyer present during interrogation,

(4) that if he cannot afford a lawyer one will be appointed to represent him. (It reads: "The warning concerning a lawyer is an absolute prerequisite to interrogation and failure to ask for a lawyer does not constitute a waiver.")

Moreover, (5) if the person indicates in any manner, at any time, before or during the interrogation, that he wishes to remain silent—that he does not wish to answer any more questions, even though he has already answered some questions—the interrogation must stop.

And (6) the person may knowingly and intelligently waive these rights—he may agree to answer questions or make a statement. But *at the trial* the burden is on the State to prove that all the warnings were given, that the defendant understood them, that he voluntarily waived his rights and that, when he did so, he understood what he was doing.

Now, with the Jury out, the point before us was, How far does *Miranda* go? Once a man is in police custody does *Miranda* fall over him like a cloak with total protection, blanketing every word he utters from that moment on? Does it stretch so far as to include statements made to other persons while the police officer was in a position to overhear? Mr. Shew argued that it does—and that before any such statement was admitted, the burden was on Mr. Wall to prove that Harry had been previously and properly advised of his rights.

Mr. Wall: "I violently oppose that, Your Honor, and I challenge counsel to show anything in *Miranda* that has to do with anything other than interrogation by police officers. In fact, my question was directed to the talk with the parents in order to show the circumstances under which the confession was later made."

Mr. Shew [lightning protest] "I object to that word—confession!"

The Judge: "This is in the absence of the Jury."

"We have reporters here."

Mr. Wall [he still bridles every time the press is mentioned] "I think the reporters should be warned relating to it."

The climate had heated up since this issue came up earlier in the day. This time the Judge said, "The reporters are firmly requested—in this case I would make it an *order*—to say nothing about a confession—"

Scars of old sores as Mr. Wall cut in, "I agree with Your Honor."

The Judge: "—until such time, if it ever arrives, that any confession or admission is admitted in evidence. [Then, turning to Mr. Shew's objection] As I have indicated before, I have no desire to expand this *Miranda* case—"

"It is not an expansion," Mr. Shew argued. "There was questioning by the police before this time—going on until this time. This was a continuation. . . . This was part of the interrogation."

Before ruling, the Judge wished to hear the testimony in the absence of the Jury.

Fuessenich added a few meager details to the nearly bare canvas. "As we went into the kitchen, Harry said to his mother, 'I am sorry,' and she said to me, 'What did we do wrong? Where did we make our mistake?' And as Harry saw his father, he said, 'I'm sorry.' . . . Before that I had told Mr. and Mrs. Solberg that we had had the conversation with Harry and that he wanted to stop and see them before he went to the Canaan Barracks where he would tell us more than he had already told us. . . . He talked with his wife in the bedroom. The door was closed. Then he later talked with his mother and his father and his wife in the living room."

The Judge turned to Mr. Shew. "What did the police do that was wrong? He requested that he be taken to his home to talk privately with his wife and his parents. And then something took place which, had it been simply a gesture—had he broken into tears—certainly the officer could testify to. Instead he apparently made voluntary remarks to his parents—not an admission or confession—just voluntary remarks . . ."

Mr. Shew [quickly] "There were certain actions taken by the police up until this time which I think were absolutely monstrous. Obviously remarks made by this young man were a result of questioning by Lieutenant Fuessenich or other officers. . . . Mr. Wall has not yet established anything about that interrogation. Now he is trying to come around through the back door and reap the benefits of what I consider very highly illegal procedure."

Mr. Shew was pushing to learn whether Harry had been advised of his rights before the interrogation began—and what happened during it.

Judge MacDonald postponed his decision until after lunch, saying that he wished to reread the exact language of *Miranda* during the recess.

• • •

Among the spectators, the luncheon conversation reached back to earlier testimony. They had suffered through the *Miranda* arguments, waiting for things to get moving again. A thin sparrow of a woman said, "She was ironing. He came in through the French door." (Her mind is made up.)

A stocky woman who has been here every day: "I don't think the State has proved a thing." (Not so sure.)

"There'll be a surprise witness."

In a group of reporters and lawyers it was all *Miranda.*

"It ties the hands of the police. We're going to have chaos."

"It gives the protection where it's needed—in the back room. By the time the police get through, protection in Court is too late."

And an interesting point not mentioned in Court. Harry was arrested in March, and *Miranda* was not handed down until June, but the focus of the language is on the *trial.* ("Unless and until such warnings and waiver are demonstrated by the *prosecution at trial,* no evidence obtained as a result of interrogation can be used against [the defendant].") In any trials after June 13, 1966, regardless of when the interrogation took place, *Miranda* applies.

"The police play the game according to the rules," a reporter said, "and then after the game is over, the Court changes the rules you should have played by, so you don't win."

• • •

After lunch Judge MacDonald was ready with his ruling. Reading aloud from the decision itself, he pointed out that the language of *Miranda* referred to informal compulsion—in-custody questioning—unfamiliar surroundings—antagonistic forces—techniques of persuasion. Harry Solberg's statements, he said, were not in any sense an admission or confession, were made voluntarily in the familiar circumstances of his own home, to his mother and father. "I can see nothing in the *Miranda* case which involves a situation even comparable to this."

◆

As the story moved forward one had the feeling that it should be moving backward as well. (This did not derive entirely from an uneasy feeling that *Miranda* was not being satisfied. It grew at least as much out of human curiosity to know what happened during those two days from Sunday morning through Monday night.)

After leaving the Solberg home that Monday night, the two officers and Harry continued on to the Canaan Barracks, arriving at about 11:30. "Harry went into the kitchen where he ate and then we went upstairs," Fuessenich said. At just before midnight, with County Detective Sam Holden present, Fuessenich began the official interrogation of Harry Solberg. Arthur Roberts, the Superior Court Stenographer (one of two working at this trial), had been summoned to take it down.

Mr. Wall posed the question to bring out that at that hour Harry Solberg was advised of his rights. Mr. Shew fired off an objection. At issue now was a police interrogation *after* the arrest. The major battle line was drawn. And the Jury was on its way out again.

Fuessenich: "I said he had a constitutional right to remain silent, that he had the right to an attorney, and that anything he might say might be used against him. I asked him if he understood that. He said he did."

Mr. Shew wished to cross-examine on this point of the warning. With his first question a new issue loomed. "You were aware of the fact, were you not, Lieutenant, that this boy was a minor?"

"Yes, sir."

"Did you tell his parents when you left them and took Harry to Canaan . . . that you were going to take him there and question him?"

"No, sir, I don't believe I did."

"Did you leave the impression with the senior Solbergs that you were going to talk to him about certain robberies or breaking and enterings that had taken place around his neighborhood?"

"No, sir, no discussion at all."

"At no time previous to this time?"

"Two days before that, yes."

Now, for the first time, details of the two days began to be filled in, although sketchily. On Sunday morning, at the Canaan Barracks, at about ten o'clock, Fuessenich received a phone call from either Mr. Solberg or Mrs. Solberg. "They said they understood that Harry was coming to the Barracks and they asked me if he would be detained. I told them that I didn't know how long he would be detained, but if he were going to be there for any period of time I would let them know."

"Did they ask you why he was down there?" They did. "And what did you say?"

[Neutral voice] "I said that we were interested in finding out about certain things that had happened around East Hartland."

"When you made that statement did you want his mother and father to understand that it was concerning some breakings and enterings?"

[Flatly] "Yes, sir, I did."

Mr. Wall objected: Mr. Shew was supposed to cross-examine only on whether there was a warning at the time of interrogation on Monday night. But Mr. Shew had introduced a new dimension to the problem—the question of the parents' rights—and the Judge ruled that, because of that question, he would allow it.

Mr. Shew [at once adding another ingredient] "I assume, Your Honor, that the Court should understand everything that took place from the time this boy was in police custody."

The Judge: "Well, not all that time. The circumstances at the time of the interrogation which apparently is about to be discussed—yes."

Mr. Shew [quick protest] "The atmosphere at that time can only be described by knowing what went before, and what the guardians of this boy understood."

Miranda, under the microscope now, was crawling with questions: Was Harry properly warned of his rights? Did he understand the warning? Did he waive his rights—voluntarily—with full understanding of what he was doing? In the case of a minor, must the parents or guardian also be given the *Miranda* warnings? And (the question of totality of circumstances) can the Monday night interrogation be considered separate and apart from the hours or days that preceded it? Broad, sprawling questions all tangled up in each other.

Mr. Shew asked what the parents were told on Sunday morning. Again Mr. Wall objected: "This inquiry relates to whether there was a warning concerning constitutional rights. We are getting pretty far afield, Mr. Shew, when we get back to the interrogation of a couple of days prior."

Mr. Shew [indignant] "Well, if the guardians of this boy were unaware of the true nature of the questioning—were unaware of why he was there—and didn't go there, didn't hire an attorney, didn't realize the seriousness of the situation, I think that is very important and it should be spread on the record. You can't just take this one statement to a minor—with his parents out of the picture—and judge on that alone!" Before this, one had the feeling that Mr. Shew was doing his best with skimpy wares. Now there was a new ring to his protest.

A few more crumbs of the story. On Sunday morning, Fuessenich said, Harry's parents called a second time. "As I recall, they wondered if I had any more information and, as I remember, I said that Harry had not yet gotten to the Barracks." And had he gotten to the Barracks then? "I don't remember." There was also a third call, about which Fuessenich remembered nothing and made no notes.

Mr. Shew: "And then what happened that afternoon?"

Objection.

Mr. Shew [heatedly] "This was a continuous process—from Sunday morning, the thirteenth of March, until Tuesday morning, the fifteenth of March, with an interval in between."

Mr. Wall: "It is in evidence that the arrest was made on the fifteenth. He was not in custody until the fifteenth. Any of these questions that were previous to his having been taken into custody had nothing to do with the interrogation which took place on the fifteenth." (It is in evidence that the arrest was made on the fourteenth at 9:30 P.M.)

Mr. Shew: "He was *in effect* in custody—"

The Judge: "He was detained against his will." (Another snarl.

When is a person in custody? Is there a difference between custody and detention? In legal semantics, perhaps—but in reality?)

With Mr. Wall fighting to keep out anything that happened *before* Harry's arrest, and Mr. Shew objecting to anything that happened *after* it, even with the Jury absent, we were getting few facts.

The legal debate over *Miranda* continued through the afternoon with the Judge carrying the burden of the argument for admission of the interrogation.

He argued that *Miranda* refers to *continuous questioning*, and that this was not *continuous* but *successive* questionings, with intervals in between. He pointed out that Harry Solberg was not held incommunicado in strange surroundings or prevented from speaking to his parents, and that *Miranda* states that the accused has the right at any point to refuse to answer and to say that he wants an attorney. At the time of this interrogation the accused had a right to say that. "According to the officer he was advised of his rights. . . . If he was given the opportunity at that point to say that he wanted a lawyer, I don't see what difference it makes if this was a part of a two-day or three-day questioning. I don't see the relevance of the circumstances surrounding the prior questioning."

Mr. Shew countered that, regardless of the interval, this was a *long* period of questioning. (*Miranda* reads: "Whatever the testimony of authorities . . . the fact of lengthy interrogation or incommunicado incarceration before a statement is made, is strong evidence that the accused did not validly waive his rights.") "*Miranda* would be meaningless if you could say that what took place at a certain instant was relevant and ignore what went on before." He believed that it was Mr. Wall's duty to bring out all the circumstances preceding this interrogation.

Mr. Wall: "Your Honor, there is no evidence whatsoever before this Court that there was any such continuous questioning."

The Judge: "This is what Mr. Shew is trying to bring out. I will allow him to show, if he can, any evidence . . . of a long period of detention in unfamiliar surroundings or of being subjected to questioning. . . ."

At this point the issue seemed to have narrowed down to the significance of the intervals between periods of questioning and, to some extent, his communication with his parents. Turning again to Fuessenich, Mr. Shew went back to the beginning.

Fuessenich filled in a few more details. Harry was picked up that Sunday morning by Detective Rebillard and arrived at the Canaan Barracks at about 10:30 A.M. "He had something to eat in our kitchen and Detective Rebillard talked with him . . . for about an hour and three quarters." During that time Harry admitted writing the Letter. Then Fuessenich, himself, questioned him—for about three quarters of an hour—about the Letter. Fuessenich did not advise Harry of his rights that morning, but Rebillard did.

"And then?"

"I suggested to Harry to clear the air—I asked him if he would consider taking a polygraph examination. He said that he wanted to talk with his parents first." Then, according to Fuessenich, he consented. (Now it became clear why Harry was at the Hartford Barracks on Sunday afternoon. He was brought there to take a lie-detector test.) They arrived at "about quarter to four."

(The time does not work out. If Harry arrived at Canaan at 10:30, ate, was questioned for an hour and three quarters by Rebillard and then for forty-five minutes by Fuessenich, that would bring the time to about 1:15. It is about a one-hour trip to Hartford, although Fuessenich said that it took an hour and a half that day. Even allowing time for fussing around and telephoning to Harry's parents, we are short of a quarter to four.)

They remained at the Hartford Barracks until about quarter to eight when Harry went home with his parents and his wife. He returned the next day, Monday, at about five o'clock.

Mr. Shew: "So he had been questioned by you or Detective Rebillard or somebody else from Sunday morning until Sunday night at eight-thirty?"

"Yes, sir. There was a lapse of time during which he ate in our kitchen and he called his parents." (In certain cases much has been made of a suspect being deprived of food. Fuessenich seemed to make the point every chance he had that Harry was fed.) "We drove to Hartford and he had a private conversation with his parents. There was a period of waiting at the Hartford Barracks."

On Monday, Harry was at the Hartford Barracks from 5:00 P.M. until they left for Canaan, stopping on the way at East Hartland.

Mr. Shew: "So that before Arthur Roberts took any statement

from Mr. Solberg, he had been in your custody for how many hours?"

"From five until roughly about midnight."

"And the day before he had been in your custody from about nine thirty in the morning until that night at nine o'clock?" (Fuessenich corrected it to eight o'clock.) "And this preceded your questioning Harry at the Canaan Barracks early Tuesday morning. Right?"

"Yes, sir."

Mr. Shew considered that he had shown that *Miranda* applied.

Still in the absence of the Jury, Mr. Wall attempted to show that it did not apply. "When was Harry Solberg arrested?"

"About nine thirty Monday evening."

"Previous to that time, was he free to come and go as he wanted to at any time?" He was. "And was there any compulsion of any sort prior to nine thirty on Monday night for him to stay in any particular place, and under any State Police control?" No, sir. (At this Harry Solberg smiled—at nobody in particular.) "Was there ever any question of any lack of consent to talk with you?" Never.

"And on Sunday, when you suggested the taking of a polygraph test, he said that he wanted to consult with his parents?"

A few more details now about Sunday. Harry telephoned his parents from Canaan, and they met him in Hartford where he discussed with them the matter of the lie-detector test before taking it. The test was administered by Lieutenant Robert Riemer, and Harry was informed of the results.

Fuessenich: "We explained to Harry that his answers . . . were not truthful answers in our opinion and that, to do away with any possible doubt, because he had been talked to before he took the examination, he would be free to go home and get a good night's sleep and come back the following day to take another examination. He said he would be very happy, he would come in after work the following day."

(One is puzzled by this testimony, even though the Jury is absent. The results of a polygraph test are not admissible in Court.)

Harry went home with his parents, and after work the following day he came back to Hartford Headquarters—voluntarily—alone and was given another test. "I told him that the results of the second test were the same as the results of the first test," Fuessenich said. ". . . Then we had a conversation and he finally said, 'Well, I want to talk with my wife. I have got a lot of things to talk over with her, and I want to talk with my parents. . . . I don't want to say any more until I have talked it over with my wife and my parents, but after that we'll talk.' "

Mr. Wall: "Prior to all this, had he been informed of his rights?"

"Yes, sir."

And so, apparently, Harry Solberg took lie-detector tests on Sunday and Monday and presumably failed at least parts of them.

Mr. Shew again. "*When* was he informed of his rights?"

"When Detective Rebillard first started talking with him on Sunday morning."

[Accusing] "It is a fair statement, is it not, that this boy was in the presence of some police officer for a period of twenty hours up until twelve o'clock Tuesday morning?"

Fuessenich agreed that it was probably close to twenty hours.

"And did you tell him that he could go home any time he wanted—he didn't have to do all this?"

[Hedging] "Oh, he understood that he was going to Hartford to prove his innocence as far as any further knowledge was concerned about this case."

[Not taking this] "Did you tell him that he could leave you at any time he wanted to and go back home?" Not in those words. "Well, what words did you use to indicate that he was free—if he wanted to be?"

"I asked him if he would be willing to take a polygraph test. He said that he would have to talk with his parents first."

"Did you tell him that he could walk out of the police barracks any time he wanted to?" No, sir, I didn't. "Isn't it a fact that the boy thought he had to stay there at that time?" No, sir, I believe it is not. "If he had turned around and thumbed his nose at you, you would have let him walk out at that time?" We would have. "But you gave him the impression that he was unable to walk out, did you not?" No, sir, I don't think we did.

Mr. Shew looked hard at Fuessenich. Plainly he did not believe this. "Did you have the room taped?"

All "conversations" with Harry were taped, except for one that took place on the first floor of the Hartford Barracks. The date, hour, and length of that "conversation" were not specified.

Coming up to the 3:30 recess there was an effort to push the question to a conclusion, with opinions and arguments summed up all around. Mr. Shew, emphasizing the length of time, repeated that after eighteen to twenty hours of police custody and questioning, any statements obtained from this boy were inadmissible under *Miranda.* "This was a twenty-year-old boy, without any experience whatsoever in matters of this kind. He was under police compulsion during this entire time—all of Sunday and from five P.M. Monday afternoon until after twelve o'clock Tuesday morning, where, so far, the evidence has stopped."

The Judge, his position unchanged, repeated his opinion that "it appears that the boy was advised of his rights . . . before the interrogation that we are concerned with at this time. [Commenting further] He was free to come and go, he was allowed to speak to his parents and to his wife. He was an emancipated minor—a boy who was working, twenty years old, married. It seems to me that the State Police might very well have been following the book that we now realize they must follow. . . . I don't see that they did anything wrong."

Mr. Shew: "It is not just a question of his being warned of his rights. He must have had a free choice. Here was a twenty-year-old boy confronted by two or three State Police officers. If he could have walked out of there, he certainly had no intimation that he would be allowed to do it. He was taken into custody and kept there—under pressure—for a period of twenty hours. . . . He did not have a free choice during this time! Maybe a hardened criminal—yes!"

The Judge believed that, on the evidence thus far, he apparently did have a free choice. Then, reaching beyond this case: "Certainly he was under some compulsion. We can't, by a stroke of the pen by the Chief Justice and four of his associates, remove all the tensions that accompany arrests and interrogations by police. But where there is evidence, as there is here, of thoughtfulness and consideration shown and an opportunity to talk to his parents—"

"These were custodial surroundings where he was held! It would be naive to say that he acquiesced willingly!"

"How can you have any kind of police investigation without surroundings of this type? You can't expect the police to question a man in his garden or on a golf link or in an automobile. In the absence of testimony to contradict, I would say that the circumstances at this particular time show no compulsion, no restraint, no unfair circumstances that would indicate he was acting other than of his own free will."

"Twenty hours should be sufficient! Twenty hours of police questioning."

"Twenty hours of continued questioning under harsh conditions— yes . . . But latitude and consideration were apparently shown. . . ."

"Continuous questioning in itself can take the place of physical coercion. That is what we certainly had here."

"Not quite."

"What is lacking?"

"There was interruption."

"I see nothing lacking in it."

"There was long questioning—but not long, continued, uninterrupted questioning." The Judge said that Mr. Shew was free to contradict the evidence that the State had given, but that was as far as he would yield.

●   ●   ●

The primary concern of the courts used to be with whether the confession was true, whether there was convincing corroboration. Now there has been a shift and the emphasis is—even if true—was it voluntary? Would the man have confessed if the police had not used certain stratagems or persuasive tactics?

The comments during the recesses today reveal that the general public is not particularly concerned with legal niceties. The public feels that a criminal should not be walking the streets, free to kill again, because of a legal technicality—and that an innocent man should not be in prison.

●   ●   ●

Mr. Shew spent the afternoon recess in conference with Mr. and Mrs. Solberg, and when Court reconvened, with the Jury still out, he asked to put them on the stand on this limited issue of the circumstances.

"Thorbjorn Solberg."

Falteringly, in a low emotional voice with a marked Norwegian accent, Tobey Solberg testified that he telephoned the Canaan Barracks that Sunday morning and spoke to Lieutenant Fuessenich. "I asked him"—Tobey struggled to get the story out—"I told him that Harry was—who I was and who my son was and he was picked up by someone and I was wondering if they knew anything about it. He said, 'Yes, in a way I do.' I asked him if he could tell me what it was all about." A very shy man, Tobey was struggling to seize this opportunity, even though he did not understand *Miranda*, to help his son. "He said, 'We want to question him about something that had gone on around the town of Hartland.' And I asked him if I could come down there and he said, 'No, that is not necessary for you to come down.'"

Mr. Shew [strong-voiced] "You asked him if you could come down and he said, 'No, it is not necessary for you to come down.'"

Mr. Solberg [very soft] "Yes."

Externally, at least, Solveig Solberg was more controlled. Speaking in a strong voice, she testified that she, too, telephoned Lieutenant Fuessenich. "I asked him why they had taken Harry down to Canaan Barracks—why they were holding him there. And he said that it was just in regards to some breaks that had gone on around in town—being that he lived in the center, he thought maybe he could give him some information."

"And did you ask him whether you should come down?"

"Yes, I asked him if we could come down there, and he said it wouldn't be necessary because Harry would be home in a little while."

"And a little later did Harry's wife call in your presence?" She did. "And she is not here today?"

"No, she is in the hospital."

Mr. Shew turned to address the Court. "Your Honor, this is exactly the kind of situation that *Miranda* is trying to protect against. Pressure was put on this boy for twelve hours on Sunday and through a large part of Monday. He was being questioned and it would be naive to say that this was done with his consent. He was in police custody for approximately twenty hours—certainly with some interruption but the pressure was still there. . . . I object to any evidence in connection with any statement made as a result of this situation."

"Your Honor, I think Counsel's mistake is one in fact." Mr. Wall, who had not participated in this *Miranda* controversy nearly so much as the Judge, came forward. "He talks about pressure, about lack of consent. Here is a man that goes right home and goes to work the following day and walks into the police station all by himself. Now his counsel says that he was under pressure—that he was in custody—and he uses words that refer to repressive measures when, as a matter of fact, this man walked right in all by himself to the police station on a particular night. . . . [Authoritative tone] Now that claim of twenty hours that he talks about is poppycock. In each of these instances, in a long period of time, the father and mother were right there all of the while. He was told that he could go out any time he wanted to on several occasions, and he was warned of his rights. Your Honor, if there is ever going to be an admission or a confession allowed in evidence, this certainly is one to be admitted."

(Not all these statements were entirely accurate. Fuessenich testified that Harry's parents were at Hartford Headquarters for about four hours on Sunday and that the police did *not* specifically tell him in so many words that he could walk out at any time.)

It was nearly four o'clock and one sensed that this battle, which began around noon, had about spent itself. The Judge was ready to rule.

"I remain of the opinion that the procedures followed by the State Police were entirely proper and in keeping with the protection of the rights of the individual. In fact, that they almost might have read the *Miranda* case before they followed the procedure. The man was not held incommunicado. He was not subject to any pressure. He was free to come and go. He was advised of his rights before this particular statement. I am not expressing any opinion as to what happened at the very outset, although there is some evidence that he was warned of his rights before the first questioning. I think that the present circumstances do not warrant the application of the *Miranda* decision. If the Supreme Court wishes to go any further than it did in that case, I would, of course, have to follow it, whether I disagreed with it or not; but I certainly am not going to carry the doctrine of the *Miranda* case as far as counsel wishes me to in this particular case."

Objection overruled. The interrogation would be admitted.

The Jury returned, and Fuessenich repeated the warning that he gave Harry Solberg before interrogating him on Monday night. "I told him that he had a constitutional right to remain silent—that he had the right to an attorney—and that anything he might say might be used against him in Court."

Mr. Shew made one last-ditch fight. "Did Harry tell you he was very tired that night?"

"Some time after this incident he did, yes."

"Did he tell you that he'd rather have you wait until morning before you proceeded any further with questioning?" No, sir, he did not. "Did you make any reply when he told you he was tired or did you keep right on questioning?" The questioning was all over at that point. "Did he tell you more than once that he was tired?" No, sir, not that I remember. "What did he say—relating to being tired?"

"As I remember, he said that he couldn't remember any more than he had told us, that he was tired, and that the next morning he thought he could remember more and would tell us more."

"Was this conversation taped?"

"No, I don't believe it was. I think this was in the hallway after we were on our way downstairs."

Mr. Shew turned away. He had no more reserves to bring up. Mr. Roberts was called to the stand.

The "Confession" of Harry Solberg

Mr. Roberts, a veteran of the courtroom, smiled and spoke right up, reading briskly from his transcript of the interrogation. "The following occurred at 12:13 A.M., March 15, 1966:

By Lieutenant Fuessenich:

Q. It is my duty to inform you that you have a constitutional right to remain silent. You have a right to an attorney, and I also want to warn you that anything you say may be used against you. You understand that?

A. Yes.

[At once to the date of the murder, June 15, 1965. Harry said he went to school in the morning.]

Q. What time did you return home? A. I don't know. I got out eleven forty-five. The bus usually gets me home around forty-five minutes afterward. [He ate, went to Granby to the lawn mower shop.] Then I went—was going to go home; and I needed some information from Arnfin Thompsen, so I went down College Highway and took another road home—and I don't know what the number of that road is or anything—I know, but I can't think; and I stopped in front of their house.

Q. *In whose car were you?* A. In my car—my father's, but it was my car . . . '59 Ford, black two-door coupe . . . Alone.

Q. What happened after you stopped in front of Arnfin Thompsen's house?

A. Went in—I knocked on the door, and she—Mrs. Thompsen—came and answered the door; and I don't remember too much after that except that I was—went in; and I can remember climbing up the ladder on the back porch and running out. That's all I can remember.

Q. *Do you remember anything about a bank?* A. Yes. I must have taken a piggy bank with change in it. Q. What kind of a piggy bank was this? A. A red plastic bank about a foot and a half long and ten inches high or something. Q. What was in the bank? A. About sixteen dollars in change.

Q. Do you remember anything else that happened in the house?

A. No, I don't. Part of it came back after I had been reading the papers, but that's all I can remember, just part of it.

Q. *Do you remember anything about a hammer?* A. Very little. Just I can remember seeing one and picking it up. That's about all. Q. What kind of a hammer was this? A. A sledgehammer. Q. Approximately how big was this sledgehammer? A. I don't know—must have been a heavy one. I don't remember how big it was. Q. What did you do with it? A. All's I remember is throwing it. That's all I can remember doing with it. Q. Where were you standing when you threw it? A. On the porch. Q. Whereabouts on the porch? A. In the part by the living room. Q. And in which direction did the hammer go when you threw it? A. Just back, I guess.

Q. *Do you remember anything else about that back porch?* A. No, except just climbing up to it. Q. Do you remember anything

about the inside of the house? A. No, not—I don't remember anything about the house inside.

Q. *Do you remember anything about a fork?* A. Just the meat
fork, that's all. That's all I remember about. I must have used it on
her, but that's all I can remember about that, too. Q. Where was
this fork when you found it? A. Must have been on the counter. Q.
Where did you leave it? A. I don't remember. I don't remember
where I left it—don't remember.

Q. *When you climbed back up on the porch, how did you get
there?* A. A ladder. Q. What kind of a ladder was this? A. Aluminum ladder. Q. And what type of a ladder was it—was it a straight
ladder or something else? A. (Witness gestures, grins.) What would
you call it? Q. Is it the type of ladder that stands by itself? A. Yes, it
is. Q. A stepladder? A. Yes, maybe—yes.

Q. When you got onto the porch, *where did you go?* A. I guess I
went out to the car, took off. Q. Toward where? A. Toward my
home. Q. What happened after that? A. I stopped on the way to
wipe off some of the blood on my shoes and a little bit on my pants.
Q. Where did you stop? A. Right down the road where there used
to be a—either a snack shop or a food stand—I can't remember
which it was. Q. Is this on the road from Arnfin Thompsen's house
to your house? A. Yes, it's right between, more or less. Q. Then
where did you go? A. I went home. I went home.

Q. *What did you do when you got home?* A. Mmmm-mm. I must
have wiped off a little bit more of the blood on my pants with a wet
rag or something. After that I can't remember too much. I don't
remember too much as it is.

Q. *Where was the piggy bank at this time?* A. In my car. Q. Did
you do anything at all to the bank that day? A. No, I was scared of
it. Q. Where in your car was the bank? A. In the trunk. Q. When
did you put it in the trunk? A. When I came out of the house.
Q. In other words, before you went anywhere, you opened the
trunk of your car and put the bank in? A. Either that or I had it
with me till I was going to wipe the blood off down the road and
then put it in. I don't remember. It was either one of them. I can't
remember.

Q. *What did you do for the rest of the day?* A. I went to work
with my father. Q. Where? A. It was in West Granby, a house he
was working in. Q. How many hours did you work over there? A.

No, I don't keep track of my hours when I work with him. Q. Did you do anything else that day? A. Yes, I unloaded a plumbing supply truck. I am sure of that. I am sure I went after the lawn mower. I know that because it wasn't ready. I went to school. That's all.

Q. But these other things were before you went to Arnfin's house?

[This is the first mention of the plumbing supply truck, and the lieutenant does not ask when he unloaded it, so this must have been discussed before, during that portion of the interrogation we have not been permitted to know about.]

Q. *The piggy bank.* When was the next time that you did anything with the piggy bank? A. It was a few days after that, I don't know—a couple days, maybe a week, I don't know. Q. What did you do then? A. Cut it open and took the change out and threw the bank away. Q. How did you cut the bank open? A. I don't remember—it was a knife or scissors, one or the other. Q. What portion of the bank did you cut? A. Top. Q. And what type of cutting did you do—did you slit the bank open or—? A. I cut a hole, I guess. Q. Do you have any idea how big the hole was? A. No, I don't remember. Q. What did you do with the money? A. I spent it, here and there. Q. Do you have any idea where you spent the money? A. No, I don't—just gone. Q. What did you do with the bank? A. I threw it out the window of the car when I was riding. Q. On what road? A. Route 20. Granby–East Hartland line. Some kids must have picked it up or something, I don't know. Q. Which direction were you heading when you threw the bank out? A. Home. Q. Which side of the car did you throw it out of? A. The right side. Q. Passenger side? A. Yes. Q. Did you stop the car? A. No, I don't think so. Q. You threw the bank out while you were driving? A. Yes.

Q. *What kind of shoes were you wearing that day?* A. I don't remember if I had my working clothes on or my school clothes on. Seems to me as if I would have my working clothes on because I—I was going to go after the lawn mower—got to pick it up and everything else. I can't actually say.

Q. Do you remember anything about a *letter?* A. Yes, part of it. Q. Will you tell me about this letter? A. I wrote it to divert suspicion. Q. What was in the letter? A. Telling how I knew her for quite a while, and I had worked in the bank with her, and that I had killed her. This is the only parts I can remember. Q. Did you mention anything about a car? A. Something about borrowing a neighbor's car, something like that—borrowing a neighbor's car.

Q. Why did you send the letter to Arnfin?

A. To divert suspicion. That's my only reason.

Q. What was the reason that you felt you had to divert suspicion?

A. Same reason I am here.

Q. *Why did you feel that people might be suspicious of you?* A. Just because my car was black, that's all; and I had the same kind of car. That's the only reason I was scared, I guess. Q. Did you have any idea that police were looking for a certain type of car? A. Yes. Q. Where did you get this idea? A. Well, off the radio—not—yes, in the paper, somebody said they saw a black '59 Ford in that area at that time. It was stopped, and requesting all about that, and my mother was saying that all the time, too—and I got scared.

Q. Why are you here, Harry?

A. Because I am accused of killing Dottie Thompsen.

Q. Did you?

A. Do I have to answer that, right now?

Q. Don't you want to answer it, right now?

A. No. I killed her. That's what you want.

Q. Is that the truth?

A. That's my answer.

Q. Is that the truth?

A. That's my answer.

Q. Is that the truth?

A. I can only give you my answer.

Q. What is your answer?

A. I killed her.

By County Detective Samuel Holden:

Q. Harry, why don't you just face up to this, now? The lieutenant is trying to get you to tell him what happened up there that day. Now, you walked up to the door, and you are claiming to draw a blank until you are walking up the stairs or throwing a hammer out. Why don't you just—if you are going to tell the truth, let's tell the whole truth. Tell him, step by step, what happened—what she said to you, what you said to her, and what happened in the kitchen and what happened in the rest of the house. A. I don't remember. Q. Is it that you don't remember because it's convenient not to remember, or you don't want to remember?

A. I don't know. I just can't remember what actually took place. I don't actually remember what happened.

By Lieutenant Fuessenich:

Q. What started it?

A. I don't know. I know I didn't have those intentions when I went there. I couldn't have. That's why I don't know what happened.

By County Detective Holden:

Q. You know you killed her, right? You know that, don't you? A. Yes. Q. And you know *how* you killed her, don't you? A. I guess I know. Q. Well, you *do* know how you killed her, don't you? A. Yes. Q. How did you kill her? A. I guess I stabbed her and beat her.

Q. *What did you beat her with?* A. I don't know.

Q. *What did you stab her with?* A. Guess it was that meat fork. Q. Was there any other forks? Or just the one? A. I can't remember any other forks.

Q. *Did you strangle her?* A. Yes, with an electric cord. Q. Was the cord still attached to the toaster? A. I don't remember. Q. What did you do with the cord after you strangled her with it? A. I don't remember that, either. Q. But you remember using the cord? A. Yes.

Q. *Do you remember dragging her out to the deck?* A. No. Q. Did you carry her? A. No, I don't remember. Q. You knew she was outside, didn't you? A. What is that? Q. You knew she was outside afterwards? A. Yes. Q. You remember her being on the ground, don't you? A. Yes.

Q. Didn't you tell the lieutenant that you were outside and *you thought she was still alive—didn't you also tell him that she had grabbed your hair?*

A. (Witness nods head up and down.)

Q. *Where did that happen*—was that in the kitchen on the floor, or was it outside? A. I don't— Q. Where was that, outside or inside? A. I don't— Q. Why don't you describe what happened in the kitchen first? A. I can't. Q. You remember what happened, don't you? A. No. Q. You know you stabbed her and you beat her? A. (Witness nods head up and down.) Q. And you used the cord on her? A. Because I remember parts when I read them, but I don't remember what happened.

Q. Well, this is—this is a pretty important happening in your life, and you certainly must remember— A. No. Q. —some of the details. The lapse of time certainly has nothing to do with that. *Did you have an argument with her?* A. No, I don't think so. Q. Well, what provoked this? A. I don't know. Q. Something had to provoke it. Were you friendly with Dottie? A. Not—just a friend, that's all. Q. How long had you known her? A. Just since she had moved into the house we rented her. Q. And all you knew her was as a friend, nothing more? A. That's all.

Q. *What happened when you arrived at the house that day?* A. All's I can remember is going in. Q. What happened after you got in? A. I don't— Q. You are going in—? A. No, I don't remember.

Q. *Where was she when you got to the house?* A. I don't know. She came to the door. Q. She let you in? A. Yes. Q. Where did the two of you go after that? A. I don't remember. Q. How long were you at the house? A. I don't remember that, either. Q. Which way did you leave the house? A. I can remember climbing up the ladder.

Q. What kind of a state was Dottie in at that time—where was she when you left? A. I guess she was outside.

Q. Now, before you said you stabbed her and beat her, and you used the electric cord on her. *What else did you hit her with?*

A. I guess I used a rock.

Q. *Do you remember using the rock?* A. No. Q. Why do you say you guess you used a rock? A. Because that's what I read, and I just recalled something. Q. Didn't you write that in a letter that you sent to Arnfin—that you hit her with a rock? A. Yes.

Q. You didn't read that somewhere, you wrote it yourself, didn't you?

A. Mm-hm-m.

Q. Do you suppose, if the lieutenant let you read that letter that you wrote to Arnfin, it might refresh your recollection about what happened that day? A. No. Q. It wouldn't refresh it? A. No. I started to read it before and I couldn't. Q. Why couldn't you? A.

Because it made me sick. Q. Did it refresh your recollection? Made you remember, didn't it? A. Not too much.

By Lieutenant Fuessenich:

Q. Harry, in your letter you said that *you wanted her to go away with you?* A. Yes. Q. Was that true? A. No. That was just somebody that worked with her before. Somebody who had supposedly sent her that letter, just somebody—just somebody else who had known her for some years before, had worked with her, that was all.

Q. In your letter you said something about *the baby.* Do you remember that? A. No. Q. Do you remember saying that you would kill the baby, too? A. I don't remember, no. I don't remember that part of it, no. Q. Did you—do you remember saying anything about killing your wife? A. Yes. I said—I think that was the first sentence. Q. No. Do you remember anything in the letter about killing your own wife? A. No. Q. You don't remember that? A. No.

Q. What was your purpose in using the rock? A. No, sir. Q. How big a rock was this? A. I don't know—must have been a big one because I wanted for some reason to do a job. I don't know how big it was.

Q. Why did you want to do a job?

A. Why did I want to do the rest of it? I don't know.

By Mr. Holden:

Q. *Must have had some reason,* Harry—right? A. I must have, but I don't know. Q. Did you have an argument with her? A. I don't remember. I am sure—about what? Q. About—? A. About what?

Q. I don't know about what.

A. Me, neither!

Q. She ended up dead.

A. Yes.

Q. You must have been mad about something. How many times have you been at that house when Mr. Thompsen wasn't home—when Arnfin wasn't home? A. I don't know if I have ever been there without my girl friend or my wife, now, being with me.

Q. What did Dorothy have to say to you when you arrived there? A. I don't remember. Q. Didn't you have any conversation with her at all? A. I can't remember. Q. You went there for a specific purpose, you say, but you don't remember whether you asked her about that? A. I must have asked her, but I can't say I did. I can't say I didn't. Q. Don't you remember any conversation that you had? A. No. Q. You don't remember how she was dressed? A. No. Q. What was she doing when you arrived, do you know? A. No, I don't know. Q. Was she doing housework? A. I don't know.

By Lieutenant Fuessenich:
    Q. *Did you make a phone call while you were there?* A. Did I make a phone call while I was there? Q. Yes.
    A. I don't remember. I don't remember. I don't remember much of what happened that whole day there.
    Q. All right, Harry, we'll go downstairs.

    "Time: 12:44 A.M."
    (There it is—a confession—the "queen of all evidence.")

Cross-Examination of Mr. Roberts
    Mr. Shew: "You naturally had a chance to observe Mr. Solberg during this examination, Mr. Roberts?"
    "Well, I saw his back mostly. He was sitting just ahead of me with his back to me." (What about the comment: "Witness grins"?)
    Mr. Shew: "Did he sound confused?"
    "In some of those places where he said repetitiously, 'I don't remember'—at that point, he seemed as though he might have been a little confused."
    With an apology, Mr. Roberts explained that to achieve the necessary speed in taking down an interrogation he works by reflex. Conscious thought would slow him down, so he does not follow the testimony or observe the witness.

The kind of silence in which no one seems to be breathing followed Mr. Roberts as he left the stand. For a long moment the witness chair remained empty. Then, briskly, Mr. Wall strode forward and with what seemed rather heartless timing, recalled Thorbjorn Solberg.
    The confession had left Tobey Solberg devastated. White-faced, hunched forward staring at the floor, he seemed at first not to hear his name called. Then, very slowly, he straightened up and found

his feet and, silently weeping, dragged himself to the stand. He took off his glasses and huddled forward over his knees.

Mr. Wall [crisp, matter-of-fact voice] "Mr. Solberg, in June of 1965 did you have in your name a black Ford, 1959, two-door sedan?"

Weeping, dazed, Tobey whispered an answer, accompanied by a nod that said yes. He nodded again to identify the documents relating to the car.

Mr. Wall: "Mr. Solberg, in June of 1965, who drove that car—did you drive it?"

"I drove it once in a while."

"But whose car was it?"

Breaking down completely, Tobey Solberg choked, "I bought it for Harry."

He left the stand and walked out of the courtroom, sobbing openly, a broken man. Bob Hansen, Mrs. Solberg's brother, who had been accompanying them to Court, followed him. Remaining in her seat, Solveig Solberg sat absolutely motionless, mouth set, eyes dry, staring straight ahead of her.

During the reading of the confession Harry remained quite calm. He had started to keep a notebook, and on the cover he sketched an intricate picture of a large-winged bee (he is quite good at this). Could it be that he had given up? Or that he knew that all this was coming and accepted it? Or was it, as some suggested, that he didn't really believe that a jury would convict him? One is reminded of reports of children in concentration camps who drew pictures of flowers while awaiting execution.

With only a few minutes left in the court day Mr. Wall asked to bring up, in the absence of the Jury, a matter that related to the confession—a matter that he wanted on the record. He recalled Lieutenant Fuessenich. "Lieutenant, at the time you were preparing to interrogate Harry Solberg, did you know what his economic situation was?"

Fuessenich replied that he knew that Harry was regularly employed at Pratt-Whitney Aircraft, and that his wife worked there, too.

"And had that been for some little time?"

"Yes, sir."

(This morning we heard that Harry was hired in February, 1966—one month before this interrogation.)

"Did you know that he had the means to employ counsel if he wished it?"

"Yes, sir."

The court day was over.

"A trial changes every day," a deputy sheriff remarked. "Last week it all pointed to the mother-in-law. Now it looks like Harry."

"That's a confession," a local reporter remarked with surprising venom. "What's Sam Rome going to say to *that?*"

In the Solberg car, up the hill beyond the green, Solveig Solberg abandoned her public courage and broke into tears.

•   •   •

The next day the Waterbury *Republican* published the full text of the "confession" under the headline: SOLBERG ADMISSION READ INTO RECORD. "I KILLED HER," COURT HEARS.

The Hartford *Courant* headline read: POLICE QUIZ OF SOLBERG ADMITTED IN EVIDENCE.

The *Republican* story, by Greg Chilson, began: "Defendant Harry Solberg, 20, confessed to police in March that he knew he killed Mrs. Dorothy B. Thompsen . . . but told them he didn't recall doing it and could remember details only after reading news reports of the slaying. . . ."

The Hartford *Courant* and the Hartford *Times* quoted extensively from the "confession," giving all the incriminating details. Both included, as they had every day, the information that Major Rome was standing by to testify as a witness for the Defense.

9

Wednesday, October 5

A confession is hard to top. The morning papers had predicted that the State was rapidly bringing its case to a close. When Court opened at 10:04, it developed that Mr. Wall had indicated to Mr. Shew a few minutes earlier that he *had* brought his case to a close, and Mr. Shew, taken by surprise, requested time to summon witnesses. Court adjourned and did not reconvene until nearly midday.

•   •   •

An hour and a half recess is a reporters' field day and if there was a split in the State Police, the press was not far behind. In the State's camp, apparently with few reservations, were the reporters from the area newspapers, old friends of Mr. Wall and of the Canaan officers. In the other camp the position, more ambiguous, was that all aspects of the case should be aired. The Hartford reporters showed open friendship toward Mr. Shew, lunched with him and with Major Rome when he was there. But Demeusy and Crowley had been covering the courts for too many years not to wait until the evidence was in before making up their minds about the guilt or innocence of Harry Solberg.

In the local camp today:

"I know he's guilty. I'm absolutely certain."

A glance at Harry, who was sitting eased down on his spine, legs stretched out, chatting with the sheriffs. "He's very relaxed—the most relaxed defendant I've ever seen."

"There was a kid who had no record of being a bad boy or getting into trouble. They picked him up because of suspicions on the letter."

"They say that he paid for that ring all in change." (Scuttlebutt.)

"They say he grew a beard in jail and played a guitar." (More scuttlebutt. And if it were true, it would hardly make him a murderer.)

"Rome is on the spot now. He'd never seen the confession."

"Why should he have seen it? He's just another cop. He wasn't on the case anymore."

"He's been on the spot for a long time. He made a mistake and they showed him up. Vengeance—that's all this is."

"We knew that the warrant on the mother-in-law was only the beginning. Cleve Fuessenich never gave up on this case."

"Cleve Fuessenich is a real smart cop."

"I don't think Rome is so smart."

"Sam Rome is only interested in a pinch—on whoever Sam Rome thinks did it."

He came in, looked around for Mr. Shew and walked out again and their eyes followed him. "He's nervous today."

"A confession is a confession. You can't get around that."

"I wonder what he said when he heard it."

(He did not hear it. He read it in the morning paper. When he was asked by Mr. Shew for his opinion of it, these were his general comments: That's not a confession! It tells you nothing! A statement isn't a confession until it's corroborated. When you get a confession you take the person right out to the scene of the crime and make him reenact it there exactly the way it happened. You make him prove it. Solberg doesn't tell them anything. He can't. He doesn't know. He says he must have hit her with a hammer, the hammer must have been heavy, he must have used a fork. They didn't ask him *where* he hit her with the sledgehammer, where he stabbed her with the fork, where he hit her with the rock. Police interrogation is an art. You have to let the person *tell you*. You purposely try to mislead him, and if you can't, then you know. You ask questions that will tell you: *Could* he have seen this? *Could* he have caused this? There's no such thing as a perfect crime, and there's no such thing as a perfect lie. Somewhere you trip him up. We've thrown out dozens of false confessions. Solberg couldn't pick up the story and take it through this crime.)

In the other press camp:

As the recess dragged on, the Hartford reporters and a few visiting lawyers went next door for coffee. The same subject matter but a different flavor.

"A confession wouldn't shake Sam. He'd need more than that. He doesn't want to tag just anyone—he wants to get the criminal off the streets."

"I remember a case where they picked up a colored man as a bank-robbery suspect," Demeusy said. (There is time this morning—nothing is happening—and Demeusy lingered over the details of this story.) "They said the guy was ready to talk. After five minutes Sam said, 'Let him go, he didn't do it.' This was an intelligent man and his alibi was the alibi of an idiot—if he was making it up he could have done better. If a man is innocent, Sam doesn't want him. He wants the person who did it."

"He's not liked in the department," a lawyer put in. "They say he's a glory hound."

"He *uses* publicity. I've had very good stories from him when he had a reason behind them."

"Another time he could have given you the story and gotten the glory and he doesn't because he's not ready," Crowley said. "If De Salvo is the Boston Strangler, Sam Rome is the man who caught him, and he never got any glory for that." If Demeusy is an authority on a dozen other cases, Joe Crowley is an authority on the Boston Strangler. "I followed that story."

"How did he get involved in Connecticut with the Boston Strangler?" someone asked, which was all a good reporter with a good story needed, especially now that there was time to tell it.

"In Connecticut there was a wanted rapist known as 'The Green Man,'" Crowley said. "These rapes occurred in different towns and at first nobody connected them up. The local police didn't call in the State Police Detective Division—they felt these were local incidents and they could handle them. But the State Police get daily crime reports over the thirteen-state teletype system, and reports of them came in. Sam watched them and became convinced that they bore the trademark of one individual. After the third one he moved in.

Right from the start Sam was pretty sure the Green Man wasn't local. He felt someone would have recognized him. The man was committing these crimes in broad daylight and wasn't attempting to cover up—he didn't wear a mask. Sam kept saying the guy wasn't local, and I remember everyone thought he was nuts.

"He talked to the women and found out everything they could tell him about the rapist—what he said, what he did, how he operated. People will talk to Sam who won't talk to anyone else. They *want* to talk to him. Then he went around and talked to rape victims in Massachusetts and Rhode Island—recent victims—less than six months. He was satisfied that they were all committed by the same man. The MO was the same. They put a map on the wall, and Ragazzi would pinpoint it from the teletypes. Ragazzi was the best man Sam ever had. Nobody worked with Sam like Ragazzi. They found they were making a lot of pinpoints around Cambridge —and Sam had learned from the interviews that when the man got close to the Cambridge area he used masks. In Massachusetts, he had told one victim, 'If you ever see me on the street and identify me, I'll kill you.'

"Sam sent the MO to Rhode Island and Massachusetts police and he got a response. The Captain of Detectives of the City of Providence, Captain John Eddy, called and told him that a man had been arrested in Cambridge and was out on bail who could fit the MO. It all fit together and Sam took two of the Connecticut victims with him and went to Cambridge. At that time De Salvo had been arrested on a sex charge and was out on a low bond—less than ten thousand dollars—so obviously nobody suspected that he was the Strangler.

"At first the women didn't identify him from the small mug shots. But by this time Sam felt that he knew. He knew his MO—and an MO is like a fingerprint. He had them blow up De Salvo's picture, and one of the women—a young German girl—almost fainted when she saw it. Sam went home to get a Connecticut warrant and came back the next day with the two women, Ragazzi, and a police lieutenant from East Hartford—where one of the recent rapes had occurred—Lieutenant Robert Flaherty. The local police took him to De Salvo's house in Malden. De Salvo's wife let them in—Sam said she was a pathetically thin forlorn creature. They looked through the house to be sure he wasn't there, and Sam went down in the cellar and spotted the telephone wire. Just as he saw it, Mrs. De Salvo came creeping down the stairs to see what he was doing, and Sam grabbed the wire and tore it out—burned his hand doing it. A little later De Salvo came up the street. 'Rags' and Sam had gone to look for him and Flaherty was with the local police watching the street. De Salvo spotted them and turned around, and Flaherty and a local officer went after him—took him at gunpoint after a wild chase through town. Later they learned that he had phoned home and hadn't gotten an answer because the telephone wire was ripped out.

"After Flaherty and Ragazzi took a statement on the East Hartford crime, and De Salvo talked to his wife, Sam continued to question him—at the Cambridge station, with the Massachusetts police listening in the next room. Before going into the room, Sam gave his gun and blackjack to Ragazzi. Then he said, 'You're a good fellow, Al,' and touched his arm. He said later it was the hardest arm he'd ever felt—he was built like a tree. He had Ragazzi slip him back the blackjack."

"You'd think he'd hesitate to be alone with him, if he was that powerful. He's not young anymore."

"I don't think Sam Rome is afraid of anything!" Crowley smiled. "And it turned out there was no need to be. Sam said to him, 'I'm the one arresting you, Al, for crimes in Connecticut. You need care—institutional care—you're a sick man.' He was alone with him for a couple of hours. De Salvo said to him, 'You're the first man who ever talked to me like a human being.' He told Sam what a rotten life he'd had—what kind of a father he'd had. He'd have done anything for Sam. He cleared up the whole mess about the Green Man—told him everything—even gave him a ring he'd taken from a woman he'd raped a few nights before in Providence.

"After they'd talked, Sam said, 'Al, you've been very frank with me. I have a couple of women here. Will you see if you can pick them out?' But De Salvo didn't fall for that. He said, 'Hey, I may need help, but I'm not insane. I'm not a whack! You tell them to identify me!' The young girl identified him right away. He had entered her apartment. She had a dollar in her bag and he took it. Then after he raped her he felt sorry for her and gave her back the dollar. He told Sam about all the other cases in Connecticut—he cleared Sam's slate completely.

"Then all at once he said, 'Major, you've had no killings in Connecticut. I don't know why you're so interested in me!' That was the break! By now Sam suspected that this might be the Strangler —and that, if he was, he should be left in Massachusetts to be prosecuted for that far more serious charge. He realized that, crazy as he was, he really loved his wife and kids, so he said to him, 'Al, you're posing a helluva problem. I have to take you back to Connecticut and it'll be a hardship on your family to visit you. Give me a case up here—an important recent case—then I can leave you near your wife and children.' De Salvo said, 'I can give you five hundred of them!' At that point the Cambridge police realized, too, that they might have the Strangler here and *they* wanted him. They rushed into the room. De Salvo took them around the corner to a woman he'd raped, who had never made a complaint. There were hundreds of them! When they came back Sam got to talk to him again long enough to get a written statement to clean up his crimes in Connecticut. De Salvo gave Sam the signed statement and then he clammed up—and he didn't talk again for three months. The next thing Sam heard he was talking to psychiatrists.

"And that's how it happened," Crowley said, standing up to go back to Court. "And there's never been a word about it anywhere."

•   •   •

Court resumed at 11:33, but not with new witnesses. Mr. Shew wished to cross-examine Lieutenant Fuessenich on the confession. "Lieutenant, at no time did Harry describe to you how this homicide had been done, did he?"

"From start to finish, sir? No, sir, he did not." (Under cross-examination by Mr. Shew, Fuessenich is less relaxed. There is a bit of the Prussian in his manner.)

"And you tried to get him to tell you, did you not?" Yes, sir, I did. "And he seemed unable to do it?" Yes, sir.

"Do you remember how many times he said, 'That's what I read in the paper'?"

[Offhand] "Once or twice, I believe." (A rereading shows four times.)

"Is there anything in these statements that Harry Solberg made to you that hadn't already appeared in the papers?"

[Pouncing] "Yes, sir, there is! About hitting the victim with a rock."

Mr. Shew [taking that in stride] "Was there anything else?"

"Not that I remember, sir."

Transcript in hand, Mr. Shew pointed out that Harry had said that he threw the piggy bank out of his car at the Granby-Hartland line, which is about five miles from where it was found. "There was a statement which couldn't possibly have been true. Didn't you think he should be questioned about it?"

"We did question him, sir."

"You made one statement about it."

"We questioned him. He gave us his answers."

"He said some kid must have changed it. Did you believe that any kid had changed it?"

"No, sir, I did not." What other statements did you consider not truthful? "Most of his statements where he said, 'I don't remember.'" You thought he did remember? "Yes, sir." But why would he give you the wrong location of the piggy bank? "I can only give you my opinion. . . . [Authoritative] That in this type of case it is quite usual that a person will withhold something for some reason best known to himself."

"What possible reason would he have to withhold the location of the bank when everybody knew where it had been found?"

[Rather pleased with himself] "Perhaps this is his reason."

Mr. Shew put down the transcript and, in a conversational tone, asked, "Have you a written statement that you or any other member of the force obtained from Harry Solberg during this time—between March 13 and 15?"

Fuessenich [a bit put off] "A written statement from Harry Solberg?"

[Emphatic] "A statement signed by Harry Solberg."

"Yes, sir, we do."

"Where is it?"

[A glance at Mr. Wall] "I believe the State's Attorney has it."

Mr. Shew: "May I have it, Mr. Wall?"

Mr. Wall [equivocating] "Well, it is not in evidence yet, Your Honor."

(But Mr. Wall has indicated that he is ready to rest, which suggests that he did not plan to offer it.)

Mr. Shew: "I am not necessarily going to put it in evidence. I am just asking you to let me take it."

Mr. Wall [protesting] "Well, it is part of the State's Attorney's files."

"Part of the State Police file, isn't it?"

[Snap] "That is right. Now the State's Attorney's files." (Mr. Wall seems intensely possessive of his files.) "I have no objection if he wants to put it in evidence and then see it—I have no—if he wants to put it in evidence I have no objection." (When Mr. Wall is upset he tends to repeat.) But for the moment this new statement stayed under wraps. Mr. Wall remained standing while Mr. Shew continued to question about it.

"Was that statement inconsistent with this statement that is now in evidence, Lieutenant?" (The "confession" statement.)

[Flat] "Yes, sir, it was inconsistent."

"Under what circumstances was it taken?"

With a half-protest Mr. Wall started forward, stopped. "This could be objectionable on the part of the defendant. This is no protection that I want, but it might be harmful to the defendant."

Mr. Shew [a hidden smile] "I'll take a chance."

Now that its existence had been revealed, Mr. Wall introduced the second statement, which, it turned out, Harry had given to the police on that same Monday night, about three and a half hours before he gave the "confession." Mr. Wall read it to the Jury.

"'March 14, 1966, 8:27 P.M., Voluntary Statement of Harry Solberg.

"'On my ride back from Granby I stopped into their house to see if my report information he had gotten for me was there. I went inside because the front door was open and the baby was crying. I was going to leave a note but I decided not to. I kept calling for someone home but no one answered. I walked into the kitchen and I saw blood on the floor and I saw it in the living room, too. Then I saw her, Dotty, out on the ground because the blood went that way. I tried to help her but she was too full of fight so I grabbed the latter [sic] and ran through the house and got out. I was going to call the police but I was too scared, so I went to work with my father. This is all I can remember except for the letter. [signed] Harry Solberg.' "

The entire statement was written in Harry's handwriting. It was witnessed by Lieutenant Robert E. Riemer.

Now that the jurors had heard two statements given by Harry to the police that Monday night, Mr. Shew wanted to make them aware of the events that preceded them. (Yesterday the few facts disclosed had come out in the Jury's absence.) He pressed Fuessenich for details of the two days. Today Fuessenich said that Harry was questioned on Sunday in Canaan from 10:50 until 1:45. There was some surprise as Mr. Shew himself brought out that the afternoon trip to Hartford was for the purpose of taking a lie-detector test. "How many such tests did he take?"

Fuessenich: "He took one test that day . . . one the following day."

"So that he had two tests in all?"

"Yes, sir. That's right."

(We are becoming aware of another puzzle. Yesterday we were told that Lieutenant Riemer administered the lie-detector tests. A few minutes ago we heard that Lieutenant Riemer witnessed the 8:27 statement that Monday night and apparently was the man to whom Harry gave it. But Harry arrived at Hartford Headquarters on Monday at 5:00 p.m. and, we hear now, took only one lie-detector test that night. Then Riemer must have played a somewhat larger role. A lie-detector test does not take three and a half hours.)

A few more details today. When Mr. and Mrs. Solberg arrived in Hartford, Fuessenich told them that Harry had admitted writing the Letter but denied any further knowledge about the case, and that the police would like him to take a polygraph test "to show us that he knew nothing more than he had told us." Then the parents and Harry talked it over in private.

"As a matter of fact, Lieutenant, he has always admitted writing that letter, hasn't he?" No, sir, he has not. "When did he admit it?"

"He admitted it, I would say, about an hour after Detective Rebillard started talking with him."

"And he's always admitted it steadfastly since then?"

"Yes, sir."

Once again through the time schedule on Sunday and Monday, and the Jury had the facts of the two days—at least as much as we did. Mr. Shew had finished.

But nagging questions remained. After being questioned all day, apparently, on Sunday and another three and a half hours on Monday, Harry admitted at last, at 8:27, that he was at the Thompsen house that day. (In this statement we must question at least one sentence: "She was too full of fight," in view of medical testimony that Dorothy was already dead or terminal in the kitchen.) An hour later, at 9:30, he was arrested. And at midnight he gave the "confession" statement. What happened that Monday night—aside from the brief visit home—between 8:27 and midnight? The more one heard about those two days, the more one would like to hear more—much more.

On Redirect, Mr. Wall brought up the rock. When Fuessenich said that until that time nothing had appeared in the newspapers about the rock, was he referring to the date of the interrogation or to the date the Letter was written?

"I was referring specifically to the letter sent to Arnfin Thompsen."

(But this was *not* his reference. Mr. Shew was cross-examining on the confession, and Fuessenich's reply was to the question: "Is there anything in these statements that Harry Solberg made to you that hadn't already appeared in the papers?")

"However, to the best of my knowledge," Fuessenich went on, "on March 15 there was no mention of a rock being used in any newspaper articles."

Mr. Wall: "Well, are you certain, Lieutenant, that there was nothing in the newspapers about the use of the rock in this killing prior to the date of the letter?"

Fuessenich: "Yes, sir, I am quite positive of that."

At 12:17 P.M. the State formally rested.

Mr. Wall had taken three days to present the State's case—and we know well enough what we have heard. The points have been made about the car and the Letter and the piggy bank and the alleged confession. We have heard Arnfin's story and those of the neighbors, Carole and Bob Stadler, and the medical details from Dr. Murphy and from Dr. Opper. We have heard testimony from only one police officer—Lieutenant Fuessenich, the fifth officer at the scene, and the man who, partially at least, directed the investigation for the first six days—who used no notes and no reports, relying entirely on memory for details of events that occurred fifteen months and six months ago.

We have not heard from Captain O'Brien, under whose supervision Fuessenich testified he acted on the night of the murder, and who gave detailed statements to the press throughout the first week. We have not heard from any member of the Detective Division, although several of them were on the scene that night and worked on the case in the days that followed. Nor from Sergeant Riley and Sergeant Chapman, the photographers. Nor from Lieutenant Fagan, the fingerprint expert. Nor from Trooper Yuknat, the Bureau of Identification man.

We have been told that, for days, articles were sent to the laboratory of Dr. Stolman, the chief toxicologist. We have heard that Dr. Stolman would be here. Last week Mr. Wall objected to certain questions, saying, "We expect to have this come out through Dr. Stolman." But his case has ended and we have not seen Dr. Stolman.

We have not heard from Major Rome, the State's Chief Detective, who took charge of the investigation six days after the murder and directed it for several months thereafter.

During the voir dire we heard the Judge direct that Harry Solberg be taken to the office of Dr. Charles Von Salzen for psychiatric examination. We have not heard the results of that examination, although, if they were significant, we can assume that Dr. Von Salzen will be called by the Defense.

Still, one feels that much has been left unsaid—that in the State's files there is much that has not been heard. And the State has rested.

The Case for the Defense

IO

Wednesday, October 5. Afternoon

"There is no alibi. Shew can't account for Harry's time that day. He can't put him elsewhere. He was *there*. And he claims a loss of memory. It would be hard to imagine dealing from a position of greater weakness. It's an almost empty bag."

Such was the general appraisal of Mr. Shew's position at mid-trial.

In his almost empty bag Mr. Shew had one interesting item—another logical version of what had happened, different from the State's version, but built out of the same State's evidence. Through careful questioning of Rome he had obtained the Major's reconstruction of the crime, which was as follows:

Dorothy was ironing. The first jab was with the four-pronged fork to the throat. There was frontal bleeding. It wasn't a deep wound but it was bleeding. She clutched her throat—there was a smear from her hand on the telephone and blood on the counter. After that first jab, *she turned her back on her attacker.* She went to the telephone and intended to use it—the phone book was opened to the Carpenter Brick Company. She certainly didn't go to telephone her husband and turn her back on a stranger who had stabbed her with a fork. She would have run out of the house. Why would she hang around long enough to let her attacker continue?

Agnes and Dorothy had an argument and Agnes got mad and jabbed her with a table fork. Dorothy didn't think she was going to do any more. There were absolutely no signs of a struggle—no defense wounds. Dorothy went to the phone to call Arnfin to tell him what his mother had done. If Harry Solberg had come in and attacked her with a fork, she would have run out of the house. You don't just turn your back on a man who attacks you and go make a phone call!

There were other deductions:

The body was partially lifted and dragged. Consider Solberg's build. He was young and Dorothy weighed a hundred and fifteen pounds. He wouldn't have to drag her—he could have lifted her.

Consider the crime. Solberg's not this mentally ill. Only a crazy person keeps going like that.

The brain wasn't damaged. If that boy had hit her on the head with a sledgehammer he would have knocked her head off.

The baby was dry. She had had a bowel movement and had been cleaned. Someone had taken care of her. Dorothy would never let Agnes take care of the baby. As soon as she could, she took care of her. She had her upstairs with her all afternoon.

Part of the porch was washed—it was wet and it hadn't rained that day—and the dress with blood on it was in the dryer. A young man wouldn't hang around long enough to wash the porch, throw the dress in the dryer, and try to make it look like another kind of crime. This whole thing didn't happen in ten or fifteen minutes. It probably took better than an hour, including time to wash the porch, put the dress in the dryer, and sand the stairs. Rome believes Dorothy was struck with the hammer and garroted in the kitchen—and that it was an afterthought to make it look like a hanging.

And finally the rock. The rock didn't stay there—it rolled off. It was on the ground. Even the police didn't know she had been hit in the abdomen until the pathologist told them. Nobody except the person who did it could have known *where* she was hit with the rock. In the letter, Solberg said it was on the head. In the confession they didn't ask him where. "I asked Agnes," Major Rome said to Mr. Shew. "I had a policewoman lying on the floor and I made Agnes show me. I said to her, 'Did you hit her on the face? Did you hit her on the side?' She said, 'No—right here.' And she pointed right to the abdomen, just above the navel."

And that was the strongest weapon for the Defense—a weapon Mr. Shew had never seen. Rome claimed that in the confession he obtained from Agnes Thompsen, she had told him how she did it and why—that she had given him twenty-two points of corrobora-

tion. As Mr. Shew began the case for the Defense the big questions
were: Would he be allowed to present Rome's conclusions in the
case? And could he get Agnes Thompsen's statements into evidence?

◆

Mr. Shew's first witness was Detective Rebillard—medium height,
about forty, dark hair and eyes—one of the quartet of officers
(along with Fuessenich, Pennington, and Sam Holden) who had
been in Court every day, solidly in the camp of the State.

"Did you take any articles out of the house?" Mr. Shew asked.

"That night?" Rebillard spoke in a low voice with little inflection.

"At any time?"

"I took several hairs from the hand of the victim and . . . turned
them over to a CSBI man."

"Were there any other articles that you took from the scene or
. . . gave to some other officer?"

[Limiting his answer] "I don't recall any others that night, no."
Rebillard arrived at 7:13 that night, remained until after 1:30,
returned the next day.

Now came an interesting study in the art of parrying questions.
"Do you recall whether any hairs were found on the sliding doors?"
Mr. Shew asked.

"Yes, there was a hair found on the sliding door."

Did you find it? "No, I did not, sir." Do you know who did? "Not
positively, no." Was it some member of the State Police Force?
"Yes." Do you know whether it was the first night? "Yes, I believe it
was the first night." At last Rebillard revealed that he thought
Sergeants Chapman and Ragazzi were involved with the hair on the
sliding door.

Mr. Shew turned to the second investigation. On Sunday morning, March 13, Rebillard went to Harry Solberg's house, did he not?
"Yes, I did." Was anyone with you? "No, they were not." And where
did you go? "I went to East Hartland." Where in East Hartland?
"To the center of East Hartland."

But after this bit of sparring, Rebillard remembered that Sunday
morning very well. "At approximately 9:30 A.M. Harry came out of
the house with a snow shovel . . . to shovel out his car. . . . I

pulled alongside the driveway and called Harry over and asked him if he remembered me and he said he did."

"Why would he remember you?"

"Because I had talked to him previously." Now it came out that Rebillard and Pennington had talked to Harry three days after the murder—on June 18, 1965. They were checking black Fords and called at the Solberg home where they talked to Harry and his mother for about fifteen minutes. The car was there that day but they did not search it.

Mr. Shew· "Why didn't you look in the car?"

"Why didn't we look in the car? . . . If we had and had found anything, it would have been thrown out anyway. . . . It would have been an illegal search."

[Sharp] "There is no rule against looking around, is there?"

"No, sir, I don't believe there is—*yet.*"

The Judge laughed. "It may come in time," he said, and the spectators laughed and Rebillard smiled, too, and looked rather pleased with himself.

Mr. Shew: "If you had a reason to look in the car, you could have asked to do it, couldn't you?"

"Yes, we could have."

(In the alleged confession Harry said that the bank was in the trunk for a couple of days or a week.)

Concerning that Sunday morning, March 13, Rebillard seemed to have almost total recall. "I advised Harry that I wanted to talk to him about a very confidential matter and that I would like him to accompany me to Troop B, Canaan. I also advised him he was not under arrest. Harry asked me how long it would be. I told him, due to the bad road conditions, that it had snowed quite heavily that night, it would take at least an hour there and an hour back and possibly several hours or more at the Troop. Then Harry mentioned . . . that it would interfere with going to church but he would go in and talk to his wife about it. So I said, 'All right,' and Harry left. . . . He went back through the snow and into his house and stayed in there approximately five minutes, I would say."

On the way to Canaan, they talked about cars, Harry's asthma, his work. At Canaan, they had coffee and doughnuts in the kitchen (food again). "At approximately 10:45 Harry and I went upstairs to a private room. . . . I advised Harry of his rights before I questioned him on any matter further. . . . I told him he did not have to make any statements, he did not have to write any statements, he did not have to sign any statements, he did not have to talk to me, he was entitled to counsel, and I believe I also added anything he said could be used against him." Then he questioned Harry about the Letter.

Mr. Shew: "Do you think that he understood what you meant when you warned him of his rights?"

"Yes, sir. I asked him if he understood and he said, 'Yes.' "

"Do you think he did?"

[Flatly] "Of course."

Rebillard testified that he questioned Harry for about an hour and a half on Sunday morning, and then Fuessenich questioned him for, he believed, about twenty to thirty minutes. Then coffee and sandwiches and milk (again!) and then to Hartford where Lieutenant Riemer took over for, as Rebillard recalled, about an hour and a half. But here his memory began to fail again.

Mr. Shew asked, "After Lieutenant Riemer got through, who took over then?" I don't recall. "He didn't leave when Lieutenant Riemer got through with him, did he?" He left shortly after. "What time did Lieutenant Riemer get through with him?" I'm not sure of that time. "Well, how long did you listen in? What time did you stop listening in?" What time did I stop listening in? (Rebillard often answers a question with a question.) Mr. Shew [growing impatience] "Listening in—on the Riemer deal. While he was with Lieutenant Riemer, what time did you stop listening in?" I don't recall that.

(The time schedule was more full of holes than ever. Yesterday Fuessenich testified that they were in Hartford on Sunday for more than four hours—from 3:45 until about 8:00 P.M. We heard of brief conversations between Fuessenich and Harry's parents, and between Harry and his parents. If the session with Riemer, which has been called "one lie-detector test," lasted an hour and a half—which is too long for one lie-detector test—what happened during the remaining two hours? This trial has developed a second mystery, already called, privately, the "Two Days") But from Rebillard there were few answers. He did not recall what time the whole thing ended on Sunday.

Concerning Monday. "I don't recall questioning Harry on Monday," Rebillard said. He believed that Riemer questioned him from about 5:15 until about 8:00. (The first statement, witnessed by Riemer, was at 8:27. One lie-detector test?)

Mr. Shew: "All that time he was being questioned by Lieutenant Riemer?"

"Not all that time, no." Well, when he wasn't being questioned by Riemer, what was taking place? "He would be sitting alone." How much was he sitting alone? "Well, he had been left for five minutes, maybe." (In the press row a muffled snort and someone muttered: "Well, *that* makes a difference!") How many times? "Oh, perhaps several." So that from five o'clock until after eight o'clock, he had rests of three five-minute periods—is that a fair statement? "It is possible, yes."

"And later at the Canaan Barracks, did you take part in any questioning then? Monday night or early Tuesday morning?"

"Yes, sir." Rebillard said that Harry arrived at Canaan that night around 11:00 or 11:30—with Lieutenant Fuessenich and Sergeant Kielty.

"And did you start in on him then?" No, sir. "Who did?" No one. "No one questioned him then?" We had coffee again. "Wasn't he questioned?" Yes, he was. "And who did it?" Lieutenant Fuessenich.

And so it went. Fuessenich began to question him shortly after eleven. Then Sam Holden took over. (This was *not* the confession interrogation—*that* began at 12:13 A.M. Another knot in the puzzle of the "Two Days." A moment ago Rebillard said that he did not question Harry on Monday; then, asked whether he questioned him at Canaan Monday night or Tuesday morning, he replied, "Yes." From the literal Rebillard we deduce that this meant Tuesday morning. But the order seems to have been that, before midnight, first Fuessenich and then Holden questioned him. Then apparently came the confession interrogation at 12:13, ending at 12:44, with Fuessenich saying, "All right, Harry, we'll go downstairs."

Then when Rebillard?

In Cross-Examination Mr. Wall, defending Rebillard and Pennington for not having asked to search Harry's car, brought out that at that time Arnfin had not yet received the Letter and that the only information they had about Harry was that he owned a black Ford.

At the Solberg home, Rebillard said, they told Harry and his mother that they were checking on black '59 Fords and possible witnesses and asked whether Harry had used his car the day of the murder. "He said, 'Yes.' He stated he got home from school at approximately 12:30 P.M. and had dinner and changed his clothes and had gone in his black '59 Ford to work with his father all day at a person's home in North Granby, whose name I believe was Howard Zimmer. . . . There was some discussion as to whether or not he had picked up a mower or something that day."

Then a new detail. Rebillard and Pennington saw Harry again the following week, on June 23, at Sharon's house. At that time they asked Harry if he had visited Sharon on the afternoon of the murder. "At first he said, 'No.' He couldn't remember; and there was a slight dispute between Harry and Sharon as to whether he had been there. Then Harry said that he did remember he had been there—at around 5:00 P.M. . . . Sharon thought it was about 2:00 P.M."

Redirect

Mr. Shew: "Was it finally decided?"

"No, we never resolved what time."

"But he didn't try to pretend he was there at two o'clock, did he? He told you he was there at five?"

Rebillard: "Yes, that's what he said, around five."

• • •

After the State rested, there were disapproving murmurs because Mr. Wall had failed to call Dr. Stolman, the toxicologist, and while it was understood that the Defense would do so, still the feeling prevailed that the State should have offered, with complete candor, the results of his findings. For Mr. Shew, before he called Dr. Stolman, there was work to be done. Last week he had asked Fuessenich about articles taken into custody (in addition to the weapons in evidence), and Fuessenich, with a list to refresh his memory, had recalled only four items taken under his supervision—the white sleeveless dress found in the dryer, Arnfin's shoes, two white shoelaces found in the driveway, and hair found in Dorothy's hand.

This morning Rebillard named one item—the hair found in the hand—and recalled another—the hair found on the door jamb.

After lunch today, Mr. Shew recalled Lieutenant Fuessenich to the stand and set about to learn the identity and to establish custody of the items taken. He began by asking again about the white sleeveless dress. "Where is it?" Fuessenich replied that he would have to check to find out.

Mr. Wall came forward. "Your Honor, if sufficient notice is given to the State, the State will at all times produce anything that Counsel wishes for exhibits here. . . ." (But this was not so simple as it might seem. Mr. Shew was still trying to find out what to ask for.)

Mr. Shew [to Fuessenich] "You know the dress that I am referring to—the one that was found in the dryer."

Now suddenly Mr. Wall protested that this was Mr. Shew's witness and he was leading. Mr. Shew replied that Mr. Wall led all last week and that he didn't complain. The Judge instructed Mr. Shew to tell Fuessenich what he wanted, which, of course, was what Mr. Shew was still trying to find out himself. Mr. Wall returned to his place and remained standing, obviously edgy.

Mr. Shew brought out that samples of water were taken from traps under Agnes Thompsen's kitchen and bathroom sinks. He asked for the reports on them, and Mr. Wall came forward with several reports in hand. "Your Honor, I am glad to produce these. I intend to object to any examination with reference to them because Dr. Stolman is not here, and if Dr. Stolman were here, he might very well tell us what these reports do state." (We heard this same protest last week when questions of this nature were asked.)

Mr. Shew [pointedly] "Will you have Dr. Stolman here, Mr. Wall?"

"I am sure he is on call. He can be here on very short notice."

"How short?"

After some discussion it was agreed that Dr. Stolman would be asked to be here tomorrow morning. Mr. Shew turned back to Fuessenich and asked whether the reports that he had in hand represented all the reports received from Dr. Stolman. In no time at all a new problem. The reports are numbered, but the numbers are not in consecutive order and do not indicate whether any reports are missing. Fuessenich could not say whether they were all here.

Making the best of it, Mr. Shew asked him to read off the numbers that he had.

Mr. Wall protested that this was a waste of time. "Dr. Stolman will be available to testify relating to these, and what numbers this witness has in hand is of no significance and is not relevant."

Obviously annoyed at these roadblocks, Mr. Shew spun around to reply. The Judge spoke up first. "I assume that Mr. Shew's purpose is to be certain that he has, for questioning of Dr. Stolman, reports of all the samples that were sent to him."

Mr. Shew: "Correct, Your Honor. I want to get everything in here. I want to make sure, because there is a lot of stuff, apparently, that would never have gotten in unless we get it this way."

Here was the fire that had been flickering just under the surface.

Mr. Wall [righteous anger] "I ask that the last remark of Counsel, to the effect—indicating that the State's Attorney is trying to prevent certain evidence from going in—"

Mr. Shew [very impatient] "I didn't say anything about the State's Attorney! I didn't say anything about the State's Attorney! [Walking away] Don't be so sensitive. I didn't mention your name."

(This was a very sore point with Mr. Shew. He felt strongly that Mr. Wall should have called Dr. Stolman and said so quite openly.)

Fuessenich read off the numbers of the reports—twenty-two in all—but each report, it turned out, listed several items: clothing, tools, and household items taken from the house and from the porch and the back yard (many of them in evidence here); plumbing parts, water samples, clothing, household articles taken from Agnes's apartment. Hairs taken from Dorothy's right hand, hairs mixed with dirt and twigs taken from her left hand, blood scrapings from all over the house. A cow manure bag containing sandpaper and shavings found in Agnes's apartment. Fingernail and cuticle scrapings taken from Agnes Thompsen. Blood specimens and hair samples from members of the family.

Altogether, Fuessenich read off hundreds of items—and for the first time one had a picture of the mountain of evidence that had been taken from this house and from these people, and of the amount of work that had been done in Dr. Stolman's laboratory. It was as though a door had opened on a whole new area, formerly closed to us.

Today there were intriguing hints. Tomorrow, we were promised, Dr. Stolman would give full details.

•   •   •

Next, Trooper Pennington—a tall slender man, who throughout the trial had been busy at Mr. Wall's side. Many times, as one watched Pennington, one sensed how much Mr. Shew must feel the lack of an assistant; and a few times the need had been quite evident when, interrupted or distracted from a certain point, he had failed to return to it. More than one visiting lawyer commented, "You can't try a murder case alone—it's impossible."

On the night of the murder Pennington was the first officer to interview Agnes Thompsen. (Ears pick up, as always, when Mr. Shew brings Agnes Thompsen into the picture. It is common knowledge that even he believes that his best defense—perhaps his only defense—is to prove Harry innocent by proving Agnes Thompsen guilty.)

"At approximately 7:15," Pennington said, "I took Mrs. Thompsen upstairs with me. . . . We sat on the couch and I inquired as to her knowledge of what had transpired."

Mr. Shew: "How long did you talk with her?"

Pennington: "Maybe fifteen or twenty minutes."

"Can you describe her condition?"

"She appeared nervous and upset. She was neatly dressed, clean. . . . I was having difficulty understanding her because she had somewhat of an accent or she spoke rather rapidly. I had difficulty getting the names of the people that lived in the house."

"Was Dr. Murphy on the scene at that time?" He arrived later. "Were you there when Dr. Murphy arrived?" Yes, sir. "And did he talk with her in your presence?"

"Some of the time. I left briefly and then returned."

Once again the time does not fit the testimony. Dr. Murphy said that he arrived at the house at 7:30 and examined the body thoroughly. (He made enough notes to prepare a lengthy report. "It was quite dark. We were using flashlights before I got through," he said.) Then, he testified, he went across the street to use the telephone and returned, conversed briefly with Arnfin, argued with the police officer to gain admittance to the house, inspected the scene downstairs enough to testify in some detail concerning it, and *then* went upstairs to talk with Agnes. So if Pennington took Agnes upstairs at 7:15, and was still there when Dr. Murphy came upstairs, then he was with her for longer than fifteen or twenty minutes. And if so, did he have time to ask more, hear more, observe more? (Like the other police officers, Pennington was using no notes.)

When he left Agnes, Pennington said, he was sent out to check the neighborhood to the south of the Thompsen home. Then he returned to the house and remained there until 1:30.

Now the stock question: "Did you take any articles from the house?"

"No, sir, not that I recall that night."

"Did you take any article that has been mentioned here and give it to any other members of your department *at any time*?"

The following day Captain O'Brien turned over the white dress to him when he found it in the dryer. Later Arnfin stopped at the house and, he believes, identified the dress as belonging to Dorothy. (This dress is beginning to smell like a red herring. Memories that have been otherwise wiped almost clean retain every detail about the white dress that was found in the dryer.)

With the reports in hand, Pennington said, he could identify the articles that he, personally, took to the laboratory.

In Cross-Examination, Mr. Wall asked, "Was the door of the dryer opened or closed when you arrived at the Arnfin Thompsen residence?"

"I believe it was closed."

Red herring or important evidence?

•   •   •

Then Ragazzi, Rome's former right-hand man—the first police officer not working out of the Canaan Barracks, the first not actively involved in this trial on the side of the State. (A visiting lawyer: "He still *works* for the State." Another: "So does Rome.")

Sergeant Orlando Ragazzi appeared to be in his late thirties, dark hair and eyes, stocky build. (One looked at him with interest because he got along with Rome, who is said to be a tough man to please.) He had been subpoenaed by Mr. Shew with instructions to bring certain records with him, and Mr. Shew asked whether he had done so. Obviously he had brought something—he was holding a bulging large manila envelope. Ragazzi replied that he had all of the Detective Division records that were in Hartford.

"And there are some other records that aren't at Hartford?"

"That would be the Canaan file."

"Why were some records in Hartford and some in Canaan?"

Ragazzi explained that he could only testify about the Hartford records of the original investigation because after that he was transferred out of the Detective Division and he had no knowledge about subsequent handling of the files.

On the night of the murder, Ragazzi was ordered to the Thompsen house "to be of whatever assistance possible to Captain Thomas O'Brien." His first assignments were to keep people away from the house and to interview Ted Thompsen. "I was then assigned to assist in the search of the Agnes Thompsen apartment. We searched the upstairs attic and the living room area and her bathroom. We didn't go into her bedroom at the time because she was in there with one of our policewomen, Virginia Butler."

"And will you tell us how you went about it?"

"As systematically as we possibly could. It was Trooper Pennington, myself, and Trooper Bonolo. We started under the eaves, which was a storage space in the Agnes Thompsen apartment, and there was quite a bit of material there and we went through everything as minutely as possible." By far the most responsive police officer so far, Ragazzi listed several items taken that night. "All of these were packaged in cellophane bags and turned over to Trooper Yuknat of CSBI."

Mr. Shew: "What did you do after you got through searching the apartment—you didn't spend all that time searching the apartment, did you?"

"Most of the time was spent right there in the apartment."

(Mr. Shew is confused—and so are we. Fuessenich testified that there had been only a cursory examination of the apartment that night. It would be simpler if we had reports rather than recollection to rely upon—and the one thing we are not getting is reports.)

"Did you have any conversation with Agnes Thompsen at that time?"

"I had no conversation with her. As I recall, Captain O'Brien and the policewoman were with her."

The next day Ragazzi checked on a contractor who had worked at the Thompsen house. "Agnes Thompsen had stated that she had seen a vehicle parked in her yard—one that resembled one owned by this contractor. . . . She said the vehicle was green and larger than an automobile."

Asked about articles taken from the house to the laboratory, Ragazzi said, "There were many many items. I could not account for all of them, trusting my memory. However, I do have a record of everything that was taken by myself or any other member of the department."

"Is that record with you?"

"Yes, it is." Wonderful! A written record!

The purpose of all this questioning about possession of the items was to lay a foundation for Dr. Stolman's testimony by establishing custody. Now it was agreed that this had been partially accomplished and that the rest could be done more quickly if the two attorneys would sit down with the list and the officers and reach an agreement.

At 4:30 Court adjourned for this purpose.

II

Thursday, October 6

This morning, as promised, Dr. Stolman was here—a neat serious man, gray suit, black bow tie, probably in his fifties. Dr. Abraham Stolman has an impressive background. He has taught and done research at the Rockefeller Institute, Columbia Medical School, NYU Medical School, the University of Edinburgh Medical School, Department of Legal Medicine, and he has worked in the New York City Medical Examiner's Office. In Connecticut his work has been almost entirely in criminal cases. As he took out his reports the overhead lights shone on his bald head and glinted off his glasses.

Dr. Stolman's first answers further complicated the problem of report numbers that came up yesterday. The reports in his laboratory are numbered in the order in which items arrive. "The year first—this year would be 66—then the consecutive number. If it's the hundredth sample received that year, it gets the number 66-100." When the items in a case arrive at different times, the numbers of the reports in that case are not consecutive. If a report is missing, this fact will not be revealed by a gap in the series of numbers.

The Thompsen case, in 1965, began with #2301. Yesterday Lieutenant Fuessenich read off numbers going as high as #2462. A snarl already—Dr. Stolman had a number as high as #2578. And he had one 1966 number, which was not mentioned yesterday at all. (Nothing in this case, it seems, is clear and simple.) In addition to the date and hour of arrival at the laboratory, the reports specified the time and place that each item was taken into custody and the police officers involved. Squaring off, Mr. Shew began to dig.

Dr. Stolman's testimony, with questions and arguments, lasted for three hours and amounted to this:

From Agnes Thompsen's apartment several articles were taken that proved to be of little interest—shoes, sneakers, dungarees, an apron, two handkerchiefs, three towels, the contents of a bathroom wastebasket. All items examined for blood and none found.

More interesting were certain plumbing items—the traps and the water in them, drained off into separate bottles, taken from Agnes's kitchen and bathroom sinks. (The trap is the lowest, U-shaped, section of pipe underneath the sink.) In the bathroom trap Dr. Stolman found no blood. "But there was a trace of blood in the water contained therein. . . ." You found blood in each trap? "I found blood in the water of each trap."

Mr. Wall, following the testimony with copies of these reports, interrupted. "Your Honor, the Exhibit should speak for itself. The Exhibit says 'a trace of blood.'"

The Judge ruled that the doctor could characterize it as he saw fit and Dr. Stolman said, "I found blood—a trace of blood . . . not sufficient to do a group typing. . . . It was human. . . ."

Next, the hair found on the inner edge of the patio door. Dr. Stolman had received samples of hair from Dorothy, Arnfin, and Agnes. "It had the same characteristics as the hair from the victim."

Mr. Shew showed surprise. (Major Rome had told him that this was Agnes's hair.) "You found the *victim's* hair on that?"

"Yes, sir."

(Later Rome insisted to Mr. Shew that this was Agnes's hair, found on the door jamb, at a point four feet off the floor.)

Dr. Stolman had received Dorothy's bloodstained clothing, her wristwatch, and a sample of her blood, which was type O. All the blood on the clothing was type O.

Next, several articles already familiar to us—the two hammers, the three forks, the door handle from the patio door, the telephone, Dorothy's eyeglasses. All human blood, all type O.

Mr. Shew turned to the next report. [Reading] "'Hairs found in right hand of victim.'"

Mr. Wall interrupted. "I think that's important for the Jury to hear, Your Honor." (We have had no difficulty in hearing either Dr. Stolman or Mr. Shew and our interest is up. This is one of four items that Fuessenich remembered, one of two that Rebillard remembered. Now Mr. Wall has called attention to it.)

These hairs, Dr. Stolman reported, were a dark color and were from one and a quarter to three inches in length. Using a microscope he found that the hairs "had the same characteristics and were the same as the hairs from the victim." (Her own hairs in her hand! How did they get there? And why was this of so much interest to the State?)

Mr. Shew moved on. "Number 2303, item J, Doctor—"

Mr. Wall came forward. He had been moving about a great deal this morning, and twice already he had interrupted on small points. "Your Honor, unless—until it is made clear to the Jury exactly where these things came from, I can see no relevancy . . . because just saying what article 'J' is, is not going to be helpful. I object to it."

Thus far the facts had been made quite clear—and the Judge remarked that he assumed that would be done in this instance, too. But Mr. Wall wanted it his way. "Well, these items all came from one place, Your Honor, and I think we can agree that they came from the downstairs apartment."

The item was the white dress found in the dryer. It had bloodstains on the bottom—human, type O—the same type as the victim. Then, the two white shoelaces found in the driveway. Both were spotted with human blood. The first had an insufficient amount to type. The second: Type B! (The first item with blood type other than O.) Dr. Stolman did not measure the shoelaces. The labels bore Rebillard's name.

Then several more items of no special interest. The white shirt found on the ironing board, the dining room drape, blood scrapings from the kitchen, the dining room, and the porch: all type O. Several hairs found on the toaster: all Dorothy's, except for a cat's hair. Items of clothing taken on June 24 from Agnes Thompsen at the Connecticut Valley Hospital: no blood. All rather dull. The Judge took off his glasses and relaxed, as though pacing himself in this rare moment of tranquility. A paper bag found in the attic section of Agnes's apartment, containing used sandpaper and shavings and several discarded items such as writing paper, envelopes, etc. No blood.

After questioning about this report (overlooking the sandpaper and shavings), Mr. Shew stated that it was of no interest to him as a Defense Exhibit. The Judge commented, "Any of these that Mr. Shew does not offer—if upon looking them over, the State decides to offer them at a later time—"

Mr. Wall [quickly protesting] "Well, Your Honor, I don't believe Counsel has a right to go and examine concerning a document and then not put it in evidence. . . . It is not even marked for identification."

The Judge [patiently] "If you wish, they may be marked for identification. But I see nothing wrong in Counsel asking the witness what the report shows. . . . If he decides that it is not helpful to him, he has a right to say so. The State . . . has a perfect right to offer it at this time or at a later date. The procedure is the only way Mr. Shew can determine what he considers would help him."

Mr. Shew [in his own defense] "I am sure Your Honor understands that these are not available. I have to dig them out."

End of tranquility! Mr. Wall sprang to his feet. "You don't have to dig them out! I'll come right over and hand them to you." Face flushed, a batch of reports in his hand, he strode over to Mr. Shew, handed him a report, whipped back to his chair.

(In the official transcript this reads, "Mr. Wall: 'What will you have?' ")

The Judge [an order] "*Just a moment!* It has been quite apparent that the State's Attorney has made them available. Mr. Shew wishes to determine, from firsthand questioning of Dr. Stolman, whether he wishes to use them. . . . Proceed along the same lines."

People who must appear often in court seem to develop a remarkable patience. Through these arguments and the tedious process of entering each report as an Exhibit, Dr. Stolman waited with stoic resignation.

The next item: A pair of shoes taken from Arnfin at 12:15 A.M. "I found blood on the outer edge of the right shoe, a small amount of blood . . . human . . . insufficient for typing." (By 12:15 A.M. Arnfin had been walking around in them for six hours—how could there be much blood left? On the other hand, whose blood do we expect to find on them besides the victim's?)

Then some articles of clothing taken at a later date, June 28, from

Agnes's apartment. (By that date, it was Rome's investigation.) One pink dress with red flowers. On the front of this dress a stain appeared to have been washed out. Tests indicated that it might have been human blood. Mr. Shew inquired whether Dr. Stolman could describe the size or location of the stain, but Dr. Stolman could not. Nor was he able to type the blood. He could only report that it was blood and that tests indicated that it was human.

• • •

During recess a local reporter said, "I was just next door for coffee. Demeusy and Sam Rome sit there at this time every day. Talk about slanted reporting!"

(The split in the press has been building up off stage. At lunch Mr. Shew's table regularly includes Demeusy and Crowley. Joe Crowley has maintained an amicable relationship with Mr. Wall and speaks to him for a few minutes each day. One reporter who talks long and often to the State's Attorney occasionally joins Mr. Shew's group for coffee. He is regarded as a spy.)

Harry's baby came home yesterday. She has been named Tiara Leone.

• • •

Dr. Stolman's testimony continued. At 2:20 A.M., on the night of the murder, in the lobby of the Connecticut Valley Hospital, Trooper Philip Salafia took scrapings from Agnes Thompsen's fingernails and cuticles and sealed them in an envelope. Concerning those scrapings, Dr. Stolman reported: "I tested them and found blood to be present. Human blood . . . just a trace amount—not enough to type it."

A good point for the Defense and Mr. Shew made the most of it. "These scrapings came from the fingernails of Agnes Thompsen?" Yes, sir. "And you found blood on them?" Yes, sir.

Next, material found in Dorothy's left hand: "Sand particles, dirt, fragments of twigs, plant fragments and several hairs. . . . The hairs had the same characteristics as the hairs from the victim."

Then, several items, coming quickly. The nail set with the electric cord. A dress belonging to Christa—no blood. The pink sponge—

bloodstained, human, type O. An icepick from Dorothy's kitchen with a drop of blood at the tip—human, not enough to type.

A dishcloth, white with yellow stripes, found near the kitchen sink in Agnes's apartment, June 18. "I found human blood to be present. I tried to type it but I came up with an inconclusive answer. There was some interfering material on the dishcloth."

Mr. Shew: "But there was human blood on it?"

"Human blood, yes, sir."

Dr. Stolman gave all this information in a flat, noncommittal voice making no comment, even by inflection, on its significance.

In the days following the murder, he said, he made three trips to the Thompsen house, the first one on June 16. On that day he examined the staircase leading to the upstairs apartment. "There was a brown stain—a very obvious brown stain—on the third step from the bottom. I requested that step be removed and taken to the laboratory . . . and I reported that out. . . . I couldn't detect any blood or any such quantity as to indicate there was blood."

"You don't know what the brown stain actually consisted of?"

"No."

Mr. Wall's turn now to attack the points scored by the Defense. "You did examine the scrapings, Doctor, and found no blood whatsoever?"

"I couldn't detect any blood in the scrapings I received."

Recalling that Dr. Stolman went there three times, Mr. Wall asked him to comment on the cleanliness and order of Agnes Thompsen's apartment.

"An exceptionally clean and orderly apartment."

Mr. Wall: "Do you attach any significance to the fact that blood was found on the tip of the icepick?" (This icepick, found in Dorothy's kitchen, was mentioned for the first time this morning. During the State's case, there was no suggestion that it had been used in the slaying.)

Dr. Stolman: "It was a little difficult to attach any significance because there was blood over many parts of the kitchen and living room. There were a lot of items that blood was splattered on, so it was difficult to tell whether it was actually used or blood was splattered on it."

"Then you would attach no significance to any blood found in the downstairs apartment . . . unless it was of some type other than type O?"

Dr. Stolman: "That's the only type that I found, and I examined a great many spots." (No surprise. The picture has been established that Dorothy did not put up a struggle.)

Mr. Wall: "This *minute quantity* of blood found on . . . this icepick—might that have had nothing whatsoever to do with the death of Mrs. Thompsen?" Objection. [A substitute question] "Is it common to find *minute quantities* of blood in any home, that might have no connection with a criminal act?" Dr. Stolman's reply answered both questions: With any sharp-pointed or sharp-edged instrument, people frequently cut themselves. The blood on the tip of this icepick could have come from a superficial wound or it could have been spattered there. Certainly the amount did not indicate that it was used as a lethal instrument.

But it was not really the icepick that Mr. Wall was interested in, except as an analogy. He turned his attention to the upstairs apartment, bringing out how meticulously Dr. Stolman went through it.

"We went through every room of that apartment, including the attic," Dr. Stolman said. ". . . I must have done fifty or sixty examinations. If I missed anything the first time, I got it the second time."

"Was there a great deal of traffic between the upstairs and the downstairs on the sixteenth by investigating officers?" There was. "And was there a possibility, as the result of that, of having some slight contamination, here and there, of blood from one place to another?"

"That's why I stopped examining the staircase. I was beginning to get blood tests all over the place including the officers' uniforms."

Mr. Wall [rocking on his heels] "Now I believe you said that there was a *very minute quantity* of blood in a trap?" Dr. Stolman explained that he had received two traps and the water from each. "And in one of them, I believe you stated there was a *minute quantity* of what might be considered human blood?"

A somewhat watered-down version and the doctor corrected him. "I think I stated that there was a trace of blood in the contents of the trap, the water—in both of them. But one trap had no blood, while the other one indicated some blood."

[Slow; building] "Now do you attach any significance to the fact that a trace of blood would be in a trap of that sort?"

"A trap is simply a reservoir and we don't know how long it was accumulated there. It really has no significance, and I have tried to tell the police that." (What about the *water* in the traps?)

"And would you say from the two items on which you found small amounts of blood—a washcloth and a dress—that it was anything to attach significance to? . . . You said you found *minute quantities* of blood."

Mr. Shew: "Your Honor, I don't recall testimony by Dr. Stolman about these minute particles that Mr. Wall characterizes. . . . I recall no such words as 'minute' before Mr. Wall used them."

Mr. Wall [crisply] "I don't think I have to use the exact words of the exhibit on cross-examination, Your Honor."

The Judge: "The word 'minute' appeared in connection with the icepick and I think that is the only time. Otherwise the word 'trace' was used a few times."

Mr. Wall [back to Dr. Stolman] "You use the words, 'Several spots of blood were detected on the dishcloth.' Does that indicate that there was any substantial amount of blood on that cloth?"

"No, just small spots. . . . I couldn't type the blood. . . . There were human bloodstains. . . . I don't know how long they were there."

[Slow] "Doctor, do you attach any significance to the finding of this quantity of blood in this location?"

"On a dishcloth? No. It is common to have accidents around a kitchen—cut yourself."

"Doctor, did you find *any* blood in the Agnes Thompsen apartment that had any significance with regard to this investigation?"

Mr. Shew objected that this was a general characterization. [Then, rather angrily] "Dr. Stolman is employed by the State. The question is very leading, and as far as I am concerned he is a hostile witness and should be characterized as such. This is stuff that I brought in that should have been brought in long ago in my opinion."

Mr. Wall [quickly] "I object to those remarks, Your Honor. Uncalled for!"

The Judge ruled that the doctor was qualified to express an opinion of that type, and Mr. Wall repeated the question. "Did you attach any significance to the quantity of blood found on any of the articles in the Agnes Thompsen apartment?"

[Firmly] "No, sir, I did not." (Score for the State!) "Whatever blood was there was in very small quantities. You had to work hard to even detect it."

Mr. Wall [wrapping it up] "And would you also explain the bodily secretions that might possibly account for slight quantities of blood . . . with respect to a female living in a household? Would you expect normally to find any small amounts of blood in the household?"

"Yes, I would expect it. In any household you expect to find blood in traps and sinks and bathrooms because even brushing your teeth, occasionally, you spit a little blood—or clearing your throat in the morning. And female secretions at certain times produce blood, or secretions that give similar reactions to blood typing."

"And does that happen to females even after the menstrual period has passed?"

"Well, yes, I would think so."

On Redirect, Mr. Shew picked this up immediately. "Do you find such secretions in the *kitchen* sink?"

Dr. Stolman: "Well, you find blood—I have found other secretions. Individuals may spit in the kitchen sink."

[Angry] "Do you find female secretions in the kitchen sink?"

"You wouldn't expect to find them in the kitchen sink, no."

"It would be most unusual, wouldn't it?"

"Yes, sir."

"All told, Doctor, there were a number of items from Mrs. Agnes Thompsen's apartment, neat as it was, immaculate as it was, which had blood on them, were there not?" Yes, sir. "And in the sum aggregate of all those items that blood was found on, do you want to go on record as saying that they have no significance in this matter?"

"Well, I would say I can't put too much significance in it, if it is a kitchen where individuals work, using sharp instruments. A bloodstain is not always easy to wash out. It takes a good thorough washing."

Mr. Shew [pressing] "Let's put it in reverse, Doctor. These stains could have *all* been made the previous day, could they not?"

"Yes, sir, I don't know how long they were there. You can't tell."

"Now—the scrapings from Agnes Thompsen's cuticles and fingernails, do you attach significance to *that*—taken at 2:20 A.M. on June 16?"

"Well, I can't explain what bloodstains were doing on her fingernails."

"So they would have some significance in this case?"

"They might have some significance, yes."

"And *all* these items could be very significant, couldn't they?"

"Yes, sir."

Mr. Wall again. "Doctor, did you know about Mrs. Thompsen having crocheted that day?"

Dr. Stolman: "No, sir, I didn't even know she crocheted."

"Is it possible that the scraping would indicate that there was some slight wound?"

"Anything with a sharp point can produce a scratch and bleeding."

"What quantity of blood was found in these scrapings?"

"It was an extremely small quantity—just particles. I had to look under the microscope to detect it."

"And it was insufficient to type?"

"You couldn't do a blood type with that amount."

Mr. Shew: "Doctor, do you know whether the State Police examined Agnes Thompsen in the Middletown Hospital to find out whether she had cut her hand or pricked her hand crocheting?"

"No, sir, I don't know that."

"You don't. But if it was found out that she hadn't, that would have been significant, would it not, Doctor?"

Dr. Stolman: "Yes, it would."

"Thank you. That's all." Mr. Shew tossed his eyeglasses onto the Defense table in a gesture of anger.

This whole discussion of a small wound or scratch from a crochet needle suggests that none of these men know that a crochet needle does not have a sharp point. It has a rounded V-shaped hook, with which it would be almost impossible to scratch oneself. The only wound that could be made with a crochet hook would be a puncture from a very strong thrust of the blunted point into the skin.

•   •   •

At lunch the amateur detectives had a romp.

"That blood wouldn't have stayed in the *water* in those traps. The water sits in the bottom of that U and when new water comes down from the sink the pressure pushes out the old water."

"You *can't* scratch yourself with a crochet hook—you could only jab yourself. It would be a big ugly wound."

"Oh, a little bloody water might back up in the trap the first few times the sink was used, but it wouldn't sit there for days if new water kept coming through."

"The place was crawling with cops that night—they could have tracked blood anywhere."

"Not on Agnes's hand, they couldn't."

"What about that shoelace with type B? Who had type B blood?"

"If she punctured her skin with a crochet hook you couldn't miss that wound. It would be a hole—with a bruised circle around it."

"A lot of blood in the water might take a few days to wash through, but not what you'd spit out brushing your teeth."

Lesson for today: The best testimony can raise a multitude of questions. Idly one wonders whether a physicist should be asked about displacement of water in traps—or a plumber? And what about the jurors? Are they asking these questions at lunch? Is one of the men explaining about traps? Has a lady juror pointed out that you can't scratch yourself with a crochet hook?

◆

After lunch Mr. Shew recalled Ragazzi to the stand and went at once to the matter of the blood on Agnes Thompsen's fingernails. "Did you or anyone in your department examine her for an injury?"

Objection from Mr. Wall: "Hearsay."

Several more questions about whether such an examination occurred were all blocked ("Hearsay" or "Proper only on Cross-Examination") with the exception of one statement that a doctor at the hospital made a general examination. (These first few minutes do not appear in the official transcript.)

Mr. Shew [exasperated] "I will ask this witness be declared a hostile witness from here on. He is a member of the State Police."

That this statement came so readily—and that no one thought it in any way remarkable—indicates how openly this rift in the police was being acknowledged. But the implications of the statement are chilling. Does it not say, in effect, that in criminal cases a member of the State Police will only give testimony willingly that is helpful to the State—that no police officer will defy the power of the State— and that in this case the officers have had their instructions?

The Judge, aware of the rift, the bitterness, the gossip, could acknowledge none of it and replied that the witness had not yet made statements that fitted that category. Which, of course, was true. Ragazzi had hardly been allowed to open his mouth.

Mr. Shew asked whether there were documents in Ragazzi's file concerning the examination of the fingernail scrapings.

"I believe they are on the State's Attorney's desk."

Mr. Shew [shocked] "Is that something *you* brought in here?" Yes, sir. "Under *my* subpoena?" Yes, sir. [Very cold] "May we have them, Mr. Wall?" A folder was located and handed over. [Sharply] "When did you give that to Mr. Wall?" Ragazzi gave it to Pennington this morning because it contained Dr. Stolman's original documents. (Yesterday, apparently, Fuessenich had testified from Xerox copies.) An explanation of sorts, but Mr. Shew was still very angry.

Ragazzi had brought a thick file into Court (one eyed it, fascinated, wondering what it held), and now he said that he would have to go through all of it to find the physician's report. It was decided that he would do this during the recess.

Mr. Shew: "Sergeant, after the first week, what else did you do in connection with this investigation?"

Ragazzi: "I assisted Major Rome . . . when he interviewed Agnes Thompsen."

The issue was before us.

Before the first word was spoken in this trial this was the acknowledged battleground. Major Rome had obtained some sort of admission from Agnes Thompsen. Those with unshaken faith believed that if it had not been a corroborated confession, he would not have closed the case.

Others pointed out that several persons in authority had access to this alleged confession—the State's Attorney, Coroner H. Gibson

Guion, Police Commissioner Leo J. Mulcahy. It is known that Coroner Guion listened to the taped interview during the Inquest—and later he issued a warrant against Harry Solberg. It is believed that Commissioner Mulcahy authorized Canaan to continue the investigation. ("Canaan went over Rome's head—could they have done it without the Commissioner's approval?") Rumors about the Commissioner are everywhere. It is said that he believes Solberg is guilty, that he is getting reports on Rome's every move in Litchfield, that he has said, "I have two good men and they have different opinions. Let the jury decide." But there is no escaping the fact that three highly placed officials have had ready access to these interviews, and nevertheless Harry Solberg is here—on trial for his life—charged with first-degree murder.

Only one man with access to Agnes Thompsen's statements—the man who obtained them—has implied, by the act of coming forward, that they contain significant admissions. If he is right, whatever else he has to offer, this is his most important evidence. This is the muscle that he can bring into Court—if they will let him. Now it was apparent that the battle was to be fought, not with Rome, but with Ragazzi, who recorded the interviews, on the firing line.

Ragazzi took out his notes. At the State's table Mr. Wall sat tense and watchful. Rome's eyes narrowed. Reporters straightened up a bit. Consulting his records, Ragazzi said that he was present on four occasions—on June 21, July 16, July 25, and August 5—when Major Rome interviewed Agnes Thompsen. The first interview, June 21, took place at the Connecticut Valley Hospital. "Major Rome requested to see Agnes Thompsen. He talked with Dr. Lowney, the Hospital Superintendent, and Dr. Miller, Chief of Professional Services, who arranged for her to be interviewed. . . . Major Rome, Lieutenant Fuessenich, myself, and one of the doctors—either Dr. Miller or Dr. McGennis—were seated in the conference room. Also one of the nurses . . . and, I believe, Arnfin Thompsen . . ."

Mr. Shew: "And there was a doctor present?"

"There was a doctor . . . present in the room or one next door where he could hear what was going on over a microphone. . . . The interview took place in a large, well-lighted, well-ventilated conference-type room with a long table and several chairs. . . . It lasted approximately an hour and a half to two hours."

Mr. Shew asked Ragazzi to read his record of that interview. All eyes flicked to Mr. Wall, expecting an objection. There was none. Ragazzi turned a few pages of his notes. Mr. Wall sat motionless.

And here is the first interview, Monday, June 21, 1965, of Agnes Thompsen by Major Rome, as reported by Sergeant Ragazzi.

Major Rome: Why did you clean the stairs? There was blood on the sandpaper?

Agnes Thompsen: I didn't notice that.

Q. You remember cleaning the stairs? A. Oh, yes. Q. What time was it when you cleaned the stairs? A. After lunch.

Q. Do you remember the argument you had with Dorothy? A. No argument.

Q. We found some blood on a cloth in your apartment. (Agnes denied this, and the Major said he asked Arnfin and he confirmed it.) She said, "Well, I had a cut on my finger." The Major said, "No, you didn't. But you were downstairs." A. There was no argument.

Q. You ought to tell the truth. When was the last time you saw Dorothy? A. A week ago today.

Q. You changed the baby? A. No. Q. The baby messed her pants. A. I didn't do it. Maybe Dorothy did it. I thought it was funny because it was so quiet downstairs. Maybe she went out. Q. Was the baby in your apartment? A. No. No, you are putting lies on me.

Q. How come there was blood on the staircase? A. I cleaned all the spots. Q. What did you do with the sandpaper? A. I put it in the trash bag upstairs. Q. How can you explain the blood on the sandpaper? How did you get blood on the towel? A. I don't know. I don't know. Q. Before you go home, tell me the truth. A. I am telling the truth.

Q. The baby's diaper was changed? A. She was in the crib from 12:45 to 6:15 p.m. I didn't have her upstairs. Q. The baby messed her pants. You cleaned her. A. I didn't clean her. Maybe it was the woman that did it.

Q. Remember the piggy bank? It was always in the living room. A. I didn't see Dottie all day Tuesday. I did not touch the baby. Q. Could you have forgotten that day? A. No, I was busy crocheting all that day. Q. Some time before did you have trouble with Dorothy? A. (She explains that when they got married Agnes wanted Ted to stand up for them.) Q. You had an argument? A. No argument.

Q. What about the cloth that was used—the one with blood? We found that in the kitchen. A. Where in the kitchen? Somebody must have been there—somebody did a trick on me. Q. Did you wash it out? A. No, I am completely innocent. Q. I am asking you to remember how the blood got on the yellow washrag? A. Someone must have done a trick on me. Q. It was found right away. A. I am innocent. Isn't it bad enough that Dorothy is dead without putting this on me? Q. A few minutes ago you didn't remember the yellow washrag. Now you remember? A. Somebody must have put it there. Q. You had no idea there was blood on the sandpaper or on the yellow washcloth? A. I washed off my finger which I pricked with the crochet needle. I heard something downstairs. Heard somebody. Saw no one.

Q. Only two people could have changed the baby, you or Dot. A. Dot must have. Q. No. She was dead at 1:30 P.M. A. I didn't see the baby before Arnfin came home. When Arnfin came home, he said take the baby—Dot was dead. I didn't know Dot was dead until Arnfin came home. Q. She was dead long before he came home. You had the baby upstairs before Arnfin came home. A. That is a big lie. Q. What time did you clean the stairs? A. About two o'clock.

Q. Are you capable of caring for your son and his daughter? A. Yes. Q. Did Dot ever let you take care of Christa? A. No, she always took her to her mother's in New Hartford. Q. She felt you weren't strong enough? A. No—that wasn't it. Q. You always wanted to take care of the baby. That afternoon you took care of the baby? (There was no answer to that question.)

Q. Who cleaned the baby? Whoever cleaned the baby tracked blood on the stairs. A. I cleaned the stairs because company was coming. Q. How much? A. Just a couple of spots. Q. What time? A. About two o'clock Tuesday. Q. Did the baby cry? A. Not at all that day. She was alone. Q. How did you know she was alone? You took care of her? (There was no answer.)

Q. We found blood in the drain, and in the kitchen drain. A. That is a lie. I want to leave. (Then she gets down on her knees and prays.)

Q. Have you been bleeding lately?

"There was no answer and at this point the interview ended and she was taken out of the room."

During the reading of this report, Mr. Wall appeared to be following along on his own copy. He dropped it on the table as Ragazzi finished.

Mr. Shew: "Sergeant, can you describe Agnes Thompsen's attitude and physical condition at the time of this interview?"

Ragazzi: "As I recall, at every contact I had with her, she appeared to be extremely nervous. She wouldn't sit still in any one position too long. At certain questions, her eyes would open up extremely wide and then she'd settle down again."

"In what manner were these questions put to her? Were they put to her in a harsh fashion?"

". . . In a normal fashion—pretty much as I read them here."

"Did she seem at any time to be in distress or suffering?"

"Well, there was always a doctor present or a nurse. I don't know what you mean by distress, Mr. Shew."

"Well—how was Mrs. Thompsen treated—could it have been done in any nicer fashion, Sergeant?" No, sir. "Courtesy was shown her?" Yes, sir. "And there was a doctor present?" Yes, sir.

"And did she seem to understand the questions?"

"I would say for the most part she did. There were times when she didn't fully understand the question and it was repeated. And there were times when she didn't answer."

(One cannot say whether that was because she did not understand or because she was reluctant to answer.)

The next interview took place on the day of the first session of the Coroner's Hearing, July 16, which Agnes attended, accompanied by a nurse. Afterward, in his office in Hartford, Major Rome interviewed her for about an hour with Arnfin, the nurse, Ragazzi, and possibly another detective present.

Mr. Shew asked Ragazzi to read this second interview.

Mr. Wall [strong] "I object to this, Your Honor."

Hardly surprised, the Judge nevertheless asked Mr. Wall to state his grounds. "The prior came in the same way—"

The objection was that the statements were hearsay. Mr. Wall said, "Your Honor, as far as the prior one was concerned, there were certain safeguards involved, and . . . although it was hearsay, I didn't object. But I can see that many collateral issues will arise out of this situation, and I believe it is definitely hearsay and inadmissible. [With finality] It would be definitely unfortunate if we injected new issues into this case that have nothing to do with it."

(What safeguards were there in the first interview, one wonders, that were lacking in the second? Police officers, the nurse and Arnfin were present. And what new issues would be injected? And how do we know they have nothing to do with this case?)

The Judge, aware that a clash—possibly a showdown—was at hand, sent the Jury from the room and again warned the press against publishing anything ruled inadmissible.

In law there are many definitions of hearsay, the strictest being that any statement made outside the courtroom, not subject to cross-examination, is hearsay and is inadmissible. The reasons for the rule are that hearsay evidence is considered unreliable and that fraud could too easily be practiced under its cloak. Organized crime, it is argued, could always produce a hearsay witness to swear that someone else had confessed to the crime. A few exceptions to the rule have developed in cases where the hearsay statement was the only one possibly available, as in the case of declarations of persons who have since died and, closely related to this, statements of persons who cannot testify because of mental illness, infirmity, senility, incurable illness.

Mr. Shew said, "I asked Attorney Frank MacGregor of the Welfare Department to be here . . . I was going to put Mr. MacGregor on to establish the fact that Agnes Thompsen is unable to be here. I believe Mr. Wall knows she can't be here. I don't want to create embarrassment—if that could be agreed upon, I could proceed."

Mr. Wall: "I think we can agree, Your Honor, that Mrs. Thompsen is in the infirmary and neither physically nor mentally able to be here. Mr. MacGregor so states." (Again and again Mr. Wall seems to seize the reins—indeed, at times he appears to be running the whole show.)

Mr. MacGregor [standing] "And that includes the foreseeable future."

The press row passed along a rumor that she had had a heart attack last week.

Now it was clear that Agnes Thompsen could not possibly be cross-examined about her statements to Major Rome. She was mentally ill and she was seriously ill physically—she was, in fact, a dying woman.

Mr. Shew went directly to his argument that insanity was an exception to the hearsay rule—and the major legal battle of the trial began. An hour and ten minutes later nothing was so clear as the fact that nothing in the law is clear-cut and absolute. The law is a conglomerate—a bit of this and a scrap of that, which can be plucked out and interpreted with one emphasis or another, and with equal logic be arranged to add up to yes or no.

Mr. Shew argued that there were two prerequisites for admission of a hearsay statement. One—that the person be absolutely unavailable. And, two—that the statement made was against one's own interest. "A self-serving statement would not be admissible. . . . But no other statement is so much *against* one's own interest as a confession of murder. . . . It is one thing to prevent gangsters from supplying alibis, but when a person admits to murder and then becomes unavailable through death or insanity—*absolutely unavailable*—it is most unfair to eliminate that statement. . . . Today we surround the accused with so many safeguards—some of which seem excessive—certainly we ought to give him the benefit of this statement if it is available."

As in the *Miranda* argument, the Judge entered very early into the debate, citing a ruling that stated, "The testimony of a third person that someone other than the accused has confessed to the . . . crime is inadmissible in favor of the accused."

Mr. Shew: "In that case, the person was not deceased, but out of the country. The evidence could have been produced in a better way—his deposition could have been taken. But in this case, this statement is the only one available. . . . I appreciate that Mr. Wall may say that Agnes Thompsen didn't know what she was doing. . . . But that is a matter of weight [the degree of credibility to be accorded the statement] rather than admissibility. To admit Agnes Thompsen's statement is only seeking the truth. And no one can be harmed by it." Today there was nothing relaxed about Mr. Shew.

He paced about the courtroom, speaking in an urgent, emotional voice. "Self-incrimination does not enter into this picture. Any statement admitted here could never be used against Agnes Thompsen later. If she were on trial, it would not be admissible. The only question here is whether she made such a statement. If she did, it was very much against her interests. *Why* should it be eliminated?"

Mr. Wall came forward to answer. [Slow, ponderous] "I dislike to appeal just to bare authority. The authority is on the side of the State here without any question. . . . However, I dislike to see evidence that might be considered proper—and that some people might think was proper—be excluded. I say, Your Honor, that this is definitely hearsay. The reason that there are ever exceptions to the hearsay rule is if there is a guarantee of trustworthiness. In this case we have listened so far to find out what has been said by the interrogator to this particular person. [Suddenly very accusing] And he has *lied* to her four times. He said, 'There is blood on the sandpaper.' Can you imagine a poor woman sitting there in an insane institution and lying to her and telling her, 'There was blood on the sandpaper. How did it get there? There was blood on the towel,' which was a lie. 'Blood on the staircase,' which was a lie. [Rising indignation] And I show you, Your Honor, that he *knew* it was a lie, the *interrogator*, because—"

Mr. Shew [cutting in] "Your Honor, this has nothing to do with the law. It goes to weight."

The Judge agreed. "We are not passing now on the circumstances under which this statement was taken . . . but on whether an admission of this type is, under any circumstances, admissible under the rule of the Supreme Court of Connecticut."

Another bit. Mr. Wall cited a case—a bastardy case—in which the statement of a deceased person was ruled inadmissible.

Another piece. The Judge cited a case—dating back to 1885 but since reaffirmed—that stated that the jury should not rule on the collateral issue of another person's guilt. " 'It would have no other effect than to acquit the person on trial and the third person could in no wise be legally affected. If he should afterwards be put on trial he would be at full liberty to show his innocence, notwithstanding the fact that the former findings of his guilt caused another's acquittal.' " (Strange logic. Is this to say that the State cannot be in the position of having *no one* to pay for the crime?) " 'It is therefore going far enough in favor of the accused to allow him to exculpate himself by showing the fact of another's guilt by some appropriate *evidence* directly connecting that person with the [crime].' "

The Judge acknowledged that opinion on this issue was divided and that there was some criticism of this rule (one is happy to hear it) but that it was the rule in this state.

Mr. Shew raised a new issue. Quoting the language of the Chief Justice in the bastardy case, he argued that this statement of a deceased person was ruled out, not because all such statements are inadmissible, but because that particular statement did not appear to be *trustworthy*.

The Judge: "What do you think Chief Justice King would think of a statement taken of a woman in a mental institution whose reason for not being at the hearing at the present time is that she is mentally incompetent?"

Mr. Shew: "That is a matter that goes to weight."

Clearly the issue of trustworthiness was a two-edged blade. There were two separate areas of reliability: The trustworthiness of the *report* (Did she make the statement that it is claimed she made?) and the trustworthiness of the *statement* (Did she know what she was saying? Was she telling the truth?).

Mr. Shew argued that the report was trustworthy. Let the Jury hear it—and hear the circumstances, too—and decide whether the statement was reliable.

The Judge continued to turn the other edge of the blade. The language of the Chief Justice referred to certain infirmities in the statement. "Here we have a woman in a mental hospital where the statement is being taken."

Mr. Shew agreed. "But under certain circumstances, elements of truth could be elicited from her. If she were on trial herself, it would be different—but she is not on trial. . . . It will be a miscarriage of justice if this testimony is not given to the Jury. They can certainly draw their own conclusions from it. This is a matter of the discretion of the Judge, considering the facts of the case."

This was Mr. Shew's most impassioned argument to date, and he was actually fighting for a pig-in-a-poke. He had never seen the alleged confession. He had Rome's word that it contained twenty-two points of corroboration. Mr. Shew did not know whether it contained twenty-two points—or half that many—or any. He was acting on pure faith. On the other hand, what choice did he have? This was his case.

He cited another decision. " 'In a capital case all doubts as to the admissibility of evidence favorable to the defendant should be resolved in his favor.' " Then an opinion from Wigmore: " 'Any rule which hampers an honest man in exonerating himself is a bad rule—even if it also hampers a villain in falsely passing for innocent.' . . . The witnesses to this statement are Connecticut State Policemen with no motive to falsify. Adequate safeguards are present. . . . The State's case is based primarily on circumstantial evidence and a repudiated confession. The *other party* had both an opportunity and a motive to commit the crime to which she confessed."

The Judge turned to Mr. Wall for his reply, reminding him that at this point we were not concerned with the circumstances under which the statement was taken. But Mr. Wall went directly to that. "Your Honor . . . our Supreme Court is very clear on the subject and the law well settled. But I wish to allude to the fact that there is no possible trustworthiness in this. . . . Your Honor would have an additional ground for throwing this testimony out if Your Honor listened . . . to what happened on July 16. [Increasing venom] There is *lying—deceit*—all kinds of things in it that would cause it to be untrustworthy."

But on this point the Judge was firm. He repeated that it was not necessary to go into that and then said that he was ready to rule. There were a number of reasons why he would exclude the statement. Principally because the State Supreme Court had expressly said it should be excluded. And because of possible untrustworthiness, in view of the mental condition of the person who made the statement. And because [quoting again] " 'The introduction of such a collateral issue [might] confuse and mislead the jury and justice may thereby be defeated. And . . . it would have no other effect than to acquit the one on trial.' " (Might not that be enough? And might not justice also be defeated the other way?)

"If this were admissible," he went on, "we would then get into all the circumstances surrounding the taking of this statement . . . whether she was sufficiently warned, whether she was browbeaten or deceived—or tired—or subjected to overzealous persuasion. It seems to me that, applying the [*Miranda*] decisions . . . if we are going to be fair to the accused individual, we must be equally fair to the State of Connecticut.

"No, it wouldn't harm Agnes Thompsen if this were admitted. She'd have to be tried again. Certainly. But the Supreme Court has been so zealous in protecting the rights of the accused . . . it seems to me if statements are taken which might also affect adversely the interests of the State—which are, after all, the interests of the millions of people . . . who might be the innocent victims of crime—then we have to be also fair to the State. We cannot allow statements to be admitted in evidence unless every safeguard was taken to be sure those statements were true and were voluntarily made . . . the safeguards that our United States Supreme Court insists upon in order to insure the truth and admissibility of statements made during police interrogation.

"For these reasons I would rule that the statement made by Agnes Thompsen is inadmissible."

Mr. Wall's face was flushed with victory.

In his notebook on this day Harry Solberg wrote: "I would like to know why and for what reason can the state object to only parts of statements such as part of Agnes Thompsen's statements and why can't they all be introduced."

•   •   •

For a deflated three quarters of an hour the day dragged on. Ragazzi had found that it was a Dr. Rucker who examined Agnes Thompsen that night. And he produced a card that read: "Mrs. Agnes Thompsen had a physical examination within an hour after she came to the hospital. No marks, cuts, bruises or blood on body . . . no evidence of bruises, etc., as of today. June 23, 1965."

At 4:15, three quarters of an hour early, Mr. Shew asked for an adjournment. "I have no further evidence at this time."

"I would not object if you are out of witnesses," Mr. Wall said, with a pointed smile, "but it doesn't appear that you are, does it?"

(Major Rome was still present in Court.) But then Mr. Wall conceded that he did not object to an adjournment and the day ended.

Why does one leave the Court with this taste of dust?

A boy is on trial for his life. Somewhere, it is claimed, there is a statement, taped, witnessed by police officers, a nurse, and at least one doctor, that would prove his innocence. And we have sat here today and listened to a ruling that that statement will not be heard. Not by the Judge, not by the Jury, not by the public, which in the end must be the guardian of its own protections. A statement exists. It is to be buried.

It is quite possible that the statement is untrustworthy. Then let us hear it and know that it is untrustworthy. Dispel our doubts. It is possible that the statement is neither black nor white, but a mottled gray—not proof, but spotted with food for thought. Then let someone hear it and let someone think! Let the Jury hear it and evaluate it and reach the best possible verdict with what is available. *Everything* that is available. If credibility is falsely claimed for the statement by the State's Chief Detective—for reasons of personal vindication or to save a perfect record, as some are saying—then let us know that, too, and judge the man accordingly.

Is it not the very minimum requirement of justice that the Judge hear it and take the responsibility for declaring it worthless? (Could he hear it and find it absolutely convincing and still find it in his law books to keep it out?) Now it is the State's Attorney who has handed down the verdict. He says this statement is untrustworthy and without bearing on this case. The judgment has been made by the man with the most to gain from that judgment. And it has been ruled final.

This has all been justified, in the impersonal machinery of The Law, with technicalities and sacred precedents. But if Harry Solberg is innocent—and if those tapes are proof and the *only* proof—can any law on earth justify what has happened here today?

12

Friday, October 7

The papers termed yesterday's defeat a serious setback for the Defense. In the *Courant* Demeusy wrote, "For Solberg the ruling from the bench might easily be the difference between life and death." In the *Times*, Joe Crowley wrote, ". . . the State took a major step in its attempt to convict Solberg." Driving to court this morning, on a brilliant Indian summer day, coming into the flaming Litchfield hills and the little village with its small shops on the green, one had a sense for a fleeting few minutes that yesterday had not really happened. But at nine o'clock a car zipped into the town parking lot behind the courthouse and had nowhere to park. The *Courant* had also reported, "Rome is standing by in the courtroom. . . . He will be summoned soon . . . maybe today." The parking lot was filled. The courtroom was filled and people had brought lunch.

The day was scheduled as a morning session only. As though getting back his wind after yesterday's bitter defeat, Mr. Shew began with three peripheral witnesses—Carole Stadler again, and two character witnesses for Harry.

"About two or three weeks before the murder, . . ." Carole Stadler testified now, "Dorothy told me that she thought her mother-in-law was getting bad again. She said her mother-in-law had come home and couldn't open the door and had to wait twenty minutes until Dorothy got home. . . . And from that day her headaches had come back—the pressure in her head—and she blamed it on Dorothy for not being home to let her in."

Carole's second statement was good for a bit of gossip. "I always noticed that Dorothy had a black and blue mark on her, one place or another. . . . She looked to me as though she had been beaten—"

Mr. Shew: "Were these really noticeable, Mrs. Stadler?"

"Oh yes, very. Once she had a great big black and blue mark here [indicating the side of her neck] and another time she had a big one on her arm and she had several on her legs."

Mr. Wall: "Now, Mrs. Stadler, this was a new home—unfinished . . . Did Dorothy do work out in the yard—heavy work, cutting brush and small trees?" Yes. "And that was practically a daily occurrence?"

"Well, I saw her out there several times. I wouldn't say every day."

And could not these bruises have been caused that way—from this heavy work?

"Yes, they could have."

Mr. Shew: "Did it occur to you before Mr. Wall asked you, Mrs. Stadler, that she might have received those bruises working around the yard?"

"Well, I had thought they might have happened that way, but I also thought they might have happened from a beating, too."

A brief cut to Harry, about whom actually we knew nothing—except that he was a poor speller and that, whether innocent or guilty, he was stupid enough to write the Letter. Today his minister, Pastor Stanley Martin Bugge, was here.

(Several times Pastor Bugge, a tall mild-looking young man, has accompanied the Solberg family to court, maintaining an outward calm which, because of the restrictive tenets of his church, has captured the interest of some of the reporters. "He keeps his cool, but I think it's a bluff." "I think actually he's shocked by the whole thing." "I think he communes with his God every night asking for strength to get him through the next day." So much for impressions of Pastor Bugge formed at twenty paces.)

On the stand Pastor Bugge, who had been minister at the Bethany Lutheran Church for five years, described the rigorous requirements for becoming an adult communicant, as Harry was, of this church. "There is a general surveillance of each potential member. In Harry's case he has been a boy in our church since childhood and his character—"

Objection from Mr. Wall. "He is already going into the answer to the final question."

Mr. Shew [exasperated] "Mr. Wall, if I'm hurting your feelings—"

Mr. Wall [acid] "You are not hurting my feelings one bit."

(Everyone on tenterhooks already and the day has barely begun.)

Pastor Bugge continued: "About three or four times a week Harry would be in church . . . for mid-week Bible study and prayer meeting . . . Junior League for High School students of which he was always a member and one year a group leader, Sunday morning and Sunday evening services which Harry almost always attended —and he also came to choir practice." (Certainly a picture of unusual devotion.)

Mr. Shew: "And what is Harry's reputation among the members of the church and of the community?"

Pastor Bugge: "It is one of great respect and high esteem for a young boy who has always had a high moral integrity in the community, in the school, among his friends, and, certainly, I have always seen this around the church and wherever I met him."

Very good for Harry Solberg. So far.

Mr. Wall [very accusing] "Pastor, do you know of an incident in a group meeting in New York involving a young lady in Brooklyn? Do you know of *that* incident involving the accused? Did you hear of *that?*" (The blast conjures up the wildest suspicions.)

"Yes, I have heard that."

"And was that favorable to his character?"

"Well, I can clarify it by answering it—"

Mr. Wall [very curt] "You may answer it. If it was or was not?"

Pastor Bugge [mildly] "What I heard was something which wasn't pleasant, but the next day he did seek out this person and apologize—"

Wheeling about, Mr. Wall returned to his chair.

Mr. Shew was absolutely furious. Lurking on the fringe of this case have been rumors that this was a sex-killing. [Sharply, before he was on his feet] "Give us the incident, Pastor."

"Well, from what I heard—Harry drove some young people from our church to and from the church in Brooklyn, and some of the girls went off and came back extremely late, so that Harry and his fiancée had to wait overtime for them. Harry was somewhat upset and showed this in some way—I am not really sure—it caused a little friction, but he apologized to them the next day."

Mr. Shew [still bristling] "Isn't it a fact—to clarify this before the Jury—that Harry was with the girl who is now his wife? . . . And that he was under instructions from his parents and from her parents to be home by twelve o'clock—and the other two girls went off on dates and prevented him from getting home on time? And he got mad at them. Isn't that what Attorney Wall is referring to?"

"Yes, I imagine so."

"And is there anything wrong in getting mad at two girls who prevented you from getting home on time when you should have?"

A protest from the Judge to that question.

"Well, let's get it straight, Your Honor. Thank you, Pastor." Mr. Shew flung his notes on the table.

Mr. Wall: "Is it true, Pastor, that he roughed up the girls and pushed one into the car and ripped her dress—is that what you heard?"

"I heard the dress was ripped as she went into the car." (Smiles in the press row; the pastor still kept his "cool.")

So the episode was not so serious, after all.

Another character witness—Mr. Phillips Skaret, elder and chairman of the church, who had known Harry since he was a small boy. "His general reputation is very good. He has a very good reputation among young people. He has attended our church regularly—was always well above average in attendance in Bible Class as well as prayer meetings, communion services and all our regular services."

Mr. Wall [bitingly] "Do you know about his reputation so far as having a violent temper is concerned?"

Mr. Shew: "Objection! There is no evidence for that question. [Incensed] I think that is highly improper and I think Mr. Wall should be censured for it. There is not a bit of evidence—"

Mr. Wall [bridling] "I have the right to bring it out."

Mr. Shew: "You are not going to do it that way!"

(Press row: "They're warming up for Rome. He's next.")

Mr. Wall: "Mr. Skaret, do you know anything about the reputation in the community of Harry Solberg as to his temper?"

Mr. Skaret: "In all my dealings with him and in all I have heard, he is, I will say, mild-tempered."

◆

We have arrived at the main event. Tomorrow's headlines would shout "ROME TAKES STAND IN SOLBERG DEFENSE."

While Mr. Shew established Major Rome's position and his credentials, Mr. Wall remained seated, with a look about him of a tiger ready to leap. Mr. Shew brought out that it was Rome's duty to investigate major and unusual crimes, that he was assigned by the Commissioner to the difficult cases, that he was not called in unless his services were required, and that he was assigned to the Thompsen case six days after the murder—an oblique indication that, at that time, the case was considered to be in trouble. A flush sat on Mr. Wall's face.

"Major, when was the first time that I ever spoke to you about this case?" Mr. Shew said. "Will you describe the circumstances—"

Mr. Wall was on his feet. "I object to it as irrelevant. . . . I feel the time should be saved for more important matters."

Major Rome stated that Mr. Shew had telephoned him, identified himself as Harry Solberg's lawyer, and asked to meet with him. Rome had replied that permission would have to be obtained from Commissioner Mulcahy and this was done. The date? Major Rome did not remember. "We run a hundred or so cases at a time. This was a small thing. I didn't make a note of it."

At Mr. Shew's request, Major Rome described the first few hours of his investigation, up to the time he went to the hospital to talk to Agnes Thompsen. Mr. Wall half stood up, sat down again. Referring to the interview that Ragazzi read yesterday, Mr. Shew asked whether Major Rome recalled it. Already a cloud was forming on the horizon. Rome no longer had access to his own files. He remembered the interview but was unable to give the exact date.

Mr. Shew: "I believe the record will show—[turning to Mr. Wall] I don't mean to lead Major Rome, Mr. Wall, but I am just trying to establish the time—[back to the witness] that this was shortly after Agnes Thompsen was confined to the hospital. Among other things, she was questioned about a substance taken from her fingernails. Do you remember such an interview with Agnes Thompsen, Major?"

"Yes, sir."

Mr. Wall [brusquely] "I object to that as leading and I ask that the answer go out."

The Judge said that Mr. Shew was only trying to fix the date. If Mr. Wall objected, he would check yesterday's transcript for it.

Mr. Shew [annoyed] "If Mr. Wall wants to save time, Your Honor—If we can't agree, we can go into a lot of things."

Mr. Wall [crisp] "I am not asking for a lot of things, Your Honor."

The Judge: "Do you object to the leading . . . ?"

Mr. Wall [holding tight] "Yes, I object to it. But I have no objection to his referring to a particular date, June 21, which was in evidence yesterday."

(And so tempers are up, tension is high and there has been a flare-up over—nobody quite knows what. Mr. Wall objected and then supplied the answer himself. But one hardly listens to the words—Rome is on the stand and the air is charged.)

Mr. Wall [bland innocence] "I don't object to the Major having notes if he requires them to refresh his recollection." (Mr. Wall knows, as does everyone else, that Ragazzi took the notes. Rome does not take notes, does not have notes, no longer has his own files.)

Mr. Shew: "Do you have notes?" No, sir, I do not. "Do you remember . . . Agnes Thompsen's statement that she had cut her hand with a crochet needle?" I do. "And she used that to explain the blood?" That's correct. "And what did you do to determine whether or not she was telling the truth?"

"Well, we checked the doctor's admittance report . . . and we knew that this wasn't so, but I checked her hands myself."

Mr. Wall: "I move that go out."

The Judge was becoming more formal. "The portion about the

report may go out. The Jury will disregard anything about the report unless the report itself is placed in evidence. The witness can testify to anything that he, himself, observed."

Mr. Wall remained standing.

"Did you check her hands, Major?" I did. "Did you see any marks or . . . ?"

Mr. Wall: "I object, Your Honor. This is long after . . . anything like that would have had any relevance. This is the twenty-first of June. If it had any relevance, it would have been the sixteenth."

Mr. Shew [whipping about] "Mr. Wall, a big mark such as she is supposed to have had certainly would have lasted that long!"

[Very acid] "A trace of blood under her nails."

Through the interruptions the Major waited, almost motionless—a solid, white-haired figure who looked like his reputation—a tough witness to get the best of, tough to confuse. Allowed to answer, he said, firmly, "She had no cut, no cut healing, no breaking of the skin of any kind on either hand."

"The facts are wrong. The letter is from a crank." He had said it more than a year ago when he first saw the Letter. Now he tried to say it again in Court.

While Major Rome examined the Letter, Mr. Wall paced the length of both tables, down to the press row and back to his place again. Mr. Shew asked, "Did you take any action in connection with that letter?"

"Later I turned it back to the Canaan Barracks with the suggestion that attempts be made to trace the writer . . . and arrest him as a crank or feeble-minded because I—"

Mr. Wall [darting forward] "I object to anything further. The question has been answered." Sustained. "I move that part go out." The reference to the type of person was ruled out.

Mr. Shew: "Can you tell us, from any statements in that letter, why you gave those instructions?"

[Emphatically] "Yes, sir. The person who wrote this letter did not have the facts in the case."

"Will you point out to us why you make that statement?"

Objection!

The Judge, remaining deliberately calm in the rising heat, said,

"If this is a question of Major Rome to point out any differences in the letter from the facts as he found them, I suppose he is entitled to do that."

Mr. Wall: "Your Honor, I object because any facts—[barbed] so-called facts—would be completely hearsay. All kinds of things that would be composite hearsay."

(How do we know that we are running into trouble? Is it the edge in Mr. Wall's voice? Is it the trigger-word, "hearsay"?)

The Judge made his first statement on this question which, at this moment, was as clear as it would ever be again. While he spoke Mr. Wall, a flush climbing in his face, paced behind the tables.

The Judge: "I mean to limit it, Mr. Wall. If Major Rome is giving his reasons for giving the instructions, and he wishes to point out differences between statements in the letter and the facts which he himself observed of his own knowledge—not through hearsay—discrepancies of actual fact . . . having to do with place, time, exhibits, matters which were known to be facts at that time—he can do that."

[Instantly] "May I further object, Your Honor—" Head thrust forward, Mr. Wall raced down the length of both tables, plowed around the lower end and darted back up through the center of the court. "On the grounds that this witness has laid no foundation as knowing any fact . . . except from reports or hearsay—that he did not come on the scene until almost a week afterward . . . and also on the further grounds, Your Honor—[rising voice] I object to it on the ground that it is immaterial what he believes to be discrepancies. If there are discrepancies, as there definitely are, Your Honor, it is up to the Jury to decide what those are from the facts as they hear them here—not just such facts as this witness makes out of his head as being considered to be fact, Your Honor."

The Judge replied, with another long explanation, that this was precisely his ruling. No hearsay. But even while the Judge was ruling his way, Mr. Wall seemed to build up steam. He moved across the room and stood in front of the jury box, rocking on his heels and jingling coins in his pockets.

The Judge: "I will limit it carefully to what he observed personally in the course of his investigation. Mr. Shew probably won't like that limitation, but nevertheless that's the limitation."

Mr. Wall [plunging on] "My objection is further that there is no foundation. He should lay a foundation that this witness actually knows of his own knowledge—"

Mr. Shew [fed-up] "Mr. Wall, I know I could get a lot of lessons from you for trying this case—"

The Judge interceded quickly and ordered Mr. Shew to proceed. Major Rome read the first statement from the Letter—"'I killed your wife. She worked with me at the bank'"—and said he knew that when the writer was found, it would turn out that this was untrue.

"I object to that, Your Honor. 'This was untrue.'"

The Judge asked whether that was not hearsay, and Major Rome agreed that it was. Then suddenly everyone was talking at once.

Major Rome: "I have to admit that was hearsay."

Mr. Wall: "I move that go out. Major Rome states frankly—"

Mr. Shew: "He pointed that out, Your Honor—"

The Judge: "He did. He pointed it out—and perhaps thought that was not contested."

Mr. Shew [trying to continue] "Major—"

Mr. Wall [leaping in] "I make the further objection that this witness should state what he knows of his own *knowledge* . . . in order that we have a foundation." (Hardly a further objection. At least a third repeat.)

Again Mr. Shew asked the Major to pick out statements that he knew, of his own knowledge, were incorrect—not based on hearsay.

Mr. Wall: "I object to this question until there has been laid a foundation of what this witness knows of his own knowledge. Was he there—did he see some physical evidence?"

The Judge tried to suggest a format. Mr. Wall wished to make an argument. And the Jury, which seemed to be spending less and less time in Court, was on its way out again.

The Jury left at 11:14 and at that time there began a winding, convoluted course of arguments repeated again and again, containing nothing that had not already been said several times—one repetition distinguished from its predecessor only by increasing confusion and animosity.

Mr. Wall [knife-edged] "This witness is no different from any other witness—and I don't believe any other witness can be asked

about discrepancies between a particular Exhibit and his own
opinion concerning it."

The Judge replied that opinion would not be admissible and
again suggested a procedure. Then he commented that if Mr. Wall
wanted Major Rome to describe everything he saw and did during
his investigation, all right. "I think it might take quite a long time."

Mr. Shew: "I think that will take us another two or three weeks—"

Mr. Wall [very caustic] "Your Honor, what I feel would shorten
this matter is to exclude the testimony entirely because I don't see
any right of the defense to put anyone on just to make comments
about a particular Exhibit."

The Judge: "But here is an officer who was in charge of the
investigation. He is entitled to explain . . . why he gave the instructions, based upon his own personal observations."

Mr. Wall: ". . . An explanation is definitely immaterial. . . . I
object to it entirely, but if Your Honor does allow it, I feel that a
foundation should be laid. . . ." (And again around the mulberry
bush.) "The Jury is the one to decide . . . based on facts—not on
what this witness thinks the facts might be. . . ."

As the argument circled and unraveled, the positions, the objections became almost impossible to define or to follow.

The Judge said, ". . . He can point out statements in the letter
which are different from known facts, based upon his own information or upon something which appears right in this courtroom
already in evidence."

Mr. Wall appeared to be saying (although no one could really be
sure anymore what anyone was saying) that the Letter should not
be used at all for the purpose of calling attention to misstatements.
But the Judge had already ruled at least once that the Letter *could*
be used. The argument wound about with increasing bitterness and
fewer points of law.

At last the Judge ruled: Major Rome could go through the Letter
and point out statements which were the basis for the order he
gave. He was to give no reasons, no comparisons, no opinions as to
whether a statement was true or false. Just point out the statements
that caused him to issue the order. "I think it would be helpful to
the Jury if they had the items which they are to consider pointed
out to them. I see no harm in that."

He explained it all again to be sure it was clearly understood. "I don't want a mistrial in this case and nobody else does—" (already there have been murmurs about this possibility). Then he called a ten-minute recess.

The ten minutes stretched to forty-five and when Court resumed it was clear, in an atmosphere more charged than before, that there had been heated discussion in Chambers. The Court Reporter read the question, first asked a very long time ago now.

Mr. Wall: "May I further object, Your Honor, that it's not particularized as to when he's supposed to have had this personal knowledge—whether it is as of today or as of a year ago."

"As of the time he gave the order." (Do we detect a weary note?)
". . . Now I am limiting this to the reason . . . that he gave the order with respect to this letter, based upon his personal knowledge. . . ."

Mr. Wall [nerves taut] "I object to it strenuously. It calls for an opinion. . . . It allows this witness to ramble on at will, *as he already has,* Your Honor—to make this totally inadmissible statement . . ." (Major Rome has hardly gotten in a word!)

The Judge: "This man was in charge of the investigation. He gave an order. . . . He may point out anything . . . based on his own knowledge . . . that are the statements of a crank or a feeble-minded person. If anything is based on hearsay I will sustain the objection."

Mr. Wall [yet again] ". . . It hasn't appeared that this witness has any personal knowledge whatsoever. . . . It calls for an opinion. . . . And also it doesn't particularize it as to the time that he gave the order." (One is beginning to suspect that Mr. Wall hopes to win this argument by attrition.)

The Jury returned. The Court Reporter read the question. Mr. Wall objected. When the Judge admitted the question in limited form, Mr. Wall appeared to be surprised. "Your Honor is admitting it! Exception!"

For the fifth time the question was read. Mr. Wall remained standing, pacing about behind the tables. Major Rome started to answer the question, going slowly as he had been instructed to do, to give Mr. Wall a chance to object. "Upon studying the photographs available to me at the time I find it impossible to believe that the individual—"

"I object to that. It is based on photographs."

The Judge: "No—no. It is for the Jury to compare the letter with the Exhibits. . . . We are trying to find any facts which the witness uncovered himself or witnessed himself."

(We are sliding into confusion. Twice the Judge has said that the Major could testify from something already in evidence. These photographs are in evidence.)

Mr. Wall [darting forward] "I might suggest, Your Honor, that this witness be allowed to state *facts*, if he has any that he knows, and then point out anything that might be different from facts that he personally knows, Your Honor."

Mr. Shew [exploding] "If Your Honor please—may Your Honor suggest to Attorney Wall that he allow me to try the case in the way I see fit!" (A gasp from a lady spectator. Why *now?*)

But the attrition was taking effect. One felt that Mr. Shew was at wit's end. He picked up the floorboard with the nail set in it, asked if Major Rome had seen it before. He had. Before or after he saw the Letter? Rome was not certain. "But I know for a fact—"

"I object!"

"Wait!" the Judge burst out. "He is going to state—"

Mr. Wall ordered that the answer relate to this Exhibit.

Major Rome: "This is not a spike. This is a nail set. In the letter the writer used the word 'spike.' " (One wonders whether Mr. Shew grasped at this harmless detail to establish a pattern so we might get on with it.)

This is a deeply disturbing picture. Here is a man with a long and brilliant record, who supervised this investigation as an officer of the State. Now he has been called to testify concerning it in a Superior Court of the State, in the trial of a citizen of the State who has not yet been found guilty. And the representative of the State is making an extreme effort to keep him from giving that testimony. Why? What is the State afraid of? For twenty-nine years this man's testimony has been instrumental in proving men guilty. Now that his purpose is to try to show that a man is innocent, the State's Attorney is working frantically to silence him.

Mr. Shew: "Are there any other statements in this letter?"

Rome [quick] "*Yes!* It is a fact that, after studying the photographs—"

"I object to that, Your Honor."

Mr. Shew [patience gone] "If Your Honor please, apparently a Donnybrook is wanted around here. I am trying to avoid it and Major—"

The Judge: "A Donnybrook is the last thing that any of us wishes, Mr. Shew, and I am trying very hard to prevent it. Now if that is a matter of opinion it's something for the Jury to decide."

"The Major started to state a fact—a fact which I don't know."

"Well, let him state a fact which he knows of his own personal knowledge. Not just from a study of the work of other investigators."

Mr. Shew: "Can you tell me any other discrepancies, Major, based on facts which you have of your own knowledge?"

"I object! Discrepancies are entirely a matter for the Jury. There are discrepancies and I don't think it helps the Jury—"

Mr. Shew [total exasperation] "Mr. Wall, whether *you* think it helps a Jury—it's not any of your business! It is mine."

Mr. Wall [crisp] "It is up to the Court, Your Honor, whether or not it helps the Jury."

The Judge substituted the word "statement" for "discrepancy." Mr. Shew asked the Major to answer the question.

Mr. Wall [an order] "The answer shall be yes or no, Your Honor."

Major Rome: "The letter—"

Mr. Wall [whipping in] "I object to any further statement at this time, Your Honor."

Mr. Shew [exploding] "Mr. Wall, will you give the witness a chance!"

Mr. Wall: "He has answered the question."

Several jurors were leaning forward, and one felt that they must be wondering what they were being denied. (As who was not?) A spectator murmured, "Why doesn't he let him talk?" But Mr. Wall's technique was working. He was bottling up the Major by objecting before he said anything and then heatedly arguing each point—the same argument again and again—until the argument became all and the question was obscured.

Ordered to proceed, Major Rome said, "It is a fact, when you look at the photographs taken of the—"

Mr. Wall: "I object to that, Your Honor."

The Judge: "Major, I am sorry but this is getting into an opinion based on evidence and not something that you yourself saw."

Major Rome's eyes, sharp and noncommittal, flicked toward the Judge, came away again. (The Judge's words earlier: "He can point out statements . . . based upon his own information or upon something . . . in this courtroom already *in evidence.*" And: ". . . He can point out discrepancies of actual fact that he observed, having to do with place, time, *exhibits,* matters which were known to be facts at that time . . .")

The Judge: "Something physical, like a board . . . is something that can be seen as tangible, but an examination of photographs taken at different times—that gets into a matter of opinion. There is a hairline distinction that an awful lot of people are going to have a hard time distinguishing, including the Court, but we will have to draw that line as best we can."

The taste of dust creeping in again. If it is that fine a line, should it not be resolved in favor of hearing what the man has to say? We have a jury of twelve ordinary and probably conscientious citizens. Can we expect them to see details and to analyze police photographs as fully and meaningfully as this expert who was in charge of the investigation and who brings to them the knowledge and experience of twenty-nine years?

A trial is a search for truth. Is the search for truth aided when the man who was in charge cannot discuss the official investigation? The State's Attorney has said, "This witness is no different from any other witness." But he *is* different. He was in charge—the only man in charge for four months—and that makes him unique. Are we to believe that he is such a spellbinder that he could sell false observations as truths? Is he so formidable that even if he is wrong, the State will be helpless to rebut his statements and, with these same photographs, this same evidence, show that he is wrong? Are we saying that we will trust these jurors to make a decision involving a man's life but we will not trust them to decide whether they actually see what a man tells them they see—and whether it means what he tells them it means?

Frustrated, blocked at every turn, Mr. Shew gave up on the Letter. He asked for the white dress which he had requested Fuessenich to bring to Court, and asked Major Rome whether he had seen it before. The Major had not! Not outside this courtroom.

(It is really the same problem all over again. By the time Rome was assigned to the case this dress had been sent to the laboratory. He received signed reports that the blood was the victim's and that the dress was found the next day in the clothes dryer. To him its significance was that a stranger would not have hung around to clean up—wash part of the porch, throw this bloodstained dress into the dryer. In Court he could say none of this.)

Unable to get past the hurdle of the six-day interval before Rome took over the case, Mr. Shew said that he wished to withdraw him and call Lieutenant Fuessenich—but the time of the half-day session had almost run out and Court was adjourned until Tuesday morning.

Out into the sunny Indian summer day—the quiet town with its sleepy pace, golden hills in the distance. But the feeling of hate walked with us.

"This is a personal fight between Wall and Rome," a local reporter said, as though that justified it.

Reflections at the End of a Stormy Week
No sane person can want this defendant, if he is guilty, set free to murder again. But can anyone want him convicted if he is innocent— a ritualistic sacrifice to the law?

I am part of the State. Did the State represent me today?

A law designed to prevent false alibis and false testimony has been used to bar evidence that might—or might not—have proved a man's innocence. In the law, for everything given, something is taken away.

13

Tuesday, October 11

"My general impression was that he was a rigidly inhibited and repressed youth . . ."

Nearly three weeks have passed since Judge MacDonald ordered that Harry be taken to Dr. Charles Von Salzen for a psychiatric examination. We had almost forgotten. If one were asked to describe Harry, after these three weeks in Court, fewer than a dozen words would come to mind; pallid, heavy spectacles, thick lips, smiling, neat, impassive, unworried, religious. This morning as Mr. Shew questioned Dr. Von Salzen, the picture opened up.

"I discussed with him first his early life, family background, siblings, history, schooling," Dr. Von Salzen began. "He told me that he had required six years to complete the four-year high school course. I asked him what year he graduated from high school. He was not sure at first if it was 1964 or 1965—he decided finally that it was 1965. We discussed his subsequent marriage. We discussed him as an individual—what kind of a person he is, what kind of interests and activities he participates in."

Dr. Von Salzen was an attractive man in his mid-fifties—medium height, lean, with a very good face, in which a scattering of deep lines gave the look of heart rather than of age—a highly regarded psychiatrist who was formerly Executive Officer and then Director of the well-known Institute of Living.

"I believe that he had lived a very restricted, narrow life. His interests were very few. He seemed to have no interest in sports or all the usual activities that high school students participate in, such as dances, parties. He didn't attend movies. He didn't dance. He didn't drink. He had a very good record so far as any minor crimes or misdemeanors—no traffic tickets—nothing of the kind. He said he attended church quite often—two or three times weekly. All in all, my general impression was that he was a rigidly inhibited and repressed youth."

Mr. Shew asked the doctor to explain in layman's terms the phrase, "rigidly inhibited and repressed youth."

"Well, he spent quite a lot of time reading the Bible . . . and he wasn't able to discuss the contents of what he had read very clearly. I also discussed any interest in girls. He told me that he never had fantasies—never thought about girls. I think, at the age of nineteen, I would consider this unusual. He seemed to have very rigid feelings in the entire area of sex and boy-girl relationships. . . . He told me that he had married on January 15, 1966, that he had been very much in love with his fiancée, and that he had gone steady with her for some time. . . . There was nothing abnormal about that."

The doctor was an articulate witness and Mr. Shew wanted to derive full benefit from his testimony. To assure complete understanding on the part of the Jury, he asked him to further explain the term "repressions." The doctor responded with an unstinting lecture on the phenomenon of banishment to the unconscious mind of "impulses . . . desires, and conflicts . . . which we do not want to know or recognize—things which are too unpleasant, too horrible to keep in consciousness." He discussed the *ego* with its instincts and drives—sexual, aggressive, acquisitive—and the *superego*—"Somewhat like conscience . . . the accumulation of everything we have been taught about right and wrong." Then he explained: "Where there is a very small superego, you see people who seem to have little conscience. . . . Where there is a very large—a dominant—superego, people feel guilty about many things which other people would not feel guilty about . . . as if every impulse arouses a sense of guilt irrationally. . . . When there is too harsh—too rigid—a superego one feels guilty about what many of us consider normal activity. . . ."

And this brought him to Harry Solberg. "I reached the conclusion . . . that he is a rigidly repressed and inhibited person and that he feels uncomfortable, uneasy, anxious about impulses, wishes, instincts which most of us learn to live with and . . . to manage in a fairly mature way."

Having established a background, Mr. Shew said, "And did you question Harry Solberg about what, if anything, he knew about June 15, 1965?"

The doctor had questioned Harry in detail. [Consulting his notes] "He stated that on June 15, 1965, he left school on the school bus and got home about 12:30 or 12:45. He thinks that he must have changed his clothes and had something to eat, and then said that he helped unload a plumbing supply truck. He then went to Simsbury to get a lawn mower repaired. Then he said that he had been having trouble with an economics report for high school and Mr. Thompsen had agreed to help him . . . so he had planned to stop at the Thompsen home to get this report. He said he walked up to the front door, which was partially opened, that he called out and knocked, received no answer. He walked into the house and called out again. He heard the baby crying. He walked into the hallway, then walked into the kitchen, then saw blood on the floor. He followed this blood into the living room, and then he told me he remembers nothing until he saw himself climbing up a ladder outside the house to the rear porch. I asked him whether he had seen the body. He said, 'I can't remember seeing her, but I must have seen her.' He doesn't recall leaving. He knows that he was going to stop at the home of a State Policeman who lives nearby, but he did not do this. He went to his home, asked his mother where his father was working because he wanted to tell his father, went to work with his father, but didn't tell him." Dr. Von Salzen looked up from his notes. "That is what he told me initially . . . as to what transpired on June 15."

(And there we have the same story that Harry first gave to the police on that Monday night last March, at 8:27, three and a half hours before the "confession," the same story that he told Mr. Shew the day after the "confession"—told again three weeks ago, at the start of this trial, to Dr. Von Salzen.)

Mr. Shew: "That's what he told you initially. Did you question him further?"

Dr. Von Salzen replied that later he reviewed the story again in detail "to see if any other memory could be brought to his mind.

There were no other memories—no greater recollection of what he had seen."

"Did he give you a different explanation later?"

"Toward the end of the examination I was continuing to ask him about his recollections of what had happened that day and he told me another story." The second story differed in some respects and in others it did not.

Mr. Shew: "Did you come to any conclusions as to *why* Harry Solberg gave different stories?"

Dr. Von Salzen: "I reached an explanation that satisfied me."

Mr. Shew: "What is that explanation?"

"I think that, at this time, even today, the defendant *doesn't really know what happened there on June 15.*"

A confirmation that Mr. Shew had been seeking for six months! He repeated the doctor's words. "It is your opinion, Doctor, that this defendant *does not know what happened on June 15?*"

"*For a certain period of time, on June 15, of 1965, I believe that at this time, he does not know what happened there.*"

"Can you tell us, in layman's terms, *why* he doesn't know?"

Objection from Mr. Wall. "I don't object to this question eventually, but . . . there has been no foundation laid for any facts upon which the doctor could base this opinion. . . . The facts that were before the doctor should first be related before he gives any opinion. . . ."

Mr. Shew was annoyed and showed it. For at least some members of the Jury, psychiatry must be an unexplored subject, and he had been making this effort to have the doctor explain his testimony step by step in simple terms in order that it might be properly understood. The interruption could confuse what might already be, for certain jurors, a confusing subject. "If Mr. Wall is worried about that, I have no objection," he snapped. "Is that what you want, Mr. Wall?"

"I don't want anything except the facts. *All* the facts."

"I am trying to *get* the facts."

The Judge ruled that if the doctor was going to explain why two different and contradictory statements were made, the Jury ought to know what the differences were. Mr. Shew asked the doctor to "be explicit about the discrepancies and then tell why in your opinion they were made." Mr. Wall objected that the question was long and involved—triple-headed, asked that the first one be read first. Mr. Shew, very angry, shot back, "I prefer it the way I asked it. If I want help from Mr. Wall—"

(The problem was Harry's other story. Mr. Shew was asking for the psychiatric explanation of Harry's reaction that day. Mr. Wall wanted "the discrepancies"—the second story, told fifteen months later—to come in first.)

Dr. Von Salzen: "From the story the defendant told me, it seems to me that, after walking into this home and seeing this blood, he then did not remember anything more after that—or his memory for it was very spotty and very fragmentary."

"And can you tell us in your opinion *why* his memory was that way?"

Objection. "I object to the opinion until the facts relating to the opinion have been introduced." The Judge said, "We haven't gotten to the discrepancies yet. This is an opinion based simply upon the first statement." But Mr. Wall strode forward to the bench. [Shoulders hunched, arms locked over his chest] "I will not object to this question after the facts have come out. There is talk about *discrepancies*—that the Jury doesn't even know about, Your Honor. . . . The Jury should first find out what the doctor is explaining in the way of discrepancies." (By now we are clear that we have another story coming.) The Judge instructed the witness to continue. Mr. Wall walked back and remained standing behind his chair.

Dr. Von Salzen: "I asked myself—what would be the reaction of a human being walking in on a scene such as this. [Indicating a photograph of the body] Although I have been a doctor for thirty years and I have seen hundreds of dead bodies, when I saw this photograph, I had a feeling of revulsion. . . . I believe that in a person such as the defendant, walking in on a rural scene on a June day expecting to get a report on economics, and walking in on a scene of blood and violence and murder and, for all anyone knew at that moment, rape—I think this would be an enormous shock to the nervous system and I think that the mind could easily reject what the senses perceived."

Mr. Shew [proceeding carefully] "And what would be the effect of the mind rejecting what it saw?"

"The effect would be similar to what one sees in combat, in

traumatic neuroses—as when a man's buddy is blown up in front of his eyes—it's so repulsive or so appalling that he cannot take it in, cannot accept it. In other words, it does not gain access to the conscious mind. This was rather common in wartime."

[Slowly, deliberately] "Is it a fair statement, Doctor, that in your opinion, it is *impossible for Harry Solberg to give a statement as to what took place June 15 because he, himself, does not know at this time?*"

Objection. The Judge commented that an opinion would be based on the entire interview. Mr. Wall added that the question was leading. Heated argument. By the time the Judge allowed the opinion, the question was forgotten and had to be read. Inevitably these relentless arguments must dissipate the impact of the testimony.

Dr. Von Salzen: "It is my opinion that for a certain period of time—and I don't know how long a period of time—on June 15, 1965, the Defendant has no memory as to exactly what happened."

"In your opinion, Doctor, has he some memories of that day?"

The doctor repeated that Harry remembered returning from school, having lunch, unloading a truck, going to Simsbury. "I think the impact of seeing this sight was the trigger—the onset of the amnesia."

Asked about psychiatric treatment for this condition, Dr. Von Salzen said that he believed it would require hospitalization for a few weeks and the use of such measures as hypnosis or Sodium Pentothal to bring back and reintegrate these lost memories.

Mr. Shew described the number of hours that Harry had been questioned during the two days. "Based upon your knowledge of Harry Solberg and the length of time he was confronted by police, would you have an opinion as to his ability to make a correct statement?" Objection. Sustained. A substitute question: "Would the effect of a long period of questioning on an individual like Harry Solberg be different from the effect on a normal boy of his age?"

Again Dr. Von Salzen replied that he had an opinion. "When there is such a memory gap . . . and the individual for the time being loses his contact with himself—then later there is an effort to make up for that memory gap . . . to fill things in. So there is a two-staged process. In stage one, there is this state of fugue or loss of memory. In the next stage, the individual gradually regains identity, knows who he is, and what he is, and tries to fill in the memory gaps. He still doesn't know."

Mr. Shew: "He still doesn't know. And the result of not knowing—what happens?"

"He makes things up or fills things in, or confabulates."

Cross-Examination by Mr. Wall

Mr. Wall did not go immediately to the second story. Arms folded over his chest, he began, "Now, Doctor, I believe that you are testifying to the present existence of a memory gap? . . . And you used the word 'amnesia.' Is that synonymous with memory gap?"

"No, not entirely synonymous. I think we all have memory gaps of one kind or another. This would be very different from a pathological state which would be considered a fugue state or amnesia."

"And . . . did you make a diagnosis of amnesia or . . . of memory gap?"

"I didn't make a diagnosis at all, Mr. Wall. I wrote you . . . that my examination was not exhaustive, and I prefer not to make a diagnosis of any kind on the basis of a two-and-one-half-hour examination."

[Ponderous tone] "In other words you recognize . . . the very definite limitations of a mere two-and-one-half-hour examination?"

[Composed] "I think I am the first one to recognize that."

"And you recognize that, without making a diagnosis, opinions relating to the motives and thoughts and truthfulness or nontruthfulness of the individual are difficult for you to evaluate?"

Some confusion over that question. The doctor asked Mr. Wall to repeat and Mr. Shew put in, "As Mr. Wall says, let's have one at a time."

Dr. Von Salzen: "Well, if Mr. Wall is asking if this is a difficult case, certainly it is difficult—yes. Is that the tenor—difficult for me to reach an opinion?"

"Well . . . you made no diagnosis, and your examination was so short . . . that a diagnosis was impractical if not impossible?" The doctor agreed. "And you made no diagnosis of any amnesia?"

Dr. Von Salzen explained that there is no such diagnosis as amnesia. Amnesia is a symptom. "In pneumonia a symptom may be a high temperature, but this occurs in many different illnesses. . . . Amnesia is a symptom which occurs in many different conditions."

• • •

Recess

"This is dynamite."

"If the Jury buys the doctor's opinion, they can't convict."

"If Harry has no memory, the confession goes out the window."

"He *said* he read it in the newspapers—"

"Rome said it from the start—about the Letter."

"It comes down to whether the Jury believes it."

• • •

After recess, at last, the "second story."

"At the conclusion of my examination," Dr. Von Salzen said, "I went over again with the Defendant the details of his entering the Thompsen house on June 15 and then he told me the second story. He gave me a rather long, involved statement to the effect that it might be hard to convince the Jury of the truth of his first story and, if the Jury didn't believe him, he could spend twenty years in prison; whereas he said that he might get only six years if he said the second story. The second story was that—when he entered the Thompsen house, Mrs. Dorothy Thompsen greeted him and offered him something to drink such as orange juice or Coke. He sat with her in the living room, and then Mrs. Thompsen made amorous advances to him. He kissed her and then when he wanted to retreat, she slapped him and said something to the effect that no one could go halfway with her. He said that at this point, he remembered nothing further; and my report states, 'When questioned closely about these two stories, he said that the first story was true, but that he might say the second story was true.'"

Clearly Dr. Von Salzen's testimony was the strongest point for the Defense to date and now Mr. Wall set about the task of discrediting it. [Rather accusingly] "Now, Doctor, did you deviate some from your report relating to what Solberg said to you about if he were convicted of manslaughter?"

"Did I deviate? . . . I don't see any deviation, Mr. Wall."

[A copy of the report in hand] " '. . . if he said the second story,'—is that in your report?"

The doctor consulted his report. "My actual report reads, 'If he were convicted of manslaughter, he might spend six years in prison.' " (Not: If he told the second story he might get six years. This is the discrepancy.) And there is nothing in the report about if he told the second story? "At the end, yes. The last sentence reads, 'When questioned closely about these two stories he said that the first story was true but that he might say the second story was true.' " But it was not in the report that he might be convicted of manslaughter if he told the second story? (The doctor did not say this!) "It was all tied up in his mind, Mr. Wall." Was it in your statement, Doctor? "It wasn't in the statement, no sir." [Accusing] And this is something you are telling today that was not in your statement? "Not in the written statement, that's true."

(What is this all about? Dr. Von Salzen, in his testimony today, did not use the word "manslaughter" first, Mr. Wall introduced it.)

Mr. Wall paced a moment. "Now—is the import of your direct examination to state that this accused is a repressed individual?"

Dr. Von Salzen [correcting him] "We all operate under repressions. . . . My report was that he was too rigidly repressed." And was that the principal finding upon which the doctor based these opinions that he had given? "No, sir. One of the major points was that walking in upon this scene and seeing this body had a tremendous emotional impact upon him—a shocking impact upon him." Were those the two principal factors, then, upon which he based his opinion: first, walking in on this horrible scene—and the other, an overly repressed individual? "That he would have, I think, reacted differently from another person entering upon the same scene."

Mr. Wall persisted. Then these were the two factors on which he based his opinion of memory gaps? Dr. Von Salzen commented that he was also relying upon his own clinical judgment and experience. Mr. Wall hastened to say that he regarded it highly. But, again, these were the doctor's actual observations—that he was an overly repressed individual and that he had come on the horrible sight of this body. Were there any other observations that the doctor made . . . in addition to these two?

Dr. Von Salzen [briskly] "I don't think that I am at all clear as to the question, Mr. Wall. Over two and a half hours, I observed many things and I considered many things important. I have not, in my testimony, condensed everything that took place during that two and a half hours."

Mr. Wall: "And whether this young man was an overly repressed individual depended upon what he told you in that two and a half hours, did it not?"

"Not entirely. No." The doctor reminded Mr. Wall that he had written to him about using certain drawings in a "projective test"—a test in which untitled pictures are used and the individual is asked to make up a story about them. "I administered a number of these pictures to him. I brought two of them with me because they do seem to indicate his marked repression of feeling."

"And is that the only conclusion that you came to from these tests?"

"Well, I think that covers a lot of territory, Mr. Wall. In my letter I said . . . that an individual such as this, when confronted with a scene of violence, would react strongly. [Firmly] I went on to say that I believe at that time behavior governed by rational thinking itself would be impossible as a result of panic."

"Panic. And this panic was the result of seeing a shocking scene?"

"In part, Mr. Wall. . . . It is not just viewing a scene, but it is what that scene does to a particular individual."

Mr. Wall [ponderous] "I ask you, Doctor, whether a repressed individual like this who *commits* a horrible crime wouldn't have the same reaction as when he viewed the horrible result of a horrible crime? Wouldn't it be even more probable that, having committed the crime, a repressed individual would then have memory gaps?"

Dr. Von Salzen agreed. "I think that is true . . . that if someone commits a crime which is alien to his ego—entirely alien to his teaching—he could well develop an amnesia for that."

Mr. Wall: "In other words this amnesia is consistent with his having committed the crime as well as just having viewed the body in its horrible state?"

Dr. Von Salzen: "Yes. I wrote you that since amnesia plays such a prominent part in each story, I would have no way of ascertaining the truth except possibly by the use of drugs. . . . The amnesia was present in both stories."

Mr. Wall asked whether Dr. Von Salzen had any personal history of this accused, and the doctor replied that he had only what Harry told him and some information about his high school record and intelligence tests. A complete, exhaustive examination, he agreed, would include other tests, interviews with various people who had known him—many things.

Mr. Wall [continuing to chop away] "Now, Doctor, were you able from the different stories he told you to determine whether his claimed lack of memory was untruthful . . . ?"

"I have no way, Mr. Wall . . . of ascertaining the truth except possibly by the use of drugs."

When Solberg said that Mr. Thompsen had agreed to help him with an economics report, did the doctor accept that as the truth? "Yes. I didn't spend much time on it. I didn't question it." And if he lied about that? "I certainly would want to know why he went to the Thompsen house. When he told me he went there for the report, I assumed this was the reason."

And would his telling or not telling the truth about that be an important factor in the doctor's evaluation of whether he did or did not remember? "I would certainly take that into consideration along with all the other things."

"Now, in his first story, he did not say anything about having any talk with the deceased, did he?"

"Well, in the first story he saw the blood and he thinks he must have seen the body . . . so he didn't have any conversation with her."

"Now . . . can you, in point of time, state where the memory gap began and where the memory gap no longer applied?"

"No. I don't know the exact moment it began. I believe that seeing this body could be a sufficient trigger to blot out this recognition of what he had seen. After an interval of this kind . . . there is a gradual return of identity. . . . I think it began to return certainly when he found himself at home, asking his mother where his father was working. . . . But it is not a matter of memory rushing back in—one moment gone, and the next moment all there. It is definitely a piecemeal type of thing."

(Could Harry, who took six years to finish high school, possibly have made up this classic example of fugue and shock?)

"And if there were memory gaps, those gaps would be filled in by remembering certain things under certain circumstances after the event?"

"Not necessarily, no. These memory gaps can be filled in various ways. For example, things that he read or heard." To illustrate Dr. Von Salzen described an organic illness known as Korsakov's Syndrome. "In this illness there are profound memory gaps. The individual does not know where he was last night or any other time. If, in talking with him, one can put an idea into his head, and say, 'Did you have a good time last night in Washington, D.C.?' he will then pick this up and put this in to replace the memory gap. In other words, one is putting ideas into his mind. He may have been in the State Hospital for two years—but this is what I mean by filling in memory gaps. It isn't just the return of one's own memory because the gaps can be filled in by other stimuli."

Now Mr. Wall stated that Harry had said, first, that he remembered nothing after he saw the body, and then, second, that he remembered nothing after Dorothy had slapped his face. "Could that memory gap have come as a result of either of those events?"

"Well, that's a question I have asked myself, Mr. Wall. And I did include this in my letter to you. I think for a state of complete blocking out of the personality, there has to be a sufficient stimulus. It doesn't happen from something minor, and, in my opinion, the stimulus here was seeing this body. I just can't believe that a stimulus of a kiss is enough to cause this great change in one's personality."

"Or a slap in the face?"

"I don't believe so, no."

"Although he did state that his memory gap started with that slap in the face, did he not? . . . And you believed him on both occasions?"

[Firmly] "No, I did not. I believed the first story. I testified that I do not believe that a kiss or a slap is sufficient stimulus to produce such a profound change in the personality."

"Then he was lying to you when he told you that he had no further memory after she slapped him in the face?"

The doctor [strong] "I don't believe that I testified to that."

Now Mr. Shew protested. "I have tried to let him have free rein, but I think the doctor testified that as far as the second statement was concerned he considers the whole statement a lie."

The Judge: "I don't believe he has gone quite that far, have you, Doctor?"

Dr. Von Salzen [firmly] "I thought I had, Your Honor . . . I would be glad to repeat it."

A final question from Mr. Wall: Does the doctor believe that Harry understands the nature of the charges against him? Dr. Von Salzen was very sure that he did.

Mr. Shew's turn to patch up the holes. He began by referring to the transcript of the "confession" interrogation, and Dr. Von Salzen said that he had read it several times and had made notes. Mr. Shew asked for his comments. Mr. Wall remained standing.

"Well, what is curious on page one, when the Defendant was told about his constitutional rights, he disregarded those and went ahead with the interrogation. On page two . . . he said, '—So I went down College Highway and took another road home. I don't know what the number of that road is or anything—I know but I can't think.' This to me was of some importance, that he knew the road, but at the time of the interrogation, he could not think. That was March 15 at 12:13 A.M. [A pause while he read his notes] I thought this was rather important. On page eighteen he was asked how the deceased was dressed and he didn't know how she was dressed. I had examined this photograph of the body for a few minutes, and I could tell pretty much how she was dressed. I thought that these points indicated some confusion in his thinking at the time of this interrogation."

Dr. Von Salzen had stated earlier that he had brought with him two of the pictures used in the "projective test." Now, at Mr. Shew's request, he explained the test again. ". . . Obviously, since there is no title and the pictures are made somewhat vague, the story which someone makes up will project his own thinking. . . . I simply used these to try to establish an emotional response."

The first picture showed the faces of a man and a woman close together. "Most people make up a story including some love or tenderness and embrace between two people. This is the typical response. The Defendant . . . said that it reminded him of a birthday party for his seventy-five-year-old grandfather, which is a good story but which to me represents a repression or pushing down of what I consider normal feelings of love."

The second picture appeared to be of a boy, a rather stricken figure, sitting on the floor, his head resting on what might be a bed or a sofa, with a small object on the floor beside him. "Most people look upon that as something tragic," Dr. Von Salzen said. "The whole tone is one of sadness and depression. The Defendant's story was that this was a boy who had been playing with a toy and got tired and lay down to take a nap. This to me indicates again repression and suppression of feeling. There is an object near him which is drawn purposely in a vague manner but I think most people look upon that as a gun, and he interpreted it as a toy, again not wanting to recognize . . . " (An interruption and the sentence was not completed, but the meaning was clear.)

Mr. Wall again. He referred to Harry's statement, during the interrogation, that he knocked on the door and Mrs. Thompsen answered it and that he didn't remember much after that except that he climbed up the ladder and ran out. "Doesn't that constitute a third different story as to the time that he stopped remembering?"

Dr. Von Salzen was losing patience. "I have already testified that in my opinion there is a lapse of memory for a certain period of time on the afternoon of June 15. I don't believe that I can answer your question any more comprehensively than that and I have testified to that."

Mr. Wall approached again, taking the stories one at a time. First, that he saw a dead body and had no memory. The doctor corrected him: He said that he must have seen the body but did not recall it. Second, after the slap in the face he had no memory. "And now this constitutes a third statement relating to his lack of memory, isn't that so?"

Dr. Von Salzen [still not taking this] "I have testified, Mr. Wall, that I believe he does not remember what happened during a certain period of time that afternoon and that I believe the trigger that started this lapse of memory was seeing the dead body."

[Crisp] "You have so testified?" Yes, sir. [Snap] "Now would you please answer the last question." Dr. Von Salzen agreed that it was a third statement relating to lack of memory.

Mr. Wall: "And having made three different statements on the same subject, Doctor, there is a pretty good chance, too, that it is a lie on each of the three occasions, isn't there?"

"As a doctor—we don't consider that amnesiacs are lying. We consider that they have a loss of memory. They may make up things to fill the gaps."

"When someone says, 'I don't remember,' when he actually remembers, that is an untruth, is it not?"

"I suppose you might say that, yes."

"And these three statements are completely inconsistent, are they not?"

"They are certainly very contradictory."

"And at least two of them are untruths, are they not?"

"I believe so."

[Turning away] "That's all."

Mr. Shew: "Doctor, the very fact that these statements are contradictory—which they are, obviously—isn't that in itself caused by the fact that the accused can't actually remember?"

Dr. Von Salzen [positively] "In my opinion—*yes.*"

◆

After lunch, Dr. Robert B. Miller, Chief of Professional Services at the Connecticut Valley Hospital. (The days seem to fall into patterns—police days, medical days, legal days. This is the day of the psychiatrists.) A serious-looking man—young face, gray hair, a deep rumble of a voice—Dr. Miller, like Dr. Von Salzen, appeared to be knowledgeable and quite at ease on the stand. He had been subpoenaed by Mr. Shew with instructions to bring with him the hospital's complete record on Agnes Thompsen. Now he said, "Mr. Shew, may I say that these are hospital records which are considered confidential. I would be glad to provide you with them if instructed to do so by the Court." The Judge gave the necessary order.

Mr. Shew asked first for the report of the physical examination of Agnes Thompsen on June 16, 1965, when she was returned to the hospital. In it one item proved to be of special interest: "Stain on palmar surface of fingers from fingerprinting."

"Does it mention any cuts or punctures on her hands?"

"There is no notation of any cuts or marks other than the stains. . . ."

Mr. Shew asked whether there had been an inquiry concerning this document from any State Police Officer or from the County Detective within the past week. Dr. Miller replied that there had been an inquiry from County Detective Holden and that he had given him this same information. (Is the implication that, while suggesting that the blood under Agnes's fingernails came from a wound, the State has probably known that no evidence of such a wound had been found?)

Mr. Shew turned to the subject of Agnes Thompsen's illness and we learned that the diagnosis appended to her chart was "Schizophrenic reaction, paranoid type"—made as early as February, 1964.

Then, from the hospital records came first a brief history of her condition up to that day in December, 1964, when she left the hospital to try an extended visit home, followed by details of her condition when she was returned in the early morning hours of June 16, 1965, after the murder.

Dr. Miller read from the record: " 'On admission she had hallucinations and delusions, mainly of a religious nature. . . . While under treatment in the hospital she frequently had hallucinations and delusions revolving around similar religious themes. In addition to auditory hallucinations, she had tactile experience of "spirits touching my finger and God touched my spine and head." . . . Subsequently she showed some signs of improvement and was permitted home on visits . . . that were reported to be increasingly satisfactory. She was able to do various forms of work at home and socialize to a moderate extent. Her son claimed that she was greatly improved and . . . expressed a desire to have her return home, feeling that she could make a satisfactory adjustment. . . . On December 22, 1964, she was over-excited and over-talkative but in good contact, fairly oriented and showing appropriate affect. [Affect, the doctor explained later, meant outward expression of feelings.] No further evidence at that time of hallucinations or delusions, so she was permitted to try an extended visit home.' "

Mr. Shew: ". . . Her son expressed a desire to have her come home in December, 1964?"

Dr. Miller: "Yes, that is correct."

Then to the night she came back to the hospital. Dr. Miller read from the report of the Resident in Training, who admitted her:

" '. . . She was brought from her home . . . by a policewoman and two State Police Troopers. . . . She had an emergency certificate signed by her local doctor, which read: "History of present illness: Acute agitation over violent death of daughter-in-law and pressure on head. Physical findings: None. Mental condition: Acute agitation? Violent? Suicidal?"

" 'The woman is . . . spry and chipper . . . appears to be somewhat agitated. . . . Neatly and appropriately dressed. . . . Hair is nicely groomed. She said that she returned to the hospital because her family physician . . . said she should come back . . . because "my younger son's wife died." She said, "She was killed. I heard two hard bangs and then I saw a man lower something down from the porch to the ground. It was dark. I saw a man in the back and I thought it was her brother. I was upstairs and didn't know anything bad had happened. I can't believe it is true. I was the only one home and I had to say what I saw to the detectives. I couldn't love her any more if she were my real daughter. She was very nice and we never had any arguments. I never bothered them, but today it would have been good if I bothered them. They have their ways and I have mine." . . . She said that the baby was left alone all afternoon and that she didn't hear any crying whatsoever . . . that her daughter-in-law died between 1:15 and 2:30 and was not found until her husband arrived home about 6:15. She then said about the baby, "She will never remember her mother."

" 'She denies hearing any voices . . . or having any nervous trouble. She complains only of pressure in her head and some vague type of stomach trouble. Patient was oriented as to time, place and person. . . . She was able to give all of the historical material. . . . Memory was good for recent and remote events. Her speech was spontaneous. . . . She was coherent and relevant. It was not possible to detect any discrepancies in her story as she told it. . . . No delusional material elicited. She frequently remarked about how happy she was at home and how well she got along with her son and his wife. She spoke of how she had kept herself busy taking care of a garden and also of her African Violets. Patient showed evidence of being somewhat agitated . . . frequently hyperventilating. She stated that her fingerprints were taken here at Connecticut Valley Hospital after she was returned. When asked if she did not think this was strange, she said, yes, that she wondered about it but she did not ask. According to verbal information received from a Supervisor, the State Troopers who accompanied the patient to the hospital stated that she, herself, had murdered her daughter-in-law. She is placed on suicidal and homicidal precautions.' "

Mr. Shew asked the doctor to repeat the sentence about the statement of the State Troopers, and Dr. Miller complied: " 'The State Troopers who accompanied the patient to the hospital stated that she, herself, had murdered her daughter-in-law.' "

Agnes Thompsen was seen on June 16, later in the morning, by Dr. McGennis, a Senior Psychiatrist. Dr. McGennis first saw her while she was assisting one of the nurses making a bed, found her calmer, still neatly groomed, coherent, relevant. " 'The only outward sign of agitation during the conversation,' " Dr. Miller read from Dr. McGennis's report, " 'was series of hyperventilation when discussing yesterday's happenings at home. No delusional material and no hallucinations noted. No significant depression, no ideas or reference to persecution or grandiosity.' "

To Dr. McGennis, Agnes Thompsen's story remained the same. " 'She vehemently denied having anything to do with the death of her daughter-in-law and consistently held to her statement about a man in a dark green car being present in her daughter-in-law's apartment yesterday afternoon. She stated that she did not see his face but saw him throw some large bundle from the porch outside her second floor apartment to the ground below. She said she heard "Two tremendous bumps" about 2:00 P.M. yesterday but did not go downstairs to investigate. She said she spent the day in her two-room second-floor apartment, crocheting, reading and doing housework. She denied any interpersonal difficulties with her daughter-in-law or her son but said that by mutual consent, she and the younger couple lived rather independent lives. She has been working two or three days a week at domestic work in the area and made about twelve dollars a day from this.

" '. . . Memory, both recent and remote, shows significant impairment. General fund of information appears in keeping with her intelligence level, in dull normal range. Judgment is impaired.' "

Dr. McGennis's note, Dr. Miller pointed out, differed from the other in that the Senior Psychiatrist felt that her memory was quite poor.

By August, Agnes Thompsen's condition had changed somewhat. A note on August 2 read: " 'Patient appeared more agitated and voluble on ward today. She had been interviewed at length by police officials two days ago and . . . she said, "They couldn't break me down because I am unguilty. They'll never get me to break down. They blamed me for it. They have lied so much. I'm at peace with the Lord. They blackened me down so terrible." She denied any pressure in her head.' "

By August 23 the change had become marked. " 'Patient shows more and more preoccupation with her Bible reading. She shows hyperventilation and athetoid-type twitching when attention is directed at her, even with conversation on neutral topics. She denies hallucinations, but her preoccupation, distractibility, and frequent listening attitude suggest otherwise. She has shown no aggressive or paranoid behavior in Ward 22'—which is a closed ward—'where she has been since admission. . . . She still assists nursing personnel, but in recent weeks she does things in a mechanical, robot-like fashion with very little conversation and a glassy, far-away look in her eyes. . . . Diagnosis: Increasing decompensation of her schizophrenic process.' "

"What does that mean, Doctor?" Mr. Shew asked.

"That means she was getting worse. . . . She was becoming more and more preoccupied and withdrawn and acting in a much more robot-like fashion."

By October 4, the date of the Coroner's Hearing, Agnes Thompsen had deteriorated still further. Dr. Miller, himself, examined her that morning and now in Court he read his own note. " 'I found her to be tense, anxious, manneristic, and with an extremely inappropriate affect. When discussing the possible Court appearance today with her, it became apparent that her reality testing was extremely poor and that she would not be capable of advising counsel. In reviewing the situation with her, it became apparent that she did not know right from wrong or the nature of her acts. . . . She is not capable

of appearing for trial. . . . Subjecting her to the confusing pressures of a Court appearance, particularly one related to a situation
so distressing, would not be feasible and might exacerbate her
illness. Consequently we shall not permit her to appear in Court this
date.' "

Dr. Miller himself went to the Coroner's Hearing and wrote a
note about it—a note that was not read at this time.

At this point there was an interruption in Dr. Miller's testimony
while the Judge inquired about the pages of the hospital record that
were being offered.

Mr. Shew: "I would like to have the whole report on record, if
possible. . . . I would take a chance and admit it now, although I
have not had the opportunity of going through it."

Mr. Wall: "I have never seen it or heard of these things before,
Your Honor, and I would like, before it goes into evidence, to have
an opportunity to look at it."

The next note in Agnes Thompsen's record was dated five months
later, March 1, 1966:

" 'This patient is fairly good most of the time, but can become
very upset and agitated. Hallucinates at times and states that she is
talking to a little God. Can become assaultive to other patients.
Helps with some work on wards. Does not attend any activities.
. . . Fully ambulant, neat, assists nurses on wards spontaneously.
Affect is blunted. At times appears preoccupied. She admits to occasional auditory hallucinations, but not in the past month. She denies
depression, reads her Norwegian Bible for hours each day. . . .
Some improvement in the last six months.' "

(In this report one notes for the first time the word "assaultive."
Also the final statement about some improvement leads one to
believe that six months ago, in August, her condition was worse
than one had first understood from the notes of that date.)

This was the last report up until the reports of her recent illness.
Also contained in this record book, Dr. Miller said, was a report that
he had made to the Commissioner of Mental Health in March,
relating to this case, and, too, a copy of a letter that he wrote to Mr.
Wall in September, 1965 (a year ago). Mr. Shew asked to see the

letter; Mr. Wall asked to see it. The letter was handed to Mr. Wall.

Mr. Shew: "Doctor, you used the phrase, 'Schizophrenic reaction, paranoid type.' What does 'paranoid' mean?"

"In reference to this case—this patient had both hallucinations and delusions which referred to concepts of persecution, bizarre phenomena, and so forth. . . . A hallucination is a false perception. A delusion is a false belief. In other words, if someone believes he is hearing voices, this would be . . . an auditory hallucination. On the other hand, if he harbors some concept such as being persecuted by some unknown and imaginary person, this would be a delusion."

"And what does schizophrenia mean?"

"Schizophrenia is a very vague disease entity . . . but basically, it means an individual who has a thought disorder, who may or may not have hallucinations or delusions, who believes and behaves in a manner which is inappropriate to reality. . . . Their response . . . is quite disproportionate to the emotion. So that an individual might be disproportionately distressed at seeing or hearing some tremendous piece of bad news—more or less distressed than the so-called normal individual would be."

"And as far back as 1964 your institution gave this diagnosis to Agnes Thompsen?"

"That is correct."

"And when a person such as Agnes Thompsen has delusions of persecution, are they apt to be dangerous?"

"Not necessarily, but possibly." There was no way, Dr. Miller explained, that he could make such a statement, specifically, about Agnes Thompsen.

Mr. Shew: "But there is certainly a possibility?"

Dr. Miller: "There is, in fact, a possibility."

"Doctor, is there anything in the records concerning any communication that Agnes Thompsen thought she had with the Devil?"

"Yes, there is." Dr. Miller turned to a report of March 5, 1964—about ten days after Agnes Thompsen entered the hospital for the first time. And here was the story of Agnes's early alarming bouts with the Devil.

" 'She stated that the Devil had gotten into her spine, and God had healed her spine and head. She stated that the Devil had been walking around her head, then touching her body. She tended to be very paranoid, suspicious, and expressed a lot of autistic thinking. . . . No memory losses. . . . This patient displays paranoid reaction rather than any depressive reaction.' "

And again on June 12, 1964: " 'Delusional and hallucinated. She feels that God has influenced her to heal her spine and head. She talks about the Devil drawn to the leg, but then revelation in kingdom come and many religious phrases. She has the idea that there is a spirit that touches her finger, and that these spirits move around in her head. "I walk on my head." She feels that she is not ill, that there is nothing wrong with her head, and she wants to go home.' "

In this note, for the first time the possibility of organic brain disease was suggested as one of the doctors expressed an opinion: "Brain syndrome with psychotic reaction."

Mr. Shew turned to another phase of Agnes Thompsen's psychiatric history—remissions—first asking Dr. Miller to explain the term.

"Remissions," Dr. Miller said, "are periods during which the pathological symptoms diminish or disappear and the patient apparently improves or gets better. The term . . . is usually used to indicate a period . . . in the course of an illness during which there has been improvement, but following which the illness continues with all the symptoms as before."

Mr. Shew: "You use the term 'apparent improvement,' Doctor. With this particular patient, was there any possibility of recovery after June, 1964 . . . when she could be considered a normal person?"

Dr. Miller: "I believe that there never would be a time when she would be considered completely normal, in comparison with other so-called completely normal individuals, even though there might be periods of time during which she . . . could effect some sort of marginal adaptation to the world around her. . . . As long as she remained apparently well or much improved, she would be considered as schizophrenia in remission. However, any additional stress beyond that which her very low level of tolerance might handle, would in all likelihood push her right back into her symptomatic phase of her illness once again."

"In other words, she would have no tolerance to face situations?"
"Correct."

"Doctor, were you present on any occasion when this woman was interviewed by the State Police?"

Dr. Miller replied that he was present on several occasions, when there were several police on the premises; he remembered many of them, not all.

Mr. Shew: "Can you describe the manner in which she was interviewed by the State Police—as far as consideration for her was concerned?"

Objection. "There is no specific time—no specific occasion—no specific person."

All such specific information, Dr. Miller said, was in the report he had just referred to, which he made to the Commissioner of Mental Health, a copy of which was included in this record. Mr. Shew asked to see the report and Mr. Wall joined him to read it. Dr. Miller sat waiting patiently, holding his eyeglasses.

Mr. Wall: "Do you offer it?"

Mr. Shew: "Yes, I do."

Mr. Wall: "Your Honor, I will object to it. I don't consider it part of the hospital records. It is interdepartmental mail and includes a great many conclusions that do not appear to be relevant here." Mr. Wall handed the letter to the Judge, pointing out that it was dated March 29, 1966. After examining it the Judge ruled that the letter would not be admitted, although the doctor could use it to refresh his memory. Mr. Shew argued that the letter was part of the hospital record, and again the question arose of introducing the entire record in evidence.

This time Mr. Wall objected. "Now that I see such objectionable matter in there, I would certainly object to it as a whole." He walked quickly down to the lower table, turned with that look of being ready to pounce, walked back. (From the telltale manner, the sudden quick edge, from the original question concerning the police interrogation of Agnes Thompsen that prompted the argument, one suspects that the subject matter of this letter was Major Rome's interviews, but once again we are left with only our assumptions.)

Just before recess there was a short discussion of one interview at which Dr. Miller was present. He described Agnes Thompsen's lack of reaction last March to the news that she was no longer a suspect. "At the time that the warrant was lifted," he said, "Lieutenant Fuessenich spoke with Mrs. Thompsen while I was present. The lieutenant attempted to explain to Mrs. Thompsen that . . . she was no longer under suspicion. He had some difficulty conveying this to her and, while waiting for a response from her, had to ask her whether she was in fact pleased by this because she, herself, made no spontaneous indication of this at all."

• • •

Recess
"Strong for the Defense."
"Nothing specific, really. Just that the poor woman was sick."
"She said she looked out and it was dark! It was early afternoon."
"She said the baby was alone all afternoon and didn't cry."
"The baby was dry."
"That remark, 'The baby will never remember her mother.' That doesn't sound so loving to me."
"She certainly stuck to her story. It was always the same."

One member of the press noted a fact that eluded most observers. In the Hartford *Courant,* Gerald Demeusy wrote: "The . . . jury heard for the first time . . . that someone else had been arrested in connection with the slaying. . . . Extreme care was taken during the first two weeks of the trial to keep from the jury that the killing of Mrs. Dorothy Thompsen was first charged against her mother-in-law."

• • •

After recess Mr. Shew brought out again that Agnes Thompsen, at the time of Dorothy's death, was home only on extended visit and was required during that time to visit the outpatient clinic of a state hospital in Hartford. "Is there any note in your records to show whether there was anything in Agnes Thompsen's behavior *previous* to June 15—not *on* June 15—to indicate that she should have come back to the hospital?"

Dr. Miller disclosed that he had received a verbal report from the outpatient clinic and had made a note of it. "Approximately ten days prior to her having been readmitted to the hospital, she had been discharged by an employer because she appeared to be acting in a bizarre fashion and seemed to be delusional and hallucinating. The people for whom she had worked felt somewhat uneasy and fearful and discharged her. . . . We also had information that she had been told by the outpatient department to return to the hospital—or rather, the family had been told to return her to the hospital because her case had palpably worsened."

Cross-Examination by Mr. Wall

Mr. Wall was concerned with the physical examination of Agnes Thompsen, performed by Dr. Louise Rucker, when she returned to the hospital on June 16, 1965. "The physical examination made of Mrs. Thompsen was routine, was it not?"

"Yes."

". . . And there was nothing . . . any more meticulous than any other examination made of any other patient?" No. "And that was made generally to determine whether there were any cuts or bruises or other mutilations of the body that would be apparent, is that correct?"

Dr. Miller: "Well, what I read indicated . . . a sufficiently thorough examination to even make notations of fingerprint ink on the fingers."

Mr. Wall: "In other words, you concluded from the fact that there had been fingerprint ink on the fingers, that the person who made the examination was a very observant person and had made a report?"

"I don't think it required that much observation to see black ink on white fingers, but at least she looked."

"And this examination was not of the type that would ordinarily disclose a pinprick or cuticle damage or a small matter of that sort, was it?"

"I could not say specifically, but I would tend to agree with you."

Mr. Wall: "That's all."

(Once again the impression is left that it is possible to make a pinprick type wound with a crochet needle.)

•   •   •

"Trooper Allan A. Yuknat."

We had already heard several times that Trooper Yuknat was the Bureau of Identification man at the house that night. Now he took the stand and was sworn, but before Mr. Shew's first question, Mr. Wall came forward. "Your Honor, there was a witness on the stand at the last time and he was taken off. Is the request made to put this witness on out of order as preliminary? Otherwise, I think the witness who was on the stand should be recalled to the stand."

(The witness who had been on the stand last Friday was Major Rome.)

Allowed to continue, Mr. Shew established Yuknat's presence at the house and then said, "In connection with this investigation, I ask you whether you had in your possession a pair of shoes?"

Yuknat: "Yes, we had a pair of shoes belonging to a male, which were black."

"Did you do anything with this pair of shoes?"

"At that particular moment I just took them into custody as I did with numerous other items."

"Whose shoes were they?"

"They were the shoes of Mr. Arnfin Thompsen."

Mr. Shew handed Yuknat the photographs that showed the footprints on the kitchen floor, and Yuknat acknowledged that he had observed the footprints that night. "Did you attempt to identify whose footprints those were?"

Yuknat: "Well, we made an attempt to compare them with the shoes you previously mentioned." What did you do? "Just a visual check, sir." (Once again the information was flowing like glue. Once again an officer with no notes.)

Mr. Shew: "When you say a visual check, did you attempt to place the shoes on the floor?"

"No, I was looking for identifying characteristics within the imprint left on the floor, which would correspond to a similar characteristic on the shoe itself, and then we would have gone further, if we had found this." (This seems strangely defeatist—

because there were no trademarks or other special marks, to forgo the opportunity to see at least whether the shoe fit the print.)

"And did you come to any conclusion as to whose footprints those were on the floor?"

"I did not."

For a brief moment Mr. Shew regarded Yuknat. In his hand he had the transcript of the first Coroner's Hearing—July 16, 1965. Here is Yuknat's testimony at that time:

Coroner Guion: "Do you have an opinion as to what [the footprints] are?"

Yuknat: "Well, on the evening of June 15, under direction of Captain Thomas O'Brien, I was given a pair of shoes which I was told had been worn by Mr. Arnfin Thompsen, and we took them to the area of these blood impressions which you see in the photos, and to the best we could determine at that time, the size and shape were similar, the holes caused by the nails holding the sole to the shoe were in the same location as the impressions on the floor themselves, but there was no outstanding identifiable characteristics that you could say would permit a positive identification."

Coroner Guion: "And so the basis of your investigation is that there is a similarity between these impressions and the impressions which would have been made by the shoes that Arnfin Thompsen . . . was wearing?"

Yuknat: "That is correct, sir."

Coroner: "Did they all seem to be made from the same source or different sources?"

Yuknat: "They appeared to be from the same source, and again without any particular identifiable characteristic a positive identification would be impossible."

Mr. Shew pressed Yuknat for better answers. "Can you tell us whether the imprints on the floor were similar in size and shape to those of Arnfin Thompsen?"

Yuknat: "They were similar in size and shape."

"And the holes caused by the nails holding the sole to the shoe were in the same location as the impressions on the floor?"

[Hedging a bit] "They were in approximately the same location."

What can be said about this? In the end the facts are wrenched out and the testimony is similar. But the impact is quite different. At the Coroner's Hearing the man appeared to believe that the prints were from Arnfin's shoes. Today the impression is left of considerable doubt.

.   .   .

When Mr. Shew followed Yuknat with a call for Lieutenant Fuessenich instead of Major Rome, Mr. Wall again injected that there had been another witness on the stand.

Today Fuessenich revealed that, on two separate occasions, hairs were sent for analysis and comparison to the Alcohol Tax Division in Washington, D.C. The dates: August, 1965, and April, 1966—pinpointing the two different suspects. The hairs in question were those found in Dorothy's hand and the one hair found on the patio door.

Mr. Shew asked whether the conclusions reached in Washington were different from those of Dr. Stolman. Fuessenich replied that they were. "The Alcohol Tax Division could not match any of the hairs sent to them with any of the other hairs sent to them. There was no comparison whatsoever."

Although this seemed rather important, no more was made of it at this time, and from the testimony alone the significance remained confused. During Cross-Examination Mr. Wall put the two reports of the Alcohol Tax Division into evidence and they were, therefore, available for examination by the Jury. The significance of the reports is this. Dr. Stolman, comparing characteristics under a microscope, had found the hair in Dorothy's hand similar to her own hair. He had also testified that the hair on the patio door was similar to the victim's hair—a point that had surprised Mr. Shew.

In Washington the hairs were subjected to a more sophisticated method of comparison, described on the report: "Hair sample was irradiated in a nuclear reactor for a period of four hours—and the chemical analysis of each hair was reported."

In August, 1965, hair samples from Dorothy, Arnfin, and Agnes were submitted for comparison with the questioned hairs (from the hand and the door). The report came back that the questioned samples "could not be matched to any other exhibits." In April, 1966, another sample was sent—Harry Solberg's hair. The report was that this hair was distinctly different from the two questioned samples previously analyzed. This time the report went even further, noting that "besides significant quantitative differences between the elements found in [the samples], qualitative differences also exist." Harry's hair was completely different from the ones in question.

On Redirect, Mr. Shew asked how the police had obtained the sample of Harry's hair, and Fuessenich replied that they got it from Harry on Sunday, March 13, at the Hartford Barracks.

"Did he know that you had taken it?" Oh, yes. "He gave it to you?" Yes.

•   •   •

With about ten minutes left in the day, Major Rome returned to the stand. Mr. Shew focused on the visit to Agnes Thompsen on August 5, 1965 (the date on which, apparently, Rome obtained her "confession"). On that date, he testified now, several police officers were with him—Sergeant Ragazzi, Detective Lester Redican, two other State Troopers. Also present at that interview was a policewoman—Valerie Hageman. Always, at all interviews, some member of the hospital staff was in attendance—the nurse, Dr. Miller, or another member of the staff. The interview of August 5 lasted between two and two-and-a-half hours.

Mr. Shew: "Do you remember whether Dr. Miller was present—either at the interview or in the next room?"

Major Rome: "He was there. I don't know whether he was there all the time. We had a microphone in the room and a speaker in the next room where the doctors and other troopers could listen."

"And can you describe Agnes Thompsen's condition?"

Major Rome: "I thought she was nervous. She is a very excitable woman although she appeared to be strong and in good health physically."

"And what precautions did you take concerning Agnes Thompsen's health and welfare before you started any interrogation?"

[Firmly] "I left that entirely up to Dr. Miller or members of his staff who were in attendance. I don't think I was capable myself of determining the true condition of her health."

Mr. Shew: "At any time did you interview Agnes Thompsen without the approval of somebody on the staff of the hospital, Major?"

"No, sir."

"And whose approval did you have on August 5?"

Major Rome: "Permission would be sought through Dr. Miller to Dr. Lowney the Superintendent. His permission was necessary. And on one or two occasions I talked to Superintendent Lowney."

"And Miss Valerie Hageman, a policewoman, was present?"

"At this interview she was."

Mr. Shew: "And did you ask certain questions of Agnes Thompsen at this interview, Major?"

Major Rome: "I asked many questions, sir."

And with that it was five o'clock and Court adjourned, with the Columbus Day holiday tomorrow, until Thursday morning.

14

Thursday, October 13

"Now during this interview did you have Valerie Hageman do anything—take any action?"

"Yes, I asked her to lie down on the floor."

Mr. Shew resumed where he had left off on Tuesday. For a few minutes he reviewed with Major Rome the details of the interview of August 5. (Policewoman Hageman and the nurse were in the room with Rome and Agnes; the other police officers listened in the next room, where the doctors could also listen.) Valerie Hageman was here this morning, sitting in the front row with Lieutenant Fuessenich. At the State's table Mr. Wall—tense, watchful—remained standing. Mr. Shew said, "And what was your purpose in asking her to lie down on the floor, Major Rome?"

Mr. Wall: "Object to the purpose. . . . What's in this witness's mind—"

Mr. Shew: "I'm not asking what was in his mind. I'm asking what was actually done."

The Judge: "He can state what his purpose was in setting up the scene . . . in a certain way. [Then, patiently] If you have some additional reason that this is prejudicial—"

"There are, Your Honor—" We had been in session only a few minutes and already Mr. Wall seemed about to explode. "And I wish to develop those by Cross-Examination relating to the circumstances that existed so that Your Honor can then determine whether or not this is admissible—[moving quickly to seize the reins] and with Your Honor's permission, may I inquire of the witness relating to these circumstances."

With some apprehension—there was an atmosphere of impending disaster—the Judge asked whether this was going to develop into something that should be in the absence of the Jury, and at once both attorneys protested that they wanted the Jury present. But Mr. Shew had misgivings about this interruption in his own examination. "As I understand it, you wish to—"

"Relating to this," Mr. Wall cut in sharply. Reluctantly Mr. Shew acquiesced. Mr. Wall had seized the initiative in a major battle.

Standing some distance from the witness chair, Mr. Wall moved about in a wide arc, holding what appeared to be a report, or several reports, in his hand. "Major Rome, you called upon policewoman Valerie Hageman for her services in connection with this investigation. . . . Now did this happen on the morning of August 5?"

"When I actually asked her to assist I do not know. I believe it was on that morning."

More questions on the time of day. [Accusing tone] "So you came to the hospital in the morning and made arrangements for the interview . . . And did you call Miss Hageman about 12:20 . . . to request her to come to the hospital?"

"I just stated that I don't know the time of day she was called. I believe it would be— [As Mr. Wall plunged on] May I finish?" Mr. Wall apologized. The Major completed his sentence. "—It would be about that time." (Nothing at all has been said in the last few minutes; the knot of tension has pulled several notches tighter.)

Mr. Wall paced about as though stalking his prey, consulted his papers. "And had you interviewed Agnes Thompsen that morning before you called Miss Hageman?" If I was at the hospital, I was there to interview Agnes Thompsen. "And had you questioned her for some time that morning?" I don't know what you mean by some time. "Did you question her at all that morning?" I said I believe I did. "For how long did you question her that morning?" I don't know.

A long pause—total silence. Mr. Wall waiting, rocking on his heels.

Major Rome: "Are you waiting for another answer?"

"Did I get an answer? Did I get an answer?"

"I thought I did. [Repeating, undisturbed] I don't know."

"I didn't hear it. I'm sorry. You have no idea whether it was one minute or two hours or five hours?"

"Yes. It would not have been a minute, and it could not have been five hours."

Mr. Wall consulted his papers. "And when you saw Miss Valerie Hageman on that day, did you issue instructions relating to what she was expected to do?"

[Emphatic] *"Yes, sir, I did!"*

[Monotone] "And will you relate to His Honor and the Jury what you—"

[Very emphatic] "I will be glad to."

[Snap] "Well, I will be *very happy to have you.*"

Rome [a grin] "Very good—make us both happy. [Briskly] I had talked to Agnes Thompsen on at least three previous occasions—"

Mr. Wall [cutting in] "May I ask, Your Honor—"

Rome: "Will you let me finish?"

The Judge [quickly] "Just a minute—" Mr. Wall interrupted to say that the answer was not responsive, asked that the question be read. The Judge attempted to comment. Mr. Wall, cutting in, insisted on the question. The question was read and Mr. Wall said, *"What those instructions were."*

The Judge explained that Mr. Wall was objecting to background information on the instructions. "That can be brought out later. At the present time, the question is just what the instructions were."

Mr. Wall [acid] "What is the response to that question?"

[Matter-of-fact] "Miss Hageman was to pose as Arnfin Thompsen's sweetheart."

"And will you relate what instructions you gave and amplify the statement that Miss Hageman was to pose as Arnfin Thompsen's sweetheart?"

[Spirited] "Amplification I will be glad to give you, Mr. Wall!"

[Caustic] "Just amplify what your specific instructions were."

Major Rome: "I explained—now this is all from memory, I have no notes on this—I explained to Miss Hageman that I was of a firm opinion—"

The Judge interrupted. "This is not responsive, Major."

Rome: "I am sorry. It is all part of the instructions."

Mr. Wall: "May I move it go out, Your Honor—'I have a firm opinion—'? [Ordering] Just the instructions, Major."

"I instructed Miss Hageman to pose as Arnfin Thompsen's sweetheart [quicker, firm] in order to get, *not a confession,* but some *information* from Agnes Thompsen which we could later *corroborate or verify* to determine whether she was guilty or innocent."

Mr. Wall paced about, consulted his papers, moved closer. [Baiting tone] "Now is that *all* that you recall of importance of the instructions you gave to Miss Hageman?"

"Well, if you refresh my memory, I'll go on, but this is all I can recall right now. You see, I made no notes myself." (Of which we have all been made aware.)

Mr. Wall [suddenly barbed] "You have been in this courtroom for about ten full days, haven't you?"

[Flatly] "No, I have not."

Mr. Shew on his feet. "Objection, Your Honor. Just hold it right there. Mr. Wall even asked Major Rome to stay out of the courthouse."

Mr. Wall [hotly] "I never said any such thing!"

Mr. Shew [furious] "Don't call me a liar again!" (This last does not appear in the transcript.)

The Judge restored a temporary order.

Mr. Wall [baiting again] "Major, what other instructions did you give to Valerie Hageman . . . ?"

"Mr. Wall, the only thing that comes to my memory now is what I have told you. If you refresh my memory I will be glad to go on. I am hiding absolutely nothing."

Explosion! Mr. Wall [boiling] "May that remark, 'I am hiding absolutely nothing' go out, Your Honor? [Very snide] Methinks he protesteth too much."

Mr. Shew: "*Objection!* I can make just as many wisecracks as he can, Your Honor, if we are going to have that! And I don't think they are very good!"

Instantly the Judge excused the Jury. A shocked, pained, embarrassed, expectant, absolute silence filled the courtroom. It was 10:33. We had been in session exactly thirty minutes.

When the Jury had gone, Judge MacDonald for the first time publicly acknowledged the ill feelings in this case. [Firmly] "I am not going to allow them to . . . erupt into anything that could cause a mistrial. I do think that Major Rome's answer was unnecessary, in which he said that he had nothing to hide. But I think the State's Attorney's observation was even more unnecessary." Then, going to the core of the matter, he asked why, since Agnes Thompsen's statements had been ruled inadmissible, it was necessary to go into the circumstances under which they were made. Once the subject was opened up the State's Attorney was entitled to go into it. But, he asked Mr. Shew, what was the purpose of going into it at all?

Mr. Shew replied at once that he felt that he had been prevented from presenting a most essential part of his case. "I am going to get just as close to it as I can. I think the Jury should know that this is being withheld from them, that I wish to produce it, and that Mr. Wall wants to hold it back." In all Supreme Court decisions in murder cases, he said, emphasis is placed on bringing out the *truth*. "The duty of the State is not just to get a conviction! It is to bring out the *truth!* And that is what I have been trying to do."

In that case, the Judge said, if Mr. Shew was going to try to communicate the nature of these statements, Mr. Wall was entitled to go into the circumstances. The questioning would continue. "But with the admonition, please—don't let this turn into a Donnybrook that has no place here."

"Your Honor, I apologize for the quotation," Mr. Wall said, with a nod to the bench, "I do wish, however— [Accusing] This witness has, on two occasions, made statements like this. Several days ago, he said, 'I am only trying to tell you the truth, Mr. Wall—' Now he comes out with this statement. A witness as trained as this man should be restrained. I think that type of statement is provocative of the type of thing that I did on this occasion." (One thinks of Rome's reputation for quick wit on the stand and for getting things in. Is this what is worrying Mr. Wall?)

The Judge agreed that Major Rome should refrain from making such statements. Then [to Mr. Wall] "And I think that you should also . . . refrain from statements that give rise to his compulsion to add something that . . . counterbalances an implication made by you. . . . I think you gentlemen know what I am talking about. So let's just call a halt—and proceed as though you two had never had words before."

On the stand, Major Rome smiled. Mr. Wall restrained a smile while standing in mid-court. He walked behind the State's table and turned away and then smiled.

The Jury returned and Mr. Wall resumed with the same question. "Now, Major . . . you requested Valerie Hageman to pose as the fiancée of Arnfin Thompsen. . . . Did you give any further instructions . . . to Miss Hageman?"

"Mr. Wall, I truly don't recall. I am sure I may have. I explained the type of person we had to deal with, and I asked her if she could go along with it, with a certain strategy to open the mind of an insane person."

[Circling, mid-court] "And now you had with you another man who was on your staff. . . . And is it so that at your direction he went in and told Agnes Thompsen that he was a lawyer . . . that he had been hired by the girl friend to . . . protect her interest?"

"Exactly what he said, I have no recollection right now. [Firmly] But I was dealing with a woman who had been committed—an *insane woman*—and I had to resort to subterfuge to find the truth in this case. [Positively] *And I did!*"

Mr. Wall [lashing out] "And that subterfuge involved your denial of that woman of counsel, isn't that so—that poor woman?"

Rome [coming right back] "That was discussed with Superintendent Lowney of the hospital. And her son—either Arnfin or Theodore—or the hospital superintendent, who was her guardian at the time, was present. The members of the hospital were present. . . . [A smile] And she didn't fall for it. She was too smart."

"That was not your fault, was it, Major?"

[Candidly] "I tried."

"You tried very hard . . ."

"Mr. Wall, I tried to get the true facts of this case—*and I did.*"

Mr. Wall: "I move that go out, Your Honor." The Judge directed that the last statement go out. Mr. Wall paced about, taking his time, while he read his papers. (In the press row, one opinion is that this is Rome's own report.) He moved closer to his prey.

[Eyes on the report] "Did you also offer to get Agnes Thompsen out of the institution if she would answer your questions the way you wanted her to?"

[Strong] "No, sir, that is only part true that you are reading."

"What part of that is true?"

"I told her, in an effort here to open her mind, because I felt the woman had the secret to this case locked in her mind—"

[Whipping about] "May that go out, Your Honor—that portion that is not responsive?" The Judge so directed. Mr. Wall asked for the question.

Rome [fast—his reactions are very quick] "I know the question . . . [Answering it] The first part—that I would do this if she would answer questions *my way,* this is something *I did not ask.*"

Now, snatching bits and pieces out of what was apparently Rome's report of the interrogation, Mr. Wall flung them at him. [Lashing out] "And you told her she would be in the best position to get out, go free, go home and forget about it, didn't you? . . . And did you say, 'You tell me where the piggy bank is, and you and Jean,' meaning Miss Hageman, 'can go right home'? . . . And did you say, 'If you are going to continue to lie to me, then you have to stay here for the rest of your life'?"

To each question the Major replied that he did not recall the exact words, but that if Mr. Wall was reading it from the paper, he would go along with it. "I used every kind of deception to get the truth. I was dealing with an insane woman. [Impatience] This wasn't a *confession* to be used *against Mrs. Thompsen!* I wanted the *truth* of this case."

[Lash] "Did you say to Miss Hageman, 'I am going to stop your marriage to Arnfin, Jean'? . . . Did you say, 'If the mother did it, you can marry Arnfin'?" That doesn't make sense to me. "Did you say to Agnes Thompsen that if she said she did it, then Jean could marry Arnfin?"

"I'll go along with that, yes. Yet I don't recall. I used everything in my bag of tricks to get the truth from this insane person. I opened the bag wide."

"Did you say, 'I'll bring Arnfin here tonight. You tell me where the bank is and I'll get a minister here to marry them'?"

"I could have said that. I deny nothing, Mr. Wall, in my attempt to get the *truth.*"

"Did you say, 'Anybody that doesn't remember has to stay in this hospital'?"

"Yes, that I am sure I would say. I believed that she knew what she did and I was trying to get it out of her. . . . I was trying to jar her into telling the truth . . . *and I feel she did!"*

"Did you say, 'When you talk this way you know what I have to tell the doctors? She can't remember. You have to keep her here for another year—five years, ten years, the rest of her life'?"

Rome [still calm] "I did everything possible in the legal manner to try to extract the truth from this lady. . . . Because in previous statements, she had stated to me that she knew, and I was there to try to get the truth. *And I eventually did."*

"You said, 'Jean is entitled to know. She is going to be your daughter-in-law—maybe tonight'?"

"I don't remember really saying this, but I feel sure this is—" Mr. Wall plunged on. Rome [fast] *"Let me finish, please.* [Instantly calm] This is in line with everything I was trying to do to extract the truth—not a *confession—*the *truth."*

"Did you say, 'I don't want to tell the doctors you can't remember. They are going to keep you here. And these nurses are worse than the doctors'?"

The Judge interrupted to say that perhaps this last statement should not go into the record because it might be the basis of some action by the nurses. But the Major, with a smile, said, "I'll take the chance, Your Honor. May I explain that? It was just a pun to the nurse at the time. There was a nurse present, and I did that more to break the monotony for this poor girl who was sitting through all this."

Mr. Wall [sarcastic] "Was this an occasion of levity to you, Major?"

"At that instant, yes—yes."

Mr. Shew pointed out that, even in Court, we have had occasional levity, and the Judge, with a smile, added that perhaps he was guilty of that, too. Mr. Wall had no time for levity. He raced on. "Did you say, 'Agnes, we are telling the truth—your memory has to be good or you stay here'?"

Still again Major Rome said that he did not remember his exact words. "This is what I would do to extract the truth—*not a confession—*but *true statements that could be verified or corroborated.* I am sorry that I had to use this kind of subterfuge but—"

Mr. Wall [biting] "You are devoted to the truth?"

Rome [emphatically] *"I am."*

[Sarcastic] "Yes. Did you say, 'I don't want to tell the doctor you can't remember because if I tell him that, you are going to stay'?"

Rome [a sudden smile] "I just thought of an answer to that question, 'You are devoted to the truth?' Can I answer that one?"

Wall: "No. You have answered it. Please answer this one. . . . Did you say, 'If you start making up things, I am going to tell the doctor you don't remember'?"

[Loud and clear] *"Yes, sir. Because I didn't want her to make up anything. I wanted the truth."*

"Now you may wish to answer that question, Major, if you are devoted to the truth. Are you? [Biting] Would you like to answer that question?"

Rome [leaning forward] "If I weren't, I wouldn't be here."

"Aren't you under subpoena here today?"

[Positively] "Because I want to get the truth out."

"Aren't you under subpoena?" I am. [Again] "Aren't you under subpoena today?" I said I am. "Then you would have to be here whether you wanted to be or not, would you not?"

"Mr. Shew knows—"

"Wait a minute. Answer my question, please."

"No!"

"In other words, you could defy the law and defy a subpoena?"

"No!" [Tapping his knee emphatically] "But if I had told Mr. Shew something else, he wouldn't have me here today." Abruptly Rome closed the door on this brief flash of emotion and sat back.

Mr. Wall paced, moving several steps away and back again. "Did you say, 'I don't want to tell the doctor that you can't remember. Look what you are doing to me'?"

"That doesn't make sense. I don't understand that question."

"Did you say, 'We got your footprints and fingerprints right here' —and you pointed to the bay window?"

"That I don't recall, but if someone with a better memory than mine says I did, I did. I was talking to an insane person and I was seeking the truth."

"Did you say, 'Don't let the doctor know—if I am talking to you and you say you don't know, I'm a dead duck'?"

"That I don't recall but if someone else does, I will go along with it."

A long wait as Mr. Wall walked to the State table and then, a bulldog look on his flushed face, crossed to where Valerie Hageman and Lieutenant Fuessenich were sitting in the front row. There appeared to be a brief conference. (The press row opinion now was that it was Rome's report *plus* information supplied by Valerie Hageman.) Mr. Wall resumed.

"You started the interrogation of Mrs. Thompsen on the morning of the fifth of August, did you not?" I testified before that I don't know the exact time. "And it was late at night before you completed your interrogation?" If you will explain what hour "late at night" means? "Had there not been darkness come upon you at the time that you just completed it?"

"No, I don't believe so. Anyway, this was under the control of the superintendent of the hospital—the hours I talked to her, when she was fed, and the time taken out. This is all under their control."

Mr. Wall: "Now, this question that was asked of you as to whether or not Miss Hageman lay on the floor on one occasion. That was after you made all those statements to Mrs. Thompsen, isn't that so?"

"I would again say yes. Yes."

Mr. Wall tossed down his papers and seemed—as he turned to the Judge—strangely exhilarated. "I object to the question, Your Honor, on the grounds that not only is it hearsay, but anything which might have been said under these circumstances, would have no trustworthiness, whatsoever."

He had finished.

The Judge took a moment to look at Mr. Wall. "Well, it was so long ago that we had the question that I'd like to know from you what the question *was*—to which the objection was made that called for the last half-hour of interrogation. Just what was it? Do you remember? [Then, troubled] I would make the observation at this time that I think I am going to reverse my former ruling concerning the admissibility of the statements."

Mr. Wall on his feet! Mr. Shew on his feet!

Mr. Shew: "I am certainly going to ask you to, Your Honor."

"One of my reasons for keeping such statements out," the Judge went on, "was that they would only confuse the issues before the Jury and make it look as though somebody other than the accused was on trial. Now I feel that, since questions were asked concerning the circumstances surrounding the interrogation, the Jury is entitled to know what the statements were that were objected to, so that they can decide themselves what weight should be given to them." (Exactly what Mr. Shew had asked from the start.) ". . . It seems to me that what is fair for one, is fair for the other, and as long as we have gone into the circumstances . . . my inclination is to allow the results of that interrogation to come in." He would hear arguments after recess.

• • •

The recess stretched to nearly half an hour, and there was plenty of comment to fill it. (Would one have a different picture without these opportunities, three times a day, to back and fill?)

To Mr. Shew, Major Rome repeated what he had said on the stand every time he could get it in—that this was never intended to be used against Agnes Thompsen in Court. Everyone knew the case was never going to trial.

He described, as he had before, Agnes's condition that day: "They told me she was deteriorating rapidly; that day she was unusually alert. These people have these lucid periods and as they deteriorate they become shorter. They can be sharp one minute and ten minutes later they're way out. You have to catch them and work fast." (Mr. Shew had questioned Dr. Miller on Tuesday about these periods of remission.) "I had a dying woman on my hands. This was getting the facts—while we still could—to prove once and for all what happened. Once she was gone, that was it. I couldn't bring her back. It was my *job* to find out the truth. I had to *know*—did this woman kill her daughter-in-law or *did I have a vicious killer on the loose?*"

(A reporter, watching him, said, "Sam wears a cool front but he's fighting now for his very existence—his name, his job, his reputation.")

"Sometime later an innocent person might be accused," Rome said to Mr. Shew. "What would people say then, if I said, 'I could have straightened the whole thing out and gotten the answer from her if I did that, but I didn't think it was proper.' Bull! This was never intended to be used against her in Court. I was the first to agree that it wouldn't be admissible. I said so at the Coroner's Hearing."

A friend and a visiting lawyer joined them.

"To do any kind of police work you don't turn your back," Rome said. "You do what is necessary to meet the situation. Any cop worth his salt does everything he can legally to get at the truth."

"Was this legal, Sam?"

"Yes! Anything obtained can't be used in Court as evidence against her, but there is no law that says you can't interrogate without a lawyer." (He's right! Reread *Miranda* and he is right. It says that unless the State proves that the warnings were given, nothing obtained by police interrogation can be used by the State against the Defendant in Court. But this case was not going to Court. Agnes Thompsen was insane and she was not going to recover.) "What I did was not illegal," he said. Then, with a smile, "Or Wall would have me arrested."

"But she was insane, Sam. Doesn't that give you doubts?"

"No!" There was no scrap of apology—no regret—in his manner or in his thinking. Only conviction. "Even from a sick mind you can get information that can be corroborated. She couldn't have dreamed these things up. Once she started to talk I purposely tried to mislead her. If she didn't do it, she would have allowed herself to be misled. She gave me a description of how this crime was done. She gave me details that could be corroborated. She told me how she did it and why. Either her story checks or it doesn't. This whole case comes down to: Is the confession from Agnes better corroborated than the confession from Solberg? No matter how ill Agnes might have been, she told me things that nobody could have known except the person who did it. She told a story that can be checked against the evidence. *And that story should be heard.*"

• • •

When Court reconvened, with the Jury absent, the Judge restated his own position: Much of what he had been trying to avoid had come out now. The Jury knew the circumstances of the interrogation, they knew from Dr. Miller's testimony that Mrs. Thompsen was originally accused of this crime, they knew that at least one investigating officer believed that she knew who committed the murder. "They have had so many hints . . . that I am beginning to

wonder whether the fairest way would be for them to know exactly
what this woman said and to evaluate the statements themselves
and decide what weight to give to them. That's my present line of
thinking. I haven't decided. I will be glad to hear arguments."

But it could not be expected that on this issue the arguments—all
of them familiar now—could be offered without new discords. Mr.
Wall repeated that the statements were hearsay and untrustworthy.
Then he said, ". . . My purpose in making this intermediate Cross-
Examination was to give Your Honor an additional reason why Your
Honor's ruling was correct . . . To allow a Jury to hear what a
schizophrenic woman said, after being plied with lie after lie and
deception after deception. Your Honor, how that could have any
possible trustworthiness is just beyond me!"

"I had already made the ruling," the Judge pointed out, "and I
just wonder why, since I had already excluded that testimony, we
had to go into all of these circumstances?"

Mr. Wall: "For this reason, Your Honor. The Counsel for the
Defendant had claimed that he was going to appeal on this ground.
He said that he felt the Supreme Court would have to decide—"

Mr. Shew [at once] "Let's stop right there, Your Honor—that is
incorrect! I never made such a ridiculous statement! I don't expect
to have to appeal!"

Mr. Wall [undaunted] "He stated that he felt Your Honor's ruling
was not correct and I felt, Your Honor, that it should be in this
record that this was an additional reason why Your Honor's ruling
was correct."

The Judge put the argument back on the track, again examining
his own dilemma. Had he heard the circumstances in the absence of
the Jury, he said, he would certainly have excluded the admissions,
unless Mr. Shew brought out something which changed the picture
completely. (Off to one side Mr. Wall, very nervous, jingling coins
in his pocket.) But now, the Judge went on, he was debating with
himself on several questions. Had the reasons for keeping the
statements from the Jury lost their meaning? Would it be fairer—to
both sides—if they heard them? Now they were left wondering
whether the statements amounted to anything. Would the Jury, if
they heard them, be in a better position to decide the case?

(How can there be any question? For days now we have flirted
with the subject of these tapes, and we are still wondering and

suffering over what is in them. Are they hysterical or are they rational? Are they confusing or are they convincing? Too many doubts have been raised now not to know. There is too much at stake.)

The painstaking debate on true justice continued.

Mr. Wall stated that the statements would only confuse the Jury. (Does the Jury even remember that Harry Solberg is on trial?)

Commenting that Mr. Wall had made a great deal of the fact that the person involved was insane, Mr. Shew cited a case that stated that insanity was a basis for admitting hearsay evidence. "The word 'insanity' is used—the Court presupposes that the person whose statement is going to be repeated is insane. . . . And what this law is about, as far as trustworthiness is concerned, is the *repetition* of that statement. Not the trustworthiness of the original statement—you can place whatever credence you want to on that—the trustworthiness of those repeating it. Now here we have five or six State Police Officers listening to certain statements being made. And if that isn't trustworthy, I don't know what is."

The Judge: "You mean we don't need to be concerned about the trustworthiness of the person making the statement?"

"That is correct, Your Honor. . . . Here we have a trustworthy repetition. It is very easy right now to establish just what was said there. There can't be any question about it. Even Mr. Wall will be satisfied, because I am sure he has got tapes of the whole darn business."

But even as the Judge discussed it, he appeared to be talking himself out of his new position: These very important statements were not made in the presence of the Jury—there was no opportunity for cross-examination. We would be hearing only the statements she made in reply to questions—asked under what appeared to be rather high-pressure circumstances. "This is not intended as a criticism," he said, "because I have often stated that I disagree with some of the Supreme Court rulings on that point. But we would have statements made by a woman whose mental condition is at best uncertain, under very trying circumstances—with no opportunity for the Jury to evaluate what her condition was at the time she made the statements, and with no opportunity for her to be cross-examined as to the truth of the statements that she made."

(Could not hospital personnel testify concerning her condition? Might not the tapes themselves reveal something about it—and about the probable truth, too?)

Mr. Shew: "Your Honor, she is not on trial. There is no self-incrimination."

The Judge [wryly] "That is what I keep reminding everybody."

Mr. Shew: "Mr. Wall has brought out the circumstances. The Jury is entitled to know the rest of it. It is absolutely unfair not to admit it. [Hotly] Why, it is an insult to this Jury when Mr. Wall says they would be confused by this."

The Judge: "I am afraid I have said it—because I think we are getting dangerously close to trying Mrs. Thompsen instead of Mr. Solberg."

Mr. Shew: "Well, maybe it has taken a great deal of effort to get at the *truth*. . . . Nobody is going to try that poor old lady. Anybody with any sense knows that she *never* will be tried. Mr. Wall said in his argument that it would confuse the Jury. What absolute utter nonsense! If anything, they are confused now! This might clear it up!"

But justice still eluded us. The Judge postponed his ruling until after lunch, and for another few hours we were left cliff-hanging.

◆

With the most critical decision of the trial in limbo, the testimony for the remainder of the morning seemed an interlude.

Mr. Shew called Trooper Philip Salafia, the officer who took the fingernail and cuticle scrapings from Agnes Thompsen at 2:20 A.M. in the lobby of the Connecticut Valley Hospital. (Salafia is something of an outsider—from neither the Canaan Barracks nor Hartford Headquarters. At the time of the murder he was with the Detective Division; now he was attached to the Groton Barracks, seventy miles away.) On the stand Salafia said that he had his notes with him and had consulted them. (Notes!)

A pleasant-looking, earnest young man in his late twenties, Salafia testified that he accompanied Detective James Jacobs and Policewoman Virginia Butler that night as they returned Mrs. Thompsen to the hospital. ". . . I inspected the woman's hands and there appeared to be a dried substance clinging to, or partially underneath, the cuticles. I scraped this into a small piece of white plain paper. I also scraped underneath the fingernails into the white paper. The paper was sealed and marked by myself, with the date, time and my name."

"And what, if any, injuries did you see on her hands, Officer?" Mr. Shew asked.

"The only thing I can positively remember, sir, is that her hands were very clean, but I don't remember if I saw any cuts or injuries."

"At that time, if there were any cuts, you didn't notice them, is that correct?" Correct. "And if there had been a cut that would have produced any bleeding, would you have made a note of it?"

"I probably would have, sir."

Did he explain to Agnes Thompsen why he was doing this? "I had a lengthy conversation with her. She was quite talkative, but whether I explained why I was taking these dried substances from her cuticles and fingernails, I don't know." He put the scrapings into an envelope, sealed and marked it, and delivered it the next morning to Dr. Stolman.

"Did Detective Jacobs observe you scraping the fingernails?"

"Detective Jacobs and Policewoman Butler were very close observers, sir."

In Cross-Examination, Mr. Wall: "Now this substance . . . was from the cuticle of the right middle finger, is that correct?"

Salafia consulted his notes. "Yes, sir, it was."

(The *right* middle finger. One wonders whether Agnes is right-handed. If so, she would have held a crochet needle in her right hand and any injury would have been to the left hand!)

"And you observed no such substance on any of the other fingers, did you?" Yes, sir, I did. "On one finger? On any other finger?" Other *fingers*, sir. "Well, did you observe something particularly relating to the cuticle of the right middle finger as distinguished from the other fingers?"

"No, sir. It was a globby substance, clearly visible."

"Yes, and you saw something that was clearly visible on the right middle finger?" That is correct, sir. "And you did not observe the same conditions on the other fingers . . . did you?"

[Not thrown off] "Not as much, sir."

(Confusion piled on confusion! A pinprick wound—impossible,

anyway, with a crochet hook—would not bleed enough to spill over onto other *fingers*. A wound from a crochet hook that would bleed so profusely would be most apparent!)

"And you then did take scrapings from all ten fingers?"

Salafia [looking at his notes] "All I have noted was that I obtained scrapings from the other fingers. Whether I scraped all ten fingers or not, I can't remember, sir."

"And did you take any special pain to examine under the fingernails to determine whether there might be a pinprick or a crochet needle prick that could have caused anything of this sort?"

"No, sir. The scraping itself was a—may I say, delicate business. I didn't notice anything—not that I can remember anyway."

Mr. Shew: "Well, Officer, if you had seen some source that might cause blood on Mrs. Thompsen's fingers, you would have noted so in your report, wouldn't you?"

"Yes, sir, I would."

•   •   •

Detective James M. Jacobs followed Salafia to the stand and corroborated his story. Salafia scraped all ten fingernails. Detective Jacobs watched him. And he, too, looked at Agnes Thompson's hands and saw no cuts or sores. If he had seen any, he would have mentioned them in his report.

•   •   •

Then Policewoman Virginia Butler, who had spent much more time with Agnes Thompson that night. Summoned for that purpose, she had arrived at the house at 9:15 and had remained with Agnes until she left her at the hospital. Mrs. Butler—a rather stocky blonde woman, eyeglasses, good posture—works out of Litchfield and Canaan.

With a series of questions, Mr. Shew elicited a picture of the mother-in-law's behavior that night. Agnes Thompson had talked about her religion, her crocheting, her friends. She was aware of what had happened. So far as Mrs. Butler knew, she had not seen the body, but she wanted very much to go downstairs. "I had to keep talking to her to calm her down a little and keep her upstairs." Then an interesting comment: "She asked me if it could possibly have been the Boston Strangler. . . . She said it was too bad it had happened. . . . She would get a little bit excited every once in a while, so I'd get off the subject and then she'd calm down again." Also, Agnes Thompsen said that she had seen a green car parked that afternoon in front of the house.

Mr. Shew: "Do you remember, Mrs. Butler, whether it is possible to see out front from her apartment?"

"As I recall, it wasn't a very good view."

(There is no front window—only a side window, from which the road at the entrance to the driveway would be at almost a ninety-degree angle.)

Did Mrs. Butler see her use her hands for anything that evening? "No—outside of reading her Bible and looking at old photographs taken in Norway. . . . She was very immaculate and when somebody would bring in dirt from their shoes, she would pick it up from the floor."

"Did you have a chance to observe her hands?"

"Yes, all during the evening when I was with her and at the hospital."

"And did you see any cuts or bruises or punctures or anything else on her hands?"

"No, sir."

Mr. Shew asked to see Mrs. Butler's report, and after reading it, he said, "There were other statements made that night, weren't there, Mrs. Butler?"

"Well, we talked about so many things . . . about her crocheting and about her daughter-in-law, that it was too bad it happened—" Did Agnes Thompsen show any remorse over her daughter-in-law's death? "Not particularly. She wasn't crying." What did you say in your report? "No, she didn't actually show any remorse." Refer to your report. "She didn't talk about it too much."

This was blowing up into a minor clash as Mr. Shew insisted and Mrs. Butler appeared to be reluctant to read directly from her report. "Will you refer to your report, Mrs. Butler?"

Mrs. Butler looked at the report. "She did make the remark that she would stay there and take care of the little child."

"*That she was going to stay there and take care of the little child.* . . . Now, did you make a remark that she took exception to—while you were with her? . . . I am not asking what the remark was. I am asking whether she took exception to one of your remarks." Yes, she did. "And what did she do?"

"She just jumped up and glared at me. . . . I changed the subject and she calmed down."

Mr. Shew offered the report in evidence. "And now the last sentence—will you read it out loud, please?"

But instead Mrs. Butler began to explain. "Well, that particular evening I felt that this woman would be—"

Mr. Shew [impatiently] "Now, Mrs. Butler, please. I asked you if you would just read that statement in your report."

Mrs. Butler complied. " 'It would appear that this woman could be capable of going from various moods up to one of violence. As stated, she showed no grief, sorrow or any emotion of any kind over the death.' "

Mr. Wall began his Cross-Examination by asking Mrs. Butler to describe the condition of Agnes Thompsen's apartment.

"It was immaculate—absolutely immaculate—except for the dirt that had been brought in by people going in and out."

And her personal appearance—was she disheveled or well-groomed?

"Very well-groomed. She had gotten a home permanent that day and her hair was up in pin curlers." Did those pin curls include all the hair on her head? "All of the hair. It was right down flat in pin curls all around."

"Were any of the pin curls out of place?"

"No, they were set just so . . . I believe her daughter-in-law had given her the home permanent . . . and the pin curls had just been left there."

Issues arise out of nowhere. Mr. Shew noted that there had been no reference to the pin curls in Mrs. Butler's report. "When did you first remember that you asked her about that?"

"Well, I remember seeing her with all the pin curls in her hair."

(The significance of this seemingly trivial detail was that Major Rome insisted that Dr. Stolman had reported that it was Agnes's hair found on the door jamb.)

Rather sharply Mr. Shew asked whether Mrs. Butler had discussed this case with Mr. Wall or with Lieutenant Fuessenich or with any members of the department. Mrs. Butler denied it. "When did the question of the hair and the curlers first come up, Mrs. Butler? Did you discuss that this morning?"

"Someone asked me about it—I think it was Trooper Pennington. . . . Just if her hair had been up in pin curlers and I definitely remember it was. . . . I think I did mention, when he asked me, that she had it done that day. She had a home permanent that day."

"And that was the first time you mentioned the home permanent—to Trooper Pennington this morning?"

"Well, it was known at the house that night."

"And you knew that Agnes Thompsen had said her daughter-in-law did it . . . and you hadn't called it to *anyone's* attention until this morning when Trooper Pennington called it to *your* attention?"

"Yes, I hadn't thought of it any more."

. . .

When does a mind make itself up? And why? Every day, if you listen, you know that a few more people have decided the question of guilt or innocence before all the evidence is in. Influenced by different testimony, succumbing for different reasons, some people hold out longer than others. But once decided, from then on, passion mixes with reason and the person sees with a prejudiced eye. He grasps those shreds of evidence that support his conclusion. He brushes aside troublesome bits that support the verdict he has rejected. An opinion is first the possessed and then the possessor of the man.

What about the Jury? Are they any different? Will a sharpened sense of responsibility keep their minds open to the end? Are their minds open now? If today, at last, we hear Agnes Thompsen's statement—and hopes are high now that we will—will its impact change opinions already rooted, hardened, befriended?

Going to lunch today a stocky tweedy lady who has not missed a session said, "That kid didn't do it." Why today?

◆

"I am ready to rule on the question of the statements by Agnes Thompsen without any further argument," the Judge said. Lunch over. The Jury absent. The Courtroom filled—absolutely silent.

Judge MacDonald commented that he had spent the noon hour reviewing the authorities submitted by both attorneys. "And I will state that I am more firmly convinced than ever that my prior ruling was the correct one and that the statements are not admissible!"

No reversal! The ruling would stand!

The Judge wanted to have his reasons on record and now he devoted several minutes to reviewing them, again quoting the Court decisions, again explaining his interpretations of them, again applying them to this case. "There are so many apparent infirmities with respect to the trustworthiness . . . her mental condition . . . the pressures she was under, whether justified or not—I am not passing on that question . . . I am simply saying that, because of the circumstances under which the statements were made, coupled with the fact that they were made without protection of oath, without the protection of cross-examination, I think that they are clearly inadmissible and I will repeat that ruling at this time."

At once Mr. Shew asked to have the Judge's earlier remarks on this question read. Mr. Tyll, the second Court Reporter who had been taking testimony at that time, was summoned and in his notes he located the Judge's comments which, three hours ago, had held so much hope for the Defense. He read: "'. . . One of my reasons for keeping such statements out was that they would only confuse the issues before the Jury. . . . Now I feel that, since questions were asked concerning the circumstances . . . the Jury is entitled to know what the statements were that were objected to, so that they can decide themselves what weight should be given to them. . . . It seems to me that what is fair for one is fair for the other, and as long as we have gone into the circumstances surrounding the interrogation, my inclination is to allow—'"

"That's all I wanted," Mr. Shew said. "So I now understand, Your Honor, that you do not mean that it is only fair to go on with this examination?"

"Mr. Shew, at the moment that I made that statement, I felt just exactly as I stated then," the Judge replied, candidly. ". . . Fortunately, I said that I would like to think it over and to review the law; and in thinking it over, I am convinced that my inclination was based on my own personal feelings of the moment rather than on sound law. . . . I think that . . . the Supreme Court would think the Court was exercising poor discretion to allow the statements to come in because of the lack of trustworthiness surrounding them. . . ." Then he added, "If the reading of my remarks indicates that I have wavered several times in reaching this conclusion, that is quite true. I have and I admit it. I feel that it is the only ruling that I can make."

Grasping at the last straw, Mr. Shew said, "Then, Your Honor, the Jury should be made aware of the fact that certain statements that Mrs. Thompsen made are being kept from them—"

"Well, they know that."

"I want to make it very clear, Your Honor. They were in on this discussion. [Pointedly] It was very obvious why Mr. Wall took so much time on it. It was absolutely unnecessary. This long interrogation with Major Rome on the stand took him almost three quarters of an hour. . . . With a slight subterfuge, he took this opportunity to get on the record what he might not have otherwise gotten on. I let him do it. Now I feel that it is absolutely a travesty on justice not to let me finish up. *This boy's life—*"

The Judge interrupted to say that he agreed that this morning's episode was unnecessary and that he had said so. But the questions were asked without objection so the Court let them in. Now the harm had been done. As for informing the Jury that certain statements made by Agnes Thompsen were being excluded, he considered that a fair request.

When the Jury returned he delivered this explanation: "Ladies and gentlemen, I would like to explain something to you . . . so that you won't think that Counsel are trying—the State's Attorney is trying to conceal anything from you—or that anyone is trying to withhold anything from you which is pertinent to this case. You are all aware, I am certain, that . . . during the course of interrogations by the State Police, Agnes Thompsen made certain statements. Certain of those statements . . . I have excluded because . . . the rules of evidence laid down by our Supreme Court clearly bind me to refuse to admit them. So I am simply pointing out to you that certain statements made by Agnes Thompsen have been excluded and will not appear in evidence before you."

Mr. Shew: "If I may add, Your Honor, that I am the one that requested the statements."

The Judge: "That, I think, was apparent. Mr. Shew has been attempting on behalf of the Defendant to get certain statements into evidence and the Court has excluded them under the rules of evidence."

The matter was closed. The Defense had lost the major battle.

In an anticlimactic atmosphere Policewoman Butler returned to the stand. Major Rome, thoroughly frustrated now, walked to the back of the room where he remained standing. Mr. Wall resumed: Was Agnes Thompsen's hair still in pin curls when they took her to the hospital?

Mrs. Butler: "Yes, sir, we didn't touch it."

Mr. Wall began to refer to the hospital records, but Mr. Shew put in that he would agree to the pin curls if that was what the record said, and Mr. Wall repeated, "That it was in pin curlers and in perfect condition." The matter was passed over without further discussion. (Which, if this is important, is rather strange. In the report of the admitting doctor, part of which Dr. Miller read aloud, the only reference to the condition of Agnes Thompsen's hair was, "Hair: Colored gray. Distribution: normal," and, "Her hair is nicely groomed." In this trial there had been no word about pin curls until Mrs. Butler took the stand.)

As Mr. Shew began the Redirect one could sense the degree of his deflation. He brought out that it was not Dorothy, but another daughter-in-law who had done Agnes Thompsen's hair and then attempted to question Mrs. Butler further on her report. Twice Mr. Wall objected that this was repetitious and that the Jury had the facts from which to draw the conclusions. Very angry, Mr. Shew snapped, "Again I will ask Mr. Wall to let me try my own case. If there is anyone that repeats around here, he does." This small point went to Mr. Shew, and he reviewed the more important points of the report. Here is Policewoman Butler's entire report (with routine descriptions of the house and family omitted).

"While with Mrs. Thompsen it was evident she was in an excitable state, she was breathing deeply throughout the entire night, she would get very restless and rush for the door to go downstairs to see what was going on. However, she spoke in a lucid manner and as long as I carried on a conversation with her she would remain fairly quiet. Her memory is very good, we talked of her photo albums, her crochet work, etc. During this time she showed no remorse over her daughter-in-law's death, merely mentioned it was 'too bad.' She is a definite religious fanatic and at one time I made a remark she didn't like and she jumped off the bed and glared at me. By changing the conversation she calmed down. According to her she saw a car in the driveway from her window, first she said it was dark green, then light green. She also stated she saw a man from her bedroom window, on the porch in the rear, just the back of him. She thought it was Dorothy's brother. I asked her if he usually visited and she said 'never.' Mrs. Thompsen also asked on two occasions if the Boston Strangler could have done it and I doubt if she knew the cause of death. She was also quite concerned about two white handkerchiefs she had washed and were in the bathroom. Throughout the night she made numerous mention of the fact that now she would or could quit her housekeeping job and remain at home to take care of Christa and the house. Mrs. Thompsen gave me the impression it was a happy home and that she and her daughter-in-law were very compatible. A small amount of dirt was left on the floor by someone's shoes and Mrs. Thompsen picked it up practically grain by grain, her apartment was immaculate, she was disturbed because she noticed a few items that had been moved during the search.

"It would appear that this woman could be capable of going from various moods up to one of violence. As stated, she showed no grief, sorrow or any emotion of any kind over the death."

. . .

"I have no further questions of Major Rome, Your Honor," Mr. Shew said.

"I would like to cross-examine Major Rome, Your Honor."

Mr. Wall picked up the board holding the nail set and then the anonymous letter. "Now, Major, I believe you made an observation that the piece of metal driven into the board was a nail set and that it was not a spike. Is that correct? That you did make such an observation, sir?" I believe I did. "Actually, wasn't the function of that nail set the same function you would expect from a spike since it was driven into the wood in the same manner as a spike?" To me a spike is a spike. I know the difference. I know what a nail set is, and I felt that was a discrepancy. I still do.

"And that it was a discrepancy of substantial importance that it said 'spike' and it was actually a nail set?"

Major Rome [calm] "No, that's just one of the discrepancies. The ones of substantial importance, I wasn't allowed to testify to."

Mr. Wall handed Major Rome the Letter and asked him if he found in it anywhere the word "spike." Major Rome replied that it was spelled "S-K-I-K-E." He assumed it was misspelled.

Five times, with increasing venom, Mr. Wall repeated the question to force Major Rome to say that the Letter did not contain the word "spike." "It says 'skike,' S-K-I-K-E, isn't that so?"

"Yes, I felt that was spike. Wouldn't you?"

[Biting] "It didn't occur to you, did it, that a nail set used as a spike might be called a skike by somebody?"

"No, sir."

[Sharp] "But it did not say 'spike' in there in any place, did it?"

The Major spelled it out. "S-K-I-K-E. [Calmly] The nearest thing that ran through my mind was spike."

[Twist] "But it didn't say 'S-P-I-K-E' in there, did it?"

"I didn't spell it, either."

[Tighter] "It didn't say *S-P-I-K-E* in there, did it?"

"It says 'S-K-I-K-E' and I took it to mean S-P-I-K-E."

[Quite worked up] "It didn't say *S-P-I-K-E* in there, did it, sir?"

"It does not."

"*It does not? Thank you!*" Mr. Wall flung the Letter on the table. Face flushed, mouth curved down in a half-circle, he turned to continue the lashing. "You gave an order in connection with that state's Exhibit K—you issued an order?"

Major Rome: "If I did, I don't remember it right now."

"Have you no recollection of giving testimony here in this courtroom that you gave an order after you examined State's Exhibit K?"

Rome: "I'm sorry, I don't know these Exhibits by their numbers. If 'K' means the letter, I did."

Now Mr. Wall wanted to find the Letter again and could not. It was on the table where he had thrown it! He searched about excitedly until Mr. Shew pointed it out on the table. He snatched it up. "And did you issue an order [pacing about] to trace the writer of this letter and arrest him for being a crank or feeble-minded or something?" Yes, sir. [Sharp] "Is there any crime that you know of in the books of being a crank?"

Major Rome [firm] "Writing letters like that is a breach of the peace in my opinion."

[Acid] "But not of being a crank—do you know any?" Mr. Wall jingled the coins in his pocket.

[Emphatic] "I was talking about *this letter,* being sent to a man who had just lost his wife. Sending this kind of letter would be the work of a crank, yes, sir—and there is a law against it, yes, sir."

[Knife-edged] "Now answer my question, please, sir. Is there any law on the books relating to the arrest of a man for being a crank?"

Mr. Shew interrupted to say that certainly some men do things for which they are considered cranks and they do get arrested—and that he didn't see the point of this.

Mr. Wall [lashing out] "If Counsel wishes to object and the witness doesn't wish to answer—"

Major Rome: "I will answer."

The Judge sounded a bit weary, a bit disgusted, as he said that the witness had answered the question and that it was not necessary to go into whether there was a law on it.

Flushed, wide-eyed, Mr. Wall paced, spun about, came right back with an almost identical question. "Is there any law on the books for the arrest of a man for being feeble-minded?" [Jingle—jingle.]

Major Rome [undisturbed] "No, sir, not that I know of."

Mr. Wall: "And that's the only order that you issued with relation to the State's Exhibit K, is that so?"

Mr. Shew: "He didn't say it was the only one."

Mr. Wall: "I am asking him!"

Mr. Shew: "If Your Honor please, I could straighten this out. I dislike being misquoted. We could save time if Mr. Wall did not do that."

Mr. Wall [snap] "Where have I been misquoting, Your Honor?"

Mr. Shew: "You did just then. Misquoting my questions."

Mr. Wall: "Did you issue any other order, Major Rome, in connection with the letter other than you have testified to?" [Jingle—jingle—jingle.]

Major Rome: "Well, I didn't issue the order you just stated. I

issued the order that I testified to a few days ago, and the order that
I am trying to repeat now. That this was a letter written by a crank.
If you find him, you arrest him for breach of the peace. *Not* for
being a crank—"

Mr. Wall [furious] "May I ask that the answer go out and the
witness be instructed to answer the question, Your Honor?"

Major Rome did not remember any other order.

Mr. Wall snatched up another paper, paced about, looking at it.
"Did you issue a press release at or about this time that was widely
published relating to the fact that this was a work of a crank, that it
had no connection, whatsoever, with the case? [Showing him] The
date was June 25."

Major Rome: "May I see the whole thing?"

Mr. Wall [ordering] "Would you just refresh your recollection
with what I show you, sir. I ask you whether this that I am showing
you is refreshing your recollection?"

Mr. Shew: "If Your Honor please, I don't think this is proper
unless Mr. Wall wishes to put the whole thing in."

Mr. Wall: "I am merely asking whether it does refresh his recollection—"

Mr. Shew: "May I see that?"

Major Rome: "I don't print the newspaper. I don't know whether
this is accurate. I don't remember having given that statement."

Mr. Shew: "I am certainly entitled to see what he is asking my
witness."

Mr. Wall: "I'll show you right here."

Mr. Shew: "You will show me the whole business." (Again the
scene was bordering on hysteria.) "May I have that paper, Mr.
Wall?"

Mr. Wall: "You may look at such portion as was shown to Major
Rome."

The Judge agreed that Mr. Shew was entitled to see only the part
that was shown to Major Rome. Mr. Wall jingled coins while Mr.
Shew read it.

Mr. Wall [back to Major Rome, sharply] "Does it refresh your
recollection?" The Major said that it did not. [Clearly accusing]
"And you have no recollection of your having issued any statement
to the newspapers . . . that this letter was the work of a crank and
had no significance in the investigation whatsoever?"

Major Rome: "I have a recollection of returning that letter—after I examined it carefully and realized that the individual who wrote it had no facts—of returning it to Canaan."

Mr. Wall [whipping about] "May I ask, Your Honor, that what the witness has said go out?"

The Judge so ruled. The question was repeated. The Major repeated that he had no recollection of making the statement to the press.

Abruptly Mr. Wall said that he had no further questions, and the emotional performance was over.

Mr. Shew: "Major Rome, do you still consider that the person that wrote the letter was a crank?"

Major Rome: *"Absolutely."*

• • •

A much-needed quiet as Mr. Shew called another brief character witness for Harry Solberg. Mr. Richard Gower of East Hartland, twenty-four years old, who had worked for eight years at Hayes' Store. That this is a strategic listening post cannot be appreciated, perhaps, except by persons who know the fabric of these little pocket-sized towns. As Mr. Gower put it, "It is the only store in town. We knew pretty close to everybody. . . . We heard quite a bit of what went on."

Concerning Harry Solberg he said that he had known him for about twelve years—was no particular friend. "I knew him when he rode the school bus. I knew him working in the store. He was always around town, very quiet. . . . His reputation has always been good."

While Mr. Shew questioned Mr. Gower, Mr. Wall, still too wound up to sit down, paced restlessly behind the tables, down and back, down and back.

Mr. Shew: "Did you ever hear anything bad about him until this time?"

Mr. Gower: "The first thing I heard was about two days ago when an incident was in the paper . . . about a trip to New York." He was referring to the newspaper coverage of Pastor Bugge's testimony at this trial.

It is interesting that Mr. Gower, no particular friend, was willing to come forward. The town, it was reported, was split right down the middle on whether Harry or Agnes was guilty, but nobody else, except officials of the church, had wanted to become involved.

* * *

Dr. Gertrude Lucille Rucker, resident in psychiatry at the Connecticut Valley Hospital—the doctor who made the physical examination of Agnes Thompsen the night she was readmitted—a neat stocky Negro lady, intelligent and composed. At Mr. Shew's request, Dr. Rucker read her report of that examination—a most detailed and thorough one—to the Court. When she had finished, Mr. Shew said, "Would you say that her physical condition was pretty good at the time?" That is correct, yes. "Good healthy woman, physically?" Yes.

"Did you examine her hands?" I did. "And did you see any cuts or anything that would produce bleeding on her hands at that time, Doctor?"

Dr. Rucker: "I did not observe any at that time."

"Do you think if there had been any there you would have observed them?"

"I would expect to, depending—"

"And you found none?"

"I found none."

Mr. Wall, picking up the sentence that Dr. Rucker did not complete: Depending on what? Dr. Rucker: "In the ordinary course of a physical examination, I would expect to find any source of blood." Would find what? "I would expect to find any lesion of any appreciable size."

"Of any appreciable size. Then what you meant to say was, depending upon the size of the lesion. Is that what you mean?"

"Yes, that is true."

"And a slight puncture wound caused by a crochet needle might very well escape your attention, is that so?"

"I am not sure that I am familiar with the wound of a crochet needle."

(At last!)

Mr. Wall: "If there were a slight puncture wound, say in a cuticle, would you normally expect that might very well escape your attention?"

Dr. Rucker: "I can only say that it is within the realm of possibility."

Mr. Wall pointed out that Dr. Rucker made a very complete examination and found no cuts or bruises. "And there was nothing to indicate that this woman had any recent personal contact of any violent nature?"

Dr. Rucker: "There was nothing revealed in the examination."

Mr. Shew: "You didn't find anything that would cause blood to accumulate on her fingernails, did you?"

Dr. Rucker: "No, I did not."

•   •   •

The ruling on Agnes Thompsen's statements had been made for the second time, and there was no longer hope of changing it.

During recess with Mr. Shew's group, Rome said, "In any trial, the State should have nothing to hide. On the last day of the trial, if the State has new evidence that would help the accused, they should bring it in. The State represents the people. Their job is to bring out the truth. The only question should be, were we honest— did we add anything against her or exaggerate her role? Otherwise they should allow everything in—open the doors. If we're wrong, we're wrong."

A moment of troubled reflection and then he burst out, "If I'm trying to convict a guilty man and the court wants to let him off—if the guy gets a break—good—O.K.—hurrah for him! He can go out and murder someone else. But now, goddammit, I have an innocent man who might be found guilty!"

Silence. Then someone asked the question at last. "Are you sure, Sam? Do you really know that—or might there be something more to it?"

The Major looked up quickly. "I had to ask myself that at the start. Was I honestly convinced Solberg was innocent or was I trying to vindicate myself? With me, it doesn't have to be just a reasonable doubt. With me it has to be a certainty. I was certain."

There are people who have doubts. The thought lingers that others have had access to this "confession"—Commissioner Mulcahy, Coroner Guion, Mr. Wall, and more—the four officers who were at the hospital that day, the policewoman, Valerie Hageman, who was openly helping Mr. Wall in Court this morning. Probably the Canaan officers who have been working with Mr. Wall have heard it. All told, besides Rome and the hospital personnel, perhaps as many as eight persons know what Agnes Thompsen said. Perhaps more. No one has come forward to back him up.

"They say you're doing this to protect a perfect record, Sam."

[Indignant] "I am like hell! [A quick, impatient gesture] How do you sleep nights if you let an innocent man go to the chair?"

•   •   •

After recess Mr. Shew asked to return Major Rome to the stand "for just one question."

Mr. Wall [riding high] "It may be a lot longer than that one question, if I cross-examine, Your Honor." Immediately the Judge warned that Cross-Examination would be limited to the question that was asked. As the Major took the stand, Mr. Wall remained on his feet.

Mr. Shew: "Major, up until the start of this trial—before the impaneling of the Jury—had you ever talked with Mr. Wall about this case?"

"No, sir."

"He *never* discussed this matter with you?"

"*No, sir.*"

Fury flashed in Mr. Wall's face.

Mr. Shew: "And one other question, Major. What was your purpose in questioning Agnes Thompsen during this interview that Mr. Wall questioned you about this morning? Why did you do it? What were you trying to find out?"

Mr. Wall: "I object to it, Your Honor, I see no relevancy to what mental processes this man went through."

The Judge: "I understood Mr. Shew's question to be—what was the reason for the interrogation. I think he is entitled to answer that."

Major Rome leaned forward, eyes riveted on Mr. Shew. In a strong, authoritative voice, seizing this last opportunity, he said, "To extract, if I may use the word, information from this individual which could be *verified* and *corroborated* to determine whether or not it was *factual and truthful,* and whether she *did* or *did not* commit this crime. That was the *sole purpose* of that interrogation."

Mr. Wall streaked forward to cross-examine. "Major, I am not unknown to you, am I, sir?"

Rome [firmly] "No, sir, you are not."

"And you know, sir, that I have been State's Attorney in Litchfield County since 1953?"

"I don't know the date, but I have worked under you before."

Mr. Wall [the words spilling out] "And you felt you had information, did you, that was relevant to this case and you didn't, at any time, get in touch with me about this case—is that so? Is that what you want this Jury to understand?"

Rome [emphatically] "No, sir, I do not! I want this Jury to understand *that you had my reports* in your possession, which were *contrary* to the reports you had gotten from others, and *at no time* was I called to your office to see *why I did arrive at a different opinion.*"

Mr. Wall [pacing; biting] "I see. Now, Mr. Rome—"

[Grin] "Is that a demotion?"

"Pardon?"

Rome: "I'm sorry."

Mr. Wall looked about, puzzled, and Mr. Shew explained. "You addressed him as 'Mister,' Mr. Wall."

Mr. Wall [turning his back] "That was lese majesty? [Elaborate gesture] *Major* Rome, you will have the title, sir."

"Thank you."

"Major, you saw then, no necessity—not even propriety—in your getting in touch with me as State's Attorney in this county [accusing] knowing that I was proceeding with a prosecution against Harry Solberg, is that correct?"

Major Rome [flinging back the glove] "Yes, sir, that's a true statement."

Mr. Wall crossed to his table, picked up some papers and

whipped around. "And is it well known, Major, that you believe, in working for the State, that you have the *right* to *lie?*"

For the first time Major Rome showed a terrible anger. His face turned white. He wrapped his fists around the arms of the chair as though if he let go, restraint would go, too. (In that second, one saw the man of whom it was said: He goes where no one else will go, he does what no one else will do—he is not afraid of anything.) *"Will you please repeat that question?"*

Mr. Wall [shrill] "Is it well known that you, working for the State, believe that you have the right to lie?"

Mr. Shew [hastily] "If Your Honor please—"

The Judge [simultaneously] "If there is objection, I will sustain it."

Mr. Wall: "I can connect it up, Your Honor. May I show you what I have here?" He thrust a court transcript up to the Judge.

Still gripping the chair, white-knuckled, white-faced, jaw set, Major Rome shot a look at the Judge. Mr. Wall frantically jingled coins, eyes wide, thin mouth down tight in a half-circle.

The Judge handed back the papers. "I see nothing in here to justify asking the question, Mr. Wall—and I would sustain an objection to it."

Mr. Shew: "I have objected, Your Honor. I am willing to have everything before the Jury except that Major Rome is a liar. [To Mr. Wall] May I see that?"

Brushing him off, Mr. Wall paced across the room, reading his papers. "I want to examine it."

Mr. Shew: "You made a statement. I want to see it."

The Judge [firmly] "I have ruled that the question is not justified by the document. It has no further place in the—"

Mr. Shew: "I think I would like to see Mr. Wall's source of information, Your Honor, for my own purposes now. Do I see it, Mr. Wall?"

Mr. Wall [testily; turning his back] "When I am finished with it, sir." From the document that had been ruled inadmissible he shot a question at Major Rome. "On March 9, 1964, in the case of—" He named another case, another court, another town, another judge— and asked whether in that case Rome was examined by a certain attorney.

Mr. Shew [furious] "I don't know what this could possibly have to do with that. Mr. Wall is trying to carry on a vendetta with Major Rome."

Mr. Wall: "There is no vendetta!"

(Now the thing that one has felt privately for days has been stated in open court. The effect was one of shocked silence, as though an unmentionable disease had been publicly admitted.)

The Judge repeated that the document was not relevant. "I assume it is for the purpose of attacking the credibility, but I don't think that it is—"

Mr. Wall [bursting in] "Your Honor, that is not my purpose. My purpose is to answer the inquiry that has been made and the reflection that has been made upon the State's Attorney's Office— [wounded] that the State's Attorney did not go to Major Rome himself to ask about this particular case; and I felt, Your Honor, that the *reasons* for it should be made apparent to the Jury."

(Is the implication that he did not call in Major Rome because he believed the Major would lie to him?)

The Judge stated firmly that no reflection had been cast upon the State's Attorney's Office by this or anything else in this case and that "the curtain should be dropped right here and now on this entire line of questioning."

But Mr. Wall was not ready to drop it. "I feel that even though Your Honor has stated that there is no reflection upon the State's Attorney's Office, the only purpose of this testimony was to reflect upon the State's Attorney's Office in his neglect of duty in not going to see the Major about this case."

"Well, it could be argued, Mr. Wall, on the other hand," the Judge replied, "that the only purpose of your asking the Major certain questions was to reflect on him. So let's call a halt to it right here and now."

(One looks at Rome. His hands are in his lap again. He is sitting back again. His face is controlled and inscrutable again.)

Mr. Wall continued: "Now, Major, you never had any reason to believe that I, as State's Attorney, was not completely cooperative with you as a Major of the State Police Department, is that not so?"

"Yes, that is correct."

In a final, ambiguous gesture, Mr. Wall said, "May I say that in any contacts which I have had, that Major Rome has cooperated with the State's Attorney's Office, prior to this particular case."

The convulsion was over.

* * *

The day played itself out with two final witnesses.

Solveig Solberg took the stand again, and, at Mr. Shew's request, described her family—five children, of which Harry is the eldest, another son, and three daughters, the youngest aged eight. One daughter had open-heart surgery a year ago. And one grandchild, Harry's daughter, born on October 1. Harry saw his child for the first time yesterday, October 12. (This actually brought tears to the eyes of a lady juror.) Mr. Shew asked Mrs. Solberg to tell what she could remember about Harry's movements on the day of the murder.

Mrs. Solberg said that he came home from school just before one o'clock and that she put in a frozen dinner for his lunch which took forty minutes to cook and was ready at twenty minutes to two. Then the details that we have heard before: He went for the lawn mower which was not ready. He helped unload the plumbing supply truck. "Well, now I am sort of mixed up on this. I don't know if the plumbing truck came right before he went for the lawn mower or right after he went, but he asked me if he should go down and help his father, being that he couldn't cut the lawn, so I said yes, but go to the store first and bring some soda down because there was no water in the place where he was working. So he left the house and went to the store and as far as I knew he went to help his father."

Mrs. Solberg said that she did not notice anything unusual about Harry's appearance when he returned from the lawn mower shop nor about any of his clothing when she did the family washing.

Mr. Shew: "Mrs. Solberg, do you remember the last time you saw Dorothy Thompsen?"

About two weeks before the murder Dorothy drove past the house with the baby in the car, saw Mrs. Solberg outside, and stopped to talk. "Then, all of a sudden, she started to cry. I said, 'What is the matter, Dottie? Don't you feel well?' And she said, 'Yes, I feel all right, but I don't like going home.' So I said, 'Why?' 'Because,' she said, 'I am afraid.' I said, 'What are you afraid of?' So she said, 'Well, my mother-in-law is so funny towards me. I'm just so afraid she is going to do something. I have the baby there and if something happens, what will I do? Every time I turn around, if she is near me, she just stares at me and she doesn't say anything.' So I said, 'Why don't you discuss this with Arnfin? After all, his first responsibility is to you and the baby.' So she said, 'Well, we just can't seem to talk to each other any more.'"

Mr. Shew: "Mrs. Solberg, do you know how well Mrs. Agnes Thompsen knew your son, Harry?"

"She knew Harry very well because when she had her own home, Harry used to go every Saturday to cut her lawn and she always made him a big lunch."

"In other words, she knew who he was very well?"

"Yes, definitely."

In Cross-Examination, Mr. Wall tried to shake Mrs. Solberg's story about the hour at which Harry left the house, but basing her calculations on forty minutes to cook the frozen dinner which she said she put in at about one o'clock, Mrs. Solberg remained firm. Mr. Wall suggested that she told Trooper Pennington that Harry left the house between 1:20 and 1:30 and that he went to take soda to his father first and then went to the lawn mower shop. Mrs. Solberg replied each time that she did not recall saying those things to Trooper Pennington, and Mr. Wall ended his questioning.

A final witness—called by Mr. Wall—a State Trooper who, last Sunday, obtained a sample of blood from Agnes Thompsen at the hospital and delivered it to Dr. Stolman.

Then a brief business discussion in which we learned that the trial was drawing to a close and might go to the Jury sometime tomorrow. One sensed that it had to be ending. It had reached its peak today.

•   •   •

On the way out a reporter said to Rome, "A Canaan man says you're lucky the tapes didn't get in. He says you told her what to say!"

"This was done in front of a roomful of witnesses," the Major shot back angrily. "Five police officers, two doctors and a nurse. It was an open room."

"What if you told her first—or some other time?"

"Every conversation was monitored. . . . She's a demented individual! If I were feeding it to her, she might turn around and say, 'You told me to say that!' [Then, eyes sharp] With all those witnesses, Wall would have put someone on the stand. He wouldn't leave these doubts. He would have allowed the tape and then torn it apart once and for all. He'd have showed the world that I told her what to say!"

In the crowd a succinct comment about the Major's impact today. As he left a man said, "I think the kid is home free."

•   •   •

In the press the split was more apparent than ever. Last week the Waterbury *Republican* published the complete text of Harry's "confession." This week the Hartford *Courant* published a nearly complete transcript of Dr. Von Salzen's testimony. After this session, a glance at the morning's headlines revealed the widening gulf.

The *Republican:* ROME ADMITS USING DECEPTION IN PROBE.

The *Courant:* ROME, WALL PULL NO PUNCHES IN FLAREUP AT SOLBERG TRIAL.

The Waterbury *Republican* story followed the same direction as the headline, placing heavy emphasis on the "deception." It began: "State Police Major Samuel S. Rome testified under prodding by the prosecutor Thursday that he used 'subterfuge' and 'deception' to get statements from [Agnes Thompsen]. . . . Defense Counsel promptly sought to introduce those statements but [the Judge] blocked them as inadmissible hearsay." (No word of the Judge's dilemma on this point.)

Already there is an impression that Rome is all evil and the State's Attorney all virtue and, as one reads on, the impression grows stronger. Describing the courtroom clashes as "tiffs," the article reports, "Wall in one told the judge Rome should be 'restrained' from improper testifying. Defense Counsel Shew . . . chided Wall for apparently trying to 'carry on a vendetta with Mr. Rome. . . .' "

The story devoted a dozen paragraphs to every detail of the deception. It quoted Rome only three times in his own defense, even then emphasizing the deception: " 'I had to resort to subterfuge to find the facts in this case and I did . . . ,' Rome said. He said he felt the strategy was necessary 'to open the mind of an insane person.'" And, "'I was just trying to jog her memory. . . . I used everything in my bag of tricks. I opened the bag wide.'" And, "'I tried to get the facts and I did.'"

An obvious low blow: "The Major conceded, under continued questioning from Wall . . . that he told the elderly woman not to tell the doctor that she wasn't answering his questions or 'I'm a dead duck.'" (No mention of the fact that doctors were monitoring the interview and a nurse was present in the room.) "Rome insisted that the interrogation did not last all day and run into the night as Wall insinuated, and that it was 'under control of the hospital and was all strictly legitimate.'"

Half the truth is not the truth. Impacts are altered by omissions. Here is the way the two papers reported the afternoon clash. The Hartford *Courant* began with this story. In the Waterbury *Republican* it appeared in paragraph 29, the second column of page 2.

Hartford *Courant*	Waterbury *Republican*
State Police Major . . . Rome and State's Attorney . . . Wall broke into angry argument . . . in Superior Court here Thursday.	Rome and Wall got into their second dispute when Rome testified that he questioned . . . Mrs. Thompsen 'to extract information . . . which would be verified and corroborated as to whether she committed the crime.'
It came moments after Rome—testifying for the defense—coolly advised the jury that Wall had never consulted him before deciding to prosecute Solberg. . . . Stung by Rome's accusation . . . Wall went at Rome with a vengeance. "Major, I am not unknown to you, am I, sir?" "No, sir, you are not." "And you felt you had information, did you, that was relevant to this case and you didn't at any time get in touch with me about this case, is that so? Is that what you want this jury to understand?"	[Omitted. The article continues as though the above statement, which preceded the clash, was what prompted it.] Wall elicited that Rome was aware of the state's attorney's position and demanded: "You say you had information about the case and didn't want to give it to me as state's attorney?"

"No, sir, I did not. I want this jury to understand that you had reports in your possession which were contrary to reports you had gotten from others, and at no time was I called to your office to see why I did arrive at another opinion."

"You had my reports that were contrary to reports from others and at no time was I called to your office to tell why my conclusions were different," Rome replied.

"Major, you saw then no necessity, not even propriety, in your getting in touch with me as state's attorney, knowing that I was proceeding with a prosecution against Harry Solberg. Is that correct?"
"Yes, sir, that is a true statement."

"You didn't see fit to see me while knowing I was getting ready to prosecute Harry Solberg?" Wall asked.

"Correct," Rome replied.

Both papers continued with the next question: " 'And is it well known, Major, that you believe, working for the State, you have the right to lie?' "

The *Republican* made no mention of Rome's anger. It reported that the Judge intervened, that Mr. Shew objected, and that Mr. Wall went on to attempt to introduce the transcript of another case, about which it said: "[The Judge] said Wall was apparently trying to attack the credibility of Rome but Wall said he was just trying to show why his office did not consult Rome. . . ."

The *Courant* described Rome's extreme anger and Mr. Wall's stubborn efforts, after the Judge ruled it inadmissible, to question Rome from this transcript.

The *Courant* devoted the second half of the article (about forty paragraphs) to the details of the deception and to Rome's answers in his own defense—that he said repeatedly that this was done to get 'not a confession but some information from Agnes Thompsen which we could later corroborate . . . to determine whether she was guilty or innocent,' and that he was dealing with an insane person who had been committed and had to resort to deception to get the truth of this case.

Both stories cover the day's events. Many of the same facts are given, but the impressions created are quite different. This goes beyond the issue of "Free Press, Fair Trial."

15

There was a feeling this morning that we were coming up to the final curtain. When two familiar witnesses appeared—Arnfin and Dr. Stolman—one had a sense of their taking their final bows. Sharon was in Court today for the first time since the birth of the baby, as though returning for the closing scene. The Jury filed in and one looked at them as eight men and four women who had probably made up their minds and thought that not much would happen anymore to change them. Everywhere a sense that the drama was ending.

The Defense took less than half an hour to wind up its case.

Mr. Shew recalled Arnfin for a few short questions. "Mr. Thompsen, what was your mother's attitude when she found out that your wife was dead?"

Arnfin, speaking in a low flat voice but composed today—and audible—acknowledged that her attitude was one of indifference. "Just a glassy stare."

"And what was the condition of your daughter's panties when you first found her—were they wet or dry?"

"She was dry. She was clothed. She had pants on."

"Your mother had recently lost her position?" Arnfin replied that she had lost two of her three jobs. "Did she think she was then going to come home and take care of Christa?"

"Not that I know of. No."

"When did you start to discuss marriage with your present wife, Mr. Thompsen?"

"About three or four weeks after Dottie's death," Arnfin said quietly.

Mr. Wall, recovered from yesterday's extreme agitation, had no questions on Cross-Examination but asked that Arnfin remain.

•   •   •

Dr. Stolman was back today at the request of both sides. Mr. Shew's purpose was to clear up the still-muddled question of the hairs, especially the one found on the jamb of the sliding door—which, Dr. Stolman had testified last week, was similar to the victim's. Now the doctor consulted his report again and said, "The color characteristics were similar to the hair samples taken from Mrs. Agnes Thompsen."

Mr. Shew: "And if the record shows that you said it was Dorothy Thompsen's—or the deceased's—hair, that is incorrect?"

"That is incorrect because my report stands at the time I made the examination that it corresponded to the sample from Mrs. Agnes Thompsen."

(Later an examination of this report showed how this mistake could have been made. Among nine items listed were this hair and also a hair found on the two-pronged fork. At the end of the report Dr. Stolman had listed the characteristics of both hairs and had written that the one on the door was similar to Agnes's sample, the one on the fork similar to Dorothy's. On the stand he had apparently misread the last sentence.)

During the Cross-Examination, Mr. Wall had Dr. Stolman remind us that Dorothy had dark hair and that Agnes Thompsen had light-colored hair. Then he asked, "With two hairs of this type is it possible to draw any very definite conclusion?"

Dr. Stolman: "No, sir. It simply classifies. It has some value differentiating dark-colored hairs from light-colored hairs or Negroid hairs from Caucasian hairs and so on. You can't pinpoint it. Like a blood typing, you simply divide it into groups."

"In other words, all that you can say is that there are similarities . . . and dissimilarities?"

"Yes, sir, that's all you can say." And that was all Dr. Stolman could say about the single hair found on the patio door.

Mr. Wall moved to another subject. Bringing out first that Agnes

Thompsen's blood was type A, Rh positive, he asked, "On any samples of blood . . . in any of these Exhibits . . . was there ever any blood found of the type, group A-Rh positive?"

"No . . . I found type O on all items I typed—with one exception . . . the shoelace found in the driveway. It was type B."

Mr. Wall had no further questions.

Mr. Shew had no more questions and no more witnesses. The Defense rested at 10:38.

The End

16

Without delay, Mr. Wall began the rebuttal. His first witness, Karen Thompsen, Ted Thompsen's wife—a small woman, carefully set hair, green dress, small dangling earrings, spike-heeled sandals, who spoke with a slight Norwegian accent and seemed nervous on the stand. Karen is a hairdresser; here was the daughter-in-law who had given Agnes Thompsen the permanent. And it was on Monday—the day before the murder—not on Tuesday, as Policewoman Butler had testified. Karen painted a picture of an amicable family relationship. "My mother-in-law used to take care of my daughter every Wednesday." Her daughter, Sonya, was two years older than Christa, and during these visits the two children would play together. On that Monday morning, Karen said, she cut Agnes's hair first and then gave the permanent.

Mr. Wall: "When you cut her hair . . . what happened to the cuttings?"

"Well, I just threw it on the floor. . . . I think my mother-in-law cleaned it up afterwards."

"And do you recall what your daughter and Christa were doing?"

"Well, they were running back and forth between apartments and especially my daughter—she came up and then she went down again and she kept on going like this."

(Press row: "There goes the hair." If the hair was lying on the floor and the children were racing about between the two apartments, the significance of Agnes's hair found anywhere in Dorothy's apartment is considerably watered down. Or is it? The hair on the sliding door was four feet off the ground.)

Mr. Wall: "And when you completed the permanent, will you describe the appearance of your mother-in-law's hair?"

"I put her hair up in . . . real tight round curls . . . and I put two bobby pins in each curl . . . and then I put a hairnet on her and she put a scarf over that." After that, Karen said, she went downstairs and visited Dorothy.

Mr. Wall: "Did Dorothy ever say anything to you concerning her relations with her mother-in-law?"

"Not till that Monday. We were talking about it and realized she was getting a little worse. [Fading voice] We were talking about maybe that next Saturday we bring her to the doctor and see what could be done for her."

"Did Dorothy ever express to you any fear of her mother-in-law?"

"No, sir," Karen said.

Mr. Shew [already speaking as he came forward] "But *you* had expressed fear, hadn't you, of your mother-in-law?"

"No, sir."

Obviously Mr. Shew had heard something. He suggested that there had been an episode involving some soup that her mother-in-law had given Karen. "I wasn't scared of that," Karen said.

"What remark did you make about the soup?"

Karen offered an explanation. "My mother-in-law was a very good cook. And it wasn't usual—[voice fading again] that she served me anything that was heated over and she did this day. It just wasn't like her." The answer had to be read back.

"Did you make a remark to anyone in town that you were afraid to eat the soup because you were afraid something was in it?"

[Rather lamely] "Not that anything was in it. But heated-over pea soup can be hard on your stomach." Again the answer had to be read.

Mr. Shew [coming out with it] "Did you ever use the word 'poison' in connection with that soup?" No, sir. "To anyone?" No, sir.

[Very sharp] "Mrs. Thompsen, do you realize you are under oath?"

"Yes, sir."

A moment of strained silence while Mr. Shew looked hard at Karen Thompsen. Then, "Did you talk this matter over with your husband?" Yes, I believe I did. "Did he ask you to make any statements that you made here?" No, sir. "He didn't?" No reply. Karen simply shook her head to indicate no. (Ted Thompsen, a stocky, angry-looking man, had been a regular attendant and was here today, watching his wife closely.)

"And you want this Jury . . . to understand that you and Dottie never mentioned the fact that you were afraid of your mother-in-law?"

[Stubbornly] "I wasn't afraid of her, no."

"Did you ever hear Dottie say she was afraid of her?" No. "Well, you were discussing taking Mrs. Thompsen to a doctor. Didn't Dottie tell you she was afraid of her at that time?" She said she made her nervous—not that she was afraid. "Did she make *you* nervous, Mrs. Thompsen?" At times, yes. "And what do you mean when you say 'nervous'?" I got nervous looking at her because she was so nervous. "As a matter of fact you were both frightened to death of her, were you not?" Karen denied it. Mr. Shew asked again what she meant when she said it made her "nervous" to be with Agnes.

"Well, it made me upset to look at her, to see how sick she was. . . . She was close family—she was my daughter's grandmother. I felt sorry for her." Pressed for still further explanation, Karen's voice became almost inaudible. "Well, she was a mentally ill person and I was afraid she might hurt herself or do something to herself."

"And were you afraid she might hurt somebody else?"

"No, I never was, sir."

One last effort with the soup, and Karen admitted that she had said at one time that the soup was not fresh but steadfastly denied saying anything else about it. Mr. Shew gave it up and Karen Thompsen was excused.

(The testimony does not dovetail with other testimony. According to Dr. Miller, the outpatient clinic had already advised the family to return Agnes to the hospital. Arnfin said she was losing her jobs. Carole Stadler testified that two weeks earlier Dorothy had told her that Agnes was getting worse. And from Karen this casual comment: "We . . . realized she was getting a little worse . . . maybe next Saturday we bring her to the doctor and see what could be done for her." And Carole Stadler testified that Dorothy had said she was petrified of her mother-in-law; and today Karen has testified that Dorothy never once said she was afraid of her. And one remembers that Agnes was not allowed to take care of Christa—and thinks of her remark that now she could stay home and take care of the child. Now Karen has told us that Agnes took care of *her* child every Wednesday.)

• • •

This late in the game there is little continuity—it is just a matter of tying the loose ends. The next witness was Mr. Raymond J. Fitzpatrick, a heavy red-faced man, a Hartford policeman and a part-time employee of the Hartford Plumbing Supply Company. In the latter capacity he made deliveries to the home of Tobey Solberg, including the one on June 15.

Mr. Wall: "On these occasions did you bring along assistants or did you come in a truck by yourself?"

"I come by myself."

Mr. Wall: "And at the Solberg residence, did you ever have any assistance from *anyone* other than Tobey Solberg?"

Mr. Fitzpatrick: "Not to my recollection. [Flatly] He's the only one that ever helped me unload at the house."

"He is the *only one* who ever helped you unload these articles?" Yes, sir. [Quick follow-up] "Do you know Harry Solberg?" I have met him, yes, sir.

"Did he ever assist, at any time that you were there, in removing the articles that you were delivering?"

[Stolid] "No, sir."

How many times have we heard that Harry helped unload the plumbing supply truck? We heard it in the "confession." We heard it from his mother. And, most important, we heard that he told it to Dr. Von Salzen and that Dr. Von Salzen believed him, along with his first story that he had walked in and followed the trail of blood and remembered nothing after that.

Mr. Shew [fighting back] "Mr. Fitzpatrick, do you remember talking with me over the phone? . . . Didn't you tell me that you weren't sure you had even delivered that day?"

Mr. Fitzpatrick: "No, sir, I said that when State Trooper Pennington came over to the house I checked if I was working on my full-time job, and I checked the invoice over at Hartford Plumbing Supply and I come to the conclusion that I had made the delivery."

"Didn't you tell me that you couldn't remember when I asked you on the telephone last summer?" At that time I wasn't positive. "What refreshed your recollection?"

Mr. Fitzpatrick replied that after he saw the invoice he remembered the delivery because there were three bathtubs to be exchanged—he had to drop three off and pick three up. "And when was the last time you talked to Trooper Pennington?" He spoke to him only once—before he spoke to Mr. Shew. "But at the time you talked with me, Mr. Fitzpatrick, you didn't know—isn't that a fair statement?" Yes, sir. "And that was sometime last summer?" Yes, sir.

(Again the feeling that this does not quite jell. After Pennington came to the house, Mr. Fitzpatrick checked the invoice and decided that he made the delivery. After that, when Mr. Shew telephoned him, he was not positive. Now he is positive, he says, because he checked the invoice. Nevertheless, his statement that Harry never helped him at any time is most damaging to the Defense.)

On Redirect, Mr. Wall produced the invoice. "Does it refresh your recollection as to what actually occurred on that day between you and Tobey Solberg?"

"Well, I don't think I seen Tobey that day."

"And did you make the delivery all by yourself on that day?" Yes, sir. "And with no assistance whatsoever?" Yes, sir.

On Recross, Mr. Shew [still fighting back] "Mr. Fitzpatrick, you are not sure whether you saw Tobey that day, so why are you so sure that you didn't see his son?"

"Because Tobey is the only one that ever helped me unload."

(In his notebook that morning Harry wrote: "I didn't have much chance to help unload after June 15 because I got a job.")

•   •   •

Mr. William Zimmer, the contractor on whose job Tobey was working that day, to which Harry has said consistently that he went to help his father. Mr. Zimmer, a rather short compact man, turned out to be a meticulous businessman, who kept a diary of the details of his business. Mr. Wall asked, "Does your diary also record whether other people are working with you in connection with your work?"

"It does, but not in all instances."

"On June 15, 1965, was Mr. Solberg, Senior, working on that job with you?" He was. "And what was he doing in connection with his work there?"

Mr. Zimmer [earnestly] "I have been trying and trying and I cannot recall what he was working on. It could have been the finish plumbing or it could have been the finish heating. I have been trying to figure out what I was doing myself. I cannot remember. That would be a big help, I know."

"And on that day did he have any one helping him at all?"

[Cautious; a conscientious witness] "I am not certain. I have put his name down as working that day. I checked last night through the first few months of the year, and I discovered that quite a few names of people who had worked there were not in the book." Mr. Wall asked whether Harry had ever worked on this job, and Mr. Zimmer replied that he had, although he had not entered that in his book.

Now the question: "Was Harry Solberg working there on that day—June 15, 1965?"

[A pause] "As far as I know he wasn't. He was not there *all* day—" (meaning the whole day). "However, *I* was not present all of the day."

"For what part of the day were you present, Mr. Zimmer?"

Again Mr. Zimmer said he had searched for this information— found that he had worked on the job for eleven hours, including traveling time. "I have a notation that I made a purchase at Beeman Hardware in Granby Center that day. How long I was there I have no idea. I do not even know what the article was. . . . It was a very small purchase—thirty-one cents." Nor did he know what time he was at the store, which is about four miles from the job.

"And except for the time that you made this purchase, you were working there all that day?"

"Yes, I would say so. I might have made other stops when I made that purchase—I don't know."

"Did Mr. Solberg have helpers on other occasions?" He did. "And on June 15, did he have any helpers?"

But once again Mr. Zimmer was not certain. "If I knew what he was working on that day it would help me. There was one job that would have been difficult to do alone."

"Did you know who the other helpers were that did come at various times to help Mr. Solberg?"

"One was Harry Solberg, and the other, I don't know."

Mr. Wall asked if there was anything significant in the diary entry about Mr. Solberg that day.

Mr. Zimmer: " 'Solberg, all day.' That is all it says."

• • •

Recess

"The pendulum has swung back again. Yesterday it looked like Harry was home free. Today there are new holes."

"Naturally the family hopes it wasn't Agnes. Karen said, 'She's my child's grandmother.' "

"Harry said he unloaded that truck. He said he was at Zimmer's job."

"Zimmer admitted he was gone part of the time. Zimmer was really trying. He admitted he couldn't remember and didn't know."

"The psychiatrist said Harry would make things up if he couldn't remember."

"The psychiatrist believed all that, though."

"That's where it's going to hurt. The psychiatrist believed that—and the rest of the first story."

• • •

After recess Mr. Wall put Dr. Von Salzen's written report in evidence—a masterfully timed stroke. As he read it aloud to the Jury certain familiar phrases stood out with a new irony. "The examination took two and a half hours . . . should not be considered exhaustive. . . . Solberg told me . . . he had lunch and helped unload a plumbing truck. . . . He went to Simsbury to see about a lawn mower. On his way home he stopped at the Thompsens' house. Solberg had to submit a report at school in an economics course and Mr. Thompsen had agreed to help him." Then the first story: into the house, the trail of blood—and nothing more. "He went home and asked his mother where his father was working because he wanted to tell his father. . . . However, he did not tell his father. . . . He said that his girl friend, now his wife, said that he visited her about 3:30 P.M. or 4:00 P.M. that afternoon. . . ."

And other phrases leap out: "Rigidity of thinking and guilt . . . in the area of sex. . . . A marked absence of strong feelings such as violence, aggression or sex. . . . Typical of this rigidity was his statement that he had never experienced nocturnal emissions or wet dreams, that he never experienced sexual feelings about girls before his marriage and that he had never had any problem with masturbation. He did not attend dances or parties, never had a fight, did not play contact sports, never demonstrated any evidence of adolescent rebelliousness. . . . The scene was one of violence, blood, assault and possibly rape. . . . Complete rejection of the scene—or repression with consequent amnesia. . . . At the time Solberg saw the body he was incapable of thinking or acting rationally. . . . Victim of panic, of irrational guilt . . ." And, at the end, that he might tell the second story.

•   •   •

Then Mr. Hamilton Pitt, the economics teacher—a thin, towering, grim man wearing a gray suit and sweater, a teacher for thirty-one years, now in the real estate business.

The question came quickly. "On June 15, 1965, did Harry Solberg have *any assignment* to submit a report in the economics course?"

Mr. Pitt's reply was short and curt. "No!"

(The single most damaging word, so far, in this rebuttal.)

"And was there any assignment . . . pending in your class . . . expected from him on June 15 or thereafter?"

[Again short, curt] *"No."*

"As of June 15, Mr. Pitt, had Solberg completed the course?"

"The examination was on the fifteenth."

"And was there anything else expected in connection with this course from Solberg?"

[The same] *"No."*

Mr. Shew: "Now, Mr. Pitt, do you remember a discussion with Harry either that day, the fifteenth, or maybe the day before?"

"No."

"Would you remember all discussions . . . with all your pupils at that particular time?"

"I don't believe I could remember all of them. . . . There would be no discussion on the fifteenth. I merely passed out exams, and he wrote the exam and left the room." Could there have been a discussion on the fourteenth? "It could be. That was our review day." And Harry hadn't done too well in economics? "Well, he had done pretty well in midyears. He had fallen off a bit in the second half." And to get a grade he had to write a theme?

Mr. Pitt explained that there was a reference paper for which the students did library research on a specific topic and then gave a classroom talk. He drew up a list of topics and they drew by chance the one they would work on. Those papers were due on the eleventh.

"And did any of the pupils have a chance to write on a second topic other than the one they selected by chance?"

[Curt, tart] "*Definitely no.*"

Do you remember talking to Harry Solberg in front of your desk on—possibly—the fourteenth of June? "I don't remember any such discussion." But it is possible that there was such a discussion? "I granted that earlier."

Mr. Shew reminded Mr. Pitt that they had talked over the telephone last summer. "And there *could* have been a discussion . . . before the fourteenth . . . about the paper he was going to write?"

"His written work was done by Friday, the eleventh, or it would not be accepted." And did he know that? "All five of my classes knew that. . . . There is a standing rule in all of them—all written work to be handed in the Friday before exams."

"Didn't you, Mr. Pitt, tell some of the pupils in your class that, if they wished, they could take subjects other than the one they drew by chance and that you would take the best work and mark them accordingly?"

"No, they could swap. A couple of them could swap if they wanted. That is all I did say. There is no second topic."

"But it is possible that you talked with Harry Solberg on the fourteenth, or a day or two before?"

"It is possible."

Mr. Wall: "What date was the assignment due on?"

Mr. Pitt: "About the eleventh was the last day anything could be handed in."

"Had Harry Solberg given his oral talk in class at that time?"

An explanation: "That particular class was hit quite a bit by senior singing rehearsals so I could not keep my exact schedule. In fact, two or three did not talk. I had to take their papers. We did not have time. We started out with five-minute talks, and then three, and then one, and finally two or three did not have a chance to talk because of other schedules." (Mr. Pitt's longest speech—none of it pertinent—about the intrusions of the senior singing rehearsals!)

Do you recall what Harry Solberg's topic was? [Consulting a list] "American Labor Leaders." Had he completed his assignment? "He had. He got an A."

"When had he completed it?"

"By the eleventh."

Mr. Shew: "What other papers did Harry Solberg write?"

Mr. Pitt said he would have to consult his book. "When you have two hundred students you don't memorize all the notes." Mr. Shew suggested that he wouldn't remember all conversations, either. Mr. Pitt agreed. In that case, Mr. Shew persisted, it was possible that he did talk with Harry on a date immediately preceding the fifteenth. Again, curtly, Mr. Pitt agreed. And it was possible that Harry understood that he could write another theme, was it not?

[Acid] "No. His written work was in by the eleventh or it would not be accepted."

"He would not necessarily know that, would he?"

[Very sour] "He had been with me two years. He should have."

Mr. Shew [pricked once too often by Mr. Pitt's needles] "Do you act that way in class?"

[Pure vinegar] "Yes, if I have to repeat something three times to an intelligent person."

[Right back] "And who do you have reference to?"

The Judge interrupted to suggest that this not be pursued. Mr. Shew regarded Mr. Pitt narrowly and said, with heavy innuendo, "Why did you stop teaching school, Mr. Pitt?"

"Personal reasons."

"What were the personal reasons?"

An objection nipped off this sudden clash and Mr. Pitt was excused.

•   •   •

Arnfin again, recalled by Mr. Wall as a rebuttal witness.

"Mr. Thompsen, in June, 1965, or at any time within a few weeks prior to June 15, 1965, did you have any conversation with Harry

Solberg relating to any assistance you might give him in an economics course?"

Arnfin: "No."

"Was there any reason that you would know for Harry Solberg to come to your home on June 15, 1965?"

"No."

Mr. Shew: "At various times had you helped Harry with his schoolwork?" Arnfin had. "And whenever he needed help, he couldn't get it from his parents, could he? You are aware of that fact?" Arnfin shrugged and murmured that he supposed they helped him some. "You know they wouldn't be able to help him, don't you, Arnfin?" No.

Mr. Shew, persisting, asked whether Arnfin had not, in fact, helped Harry with school problems over the past four or five years, and Arnfin acknowledged that he had—possibly three or four times.

Mr. Shew: "And you wouldn't know whether he asked your deceased wife, at any time, to get some help from you, would you? He might have asked her, and you wouldn't know?"

"Well—unless she told me."

"That's right. But she might not tell you. You didn't speak very much with her just before June 15, did you?"

"Sure I did."

"Well, you were only home a couple nights a week, right?"

"Weekends," Arnfin murmured. He was home weekends.

·　　·　　·

And now a small forlorn-looking old man who had been in Court every day—Mr. Asa Burdick, Dorothy's father. Baggy green trousers, dark-blue buttoned sweater, watery bewildered eyes—formerly a farmer, now a watchman. Mr. Burdick shuffled up to the stand.

Mr. Wall: "At any time . . . prior to her death, did your daughter ever say anything to you about any fear of her mother-in-law, Agnes Thompsen?"

[On the edge of the chair, hands fidgeting] "She did not."

Mr. Wall turned away, satisfied. "You may inquire."

Mr. Shew: "Do you recall talking with Major Rome—you and your wife—in connection with this?" Yes. "And did either of you tell him that Dorothy wasn't getting along with her mother-in-law?" No, sir. "Did you ever hear your wife say that?" No. "Did you know whether or not she was getting along with Arnfin?"

Mr. Burdick: "Not to my knowledge."

(The phrase does not answer the question, is out of character coming from Mr. Burdick. Has he picked it up during three weeks in Court, liking the professional sound of it? Or has someone advised him that it is a proper answer in certain situations?)

Mr. Shew: "You don't—to your knowledge—what?"

"Well, what did you ask me?"

"Do you know whether she was getting along with her husband? Was your daughter getting along with her husband?" They were getting along. "They *were* getting along?" No answer. Mr. Burdick nodded his head up and down.

Mr. Shew: "She never discussed the fact with you that Arnfin stayed out most of the night, maybe came home only two nights a week?"

"She did not."

"So that, as far as you knew, Mr. Burdick, your daughter was happily married, is that correct?"

"Yes, that's right."

"And she was happy in the house she was in?"

"That's right."

Suddenly it was over. It had ended with a whimper. The State rested at 12:32. The final arguments would start after lunch.

◆

"I am not going to try to persuade you to convict. I am only going to sum up the evidence for you."

Mr. Wall addressed the Jury first. Mr. Shew's argument would follow, then Mr. Wall's rebuttal, and finally the Judge's charge. Then everything would have been said, and the twelve men and women would retire to decide the fate of Harry Solberg.

Slowly, deliberately, Mr. Wall read the indictment. When he finished, he reminded the Jury that they would first decide whether the Defendant was guilty—and then, if that was their decision, the degree of his guilt—murder in the first degree, murder in the second degree, or manslaughter. "I am not mentioning this," he said, "because I believe it was other than first degree." He turned to the evidence.

First there was the anonymous Letter, mailed two days after this vicious crime. "I'm not going to tell you *how* vicious. You've seen the photographs . . . of this very vicious crime." He moved to the table, where all the Exhibits were collected now, and picked up the Letter. Once again he read it to the Jury. "I killed your wife . . . I stabed her with a meat fork. I stamped on her face. . . . I draged her . . . with an electric cord . . . I used a hammer to pound in the skike to hang her. She fell to the ground. I bashed her head in several times with a large rock . . ." (The items are all there on the table. Images come to mind of each one introduced, of witnesses testifying concerning them, of heated arguments.) ". . . I used a nabors car . . . a '58 Ford . . . I'll kill the baby someday soon. I'll kill the baby, too, and my wife."

(How does the Letter sound to the Jury today? Is its impact different after three weeks of testimony?)

[Looking at them] "This was a *horrible, horrible* crime. . . . The type of person who could write *this kind of letter* to a family under these circumstances [weight on every word] is a person who could commit this vicious crime."

Turning to the sensitive subject of Agnes Thompsen, Mr. Wall acknowledged that she was an early suspect. [Rational tone] "But when the piggy bank was found far from the house where she couldn't have gone—she didn't drive—then it became obvious that *she* could not have brought the bank to that spot. . . . [Ringing] I am *proud* of the Canaan Barracks that reopened this investigation and found Harry Solberg."

(Lieutenant Fuessenich and Detective Rebillard, their wives with them today, wearing discreet looks of pride.)

[Logical; ingratiating] " . . . You heard the voluntary statement of Harry Solberg, made on March 14, 1966, at 8:27 P.M. In it he said . . . she was 'too full of fight.' *You* know and *I* know that there was never any question that the victim was dead by the time she landed on the ground. It was a complete lie. She couldn't have been alive at the time.

"Further investigation was necessary. . . . Then came the interrogation of March 15, 1966—and Harry Solberg *admitted that he
was the murderer.*"

(A pause, as there must be. Absolute silence.)

[More moderate tone] ". . . He told a lie to Dr. Von Salzen in
regard to the economics paper. I asked Dr. Von Salzen whether a lie
would knock out the props of his statement. . . . The statement of
the basis for his going to the house was absolutely false. [Including
the Jury with himself] *We* who know the facts, know they were
erroneous. [Tolerant] The psychiatrist attached importance to the
fact that his mind became blank. . . . His mind became blank in
each of three versions. The psychiatrist believed him. [Proprietary
pride] *Lieutenant Fuessenich* said he did *not* believe everything.
He said, 'I don't believe the part where he said: I don't remember.'
Lieutenant Fuessenich had more horse sense, more common sense.
. . . The psychiatrist didn't have the *facts*. Lieutenant Fuessenich did. . . . Lieutenant Fuessenich had the letter, the voluntary
statement, and the testimony of the confession.

[Confident] ". . . Except where the accused in a clumsy way
was trying to throw a curve, he *remembered*. He *did* do it. He
committed this crime. . . . He didn't say he *didn't* do it in any of
his statements to the doctor. And he gave the *motive* in his second
story—the one in which he said it would be hard to convince the
Jury of the first story and he might get twenty years. . . . If he told
the second story he might get manslaughter and get only six
years. . . .

"There was one very pertinent observation by Dr. Von Salzen, I
think, that impressed all of you as it did me—that memory gaps
could be caused just as easily if he had actually committed the
crime.

". . . *He didn't deny it in any of the statements.*"

A return to a quiet, logical tone. As to the degree of the crime, the
Jury must believe there was premeditation to find him guilty of
murder in the first degree. "The only evidence of premeditation is in
the letter. The case is very weak on premeditation." (A concession
that he is not asking for first degree—that he is eliminating the
possibility of the electric chair?) Acknowledging that the Jury's
duty was an unpleasant one and that "you don't convict anyone if

you don't feel proof was there," Mr. Wall yielded to Mr. Shew. He had not fired all his guns. He would be back for rebuttal.

At once Mr. Shew said, "If Dr. Von Salzen had heard Mr. Wall's statement, he would be more shocked than I am . . . [Defending the doctor's opinion] *The boy doesn't know what happened.* He has *tried* and he *can't* remember. . . . Here is this boy, not twenty-one years old, from the smallest town in the state. He went to church three or four times a week. He was out of the state only once in his life. He walked in on this scene and from that point on, he *doesn't remember.* He *doesn't know what happened.*

". . . There is tragedy here—certainly . . . that Dorothy Thompsen was murdered . . . that Christa will be brought up by the woman her father was with the night before . . .

"But it is a tragedy, too, that this boy happened to walk in. . . . This could happen to anyone! If he had had any worldly experience at all he would have reacted differently. But he didn't. He went to church three times a week. He thought sex was bad. He sublimates his energies and he goes to church.

". . . *I have spent all this time trying to get the truth.* [Compassionate] I don't want to blame poor old Agnes Thompsen. . . . Her other daughter-in-law said they were going to take her back to the hospital. Dr. Miller said they were going to bring her back. A few years ago Dr. Murphy was called to calm her down and found her with a carving knife that she was going to use on the devil. . . . The victim was stabbed with a fork. Now we have all seen pictures of the devil with a fork in his hand! This woman was obsessed by the devil! She was waging a running battle with the devil!

"I had to spend all this time dragging information out of the Canaan police. . . . Mr. Wall has the whole State Police force at his disposal. I had a home who-done-it kit! . . . This young boy was married and allowed to live with his wife only two months. He saw his baby for the first time in jail—two days ago.

"I have thirty reasons here [waving a sheaf of papers] why Mrs. Agnes Thompsen is guilty. . . . Dr. Stolman said there was blood in the sink, blood in the other sink, blood on Agnes Thompsen's hand, which they said was from a crochet needle. *I* had to bring you proof that she didn't do it with a crochet needle. [Rising indignation] Mr. Wall should bring the truth before you. He shouldn't conceal anything. . . . The State has *not* brought everything before this Jury. And it is his job to do so. . . . A yellow cloth with blood spots was found in Agnes Thompsen's apartment. . . . She sanded the stairs that afternoon. Why would she do it? . . . Her hair was on the sliding door of the patio. . . . A bloodstained dress was found in the clothes dryer. Would Harry Solberg put a dress in the dryer? That is not a man's work! . . . Mrs. Butler, the police-woman, said something Agnes didn't like and she became ag-gressive.

[With respect] " . . . Major Rome—the greatest investigator the State Police Department *has ever had*—investigated this case. The Jury knows what his convictions are. At great cost to himself he has come forward. . . . Even though I have been stopped from bring-ing his evidence before you, you *know what his convictions are.*

". . . Mr. Wall tried to say there was no animosity between Agnes and Dorothy. Dottie told Carole Stadler that she was deathly afraid of her mother-in-law. Mr. Wall's own witness! . . . And Karen Thompsen said, 'We decided we had to take her to the doctor.' She said that her mother-in-law made her nervous. . . . And Mrs. Solberg said that Dottie was crying, she was so afraid of her mother-in-law. . . . And Bob Stadler heard the mother-in-law say, 'Is she dead yet?' The mother-in-law said that. 'Is she dead yet?'

[Reasonable] ". . . You heard Dr. Opper say that this killing took at least ten minutes. Is it conceivable that this boy was hanging around? He knew Agnes Thompsen was upstairs. She knew who he was—she could call anyone and tell them. Anyone with sense would do the job and get out. Whoever did this was messing around *a long time!* . . . Would this boy use a fork? This strong boy? This was a woman's utensil. . . . Agnes Thompsen had to drag the body. This boy could have picked it up and carried it. This was a woman's work. . . .

"Dr. Murphy said she was animated—in high spirits. He was the first one there. . . . [Again compassionate] I don't blame Agnes Thompsen . . . [then accusing] I blame the people who had con-trol of her. Dottie Thompsen did *not* have control.

". . . Arnfin said he knew the piggy bank was there that morning. You know that after being out the night before, he didn't look at it!

". . . At no time has anyone given *any reason* why this boy would kill her. Not a single motive has been suggested by the police, by Mr. Wall, by anyone. This boy had no motive. But who did? Poor old Agnes Thompsen wanted Christa and she wasn't allowed to have her very much. . . . Agnes Thompsen hated her daughter-in-law. She was jealous of her. And only she could have done it *in the way in which it was done.*"

(For a moment, Harry, quite pale, put his face in his hands.)

Mr. Shew turned to the matter of the various statements that Harry had given. "If Dr. Von Salzen heard Mr. Wall tell of his confusion he would be shocked. . . . As to the 'voluntary statement' given Monday night at 8:27, that is a term put on by the police." Then to the confession. "A boy like this has a low breaking point. There was thirty hours of police pressure on a boy with a low IQ, who took six years to get through four years of high school. . . . Sure they gave him a sandwich and a drink. He was still under pressure. He was even allowed to go to work—and he came back voluntarily—but he knew he was going to be questioned by the police, and over that whole time there was pressure.

". . . In good police reports they try to get corroboration—there are lots of false confessions. . . . In this so-called confession there is *not one single word of corroboration.* In fact it's a disorganized mess because that's the way his mind was."

And finally to the facts about Christa. "She came downstairs with her grandmother and said, 'She killed, she killed.' She wouldn't know that unless someone told her. Arnfin wouldn't run up and tell her. She got it from Agnes. . . . And she was *dry.* Since noon? Until seven o'clock! Someone had to change her. Only Agnes could have done it. Agnes was in the picture. Christa's pants had been changed. She wasn't hungry. She'd been taken care of all afternoon. This boy didn't hang around to change her."

Appealing to the Jury to use common sense in reaching a verdict. "How can you find this youngster guilty? You can't *think*—you have to *know*—if you say he is guilty. He has already been deprived of seven months of freedom because a mistake has been made. . . . Truth is stranger than fiction. . . . These were not lies that he told. *He doesn't know.* If you check that letter with the facts you will see that everything is confused. He is absolutely unbelievably naive."

Imploring them to bring in a verdict of acquittal, he said, "You can't buy back this boy's lost freedom. Let him go back now to his wife and to his baby."

Mr. Shew had touched the area about which Mr. Wall was most sensitive, and he began his rebuttal with an indignant statement in his own defense. "I have never—in this case or any other case— tried to conceal anything from the jury. . . . The fact that I didn't produce these things doesn't mean I concealed them. . . . Counsel brands me as unprofessional for not giving you evidence that Dr. Stolman said was unimportant . . ."

Turning to the accusations against Agnes Thompsen—"a poor, unfortunate woman"—he urged the jurors not to be misled. There were no marks on her body to show she had been in any kind of combat. The amount of blood in her home was what might be found in any normal home. Pin curls in her hair were undisturbed. "If *anything* has been established in this case, it has been to *eliminate* Agnes Thompsen as a suspect in any way."

Then on to attack other points that Mr. Shew had made. ". . . The story about the economics paper was a complete fabrication. . . . Counsel says that Harry Solberg knew Agnes Thompsen was upstairs—but it was only during the previous week that she had lost her Tuesday job. . . . He expected that she was out doing housework. . . . He didn't know she was there."

". . . You heard the statement of the water board man who saw the car and saw a man getting out of the car. . . . Dottie kept the door locked. She knew Harry Solberg. She would open the door to admit a friend—not realizing that she was admitting a fiend! . . . *Harry Solberg was there.* He was on the scene. There is corroborated evidence of that."

(Tobey Solberg staring at the floor; Solveig staring hard at Mr. Wall; Sharon, anxious, licking her lips, twisting her fingers.)

As to Christa, "She said, 'She killed, she killed.' But . . . she did not want to leave her grandmother. If her grandmother had hurt her mother, she wouldn't want to be with her grandmother."

Again Mr. Wall claimed that in none of the statements did Harry deny the killing, but that there were other inconsistencies. "Dr. Von Salzen is a bright man, he expounded a good theory. He just didn't have the facts. He talked to this man for an hour or so. *You* have the facts. *All* the facts. . . . The doctor had just a few facts, and with the few he had, he himself was beginning to have some trouble."

Concerning the motive, there was the piggy bank—someone ran off with the piggy bank. "But the original motive was not to take the bank. . . . He wanted her and no one else was going to have her. The motive was sexual. His effort to twist this to defending his chastity from the wiles of this woman is further indication that the motive was sexual. . . . But His Honor will charge you and will tell you that no motive is necessary.

". . . The matter of corroboration is one that neither Counsel has touched on. . . ." There is the piggy bank (lifted up from the Exhibits—pink pig, red ears and snout—displayed once again for all to see). "Harry Solberg stated in the confession that he opened the bank with a knife or a scissors and took about sixteen dollars in change. . . . The crudely cut hole on top is just where he said he made it."

There is the anonymous letter. "In it mention is made of the use of a large rock. There was no indication by police that a rock had been used. No papers carried anything about a large rock. The only one who knew about the rock was the one who committed the crime. The only mention of it was by the accused in the letter. That rock was known only to the murderer himself. *He* had to know. Having known—he *told*.

"Harry Solberg is the responsible party here—and he, and he alone, committed this horrible, horrible crime."

And now everything had been said that could be said for and against Harry Solberg. His fate was out of the hands of lawyers. The Judge would charge the Jury after recess.

•   •   •

Recess

The predictions have started.

A deputy sheriff: "What do you think?" What do *you* think? "Murder two."

Another deputy: "How are you voting?" How are *you* voting? "Wait until I hear the charge."

All this while Harry is standing less than three feet away, talking to the sheriff, who accompanies him back and forth from the jail.

◆

At ten minutes to four Judge MacDonald began his charge to the Jury—repeating, of necessity, those familiar courtroom phrases: The burden is on the State to *prove* the guilt and prove it beyond a reasonable doubt. The law presumes an accused person innocent unless and until his guilt is established by the evidence, beyond all reasonable doubt.

"This means that, at the moment when this accused was presented for trial . . . so far as you were concerned, he was then innocent; and he continues to be innocent unless and until such time as the evidence . . . produced here in this courtroom . . . satisfies you beyond a reasonable doubt that he is guilty. . . .

"This presumption requires that if a piece of evidence . . . is capable of two reasonable constructions, one of which is consistent with innocence, it *must be given that construction.* If you entertain a reasonable doubt between a lesser and a greater crime . . . *your verdict should be for the lesser crime. . . ."*

Sober, detached, judicious, the Judge continued to explain and to illustrate his instructions in layman's terms to be certain that everything was understood.

Concerning the credibility of witnesses the jurors should use careful judgment. "You should have in mind all those little circumstances which point to his or her truthfulness or untruthfulness. You should consider any possible bias or prejudice for or against the State . . . or for or against the accused . . . any interest or lack of interest in the outcome of the trial. . . . The testimony of a police officer is entitled to no special sanctity. . . . You should weigh it as carefully as the testimony of any other witness."

Concerning proof, ". . . You will take only the evidence admitted by the Court. . . . Excluded evidence must not be considered."

Concerning certain statements made out of court by the accused, ". . . My ruling admitting them is not to be taken by you as giving to those statements any more weight . . . than you conclude they should have. I should also say this to you: Such statements by an accused person are not, in themselves, sufficient to prove the fact that the crime was committed by someone, the accused or another."

After another few minutes the Judge turned to the matter of the verdict: The charge is of murder in the first degree. However, the Jury may find the indicted person guilty of homicide in a lesser degree than that charged. ". . . The Jury in this case may bring in a verdict of guilty of murder in the first degree, guilty of murder in the second degree, or guilty of manslaughter. Or, of course, simply: Not Guilty."

The Judge had been speaking for half an hour. Now he devoted nearly another half an hour to meticulous definitions of each of the possible verdicts:

". . . Murder is the unlawful killing of a human being with malice aforethought. Manslaughter is the unlawful killing of a human being *without* malice aforethought.

The distinction between murder in the first degree and murder in the second degree: . . . "If the State proves . . . that the killing was *willful, deliberate, and premeditated,* it then becomes murder in the first degree. . . . The deliberation need not be for any great length of time. Nor need the intent to kill be formed a considerable time before its execution. . . . There must only be time enough for the accused to form a willful, deliberate, premeditated and specific intent to kill the deceased . . . before the execution of such intent . . . time to permit the making of a choice—to kill or not to kill. [Summarizing] If you find that the State has proved to your satisfaction, beyond a reasonable doubt, that Harry Solberg while of sound mind killed Dorothy Thompsen unlawfully—*with malice afore-thought* . . . and that the killing was *willful, deliberate, and pre-meditated,* then your verdict will be guilty of murder in the first degree."

Remove the last element, "*willful, deliberate, and premeditated,*" and it is murder in the second degree. Remove from that the next preceding element—"*malice aforethought*" and it is manslaughter. ". . . If you find that the State has failed to prove that Mr. Solberg was the person who killed Dorothy Thompsen, your verdict must be: Not Guilty."

If the Jury finds that the State has *proved* a case of murder in the first degree, it may not render a verdict of a lesser degree of homicide. But, emphasizing again that the Defendant must be given the benefit of all doubts, "If there is a reasonable doubt as between the greater and lesser of the two crimes, the verdict should be for the lesser of the two.

"To support a verdict it must be unanimous.

". . . The State of Connecticut does not desire the conviction of innocent persons or of any person of whose guilt . . . there is a reasonable doubt." (The specific instructions are over; the Judge is reaching the end of his charge.) "The State is as much concerned in having an innocent person acquitted as in having a guilty person punished, but for the safety and well-being of society, the State is concerned in securing the conviction of persons who have been proven by the evidence beyond a reasonable doubt to be guilty."

A change of tone and a sober comment on the gravity of their responsibility. (That the jurors feel this weight is clearly apparent in their faces.) "You are sworn to act fearlessly and faithfully. You will leave sympathy and sentiment, prejudice and bias behind you when you enter the room for your deliberations. . . . You will let your verdict, whatever it may be, reflect your sound, sober, honest judgment, unwarped by any consideration which your oath as jurors will not justify and approve."

A few routine instructions, the alternates dismissed, and it was over. It was five o'clock on Friday afternoon—ordinarily the hour for the end of the day and the end of the week. But we would remain. The Jury would deliberate until six o'clock, adjourn for dinner, then continue until about nine o'clock. If they did not reach a verdict tonight, they would return in the morning.

17

To deliberate "fearlessly and faithfully, with sober and honest judgment," the twelve men and women moved single file to the jury room and the door closed.

"This Jury will be a long time."

"How would you vote?"

"I don't know—I don't know—"

"Then you'd have to vote *Not Guilty*. You have a reasonable doubt."

"I could argue it either way. I'd have argued stronger for acquittal yesterday."

"The one thought that sticks is that I'd like to know more."

"You won't learn more now. It's over."

"That's the trouble, isn't it? They've left as many questions as they've answered."

6:00 P.M. Dinner. The Jury sent to a private dining room. Harry taken back to the jail.

In a local restaurant, at a rear table, Joe Crowley and another reporter stopped to speak to Mr. Wall. "If I am beaten in this case, it will have been the press that beat me—especially the Hartford *Courant*," Mr. Wall said. He added frankly that he thought Crowley's coverage, too, had been biased. "You know I totally defeated Rome on the stand. I beat him on every count. I made him look terrible. But the press didn't report it that way. The *Courant* headline was 'Rome-Wall Pull No Punches'—Rome, first." (Here, in a single speech, was a key to the issues that had emerged in this trial.)

Not everyone would have agreed with Mr. Wall. Many people felt that, even though Rome had not been allowed to testify, and in spite of the abuse hurled at him, his integrity and conviction came through and had a strong impact on the Jury.

"In the end *why* do you have a reasonable doubt? Because of Rome. For a lot of people this morning's rebuttal blew Dr. Von Salzen's theory full of holes. So what have you left on Harry's side? Rome."

"What you have left is Rome's reputation—because nobody knows what he had to say." (Which is really what Mr. Wall was saying, too.)

At Mr. Shew's table the conversation turned to Harry. "Your client doesn't seem worried, Bill."

"He's impressed with this trial. He says when this is over he knows Sam Rome and he's going to ask him for a job."

"He's sure it will end that way?"

"I don't think it's crossed his mind—still—that he could be found guilty. [An exasperated smile] It's been a problem from the start. He's been impressed with the attention. It's the first time he was ever important. At the Coroner's Hearing he was smiling and waving at the crowd. Same thing at the Grand Jury Session. It made a lot of people decide he was guilty. The Burdicks, for instance. After the indictment, old Mr. Burdick said, 'He's not smiling now.'"

"The Burdicks would hope it wasn't Agnes. Christa is still their granddaughter. And Agnes's, too."

"I even think Harry's enjoyed the time in jail. He's a celebrity. A first-degree murder charge gives him status in jail."

"What prompted him to write that letter in the first place, Bill? Did he ever say?"

"He told me his mother was on his back. They were looking for a car like his and she wouldn't leave him alone. She wouldn't let him drive it. So he wrote the letter to throw them off. With his mentality he thought it would work."

The conversation goes to Harry but it never stays there.

"If this kid is found guilty, Sam Rome is finished."

7:00 P.M. The Jury returned to the jury room. The crowd drifted back slowly from dinner. A reporter stopped to talk to a girl who had known Dottie. "Was she afraid of her mother-in-law?"

"Was she! She was scared to death! She talked about it all the time."

"Do you know Harry?"

"I don't—but a friend of mine went to their wedding. She was terribly impressed. At the wedding reception Harry made a speech and included God as a third person in the marriage. He said he knew that he and Sharon and God were going to have a very happy future."

Upstairs people clustered in small groups, talking, waiting. A feeling now that it would be a long wait. "We'll be back tomorrow. They won't decide tonight."

9:00 P.M. The hour at which the Judge said he would dismiss the Jury for the night. No word from the Judge. No sound from the jury room.

"This Jury is deadlocked."

9:15 P.M. Word went out for the lawyers. As the Jury filed in, one studied their faces. How do they look? Grim, determined, tired, patient, impatient, unhappy. Single file—always single file, in and out—they moved to the jury box.

A change! In the jury box they are taking different seats. They have shuffled about their usual seating order. Is this significant? Are those with similar opinions sticking together? All through this trial one has viewed the Jury as a single unit. Now suddenly they have become two sides.

The Judge asked whether they believed they could reach a verdict in another half-hour or whether they preferred to resume in the morning.

Now we learned that the foreman was Mr. Ronald E. Glander, the youngest member. "I think we'd rather come back in the morning," Mr. Glander said.

"Then we will adjourn until tomorrow morning at ten o'clock."

Sharon gasped, closed her eyes, gave a deep despairing sigh.

The press row: "How do you read them?"

"Six to six."

"The six in front for acquittal. The six in back for guilty."

"I think a few in the back are wavering."

•   •   •

On Saturday morning the jurors walked through an almost empty courtroom to begin again. Nobody expected a verdict early this morning.

Idle postmortems. (One must say something.) "The trouble with this trial was that the reporters were trying to be the lawyers," a Litchfield County police officer said.

"The reporters and Sam Rome."

"Old Sam made his big arrests when all this was legal."

"He's an old-timer. He can't change to the new ways," a reporter said. "Ten years ago his methods were acceptable."

The anti-Rome campaign has taken a new twist. They speak of him with condescension—picturing him as a tired old man, a has-been. "Sam's old. He can't operate in the new system."

Nearby another reporter muttered, "Neither can they. They just don't make the arrests."

(Last week at lunch one day someone called out to Rome and said, "Sam, what do you do now that you can't interrogate them any more?" And Rome grinned and said, "They know we're having trouble. They come in with their confessions in their hands.")

"Sam is a great interrogator. People will talk to him who won't talk to anyone else. They *want* to talk to him. Now with *Miranda*, they've taken away the thing that made him."

"This is the beginning of the end for Rome."

During the morning this reporter went into Chambers to speak to Judge MacDonald, who was in the process of cancelling a Saturday afternoon appointment over the telephone. Ultimately, the Judge believed, the Jury would bring in a verdict of manslaughter. "I doubt very much that they will bring in a verdict of murder because they will have some doubts," he said. Then he commented, "That letter is important to me. And he knew about the rock. There was no mention of the rock in the papers." (But, according to Rome, so did Agnes. She knew more. Only we never heard it.)

"I understood the law as you read it," I said, referring to the ruling on Agnes Thompsen's statements. "I understood what you were saying, but I think it's a bad law."

Judge MacDonald smiled.

"Did you understand what Rome was trying to say?" I went on. "Did you understand that he wasn't trying to get in the hysterical confession of an insane woman, crying, 'I did it, I did it!'—that he was trying to report, not a confession, but a *description* that Agnes Thompsen gave him of how the crime was committed? After all, she went to the hospital that night—before any newspaper had been published. There was no way she could have known the facts. Rome wanted to get in that *description*—details she could not have known if she hadn't been there. Sane or insane, sick or well—you can't get out of a mind what is not there. She couldn't say what she didn't know."

Judge MacDonald looked as though he were still as much troubled by this dilemma as on the day it was argued in Court, when he had said quite candidly that legal precedent seemed to indicate one decision and his sense of fair play another.

The trial was over and everyone still had his private area of concern.

12:30 P.M. The Judge summoned the Jury. (Again one studies faces. One end of the press row thinks that now it looks like nine and three.)

"Do you feel you are close enough to reach a verdict in half an hour?"

"No, Your Honor, I don't feel so—speaking for everyone on the Jury," Mr. Glander said.

(They are sitting in the *new* places, the ones taken last night. How did this new arrangement come about? Do those with similar opinions sit together in the jury room—and then walk out in order and so into the jury box? The six in the front row look tired. Three—or two?—in the back look harassed and defiant. They have the bright, wounded eyes, the tight-set mouths of conviction hardening into certainty.)

The Jury had been deliberating for nearly six hours and now the Judge gave additional instructions, asking them to listen with an open mind to the opinions of their fellow jurors. "I am not urging a small minority to give in," he emphasized. "You should stick to your

opinion if you are convinced. I only urge you to consider carefully
the arguments of others."

(The Judge, too, uses the term "small minority." Does he see the
sides as we do—this Judge has looked at hundreds of faces through
dozens of trials—or does he find other clues and see a different
picture?)

"How do you read them now?"
   "Nine to three. Three in the back row are sticking together."
   "Or ten to two. One may be wavering."
   (Are we seeing things that are not there?)

12:45, lunch—a long, leisurely lunch. No one believes there is any
reason to hurry.

June Shew arrived and reported that already, in East Hartland,
talk is running wild and pieces of information have surfaced that, if
true, would have been pertinent. "The people didn't come forward
because they didn't want to become involved."

A reporter looked pained. "I am always amazed at the way people
can close their minds and refuse to admit how serious this is. Even
in court the oath is taken very casually—people solemnly swear
with their fingers crossed."

"Nobody really believes there will be any punishment for a few
convenient lies. I think in every trial the Judge should address every
witness—before he gives a word of testimony—and inform him
about the penalties for perjury. In our courts today the oath goes
very cheap."

2:15. A call for the lawyers! Fifteen minutes to summon everyone
out of the restaurants. But it was not a verdict. The Jury had sent
out a question and had come out into the jury box to hear the
answer.

The Judge read the question: " 'Would it have been possible,
from the window of Agnes Thompsen's apartment, to see a person
at the edge of the porch lowering some object? Does this appear in
evidence or can we get this information?' "

The twelve faces, turned to the Judge, suggested that there had
been heated argument.

"Such a statement by Mrs. Thompsen was in the record," the

Judge said. Dr. Miller had read the statement which was made by Agnes Thompsen to the admitting psychiatrist. Now Judge Mac-Donald read it again: " 'She was killed. I heard two hard bangs and then I saw a man lower something down from the porch to the ground. It was dark. I saw a man in the back and I thought it was her brother. I was upstairs and didn't know anything bad had happened.' "

Looking up, the Judge told the Jury that this was the only testimony on the question. The Jury would have to decide for themselves whether Agnes Thompsen could actually have seen this. The only other source of help, he said, might be the picture in evidence of the rear of the Thompsen house. (The picture is a full view of the back of the house, not a side view that might show the line of vision. It will not be much help.) "This is the only evidence," the Judge said. "If any new evidence is submitted it is a matter for a new trial."

(What can we say about this—the only question the Jury has sent in? A hearsay statement of an insane person made at the time she was being returned to the institution. The report that she made the statement is trustworthy. There is no evidence to support the trustworthiness of the statement itself—not made under oath, not subject to cross-examination. There is no evidence to show whether it is even physically possible for it to have been true.)

Before sending the Jury back, the Judge asked whether they were at an impasse. Mr. Glander said, "I think that, given another half-hour, we can reach a verdict." The Jury filed out again.

Press row: "Nine to three."

"Or ten to two. Those two aren't going to change. If it were just one, she'd give in. Two will stick together. This jury is hung."

"I'm a hung jury myself."

3:10. Another call. "It looks like another question."

Five minutes later Mr. Wall and Mr. Shew emerged from Chambers and walked to their tables. This seemed to be more than a question. As he passed Greg Chilson of the Waterbury *Republican*, Mr. Wall whispered, "Disagreement definitely."

The Judge in. The Jury. Harry, his mother, his father, his wife—pale and apprehensive. Their agony prolonged while the clerk called the roll of the Jury.

The Judge read the note: "We regret to inform you that we cannot reach a verdict and we feel that more time will not help us."

(It is October 15, 3:20 P.M. This trial began on September 22. It has all been for nothing.)

The Judge said, "Do you feel there is hopeless disagreement?"

"Yes, Your Honor, I'm afraid so," Mr. Glander said.

The Judge's eyes traveled over the entire Jury, and he put the question to them again. About half the jurors nodded their heads, unhappily.

The Judge [accepting it because he must] "I feel that I have said all that I can say. I will not twist your arm. I am unhappy and unsatisfied. It doesn't help the State. It doesn't help the accused. The accused will have to stand trial again. . . ."

Emotions, controlled over so many weeks, broke past their guards, and Harry's mother and his wife wept silently, convulsively. His father hunched forward and looked at the floor. Harry—white, very still—stared at the table at nothing.

The Judge continued speaking. The words rolled out over the courtroom; one hardly heard them. ". . . The fact that you disagreed is no discredit to you. . . . You were an unusually attentive, conscientious Jury . . ."

Mrs. Solberg, who never once broke down throughout the long three weeks, sobbed uncontrollably now on her husband's shoulder. Harry was the first to regain composure. He looked up from the table and found his wife's eyes across the room and spoke a silent word to her—"Smile." Then he looked down again and fumbled with his eyeglass case.

The business of the Court droned on. Mr. Wall said he would announce his next move on Wednesday at the Criminal Court Session. The Judge dismissed the Jury, and the twelve men and women walked out, single file, for the last time—some of them letting their eyes slide over to Harry as they moved past him, some avoiding this last painful look. The Judge rose, and a sheriff touched Harry's arm and he groped to his feet.

One terrible outburst from Solveig Solberg. "I can't take any more!" And then, with a visible effort, she gained control and stopped crying. Sharon, hysterical now, threw herself onto her shoulder, and sobbed, "I can't take any more. I can't stand another trial." The clerk, Mr. McDermott, made his way to the Solberg family and took them into a side office.

On the courthouse stairs, the Judge stopped to speak to Mr. and Mrs. Shew. "Maybe you should think about letting him plead guilty to manslaughter," he said.

"I wouldn't let him plead guilty now to breach of the peace," Mr. Shew replied.

In front of the courthouse the crowd stayed on as though reluctant to accept this inconclusive ending. A doctor arrived—summoned for Sharon. The Judge came out and spoke a few words to the waiting press. "You see before you a crestfallen judge. The result is unsatisfactory to Solberg. He's still in jail. His wife is upstairs in a state of shock—" With a shake of his head he broke off and walked away.

In the milling crowd, Ted Thompsen said, "I'm disappointed. I feel he's guilty." The doctor came out and told the press that he had given Sharon a sedative. Tobey and Solveig with Sharon between them started out the front door. Chilson snapped a picture and Sharon screamed and rushed back into the courthouse and was taken out through a rear door.

One by one they left—the Judge, Mr. Shew, Mr. Wall, spectators, reporters, witnesses, police officers. Then everyone was gone and Harry Solberg was back in the Litchfield jail across the little town green.

PART
THREE

INTERIM

18

The Connecticut Bar Association meeting, attended by judges and lawyers from all over the state, was held at the Statler Hilton Hotel in Hartford on the following Tuesday, October 18. Whether by design or not, the Hartford *Times* in an editorial that evening published a scathing attack on Major Rome. The editorial, entitled "Despicable Deception," stated that Rome had practiced "a double deception" (which it described) ". . . on an elderly woman who was confined in a state hospital for the mentally ill." It stated flatly, "He did this in order to try to get a confession from the woman," and equated the act with sending in a "phony priest to invite . . . a confession . . . which the police could use in their investigation and the state might try to use in its prosecution." It charged that her constitutional right to counsel was violated and commented that the reputation of the Connecticut State Police was badly tarnished. "What, if any, disciplinary steps are taken against Major Rome are up to Commissioner Mulcahy," it said, adding that at least the State Police should announce publicly that such a thing would never happen again.

The editorial made no mention of Rome's repeated statement that the woman could never go to trial. It suggested strongly that the intention was to try to use the confession against her. The writer of the editorial apparently found nothing to trouble his conscience in the fact that evidence had been smothered that might—or might not—have proved the innocence of a man accused of first-degree murder.

Now you didn't have to ask around about Sam Rome. Now that he was vulnerable, the rats came out of the walls, with grudges they had cherished for years, to bite him. Wherever lawyers gathered over their drinks before the bar association dinner you heard it—all the old accusations, reinforced with new ammunition:

"Imagine a man trying to come into court with a confession he forced out of a poor old insane woman."

"Why, that man was reversed ten years ago in the U.S. Supreme Court!" (Nobody remembers the case. It was Culombe.)

With feelings of futility a handful of his friends worked at hurling up sandbags against the rising flood:

Demeusy said, "Ten years ago when he caught Taborsky and Culombe the people of the state were on their knees in gratitude. He could have run for governor and gotten elected. People quickly forget this. The public is so willing to blindly swallow all this stuff about violation of constitutional rights. And then they scream because the crime rate is growing five times as fast as the population. Sam Rome need never apologize for what he's done. He's run himself into the ground physically and literally for the people of this state—and now they turn on him. He's taking an awful beating."

A sympathetic lawyer, one of the few, said, "Sam gets the unusual cases—the ones the others can't solve, so he's in an unusual position. If they're easy they don't get to him. He doesn't have to go through this. He could retire tomorrow at seventy percent of his pay."

And Joe Crowley, particularly disturbed about his paper's editorial, said, "The best thing that could happen would be if guys like Sam Rome would disappear. Then crime would run rampant and people would see—"

In the cocktail lounge, a reporter said, "These lawyers get hot about Sam, but he gets hot about them, too. He says, 'I think what lawyers do is worse. They make every effort to free the client even if he is guilty. They want to send him out to kill again.'"

At a reception on the first floor a lawyer said, "If a drunk, a child, or an insane person makes a statement that can be corroborated, I think it deserves more weight because he can't use reason—it just comes out. A sane person can reason and avoid saying things that make him look guilty. People don't want confidences with drunks. They talk too much and they speak the truth. If an insane person describes what happened and it fits, are you going to assume he wasn't there?"

Mr. Shew read the editorial in the hotel lobby and said, "How can you have a fair trial anyplace in the state after this?"

Ironically, Mr. Shew had a memorandum in his pocket from Judge MacDonald that had arrived in his afternoon mail. The Judge had prepared a list of suggestions that might expedite the second trial and had sent duplicate copies to Mr. Shew and Mr. Wall. He suggested, first, a change of venue "because of the extensive publicity given to the trial throughout Litchfield, Hartford and parts of New Haven Counties." He suggested that the State seek only a second-degree murder conviction in order to eliminate the problem of capital punishment in selecting jurors and the problem of proving a willful, deliberate and premeditated killing. He listed several legal procedures that might, if agreed upon, considerably shorten the second trial.

The final suggestion was: "Admission of the statements made by Agnes Thompsen to Major Rome during interrogation, together with all the circumstances surrounding the interrogation, *not as an admission or a confession but to show the consistency or inconsistency of facts described by her with those actually found with respect to the killing and surrounding circumstances.*" (Underlining is the Judge's.)

A lawyer who had stopped at Rome's house this evening came up to Mr. Shew's table. "He's hurt. He feels no one is interested in whether he's right and the State is wrong. He said, 'I'm afraid after this all I can do is teach—let the murderers walk the streets. Meanwhile cases go unsolved. I have a house with burglar alarms, sirens, guns. I can protect myself. Who protects other people? People think it's too bad this happened to Dorothy Thompsen but it would never happen to them. It *could* happen to them.' When I left, he said, 'What in hell am I fighting for? Only I can't change.' "

At the first floor reception a former State's Attorney said, "I don't blame Tom Wall for being sore at Rome coming out for the other side. I'd be sore as hell." (Lawyers develop a strange myopia.)

At Mr. Shew's table, Joe Crowley said, "If anything should happen to anyone in my family, I'd want Sam Rome in on it. They might not convict him because of a technicality, but I'd know Sam would get the guy who did it."

And at the bar, someone said, "Rome is finished."

"He's all washed up. He's through. They won't kick him out but

they won't give him the work. They won't assign him the cases."
Jubilantly, "This is the fall of the Roman Empire."

Nowhere did the question arise of whether Harry Solberg was
guilty or innocent. Nobody mentioned his name.

◆

The next day, Wednesday, the nineteenth, Mr. Wall and Mr. Shew
appeared in court in Litchfield to discuss a new trial. Now there
was no crowd of expectant spectators—only a handful of lawyers
and clients, awaiting their turn in Court. Mr. Wall stated that he
would be ready to proceed with a new trial next Tuesday to
forestall criticism over the length of time Harry Solberg had been in
jail. Mr. Shew made the obviously necessary request for a change of
venue and then bitterly criticized the editorial in the Hartford *Times*
for attacking an important Defense witness when there was to be
another trial. He called the timing of the article stupid and its
contents distorted. "Everyone knows that Major Rome knew . . .
she would never be prosecuted for this. It would appear now that
he did it for some malicious purpose. . . . I am not criticizing in
any way the coverage of any of the reporters that have been in
Court . . . but apparently the Hartford *Times* has a civil war going
on within their own barracks. They report fairly on one side and
then publish an editorial which is horribly prejudicial. . . . I don't
see how we are going to get a fair trial anywhere in the state of
Connecticut now."
   But if Mr. Shew had no criticism of the reporters, Mr. Wall did.
He asked to make a statement relating to the motion for a change of
venue, and with this he began a complaint against the press that
consumed the remainder of this hearing.
   "At the start of this trial," he began, "there was a person prominent in the State Police who had his photograph in the newspaper a
couple of days in succession and . . . this was brought to the attention of the Court. . . ." It was as though three weeks had not
elapsed since this issue erupted during the voir dire. All the rancor
was still there, intact.
   In connection with the motion for a change of venue, Mr. Wall
said, he wanted to get this matter on the record. ". . . Particularly

the issue of the Hartford *Courant* and its flagrant violation of the spirit of what Your Honor stated here, at the beginning of this trial, relating to what this witness was going to say." He read a list of quotations—thirteen in all, quite short—from the Hartford *Courant* which he felt "were in complete violation of Your Honor's orders and . . . were highly unfair and inflammatory, and designed to influence this trial." (About half of them stated that Rome had originally charged Mrs. Thompsen with the murder; the other half, that Rome had not changed his mind that Mrs. Thompsen was the killer. Two stated that his testimony indicated he believed Solberg was not the killer.) Mr. Wall said that there were half as many such statements in the Hartford *Times*.

He charged that both papers had misrepresented the testimony. ". . . Both papers said that bloody articles were found in Agnes Thompsen's apartment that were of the blood type of the victim. Absolutely nothing in the testimony about it, and those were the kinds of misrepresentations that those newspapers made. . . ."

Judge MacDonald: "Was there such a statement in either paper? I have all of the papers in my file—"

Demeusy [from the press row] "There was no such statement."

The Judge: ". . . If a statement such as that was made, that's most damaging—"

Mr. Wall responded by reading from the Hartford *Times*, October 14, which did indeed contain this misstatement. "There is a similar statement in the *Courant*. I don't happen to have that right here. It didn't say blood type but it did indicate—"

The Judge asked to have this particular article set aside.

Mr. Wall: "I feel that in any place where there has been miscoloring of the case, this building up of this *great, great* man who was going to testify and solve all our problems . . . where these newspapers have deliberately contaminated the atmosphere day after day after day . . . entirely disregarding Your Honor's injunction. They *defied* it, the *Courant* defied it, day after day. Now that's not all. The testimony has been colored in the *Courant*, Your Honor, to such an extent that anyone reading it was completely misled on a number of items and I can document them."

The Judge interrupted to state that his specific injunction was that nothing be printed in the papers which had to do with evidence discussed in the absence of the Jury. "I didn't feel that that injunction was disregarded. I feel that the papers did adhere to that." He repeated that he was concerned about the statement about the blood type.

"Well, Your Honor, I could go on with misrepresentation. The *Courant* was completely colored day after day." As an example, Mr. Wall cited that the *Courant* had quoted Christa's words, "She killed, she killed," without mentioning that the child had not wanted to leave her grandmother. "I feel that there has been a terrible injustice done to the State."

Referring to the newspaper articles to which he had objected during the voir dire, he continued, "I think that when the newspapermen felt that I was in here complaining about that, then that was the way to needle me. They had it in every day—the very same thing that I made complaints to Your Honor about, very early in the trial. . . . I feel that . . . if there is a change of venue, it ought to get as far away from that type of terrible misrepresentation which has gone on . . . particularly in the Hartford *Courant*."

"Well, let me say this," the Judge commented. "This has been a trial in many senses of the word. Unfortunately there has been needling of many kinds. . . . This is all past now. . . . I don't think that the courts can . . . dictate the way in which newspapers report trials as long as they don't publish matters which the Court expressly forbids them to publish." Concerning the change of venue he agreed that it would be difficult now to find a jury without definite opinions in Litchfield County. And, he added, certainly not in the Waterbury district. (The first reference to the fact that the Waterbury *Republican* has leaned in one direction.) Nor in Hartford County. The change of venue would have to be to a remote county.

Still trying to establish a peace, the Judge continued, "I think that it is not going to do any good to rake over certain controversial things again and again. Perhaps Major Rome . . . in some ways can be the subject of fair criticism. On the other hand, here is a man whose character and value to the State Police may have been pretty effectively assassinated by the editorial which appeared in yesterday's paper!

"I would suggest that, before we go any further into . . . the various views, vendettas, criticisms—some of which are justified—that we have a quiet and, insofar as possible, friendly talk about what would be the most efficient and effective way to bring about another trial for Harry Solberg as promptly as possbile" (the one matter that no one ever seems to dwell on very long; it gets a passing nod and melts away before the heat of other issues) "under circumstances that will assure as fair a trial as possible in a part of the state which is as unaffected as possible."

But Mr. Wall was unsatisfied. "I realize that anybody that ever starts to tell the press off, usually gets the wrong end of the deal; and I realize that Your Honor doesn't intend to give them ammunition, but I can just see, after Your Honor using the word 'vendetta,' a headline by these people . . . attributing it right to me. . . . I know exactly the way those fellows act. . . . When they were told, right at the very beginning, concerning this Major Rome business— to have the *Courant* put it in fourteen times as their lead story and the *Times* six times . . . all after the matter had been brought to Your Honor's attention, is, to my mind, inexcusable. . . ."

The Judge: "Perhaps my use of the word 'vendetta' was unfortunate. I would ask that the word not be used, and I will substitute the word, 'disagreement.' " With that, the Judge called a recess in order to have a conference with Counsel and went into Chambers.

Like a shot Demeusy was at Mr. Wall's side. "I'm going to get a lawyer," he said, furious. "I want that out of the record."

Mr. Wall whipped about. "You're not getting anything out of the record!" He snatched up his papers and strode toward Chambers.

Demeusy rushed to a telephone to ask his publisher to send a lawyer to Court immediately. While he waited for his paper to call back with instructions, he said, "If that's in the record it's a lever to say we did do improper things. I have no standing in this Court. We can't come back tomorrow and straighten it out. We should answer that diatribe." In defense of his paper, he said, "My publisher feels that if there's a split in the State Police, that's news and should be published."

The hostility unleashed that day remained, and the question of press coverage of the trial, a sore point from the start, took its place alongside so many others, as a major issue of this case.

The "Free Press, Fair Trial" issue in this case has taken a reverse twist. Protests against the press usually originate with lawyers attempting to protect the rights of the Defendant. In this trial the protest comes from the State, and it is directed against a newspaper that published that there was a difference of opinion within the State Police and that the State's chief investigator, presumably believing that the accused man was innocent, would testify in his defense.

It was these facts, publicized by the newspaper with the largest circulation in the state, that put the case so conspicuously in the public eye—some people watching for the sensational aspects, some for the political aspects, and some asking troubled questions about justice.

That evening the Hartford *Times* published a feature story by Bill Huebner, whom it described as a veteran staff-writer who had observed Rome's work many times. Entitled "Man of Strong Conviction: Rome Creates Unprecedented Paradox," the story began: "When the Solberg trail comes to an end, it will be remembered for a man who stood by his convictions and thereby created . . . an unprecedented paradox. . . . Who is Sam Rome? Is he infallible? . . ." It went on to describe his talents as an investigator, it recalled his most famous cases, it noted his public courage. "He sticks his neck out, criticizes the Supreme Court rulings that give the criminal more rights than the victim and he's blunt about it." It applauded his work with children, for which he is well known. Altogether it was a glowing tribute to the man said to have been destroyed by the editorial of the night before.

On the same night the *Times* ran a story by Joe Crowley, quoting Mr. Shew's statement that the editorial made it impossible to get a fair trial anywhere in the state. " 'Everyone knew Agnes Thompsen would never stand trial, . . .' Mr. Shew said. 'Major Rome . . . never intended to use the statement against her in a court of law. A dedicated investigator has been wronged by an editorial which does not show the true facts of the case.' "

The following night in New London—forty-five miles from Hartford, seventy miles from Litchfield—a lady said, "I think it's awful. That idiot boy did it and they're trying to make it look like it was that poor woman. I hate that Sam Rome, he's so arrogant. He made a mistake and now he's covering up."

"What if he didn't make a mistake?"

"Of course he did. And he won't admit it. How could that poor old lady do a thing like that? Pick up those heavy things—kill her like that?"

"The grocer said she used to pick up a fifty-pound bag of fertilizer."

"When? Twenty years ago? That boy did it. He was there. He was a friend of the family. They were having an affair."

"How do you know he did it?"

"I read all about it in the Hartford *Courant!*"

And in Hartford, a lawyer said, "He's taken a helluva beating just to prove an innocent man innocent. For all the papers have attacked him, there's not one who wouldn't ask for him if they needed an investigator."

The controversy over Harry Solberg was quiet. The one over Rome went on and grew.

A Reporter's Diary

19

Saturday, October 22

For weeks in Court, Dorothy Thompsen was "the victim," with all the gory details of her final condition revealed. But in all that time she never emerged as a person. One never heard about the girl who had lived thirty years in that area—attended school, worked in the bank, shared a life with a husband, a child, parents, sisters, a brother, friends. Now that the trial was over, June Shew arranged an interview for me with Carole and Bob Stadler to talk about Dottie.

Before going to the Stadlers' house we sat awhile in the Shews' den and talked about the trial. If anything, Mr. Shew's feelings have hardened on the point he made so often in Court—that the State should have produced all the evidence, allowed in all the evidence, and that it had not.

"This was an impossible case because Harry didn't tell me anything," he said. "And it was impossible because there wasn't a great deal of money. A rich client would have had two or three investigators, which Wall had. He had the State Police."

(This is one of the inequities of our judicial system which took on particular significance in this case. The State has the free hand, the authority and the manpower to gather information. The Defendant supplies his own information. If he has a good alibi and witnesses, the problem is not so serious. Otherwise, if he can afford it, talented investigators may be hired. But information does not surface easily, and good investigators are expensive. If the Defendant cannot afford a private investigator, his attorney, perhaps already working for a low fee that will not begin to cover his time, will probably make an effort, as Mr. Shew did, to get what information he can and do his best with it, hoping to dig out more facts through Cross-Examination during the trial. In this case the Defense Attorney did not even enter the case until nine months after the crime; the first trial took place fifteen months after the crime. The trail was cold when Mr. Shew began, and it is colder now. The scene could not possibly be examined. The evidence has been taken into custody by the State. People forget—or they have been bothered so much they are reluctant to talk about it any more. An expensive full-time investigator might dig until he found something. But what does Counsel for a poor man do? A verdict will be based on the information he can produce. Where does he get it—and how?)

"I should have had a copy of the transcript every night," Mr. Shew went on, "but it cost fifty cents a page. The State had it. And I should have had an assistant. Wall had Pennington keeping track of things and all those other Canaan men to check things out."

"What about that sentence, 'She was too full of fight,' in the first statement?" I asked him. "Did you ever question Harry about that?"

"He says they kept telling him that she had hair in her hand. They'd gotten a sample of his hair and they told him it would be tested and that the hair in her hand was going to turn out to be his hair. He couldn't remember what did happen, and he thought she might have grabbed his hair. Then it turned out it wasn't his."

"And the economics paper? That last morning was very bad for Harry."

"Harry sticks to his story. He asked if I could get that teacher in there to talk to him. He said to me, 'I think I can convince him that we did talk about it. Maybe I didn't understand him. But we did talk and I thought I could do a second paper. It's important to me to prove to you that I'm telling the truth.' And he insists he helped unload the plumbing truck."

Mr. Shew has begun to receive letters telling him he is wrong to defend a murderer. Some of them have even threatened his life.

He went to trial with serious doubts about his client. Now, more and more, he believes that Harry is innocent.

•   •   •

"Dottie was very quiet and nervous," Carole Stadler said. "She was a flat person—colorless—not especially attractive." (June Shew does not agree. She used to see Dottie at Hayes' Store, says she was very thin, but a good-looking girl.) "She was withdrawn—and Arnfin, too. I don't remember Dottie ever saying they went out anywhere together. Dottie never went anyplace except sometimes during the day to her mother's." Then Carole said, "I thought Agnes was a very sweet person. She used to talk to me but that night she didn't know me. She looked like the cat who ate the canary."

"She never talked to me," Bob said. "I'd say, 'Good morning,' but I wouldn't get an answer."

Carole said, "Dottie complained that Arnfin and Teddy gave in to her. She was upset that Agnes dug up a long patch in the front lawn and planted flowers." (Across the street the bare strip could still be seen in the front yard.) The conversation always comes back to that night. "The shrubs under the bay window had been watered. Each individual shrub was wet and it didn't rain that day. Agnes had a watering can and she regularly watered the shrubs."

For more than a year now these people have lived with this murder, questioning the significance of the things they remember. Carole said, "Dottie wouldn't have opened the door to a stranger. She told me that. The milkman said she always kept the door locked. Randy always had to knock for them to open the door."

Bob believes that he was away from Arnfin for about three minutes as he ran around back, saw Dottie, and raced back to the front hall. He wonders whether that was enough time for Arnfin to go inside, find the baby, take her upstairs, speak to his mother, and come down again.

"Dr. Murphy phoned in his report from our phone," Carole said. "At first he said it looked like she'd been dead about twelve hours. And I said, 'Oh, no, she wasn't!' And he changed it to one-thirty."

Suddenly Bob came up with a piece of information. He said that he saw Teddy, Arnfin, and Christa—he believes the next day—at the corner of Martin and Westwoods Roads, just past Mrs. Clark's house, stopped at the stop sign on the side of the road where the bank was found. Teddy was driving, Arnfin was on the passenger side. Mr. Shew sat up at that and questioned Bob closely, and Bob said he believed it was "after supper on the sixteenth." He was with Carole's brother, whose name is Ronnie LaCasse. Mr. Shew will check with Ronnie LaCasse to learn what he remembers.

In spite of all she has said, Carole appears to think that Harry did it. "I think it was an outsider." Bob appears to think it was Agnes.

We crossed the street to the Thompsen house and went around to the back yard. Mr. Shew paced off from the porch to the spot where, according to Carole, the hammer was found—thinks it is less than eighty feet. From the side of the house June Shew took Polaroid photographs in an effort to show whether the overhang cuts the line of vision from Agnes's bedroom window to the edge of the porch. The pictures are inconclusive.

Later we drove past the Solberg house—a neat red Cape Cod cottage near the road with the smaller green cottage that Arnfin and Dottie rented in the rear. The mailbox is not on its post. There is no name to indicate who lives there. The Hartford *Courant* delivery box is still there, close to the road. The property is neat and well-tended. There was no sign of anyone home.

Monday, October 24

Today I went to the files of the Hartford *Courant* to try to answer the question: Could Harry Solberg have learned the details that he wrote in the Letter—postmarked June 17—from the newspapers of that morning and of the day before? Had these details been published by that time?

Here is a comparison of the Letter with a passage from the *Courant* story of the morning of June 17:

Letter	Hartford *Courant*, June 17
I *stabed* her with a *meat fork*. I stamped on her face. I *stabed* her with a *fork*. I *draged* her through the house with an *electric cord*. I used a *hammer* to pound in the skike to hang her. She fell to the ground. I bashed her head in several times with a large *rock*.	Headline: HAMMER IS FOUND . . . Captain O'Brien said she had been *stabbed first* in the back with a large *fork* . . . the type used for *meat* roasts. . . . There were other . . . wounds caused by a . . . *table fork*. . . . A trail of blood led from the kitchen through an adjoining room. . . . "It would appear she had been *dragged* out," O'Brien said. . . . The track led out a rear . . . door onto the sunporch and across the porch. . . . The body was found face-up in dirt beside a pile of small *rocks*. . . . Captain O'Brien said that the *electrical cord* was

around the . . . neck and attached to a nail-punch driven in
the edge of the porch. . . . "The
cord was attached and broke when
she dropped," he said. . . . He
added he believes the nail-punch
was not driven into the porch
earlier from what the husband says.

The sequence is exactly the same in the Letter as in the newspaper. Even the sequence of the fork wounds, which is incorrect, is
the same—first the meat fork, then the other fork. The vocabulary is
the same: "meat fork," not carving fork—"dragged," not pulled—
"electric cord," not appliance cord or electric wire or toaster cord.

What about the rock? Early in the article is the statement, "She
was beaten about the head with a blunt instrument until her skull
was fractured. Then she was hung by the neck with an insulated
electric cord." Then, later, "She fell beside a pile of small rocks."

One can almost picture Harry writing the Letter with the newspaper in front of him—fixing things up a bit "to divert suspicion" so
it wouldn't be obvious that he had copied it. (There is a Hartford
Courant box in front of the house.)

(Rome: "The letter is from a crank. He has written everything
that was printed in the newspapers. And when he goes beyond what
was in the papers, the facts are wrong.")

Saturday, October 29

It is rumored that the Judge believes that the final jury
vote was ten to two for guilty. The sheriff who was in charge of the
room is said to have found slips divided into two piles, ten in one,
two in the other. Could it have been the other way around?

Sunday, October 30

The Coroner's Inquest on the case is a pesthole of nagging
questions. I read the transcript today. (Reading it at this time is
turning back the clock. Coroner H. Gibson Guion held four sessions—three of them with Agnes as the suspect—over a year ago;
one, with Harry as the suspect, six months ago.)

The first session took place on July 16, 1965, one month after the murder. Agnes Thompsen attended this session and was represented by the Public Defender. Lieutenant Fuessenich, a major witness at the trial, did not appear at all. Nor did Rebillard, nor Pennington. County Detective Sam Holden attended as an observer. Captain O'Brien—never seen at the trial—testified at the Inquest that he was officially connected with the investigation from the beginning. (Fourteen months between the Inquest and the trial seems to have produced casting changes.)

At the Inquest, seventeen photographs were introduced, all taken that night. Photograph #1 reads: "Taken at 8:00 P.M." Photograph #17 reads: "Taken 10:45 P.M." A period of two and three-quarter hours. (At the trial Lieutenant Fuessenich testified that the photographs were taken under his direction from "Oh, about 7:30—to 8:30 to 9:00." A period of not more than an hour and a half.) If two photographers worked nearly three hours instead of, at the most, an hour and thirty minutes, is it possible that there are more pictures?

At the Inquest, Arnfin testified that Christa was put in her crib for her nap every day at 12:45, and that she was out of diapers; but "once in a while if she hadn't gone to a toilet before a nap or something like that, Dottie would put diapers on her." (What does this do to the suggestion that Christa might have gone the entire afternoon and remained dry?)

Arnfin also testified that he did not tell his mother anything about the wounds or about a cord around the neck or blows on the head. He did not tell her anything about the manner in which the death occurred.

Ragazzi's testimony contained details that did not come out at the trial.

Concerning the analysis of the material from the sanding of the stairs: "It was negative because . . . the particles were so minute that my understanding from Dr. Stolman is that they couldn't possibly produce . . . any evidence to indicate that there was blood on the sand scrapings." At the trial we were told simply that no blood was found. This puts the matter in a somewhat different light.

Concerning an interrogation of Agnes Thompsen at the Connecticut Valley Hospital (the date is not clear, but obviously it was before July 16 when this hearing took place): ". . . She made certain admissions to me and Lieutenant Paige when we were talking to her. . . . We were talking about the crime and what must have happened, and we said that there were indications that Dorothy had gone to the phone, and she said, 'Yes, I saw Dorothy go to the telephone to call Arnfin.' Then, when I said, 'You saw Dorothy go to the telephone?' she said, 'No, no, Arnfin told me that Dorothy was going to the phone to call him.'" (Here are some questions! Where did Agnes get this information? She went back to the hospital that night—and Arnfin has testified that he told her nothing.)

Ragazzi also testified that Agnes said she did not hear the telephone ring at all that afternoon and that the child had been in her crib from approximately 12:45 until 6:15 when Arnfin came home.

(Mrs. Burdick, Dorothy's mother, had testified that she telephoned Dottie that day four times between 4:30 and 5:50, on each occasion letting the telephone ring about five times, and that the telephone could be heard throughout that house.)

Major Rome testified that ultraviolet light turned onto clothing in Agnes Thompsen's closet revealed two dresses with stains in front, below the neck down almost to the waist. The nature of the stains was not identified, but "later when we talked with Mrs. Thompsen she described this pink rosette dress as the one she wore the day of the crime." He said that he had learned from Dorothy's parents that she and Agnes did not get along well and that Agnes was not permitted to play with Christa, whom she loved. To him Agnes's statement that she heard " 'Two noises, as if it was done by something heavier than a hammer' " was significant because a small sledgehammer which was heavier than a hammer had been used. Other investigators had told him that Dorothy didn't iron to Agnes's satisfaction. Because of the bloodstains on the shirt, he believes that an argument started that day near the ironing board.

And here is something.

Trooper Yuknat: "There were [footprints] in several areas in the kitchen . . . over near the dining room door, and then there were some *leading to the area in front of the hearth in the living room.*"

(No word of *this* in the trial, with all that was made of the piggy bank on the hearth. And Yuknat did say at the trial, coaxed by Mr. Shew with an eye on this transcript, that all the footprints appeared to be from the same source and that they were similar to Arnfin's shoes in size, shape, and location of nail holes.)

Questions—questions—many of them trivial—but the trial is over, not just beginning, and too many are still unanswered.

But here is something that is not trivial! Tucked into this transcript of the Inquest are two scraps of information, seemingly unrelated, given almost in passing—one hardly notices—which add up to a startling piece of information.

It has long been accepted that Dorothy was killed at about one o'clock. The time has fluctuated up to one thirty—the hour at which Mr. Flagg passed the house and saw Harry. How was this time of death established? At first it was vague. On June 17 the Hartford *Courant* reported, "Police believe that Mrs. Thompsen was killed in the early afternoon. . . . Dr. Murphy said Tuesday night . . . she had apparently been dead eight to twelve hours. But the Stadlers' three-year-old-son, Randy, . . . played with Thompsen's daughter from 10:00 A.M. to noon on the day of the murder." One o'clock became the estimated and then the accepted time. Nobody challenged it. The exact hour was unimportant. Later, when evidence was gathered against Harry Solberg, one o'clock was a near-fit.

But here are the two scraps of testimony at the Inquest—unimportant then—on July 16, 1965.

Dr. Opper: "There was a *considerable amount of undigested food in the stomach,* which *had not passed on farther into the duodenum.* I would say that the death occurred *very shortly* after eating, and the normal time for eating is *about one o'clock.*"

On that same day Arnfin was asked a question that he was not asked at the trial.

Coroner Guion: "What was the routine as to feeding the baby in the daytime?"

Arnfin: "Well, she'd give the baby breakfast after I left for work and then *they'd eat about quarter to twelve*—and she'd give the baby another snack about four o'clock. . . ."

And Randy Stadler came home at quarter to twelve because they were going to eat lunch. And "death occurred very shortly after eating . . . she had not digested her lunch." *Now* the time does not fit the hour of Harry Solberg's arrival! At 1:30 Dorothy was already dead!

Does this hold up? I telephoned a doctor. "Digestion begins immediately," he said. "It can vary with different people and with different foods—meat takes longer—what did she eat? The average person would probably digest a light lunch in the stomach in half an hour. An hour at most. If there was a large amount of undigested food still in the stomach which had not passed at all into the duodenum, which is the next step, it appears that she died very shortly after eating!"

The second session of the Coroner's Inquest took place eleven weeks later—on October 4, 1965. In eleven weeks there had been changes. Major Rome had obtained the August 5 statement, and Agnes Thompsen had deteriorated and was unable to attend the hearing. Both County Detective Sam Holden and Detective Rebillard were present. (Why Rebillard? It had been some time since he had been connected with the case, and he had not attended the earlier hearing, which had involved events of the night of the murder when he was on the scene. Was Canaan already starting its separate investigation?)

There were only two witnesses that day—Major Rome and Dr. Miller from the Connecticut Valley Hospital. With a certain curiosity one starts to read Major Rome's testimony. All through the trial he protested that he never intended to use Agnes's statement against her in Court and that he had said from the start that it would be inadmissible.

Although not present, Agnes Thompsen was represented by the Public Defender, Mr. Henry C. Campbell, and at this time came the first protest that this interview violated her constitutional rights. (The date of this session was eight months before the *Miranda* decision but after the *Escobedo* decision.)

Here are Rome's first words on the subject, spoken at a time when the case did not yet have the heat it was to generate later.

Coroner Guion: ". . . I am inclined to go along with Mr. Campbell. . . . I don't believe this statement is admissible in a court of law. . . ."

Major Rome: "We go along with you on that. I go along one

hundred percent. I don't think it would be admissible in a court of law."

(One must grant that implicit in his statement are the words "against her." At this Inquest, she was the suspect. During the trial, when Rome fought to have it admitted, Mr. Shew argued that she was not the defendant—that it was not being used against her.)

At this session of the Inquest, Dr. Miller testified that Agnes Thompsen was unable to be present—that her condition had steadily worsened since about the first of September and that there was no question of her inability to stand trial.

"She had been continuously mentally ill for a long period of time," he said, "but has periods of remission of her illness during which she could be considered competent." And: *"On August 5 she was in a state of remission,* in that whereas she was unquestionably mentally ill, she was capable of knowing right from wrong. She was capable of knowing the nature of her acts and was capable of advising counsel."

Coroner Guion questioned him about the circumstances of the interview and Dr. Miller replied that he was present—or another doctor or a registered nurse—always—when Mrs. Thompsen was being questioned. "The considerations extended to her by the police were above and beyond the medical demands of the situation," he said. "We were there to safeguard her physical and mental health . . . but there was certainly no need—she was never taxed. She was never pressed. Never held against her will. She was given frequent rests and refreshments."

Coroner Guion: "Throughout the interview you felt there was no necessity of your intervening in terms of her mental health and physical health needs?"

Dr. Miller: "Absolutely not."

Asked whether, on August 5, Mrs. Thompsen was able to comprehend that she had a right to counsel, and whether he felt her responses were voluntary in that she knew what she was saying and knew of her right not to say anything, Dr. Miller replied, "It is my belief that this is so."

His prognosis for Agnes Thompsen: ". . . The prognosis . . . is particularly important since in addition to her general mental condition . . . *she is also showing some signs now of cerebral arterio-*

sclerosis which would then produce this organic brain disease as well."

(Rome: "She was deteriorating rapidly. We had to work fast. If I lost her, I couldn't bring her back.")

After Dr. Miller's testimony, discussion was resumed on the admissibility of the statement at the Inquest. Mr. Campbell protested that Agnes was not present and Coroner Guion replied that any time he wanted a hearing for her to refute or testify, it would be accorded him.

"Well . . . she is deteriorating, so that I doubt very much that there will be any advantage," Mr. Campbell said.

Everybody at that time, it seems, accepted the fact that Agnes Thompsen was not going to recover and was never going to stand trial. Only now have the sinister strokes been added—in court and by certain segments of the press—of dark and devious purposes.

And here too, before *Miranda,* is a hint of what was to come:

Major Rome: "I don't think it would be admissible in a court of law. I can't quite go along with you that it was taken illegally. Mrs. Thompsen was not in custody. . . . I feel that the police officer has a right to ask questions."

Coroner Guion: "That is a shadowy area of the law to me."

Major Rome: "Then there is no use of the police trying to ever obtain an admission and trying to clear up a matter as delicate and complicated as this."

Because of mechanical difficulties the playing of the tape was postponed until October 11. Then it was heard off-the-record, so that it is not included in this transcript, but it is apparent, in the testimony that surrounds it, that many things came out voluntarily that day that were viciously attacked later. During the trials one was given the impression that an investigation—almost in a crusading spirit— had uncovered this "deception and subterfuge" about which the cry still continues.

But in the transcript of the Inquest it is clear that doctors, nurses, and several police officers were present—a very large audience for a topnotch detective to gather about himself if he intends to effect any personal gain from "deception and subterfuge"—a man about whom his enemies have said many things, but never that he was a fool. And, in addition to providing himself with a large collection of witnesses, he taped the interview and turned in the tape. It was played that day at the Inquest at Rome's insistence—prefaced by his statement that it could never be used in court—in an effort to wrap up a case that would not go to trial, close it and put it to bed.

After reading the transcript of the Inquest, can anyone say that the State has been entirely fair to him? Or the segment of the press that has cut him apart? Or the public that is screaming for his head?

The Coroner issued a finding of "reasonable cause to believe that Agnes Thompsen was criminally responsible for the death." He said that he had not considered the tapes—heard off-the-record—in reaching his decision.

We still do not know what was in the tape. We still don't know what Agnes Thompsen said. Never has a piece of information been so wrapped in silence!

•   •   •

The transcript of the three-part hearing which concerned Agnes Thompsen is a hundred and twenty-four pages. When the Inquest was reopened on April 18, 1966 (six months ago), with Harry Solberg as the suspect, there was one session, five witnesses—Mr. Flagg, Lieutenant Fuessenich, Arnfin, who identified the Letter, Mr. Liberi, and Detective Keller, who obtained the handwriting sample. The transcript runs twenty-seven pages.

Lieutenant Fuessenich was the major witness. He testified that he interviewed Harry on Sunday, March 13, and on the following day, the fourteenth, with Detective Holden, Sgt. Kielty and Detective Rebillard present. Far less information is given about these interviews than we heard about the interviews of Agnes Thompsen. There is no word of Rebillard's interrogation of Harry on Sunday morning, nor of Lieutenant Riemer's interviews that afternoon and the next evening. There is no hint that Harry was ever at Hartford Headquarters at all, on Sunday or Monday. There is not a word indicating that the interrogations were taped (Rome offered this information and offered the tapes) or that a stenographer was

called in to take down the statement. The length of these interviews
is never mentioned; the question is not asked. (With Agnes Thompsen it was asked and answered.)

The facts of the alleged "confession" come out glibly, as though
they were given willingly. "He said he killed her. . . . He said he
stabbed her with a metal fork, he wrapped an electric cord around
her neck and he hit her with a large rock, and that he took the piggy
bank."

More and more, curiosity is focusing on these two large chunks of
information that we have been denied—the police interrogations of
the two individuals who allegedly confessed to this crime. How
were the confessions obtained? How much did they really know?
What happened in the Connecticut Valley Hospital? And what
happened to Harry?

Friday, November 4

Agnes Thompsen died today at the Connecticut Valley
Hospital.

Thursday, November 10

To Litchfield today for a closer look at the evidence introduced during the trial—presently in the custody of Mr. McDermott,
the Clerk of the Court. Three revealing items. One is Harry's first
"voluntary statement" (8:27, Monday night)—written in script, not
printed, in a very shaky hand. In the folder there is another sample
of Harry's handwriting in script—part of the job application—in
which the letters (for example, the "k," the "g," and the "o") are
bold, upright and round. In the "voluntary statement," these letters
are reed-thin and slanted way over to one side, formed with wobbly
irregular strokes. Looking at it, one can only wonder again about
the Two Days. The writing seems to indicate great fatigue. And still
he told only the first story.

The other two items are parts of the hospital record that were not
read in Court.

A note of July 6, 1965 (three weeks after Agnes Thompsen's
return to the hospital), read: Patient is "generally moderately

anxious when spoken to and volunteers that her heart 'is at peace as she didn't kill' anybody. . . . Answers are short, coherent, but sound as if they were overrehearsed, with 'Wasn't it terrible,' 'We got along so well,' 'We never had an argument,' etc. repeated almost in sequence when she is spoken to. . . ."

A note that Dr. Miller wrote on his return from the Coroner's Inquest on October 4, 1965, making his points even more emphatically than at the trial. "I gave testimony that . . . it was my belief that the information she was purported to have given in the alleged confession would have *sufficient validity to be entertained as a factual document.* . . . I also stated that *I did not anticipate a remission of her illness in the reasonably foreseeable future.*"

On a two-hour drive home from Litchfield there is time to think. How much easier on Rome if he had ignored this information that Agnes Thompsen was deteriorating rapidly! The evidence was all in and had not produced a positive answer. Why bother to go further? For his own sake he should have played it safe—played it "by the book." No one would have known the difference. Sins of omission pass unnoticed. The question was, where was his first obligation? To himself? To a woman whose fate was already sealed by incurable illness? Or to the people who might still have among them a murderer who could enter another house where a woman was alone—or with only her small children—and repeat this vicious crime? The public has expressed itself loud and clear on this case— the State and members of the press and the general public. They have risen up en masse against him. They are out for blood. He is abused and in virtual disgrace and he cannot reply. He has been ordered to remain silent.

He should have turned his back. If a murderer was loose, perhaps next time he would leave more clues. If not, this would be one more unsolved murder. Who would care? Years later someone might say, "They never did find out who killed that woman up there around East Hartland, did they?" And eventually, perhaps, the police would have come to Harry Solberg, so a suspect would have been delivered up, after all, and the public and the State and the press would have been content that all was right with the world. There was nothing in it for him. He should have turned his back.

Saturday, November 12

Mr. Shew has heard that the final vote was ten to two for acquittal. The report comes from a young law student whose father is a friend of one of the jurors. Can one rely on news that has traveled so circuitous a route? It doesn't really matter, but Mr. Shew feels better to think it might have been that way. With what he has now he believes next time he can win.

When Rome heard about the new deductions concerning the time of death he said, "Anything that's found from here on out could only tend to prove that Agnes did it. They can't get anything more on Solberg."

Probably Mr. Shew's new confidence stems in part from the fact that now he, too, feels this way. He believes absolutely now that Harry Solberg is innocent.

Sunday, November 13

The more I ask about Dottie, the more I hear about that night. Today Bill and June Shew arranged an interview with Dr. and Mrs. (Eunice) Stadler. Also present were Paul Stadler, their younger son, who attends Springfield College, and Eunice Stadler's mother, Mrs. Sadie Mann. Later Carole and Bob came in.

Paul Stadler was one of the first to arrive that night. "Arnfin and Bob were on the front stoop and Arnfin was having a slug—straight liquor in a waterglass. He was pale—white—and he still had his tie up tight. I don't know why I noticed that. I looked through the window. The first thing I saw was bloody foot tracks on the floor, right inside—in the hallway. And I sneaked around and saw the body. She was all mangled—her face was all cockeyed—a hole as big as a small apple on the side of her head. My first thought was that someone had to be insane to do it. I was sick and afraid. I wished to hell it never happened to me—that I saw her. I was afraid—just afraid. I was chilled that this could happen right next door. You read about things like that."

Eunice Stadler, a bright articulate woman, is the person who found the first white shoelace. "It was lying in the driveway right beside the police cruiser. I saw it right away. There was fresh blood on it—only the outer circle had turned brown. The center was red to pink. The bend marks were still evident. I had the feeling it was never in a shoe. There were no lacing marks." (Mr. Shew thinks the shoelace was a plant. "Would the murderer run out of the house and stop in the front yard to take out a shoelace?")

After a few minutes Dr. Stadler—an outdoor-type man with a lean weathered face—joined us. His comment about Agnes: "She was powerful as an ox. One hot day a few weeks before the murder I saw her over there. It was a real warm day and she was wearing an overcoat and hat, boots and gloves, wielding a pick and shovel, digging a ditch." (This was the flower garden strip in the front yard—the one Dottie resented.)

"It was chaos that night," Eunice said. "Everybody seemed to be going off on a tangent on their own. All Indians and no chiefs— everyone on their own. Everyone was asking us questions. It was absolute confusion."

But during every interview, it seems, one piece of information comes out suddenly, without warning, next to which everything pales in comparison.

Mrs. Mann, Eunice Stadler's mother, came in—an outspoken and positive old lady. And now it turned out that at about nine o'clock on the night of the murder some police officers questioned Randy at Dr. Stadler's house, where he had remained in Mrs. Mann's care since his mother sent him there earlier. Paul Stadler and Mrs. Mann were present during the questioning. There is some confusion among the Stadlers as to who the policemen were. Paul and Mrs. Mann say there were two policemen and, they believe, a reporter. One officer was "a tall detective with a very thin face, who smoked a pipe." The other one did not stay long. This is how they report the interview.

Paul Stadler

"They asked Randy, 'Why did you go home?' and Randy said that Christa's mama sent him home because they were going to eat."

(Carole said, "This was a regular schedule. Randy would go over there and Dottie would send him home at quarter to twelve when they were ready to eat. He came home at quarter to twelve that day.")

Paul: "They asked him, 'Who was in the house when you went home?' And Randy said, 'The Christa and The Mama and The Gramma.' "

(Eunice explained that this was the way Randy talked at that time, the way he used to refer to Christa and her family.)

Paul: "The officer said, 'What did the man say?' And Randy said, 'Didn't say anything 'cause there wasn't any man there.' The officer said, 'What was the Gramma doing?' And Randy said, 'She wasn't doing nothin'—only sitting by the ironing board.'

"I know Randy," Paul said. "And he wasn't fooling around. He wasn't lying."

Mrs. Mann

"The officer said, 'Who was the man?' And Randy said, 'Didn't I *told you* there wasn't any man?'

"The officer said, 'What was the Mama doing?' And Randy wouldn't tell him. They urged him to answer and finally he said he would tell me. And he whispered that she was cleaning the little girl's potty-chair. He was embarrassed to say it out loud to the police.

"Then the officer said again, 'What was the Gramma doing?' And Randy said, 'Nothing—just sitting by the ironing board.' "

Paul

"The police would talk about something else, unrelated, and then come back to it and say, 'What did the man say?' and Randy said, 'Didn't I told you there wasn't any man?' "

One cannot ignore the fact that Randy was only three and a half years old. But could he have imagined this? Somewhere there is a police officer who has this information that Randy said Agnes Thompsen was downstairs, sitting next to the ironing board when he left. Where is his report?

Wednesday, November 16

Word that the Canaan police are checking very carefully the pieces of information about the time of death—the time that Dorothy ate lunch and the autopsy report. How did this leak out?

A strange insidious fear is spreading among people who are

discussing the defense of Harry Solberg. They are afraid to talk about it over their telephones. When I call Mr. Shew he calls back from a neighbor's house. Other people—potential witnesses, interested persons who are becoming more and more involved—arrange to meet him in person rather than talk over telephones. It is probably all imagined, but the fear is a symptom of the infection that is running wild in this case.

There is a rumor that there is trouble finding a place to hold the second trial. It is said that no judge really wants to try the case.

There is a rumor that the new trial will begin around December 6 to bring the verdict up to around Christmas Eve. Whatever happened to Judge MacDonald's suggestions for a speedier trial? Where do these rumors come from?

Sunday, November 20

For more than a week something has been brewing. Not the least of the unanswered questions in this case is whether Harry Solberg truly has no memory for a period of time on the afternoon of June 15. To answer the question, there has been talk of a complete psychiatric examination for Harry, which among other measures would include the use of Sodium Pentothal. The matter came to a head about ten days ago, and Dr. Von Salzen stated the conditions under which he would be willing to undertake such a study and the results that might be expected. From a layman's point of view, the anticipated results are devoutly to be desired. The doctor would probably learn whether Harry is innocent or guilty. If he is amnesiac, even if guilty, he would receive treatment. If he is amnesiac and innocent, he would remember what happened that day and would know that he is innocent. Innocent or guilty, his memory would be restored which, for Harry, would be therapeutic. It sounds marvelous!

It is crawling with problems!

There is danger of an accusation that psychiatric techniques are being used to obtain a confession. Also, Harry must give his consent—if he is guilty he is exposing himself to great risk—and, since Harry is a minor, his parents must also consent.

And there is more. Last Sunday evening Judge MacDonald discussed some of the legal problems. "Mr. Wall argues, with some justification, that if they go into it, it shouldn't be just one-sided," he said. "But then, if he is guilty, and under the truth serum he confesses, you get into the situation of a man testifying against himself."

"Would it be legally admissible as evidence?"

"There would be a problem. Even if Mr. Wall and Mr. Shew agreed that however it came out, it would be admitted, it would not necessarily be binding. If he took the truth serum and blurted out the whole story—if Mr. Shew withdrew from the case and another lawyer came in, he could argue that using it would be a man incriminating himself—and he would win. The Constitution says a man cannot be forced to incriminate himself—so the step can be said to be one-sided."

Agreed. But should this deter them? Should not the first interest, even of the State, be to learn the truth? If Harry is innocent, can there be anyone who does not want to find it out? If he is guilty, even if the State could not use this confession in Court, at least then Mr. Wall would be absolutely certain in his own mind. (In a case where there is so much doubt, so much smoke, is it possible that he has no misgivings?) He could still make the same effort to convict him with the same evidence he has now. And if Harry confessed under truth serum, it might become easier to convict because Rome would probably withdraw from the fight. He would be stunned—he is absolutely convinced of his position. But, as Joe Crowley said, "If the State came up with convincing new evidence, I think Sam would switch." In his effort to convict the guilty, Mr. Wall has nothing to lose.

For Mr. Shew there was a different dilemma and he wrestled with it for a week after Judge MacDonald presented Mr. Wall's terms. If Dr. Von Salzen, after the use of Sodium Pentothal and possibly other measures, was absolutely satisfied that Harry was innocent, Mr. Wall would nolle the case. But if Dr. Von Salzen said he was guilty, Mr. Wall wanted Mr. Shew to agree to plead guilty to second-degree murder. Mr. Shew felt he could not bargain this way. He believed he could get manslaughter but still he felt he could not bargain. "If something went wrong, the family would never forgive you."

(The idea of manslaughter in this case seems totally unacceptable. If Harry committed this crime, he belongs in an institution. If he did not, he should be free. This was no halfway crime and there should not be a halfway verdict.)

During the week Mr. Shew discussed the offer with Harry, who was very cool to it. "He doesn't know—that I'm sure of," Mr. Shew said. "The one thing he's afraid of is that he might find out he did it. As an excuse he said to me, 'I was impressed with the jury trial and I want a jury to say I'm innocent.'"

The elder Solbergs seemed to agree that it was the thing to do, but they felt that if Harry remained opposed, they would not be able to make him accept. The week dragged on, while the offer dangled like a juicy apple on a string that no one dared bite into.

Except Rome. When Mr. Shew described the offer, adding that no lawyer could bargain that way, Rome looked at him and said, "Take it. The kid will come out clean."

Today (Sunday) Harry turned the offer down. The Solbergs told Mr. Shew this morning that they felt a jury must decide. The reactions of the Judge and Mr. Wall were similar. They said, "So he doesn't want to take the truth serum?"

Mr. Shew replied, "If he's going to be found guilty, he wants it to be by a jury of twelve men—not by a doctor."

Privately Mr. Shew believes that the Solbergs are afraid of and shun psychiatric treatment. Whatever the reason, the possibility of that solution is gone, and everyone is back in the same place again.

Monday, November 21

Mr. Shew says there was no leak on the new information concerning the time of death. He told Mr. Wall himself, hoping that, with this strong piece of evidence, he would decide not to proceed with the second trial. It was a calculated risk that did not have the hoped-for effect. Instead, the State is going to work, trying to refute it.

Everyone accepts the idea now that there will be a second trial.

Wednesday, November 23

Mr. Shew has an assistant! John McKeon, a young lawyer with considerable trial experience, has volunteered. Until last sum-

mer, Mr. Shew and Mr. McKeon had adjacent offices and had discussed the case several times. Mr. McKeon is a compact, wiry man
in his late thirties—quick and articulate. He is a close friend of
Demeusy's; he has had differences in Court with Sam Rome—a new
twist in the case.

Sunday, December 4

The trial will not be before Christmas, but everyone
knows that it must be soon and the pace is quickening. Today with
Mr. Shew I went to the Thompsen house, rented now to someone
else, and went upstairs to the rear window of what used to be
Agnes Thompsen's bedroom. (After the trial, according to Mr.
Shew, Tobey Solberg and Pastor Bugge called at the house and
asked to be permitted to look out the window and were denied
admission.) This week Mr. Shew made the request and arrangements were made for Rebillard to meet him at the house today.

At the window I crouched down to a height of five feet, which
was Agnes Thompsen's height. I was not able to see the edge of the
porch floor. I would not have seen the nail set. I would have seen
the head of a man standing up at the edge of the porch.

Tuesday, December 6

A few days ago, John McKeon went to the Litchfield jail
to talk to his new client. From his jail cell Harry could see him as he
entered, and his first words to McKeon were, "I thought you were a
dick." ("Harry is learning quite a bit in jail," McKeon commented
afterward, "including the lingo.")

The interview lasted several hours, and McKeon came away with
mixed and complex impressions. "I had to treat him harshly—as
harshly as the State's Attorney would treat him," he said later. "A
big question in my mind was whether to put him on the stand. I
bore down on him relentlessly—and I couldn't shake him.

"In jail he is slovenly—he's developed a pot belly—shirt unbut-
toned, protruding out over his slacks. But his hair was carefully
combed, every hair, every wave in place. I felt he had strong
feminine traits. He wore his glasses at the start of the interview and
then took them off. He needs glasses, but whenever he knows his

picture will be taken, he takes them off. He's very vain. He's a hero at the jail. They treat him with unusual deference. He's a celebrity. He's achieved a status he never had before and couldn't get anywhere else—in any other way.

"I tried to get a complete account from him of everything that happened." (And Harry told him the first story about hearing the baby crying and going in, etc.) "I asked him about the piggy bank and he doesn't remember. He says he drove down the street and then just drove around. He stopped in front of the residence of a State Trooper whom he knew. 'I was going to tell him. Then I changed my mind.' "

In reply to McKeon's questions, Harry repeated the details he had told Mr. Shew—that he came home on the bus, changed his clothes, ate lunch. Then he said he was going to pick up the lawn mower, and his mother gave him money for the lawn mower. Then he helped unload the plumbing truck, went for the lawn mower, which wasn't ready, and on the way home stopped at the Thompsens'.

"We talked about the paper," McKeon said. "He remembers very clearly that the first title he got was 'Marketing'—something about a farmer who has to invest thirty cents an acre producing potatoes. Harry felt he couldn't cope with this subject and asked for another. He was assigned the subject 'Great Men,' and he wrote the paper and got an A. Then he thought that if he tried to carry out the original assignment, too, he might get a very good grade in that course, so he asked Arnfin for help."

McKeon repeated their conversation on this point, as follows:

McKeon: "How could you expect Mr. Thompsen to be home in the daytime? You were going over to see his wife."

Harry: "I had phoned them and they said they would have it ready."

"Did you call the day before?"

"I talked to them on the phone (he couldn't remember whether he talked to Arnfin or Dottie) and they said it would be ready and I could pick it up."

"Then he repeats his story of going in, seeing the disorder, climbing the ladder—" McKeon went on. "He goes up and down a side road, meditating—but it was an inarticulate conflict. He didn't know *why* he wanted to find the police. He drove around a bit and went home. He was going to tell his mother."

Again the conversation with Harry:

McKeon: "For God's sake what were you going to tell her?"

Harry: "I don't know. Then I decided to tell my dad. I asked my mother where my dad was working, and she told me in East Granby. She said, 'Go get some soda at Hayes' Store to take over there' and she gave me the money."

McKeon: "You told me you had money from the lawn mower."

"Well, I must have given it back to her. . . . I drove down and worked with my father the rest of the day." And did you tell him? "No, I decided against it."

McKeon: "*What did you have to tell him?*"

Harry [blank]: "I don't know."

"He worked with his father the rest of the day. Came home, had supper and went to his girl friend's house."

McKeon: "Didn't you feel upset?"

"No."

"What was the first inkling you had that there had been a death?"

"My father came in from a meeting at the church and told us that Dottie Thompsen had been murdered."

McKeon: "Why didn't you say then that you knew something about it?"

Harry: "I didn't know something about it."

McKeon: "Did you kill her?"

Harry: "I don't know."

"Did you sleep that night?" Sure. "What about the letter? You wrote the letter."

"A few days later. Because they were looking for a black '59 Ford. My mother was bugging me." Why? "To divert suspicion. The police came and took my fingerprints. They said they were taking the fingerprints of everyone in the area who owned a black '59 Ford." [This probably happened at a later date.]

McKeon went on to the events of Harry's arrest:

McKeon: "What happened there in front of the house that Sunday?"

Harry: "A policeman came to the house and asked me to come with him."

"Did you know why he was there?"
"Yes, I knew he was there about the letter."

"They drove along. It was slow going, there had been a heavy storm. A call came in over the police radio that the Solberg parents phoned. Here everything jibes with police testimony. The detective takes him inside. First they have coffee. Then he sits him in a room and questions him."

McKeon: "Did they tell you about your right to have a lawyer?"
"No."
"What did they tell you?"
Harry: "They told me I didn't have to say anything."
McKeon: "Why didn't you keep quiet?"
Harry [a little surprised] "I wrote the letter!"

"Then—" McKeon continued, "after a few questions the officer took a piece of paper and drew a line making two columns and wrote 'True' and 'False' and said, 'Each time I ask you a question and you answer it, I'm going to evaluate your answer and mark it True or False, and at the end of the game we'll see who wins.' And he commenced the questioning which lasted for some time. Then one of them said, 'Why don't you clear yourself? Why don't you take a lie-detector test? Then we can forget about you and go about our business.' By now his parents were phoning in. His parents were told he was going to Hartford, and they said they would meet him there. In Hartford the police explained to the parents that they were going to give Harry a lie-detector test. His parents signed a release.

"Harry thinks of Riemer who administered the test as a doctor. He said, 'I call him Doc.' Riemer put a series of questions to him but never used the word 'killed.' The questions would be, 'Are you wearing a flannel shirt?' 'Did you harm the Thompsen woman?' Then another nothing question. Then, 'You'd been going with her— were you at the house alone with her on any other occasion?'

" 'That was the first time I was ever in that house alone,' Harry said. 'I was always with Sharon or Arnfin or my parents.' He helped Arnfin with building the house and helped his father with the plumbing.

"Then Riemer went out, came back, and administered the same

series of questions all over again. Then he said, 'These aren't the best conditions. This isn't a good time. You should go home and rest—come back and take it again.'

"When he went out it was dark. His parents drove him home.

"The next day—'After work I drove over to the police station in Hartford,' Harry said. 'They were waiting for me—three of them, including the Doc. They said to me, "Are you aware of your rights?" and I said, "Yeah." We went upstairs and they gave me another exam—the Doc did.'

"Then they said, 'The lie detector says you're lying. Write out in your own words what happened.' This is when he wrote out the first statement. Then with this version, they came back and said, 'This account is no good. It's a lie. Why don't you tell the truth?'

"Harry said to me, 'Right then and there I realized I was getting into something.' "

(Is it possible that up until this point it had not occurred to him that somebody would not believe him!)

"Harry said, 'All right but I want to go talk to my father.' Then they said, 'All right, we'll take you up and you can talk to your father and then will you come back with us?' And he said he would.

"He went home in the company of the police and left with them. They made arrangements to go meet somebody. This turned out to be the Court Stenographer, Roberts."

McKeon: "It was late at night. Were you tired?"

Harry: "Yes, I was tired. . . . A man came with a machine and they questioned me some more. All this stuff they told me about."

"In the confession you admitted using the hammer, using the fork. Why?"

"Because that's what they said. They said that's what I did."

"How about 'still full of fight'?"

"That's what they told me to say."

McKeon: "Now after all this you're still telling me that's all you remember. How in hell could you sit there saying all that to police officers, hanging yourself?"

Harry: "They said that's how it happened. I don't remember."

"In the confession three or four times they asked if you killed her and you kept saying, 'That's my answer.' Why?"

Harry: "I didn't remember. Why would I kill her? I had no reason to kill her."

"He doesn't recall the exact hours. He knows he had something to eat. Then next thing he remembers is going to the Winsted Court House on the morning of the fifteenth. They ushered him into a room to talk to the Public Defender."

McKeon: "Did you ever have a lawyer?"
Harry: "No. My father knew Mr. Shew. The Public Defender told me from now on to say nothing. . . . After Court they drove me to jail and asked me some more questions."

"He told them the Public Defender said not to say anything more. They still asked more questions. They couldn't have thought they had a very good case if they were still pressing him."

During their talk, McKeon said, Harry sipped coffee and smoked a great deal. He smiled frequently. "He was impassive. At no point did he indicate emotional change."

Out of the entire interview one point remained uppermost in John McKeon's mind.

"I knew of the arrangement with Von Salzen to subject him to psychiatric treatment including possibly drugs and hypnosis in an effort to reconstruct the crime. Near the end I said to him, 'Why in hell didn't you take it? If you're innocent, it was all in your favor. If you have nothing to hide, you had nothing to lose.'

"He looked at me with that myopic stare—he didn't have his glasses on—and he said, 'I would rather go to jail for life, sent there by a jury, than to find out through an examination that I did this.'

"To me that is a complex statement," McKeon said. "I came away thinking he is either very stupid or very complex and I wasn't sure which."

Thursday, December 8

John McKeon has been pursuing the question of the hour of death. A few days ago he asked his personal physician, Dr. Maxwell Goldstein, of Hartford, an internist, for an opinion. Dr. Goldstein asked to read the official autopsy report, and McKeon delivered a copy to him.

Now he has had an answer. Dr. Goldstein said, "It is more likely that I could cross the Red Sea on foot than that that girl could have lived more than a few minutes after eating."

McKeon says the doctor is prepared to come into Court with charts and graphs to illustrate.

Friday, December 23

Earlier this week John McKeon went to visit the Burdicks —Dorothy's mother and father. "The house is like a Rockwell painting," he said. "Stark, barren, a plain kitchen—severe. The mother is stout and takes glycerine for her heart. They have very strong opinions against Solberg. They didn't talk about proclivities or tendencies, or say, 'We know he's the type.' They talked about his behavior at the trial—the way he was half-laughing. They didn't like his conduct. The fact that he slapped a girl was important to them."

Mrs. Burdick said that Dottie called her at 8:00 and at 10:20.

"What time did she eat lunch?" McKeon said. "One or two o'clock?"

Mrs. Burdick replied, "No. Every day at quarter to twelve."

Wednesday, December 28, 1966

The date and the place have been set. The trial will begin in Bridgeport on January 10. It will be held in a special courtroom in the Federal Courthouse, and a Judge has been especially assigned. He is Judge Douglass B. Wright.

Tuesday, January 3, 1967

Trial fever is building. The lawyers are rounding up witnesses. Dr. Opper is no longer in this area; he has moved to Maine. Mr. Shew has been trying to telephone him there, finally reached him at the hospital. Dr. Opper remembers that the contents of the stomach were mostly vegetable matter and fluid, which would be easily digested. Fluid passes through almost immediately. After rereading his report, Mr. Shew says, he told him that his estimate of the time necessary to digest this material would be about half an hour. In the event that she was tired or nervous, an hour at most. Dr. Opper is expected to come back to testify at the trial.

Mr. Wall has asked whether Mr. Shew is going to use Rome in the second trial, and Mr. Shew has said he doesn't know. The truth is that he has some doubts. The feeling against Rome is still high. Who is keeping it alive this way? This week a lawyer who has been active in state politics for many years commented, "Where did this hostility come from? And *why?* Why would a man go to trial without first consulting with the chief investigator whose reports he had, saying that someone else did it? Why would anyone even authorize issuance of a warrant—especially when it involved throwing away a first warrant that said somebody else did it? There was no rush. Time was no factor here. Nobody was getting on a plane and leaving. There was plenty of time to talk to him. And where was the Commissioner in all this? If he didn't know Canaan was going off on their own, why not? When the Canaan men came in with their findings, all he had to say was, 'Let's call Sam in and hear what he has to say.'

"Sam Rome has devoted his life to protecting the people, and the very people he's protecting are turning on him. And there's a powerful criminal element in this state. The Mafia would like to be rid of him. If everyone turns on him, he can't stand alone. He can't fight them all, although that's what he's doing now.

"He's a tremendous public servant—and who is there to defend him? He's one of the greatest defenders of our freedom we have!" Then, as though checking this emotional outburst, he shrugged. "At least someone should give reasons why he shouldn't be considered a public enemy."

This is the climate in which the second trial of Harry Solberg will begin—one week from today.

PART
FOUR

THE
SECOND TRIAL

20

The setting could not be more different. In Litchfield you would step out of the courthouse, on an Indian summer day, onto the sunny street bordered by the village green and the little shops, and a sense of incongruity would set in that in this storybook tranquility a murder trial was unfolding only a few yards away. Now on a gray raw day in January we came to an ugly bruised section of Bridgeport, to a former Underwood typewriter factory converted into a court building—an area of warehouses and smokestacks, pocked with gaping wounds of demolition and construction, with a low-cost housing project rising on one side, a superhighway overhead on the other.

But the players were the same. Mr. Wall, Mr. Shew, the Canaan Police, the reporters—Demeusy, Crowley, Chilson of the Waterbury *Republican*—the Solberg family, Harry. And two new players— John McKeon and Judge Douglass B. Wright. Aware that Judge Wright had been hand-picked for this special assignment, one awaited his arrival and watched with curiosity as he walked from the parking lot. (The reporters have supplied advance notices on him—a strong judge, a scholarly judge, the author of several volumes on Connecticut law, an intelligent and sensible man.) He is a striking-looking man—six feet four inches tall, slender, gray hair, a young face, fine-featured—a purposeful gait as he moved across the street to the court building. The federal courtroom, made available for this special trial, is on the fifth floor.

The first clash came before anyone had set foot in the courtroom. As soon as the Judge arrived Mr. Wall asked for a conference, and someone was sent to look for Mr. Shew, who at that moment was looking for a room he could use. As in Litchfield, there was an office for the State's Attorney but none for the Defense. Mr. Shew and Mr. McKeon entered Chambers and apparently within seconds all parties got off their first shots and several more. Mr. Wall charged that Mr. McKeon did not belong here, that he was in the case not to represent Harry Solberg but at the request of Rome and Demeusy, "who had an interest in seeing that Solberg did not enter any plea other than not guilty," and that he felt the Court should be satisfied that Solberg was represented by an attorney of his own choice.

"When he said that John was hired by Rome and Demeusy and the Hartford *Courant,* I absolutely exploded," Mr. Shew said later. "I said, 'Damn it, you're not in Litchfield now! I put up with all this stuff in Litchfield and I'm sick of it.' John had never discussed the case with Rome—he's not even on good terms with Rome and I told him that."

Mr. Wall produced an article from Monday morning's Hartford *Courant* and asked the Judge to note statements "attributed to Counsel for the Defense." The article read: "DEFENDERS CONFIDENT OF SOLBERG ACQUITTAL. Defense lawyers . . . said Sunday they are confident of an acquittal verdict. . . . [They] said they have uncovered 'startling new evidence' that fully supports Solberg's claim he is innocent. . . . This evidence, they added, will enable them to reconstruct the murder as it actually happened and to identify the real killer." (It also reviewed the history of the case and included Rome's opinion on who committed the crime.)

Mr. Shew denied that he or McKeon had made the statements. Mr. Wall shot back that the statements were similar to statements Mr. McKeon had made in interviews with witnesses and their neighbors. Mr. Shew said later that there were threats of going to the Grievance Committee—talk of having McKeon disbarred.

Mr. Wall emerged from Chambers, face red, head thrust forward, a thundercloud bent on destruction—with Mr. Shew right behind him, looking just as angry. John McKeon, totally unprepared for this encounter, was white. "If I'd been in this case alone, I'd have been out on the street by now!" he said to Demeusy. "You have to hand it to Bill, the way he gives it back to him."

On this happy note the voir dire began.

". . . The mere fact of his arrest carries no imputation of guilt—no taint of any sort," Judge Wright instructed the panel. The Judge has a sensitive, intelligent face and a restrained and patient way about him, but he speaks with authority. "He starts in your mind as innocent as a newborn baby, and he continues innocent in your mind until such time as the State proves beyond reasonable doubt that he is guilty. The burden of proving guilt beyond a reasonable doubt is on the State."

The panel was escorted to the jury assembly room. The first prospective juror, a lady, was called. In his slow, deliberate monotone Mr. Wall began. "Harry Solberg, the accused, has been indicted by the Grand Jury of murder in the first degree . . ." And on to the questions:

"Do you have any strong feelings on capital punishment?"

"Could you decide on the facts as you hear them in the courtroom?"

"If the Court charges you that sympathy has no place in your decision, could you take the law from the Judge?"

"What newspapers do you read?"

Mr. Shew's turn. "Have you read about the case in the newspapers?"

"Are you acquainted with any members of the State Police?"

"How do you get along with your mother-in-law?"

"Have you ever had a problem in your family with regard to care of the mentally ill?"

This is a stark, businesslike courtroom—light-oak plywood paneling, bright efficient lighting—smaller even than the court in Litchfield, with none of its charm. There is the traditional arrangement of the witness stand next to the bench with the jury box beyond it, against the wall. The attorneys' tables face the bench, with the State's table to the right, closer to the jury box, the Defense table to the left, closer to the press table, which is along the left wall. In the back of the room is a small section for spectators, and here, close together in the first row, sat Tobey and Solveig and Sharon Solberg. In the back row next to a center door were the Canaan police, who apparently were checking information on prospective jurors. They would duck out, return a few minutes later, and pass notes to Mr. Wall. Scattered about were a few court officials. Otherwise, there was no one.

In contrast to the packed courthouse in Litchfield, the room was almost empty.

"Do you have any preconceived ideas about capital punishment?"
"As long as I don't have to pull the switch, it's all right with me."

"Do you get along with your daughter-in-law?"
"She has turned my son against me. I'm an unwanted mother. They don't come to see me and I don't go to see them."

"Harry Solberg, the accused, has been indicted by the Grand Jury of murder in the first degree . . ." Mr. Wall had opened his questioning of each prospective juror with this statement. After a half-dozen persons had been questioned, Mr. McKeon objected to it and asked that the term "Grand Jury" be omitted. "It creates an inference of guilt in the mind of the uninitiated," he said. "To the average layman it predisposes the notion of guilt."

Mr. Wall was instantly indignant. "I think I am entitled to use it. That is a fact. Your Honor told them at the outset that the Defendant was as innocent as a newborn babe. That carries a great deal of weight."

"This insinuation is with them before they take their seats," Mr. McKeon persisted. "This is the lay mind."

Mr. Wall: "I believe the jurors are entitled to know."

Mr. Shew: "They already know."

The Judge suggested that Mr. Wall substitute the phrase, "Mr. Solberg has been indicted."

Mr. Wall [injured] "If it is considered improper—"

The Judge [calmly] "It is not improper, but if the fear exists, perhaps you might exorcise those words."

When he resumed, Mr. Wall said, "Harry Solberg has been *indicted* and *charged* with murder in the first degree in an *indictment* and if found guilty of murder in the first degree as *charged in the indictment* . . ."

By the end of the morning one juror, a man, had been accepted.

During the luncheon recess the second crisis erupted in Chambers. By now Mr. Wall had seen a copy of the previous evening's Bridgeport *Post,* which had carried a page-one story about the case, with statements similar to those in the morning Hartford *Courant.* Mr. Wall wanted another conference.

Later Mr. Wall prepared a written memorandum on both clashes in Chambers that day. In it he wrote, "I pointed out that the statements were clearly improper and that action in the nature of contempt proceedings against those responsible for printing them might be required. . . . Mr. Shew stated that I was out of my jurisdiction of Litchfield and that I could no longer be a 'little Hitler' as I was in my bailiwick and that if anything like this were resorted to he would have me cited for contempt for calling one of the witnesses a liar."

Mr. Shew's version: "Wall said he was going to report me to the Grievance Committee and I said, 'All right, let's stop right here. Everything. I want to report *you* to the Grievance Committee for calling Sam Rome a liar in open Court before the trial even started. Let's stop and we'll both go to the Grievance Committee.' Then Wall said McKeon was just here for Demeusy and Rome—to make sure we didn't plead guilty. And I said, 'Damn it, you're not in Litchfield County now. Stop being a Hitler.' "

The Judge asked Mr. Shew whether there was a possibility that Harry might plead guilty and Mr. Shew replied, "I might possibly let him plead guilty to passing a traffic light!" Mr. McKeon added, "Maybe following too closely."

The second lady questioned after lunch put a torch to the already smoldering fire. In reply to a question from Mr. Wall, she said that she had read last night's Bridgeport *Post* this morning in the jury assembly room! She hastened to add that at lunchtime she had put the newspaper in her car. Now, the heat generated in Chambers spread into open Court. Mr. Wall referred openly to the "inflammatory" story in the Bridgeport *Post, planted there* by the Hartford *Courant.* Mr. McKeon objected to Mr. Wall's statement that the story in the Bridgeport *Post* was planted by the *Courant.* He said this was prejudicial to the Defendant and asked Judge Wright to put a stop to it.

Instantly Mr. Wall was on his feet with a counterthrust. "An attempt is being made to prejudice prospective jurors against the

State in Fairfield County. . . . [Bristling] I'd like to call Mr. Demeusy to the stand."

Judge Wright firmly dismissed that demand. "We are not trying any collateral issues."

Mr. Wall raced on. "The statements in the article attributed to Counsel were highly improper. . . . If made, they represented a breach of ethics by the attorneys for the Defense. They claim they never said it—"

Abruptly Judge Wright cut in. "This trial will be conducted with all decorum if I have my way—which I intend to have." (This is a strong judge.) "The phrase 'planted by the Hartford *Courant*' should not go to the juror. You should restrict yourself to the question: Has he read the article."

Mr. Wall [crisp] "I did not wish to have inference that the Bridgeport *Post* is responsible. They are innocent. The article is a rehash of the Hartford *Courant*. Mr. Demeusy is here. I'd like to call Mr. Demeusy to the stand."

Mr. Shew: "I object to efforts to try the Hartford *Courant* and Major Rome and a lot of other things as before."

Mr. Wall continued to air his grievances, "I telephoned the publisher of the Hartford *Courant* and told him there had been highly inflammatory articles in the first trial. He agreed to look into it. I never heard from Mr. Reitmeyer. This article was designed on the part of Mr. Demeusy to bring about the same kind of atmosphere that existed in Litchfield. It shows his solidarity with the Defense Counsel."

The Judge: "If some of the articles get out of line, in accordance with the *Sheppard* case the Court may have to interfere with the conduct of the press. I don't expect that to happen. [To Mr. Wall] You may ask whether they have read the papers and ask them not to read them and I will back you on that. [Clearly ending it] This is the trial of Harry Solberg and nothing else."

At the press table Demeusy looked undisturbed. Richard Ondek, the young man from the Bridgeport *Post*, a newcomer to the case, looked perplexed.

[To a lady] "Did you read the Bridgeport *Post* yesterday?"

"I remember that the mother-in-law was accused and when they picked up the young man they dropped the case against her and she has since died."

"Do you remember reading quotations of statements by the lawyers?" No. "Do you remember whether it stated what Major Rome thinks now?"

"No, I don't remember that."

Excused by the State.

"Do you have any strong feelings on capital punishment?"

[An Irish brogue] "I don't like to see anyone die—have it on my shoulders."

Mr. Wall: "I'm sure you don't think *I* like to see anyone die."

[Soberly] "Nobody does." Then the most refreshing comments of the day. "I'd have to follow my own conscience . . . I'm a human being—right? I have sympathy for both sides. . . . I read that new evidence was being introduced and I guess that the Defense was confident of an acquittal."

The Judge: "Did the article affect your thinking about the case with impartiality?"

"We all read what one man says and we don't have to believe it. Like you said, all the evidence has to be in. This is a new case. [The brogue has a lilt to it.] I'm not affected. It's just something that somebody wrote—right?" Excused by the State.

After the afternoon recess the Judge handed copies of the criticized newspaper articles to all three attorneys. Immediately Mr. Wall asked to introduce them as Exhibits "in connection with the atmosphere that existed during the voir dire." Mr. Shew objected.

"There is no foundation yet, . . ." the Judge said, "but they may be marked for identification."

Mr. Wall: "I'd like to call Mr. Demeusy to the stand."

Mr. Shew: "I'd like to proceed with the trial."

"We are now engaged in picking a jury," the Judge said. "The news media is not the subject of our inquiry. The only question is whether any jurors have been so swayed as to be incapable of impartial opinion."

Mr. Wall [doggedly] "The articles should be available for jurors in the event they are examined relating to them. There is a question of fair trial here. I want to call Mr. Demeusy to the stand to testify whether they did appear. . . . Copied into the Bridgeport *Post* are the essential features of Mr. Demeusy's propaganda."

"Have them marked," the Judge said again. "If it becomes evident that some jurors have been swayed you may raise your question again."

The day ended with twenty-three persons having been interviewed and only three jurors selected. Four had been excused by the Court, nine by the Defense, seven by the State. With an emphasis born of the day's skirmishes, the Judge instructed the panel not to read about the case in any newspaper, or listen to radio or television reports or discuss it with anyone.

Then, at the close of the first day, Mr. McKeon introduced a new and more important factor into the trial. Yesterday, he said, the Defense had had a subpoena served on Lieutenant Fuessenich, instructing him to appear in Court today with all the tape recordings of the police questioning of Harry Solberg. Lieutenant Fuessenich had apparently ignored the subpoena. At once Mr. Wall came forward to say that it would be an imposition to ask Fuessenich to be in Court with the tapes when the trial had not even started. Mr. McKeon replied that the lieutenant was not at liberty to ignore a subpoena. The Judge, turning to Mr. McKeon first, asked his purpose.

"I want the witness to appear with the tapes," Mr. McKeon replied. "I want to be sure the tapes remain in the custody of the Court."

Mr. Wall [authoritative] "The Defense will have them at the proper time."

The Judge: "Are you claiming the tapes might be altered?"

Mr. Wall put in that there was no possibility of the tapes being cut. "If Counsel had asked me to have them here, we would have. It is an imposition to ask Lieutenant Fuessenich to remain—"

The Judge turned to Mr. Wall. "Do you oppose the Defense seeing and listening to these tapes now?"

"I do, Your Honor."

To put the picture into proper perspective, the Judge asked whether the tapes were played at the first trial. Then, reasonably,

"Why can't the lieutenant deposit them with the Court and go about his business?"

"I'm not sure that it is proper—" Mr. Wall began.

"I'm not passing on whether it's proper. He can deposit the tapes with the Court and not sit here for ten days."

"They're not entitled to them!" Mr. Wall protested.

The Judge ended the matter by ordering Pennington to tell Fuessenich to bring the tapes to the courthouse the next day at his convenience. The first day was over.

•   •   •

On Wednesday morning the Hartford *Courant* headline:

Solberg Defense Wins Point
POLICE MUST SURRENDER TAPES

The article reported that Judge Wright, over Mr. Wall's protest, ordered that Fuessenich bring the tapes to Court today, and that Mr. McKeon had complained that Fuessenich had apparently disregarded a subpoena. "Judge Wright asked Wall if he had any objection to the defense listening to the tapes. Wall said he did object. . . . Wall insisted the defense 'is not entitled to the tapes.' "

Also reported was Mr. Wall's charge that the *Courant* had planted the "highly inflammatory" story in the Bridgeport *Post*.

When Court opened, Fuessenich was there with the tapes, and Mr. Wall promptly said that the lieutenant wanted to make a statement "to overcome the impression in headlines in the Hartford *Courant* that the State was suppressing evidence—and that he had disregarded a subpoena." Fuessenich's statement was that he had tried unsuccessfully to telephone Defense Counsel to find out when he was expected to appear.

Mr. Wall: "I think we're entitled to an apology from the Hartford *Courant* and the attorneys."

Mr. McKeon: "We are not apologists for the Hartford *Courant*, but we will stand on the record of what was said on Tuesday concerning the subpoena."

With Lieutenant Fuessenich on the stand, Mr. McKeon determined, in preliminary questioning, that altogether there were seven tapes—two covering the questioning in Canaan on Sunday, March 13; two covering the questioning later on Sunday by Lieutenant Riemer in the polygraph suite in Hartford (hinting at what we have long suspected—that the lie-detector tests were quite a bit more than just that); two more covering Riemer's questioning on Monday, March 14. And a seventh tape recorded in Canaan very late March 14 and early March 15, after Harry was officially arrested.

Over repeated objections by Mr. Wall to this questioning on the tapes, Mr. McKeon asked, "After this was over and the tapes were put into boxes for storage, where did they remain? . . . Have you heard them played back lately? . . . Do they substantially resemble those interviews as you remember them?"

But this morning Mr. Wall had advised Judge Wright that he was willing, after all, to play the tapes for Defense Counsel and a time and place had already been arranged. They were to be played tomorrow evening (Thursday) beginning at 7:30 in Mr. Wall's motel room. The Judge asked a single question of Fuessenich. "Were any alterations made in the tapes?" and Fuessenich replied, "No, sir." The Judge indicated that the discussion was over.

A final statement from Mr. Wall: "There has been an inference in the Hartford papers that I am trying to suppress these tapes. I want it understood that the State has always been willing to produce them. There was never a request until this outburst yesterday."

So the tapes, so carefully circumvented last time, are going to be heard at last—at least by Counsel for the Defense. Among veteran observers of this case there is a feeling, for the first time, of the clenched fist of the State beginning to open.

The voir dire continued.

A gentleman who had followed the first trial in the papers. Did he reach any conclusion? "I reached the conclusion that it was all mixed up. That was the conclusion that I reached."

A lady who followed the last trial very closely—feels she *knows* who did it. Excused by the Court.

"I feel everyone called to jury duty should serve." Accepted.

"The punishment should fit the crime." Excused by the Defense.

A man who, for no particular reason, tells us that in 1927 he drove a Model T from Los Angeles in sixteen days, wishes he could find one today, but you couldn't get new parts. Excused.

Just after lunch the first panel was exhausted and a new one brought in, addressed by the attorneys, and instructed by the Judge.

"I couldn't consider the death penalty. I can't see where it would be up to me to take another person's life." Excused by the Court.

A lady who has a married son living next door. "I get along with his wife better than he does." Excused by the Defense.

A lady who was sick with worry. "I lost a night's sleep. I work so hard to save lives—for organizations like the cancer society—I don't know if I could live with myself the rest of my life." Excused by the Court.

By the end of the day, four more jurors had been picked. In two days fifty-three persons had been examined. Eighteen had been excused by the Court, eighteen by the Defense, ten by the State. Seven had been accepted. The Jury now consisted of four women and three men.

* * *

On Thursday morning, a third panel. The judge instructed them: ". . . The mere fact of his arrest carries no imputation of guilt, no taint of any sort. He starts in your minds as innocent as a newborn babe . . ."

Mr. Wall: "Harry Solberg has been *indicted by the proper authority* and charged with murder in the first degree in an *indictment* and if found guilty of murder in the first degree as *charged in the indictment* . . ."

Mr. Shew: "Did you ever hear the name Major Samuel Rome?" The question was being asked regularly, and each time Mr. Wall seemed to bristle, although Major Rome had not yet appeared in Court in Bridgeport.

Mr. Wall: "If you were *sure* the person was guilty of murder in the first degree and if the crime were so aggravated and so brutal . . ."

Mr. McKeon: "Could you follow the law that the Defendant must be proved guilty beyond a reasonable doubt?"

Mr. Wall: "Harry Solberg has been *indicted by the proper authority* and charged with murder in the first degree in an *indictment* and if found guilty of murder in the first degree as *charged in the indictment* . . ." Having been asked to delete his reference to the Grand Jury, Mr. Wall was delivering this lengthy statement to each prospective juror.

The explosion was inevitable. It came just before lunch. When Mr. Wall finished questioning the prospective juror on the stand, Mr. Shew strode forward. "Do you know what an indictment is?"

"I'm not sure. It has something to do with a Grand Jury."

Mr. Shew: "Do you know that at the Grand Jury a Defendant has no opportunity to defend himself?" Mr. Wall leaped to his feet. Mr. Shew swung around. "Do you want to say something, Mr. Wall?"

"Not while *you're* talking!" Mr. Wall whipped around and took his seat.

When Mr. Shew finished, Mr. Wall had a great deal to say. "Your Honor *requested* me, *not ordered*, to refrain from asking questions including the word Grand Jury. I have acceded to the *letter* of Your Honor's request. Now questions asked by Counsel for the Defense have brought out matters involving the Grand Jury. . . . I have voluntarily muzzled myself from use of those words. . . . It is unfair to imply to this juror that there is something unfair in the use of the word indictment. . . . It is manifestly unfair to ask the State to observe voluntarily this restriction while the Defense implies there is impropriety to use of the word indictment."

Mr. Shew [indignant] "Mr. Wall repeated three times 'indicted by the proper authority'!"

Mr. Wall [challenging] "Then I am released from restrictions on the use of the word?"

Mr. Shew [to the witness] "Could you consider Harry Solberg as innocent as a newborn babe unless the State proved otherwise?"

Mr. Wall: "I have objection to the use of the simile, 'innocent as a newborn babe.'"

Judge Wright showed surprise. "He quoted me."

Mr. Wall: "I object to the question being asked of the witness. I object to the Court use of a simile as strong as that. A newborn baby couldn't possibly have committed this crime and this defendant *could* have."

The Judge commented mildly that he was required to charge the Jury that they should begin free of bias and prejudice.

Mr. Wall: "The second time Your Honor didn't use the phrase. I thought Your Honor had eliminated it." (With the third panel the Judge had included the phrase again.) Mr. Wall dropped into his chair and, for some reason, threw a cold smile at the press table.

The Judge took off his glasses and smiled. "I have used the term for fifteen years and it has always stood up until now. This is the first objection I have had to this term."

Mr. Shew [disgusted] "Mr. Wall likes to have an advantage before he begins. He doesn't like to play unless he has an advantage. We will try to see this time that he does not have one."

Mr. Wall to his feet again. "I think it is unfortunate that Counsel has related dissatisfaction with my conduct in the past. I move that the words be stricken from the record."

The Judge: "It was in the absence of the Jury and no harm has been done. [Then abruptly] If you feel that the State has been prejudiced by the statement, I will release this entire panel and get a new panel."

Mr. Wall [stunned] "I don't want this panel excused! I don't want this juror excused!"

(We had almost forgotten that there was still a prospective juror on the stand.) Then suddenly both Mr. Wall and Mr. Shew said they had no objection to this juror and no further questions of him and the juror was accepted! He went into the jury room. One could imagine him telling his fellow jurors that this promised to be quite a trial!

The second lady questioned after lunch was accepted and became number twelve and the Jury was complete. As in Litchfield, it appeared to be a representative cross-section—six men and six women, old and young, college graduates, salespeople, factory workers, housewives, retired businessmen, all ethnic groups—Italian, Negro, Polish, English. Two alternates, a man and a woman, were accepted quickly, and at three o'clock the voir dire ended.

Once again it had been the seedbed in which issues were nurtured and animosities put down strong roots. The Hartford *Courant* appeared to have pushed aside all other contenders as Mr. Wall's most favored enemy. The issue of press coverage of the trial could no longer in any sense be considered peripheral. Mr. Wall's resentment of Mr. McKeon had become openly apparent. And, most important, the issue had been raised of the police interrogation of Harry Solberg, who was still the Defendant in this trial—even though for hours at a time this fact was obscured by smoke from hotter fires.

The first few tapes were to be played tonight in Mr. Wall's room at the Howard Johnson Motor Lodge in Stratford, just a mile or so up the highway. According to Mr. Shew, even while they were making the final arrangements, Mr. Wall charged that this was just another excuse to make headlines for the Hartford *Courant*.

• • •

At 3:11 the Clerk of the Court, Mr. Ralph Scofield, read the indictment and the trial began—this time with Lieutenant Fuessenich, not Arnfin, as the first witness. In the remaining two hours of the afternoon Mr. Wall, through the witness, set the scene and began to fill in the details of the crime, ending the day with the introduction of a single photograph of the battered body.

And now the reaction of the Jury—the sudden shock produced by the photograph—the reluctant insight into brutality pushed to this extreme—eyes frozen a long moment on the picture and then, pained and puzzled, raised to look at Harry—searching to see whether this mild-appearing boy could have done this hideous thing—not expecting to find the answer—just looking. And the day ended.

• • •

It was inconceivable that the listening session that evening would go off smoothly and it did not. It got off, at once, to a bad start. A few minutes after Mr. Shew and Mr. McKeon entered the room, one of the police officers picked up a damaged disk that had broken off the door knob and said, "Look—someone's been fiddling with the lock!" The episode hung over the evening like a lead weight.

The tapes began with the warnings of his rights given Harry that Sunday morning in Canaan by Rebillard. Mr. McKeon was shocked. (The next day he said, "When they told him of his rights it was all delivered in the same stroke—the same breath. It meant absolutely nothing. They said it so fast and he was so nervous. They said, 'First I gotta tell you, Harry, you have a right to remain silent.' They just tossed it off. 'And—uh—you've got a right to counsel. . . .' And Harry said, 'Yeah.' It was absolutely meaningless!")

The tapes revealed that Rebillard questioned Harry first, and then Fuessenich took over. In Shew and McKeon, furiously taking notes, a slow burn set in. (Mr. Shew—the next day: "They played with him like a cat with a mouse. It was like pictures I'd seen of a leopard toying with his prey. Those devils could have gotten him to say anything. At the end of the evening I was so burning mad I said, 'If you sons-of-bitches did that to a son of mine I'd gut-shoot you!' Wall said, 'I think it was a very clever piece of police work.'")

At 10:55, after a little more than three hours, the tapes covering the Sunday interrogation at Canaan ended, and Mr. Wall invited his guests to leave. Once outside, McKeon turned to Shew. For three hours he had been growing increasingly worried about the episode of the broken door disk. What had seemed at first only a bad joke took on an ominous flavor, and McKeon was actually afraid that he and Shew might be accused of jimmying the lock to get the tapes. He insisted on reporting the incident at the motel office. Finding a notary public on duty, he gave him this sworn statement:

"Statement taken at 11:09 P.M. January 12, 1967.

"I, JOHN MCKEON, over 21 years of age, being of sound mind and body, do hereby depose and say:

"At approximately 7:45 P.M. William Shew and myself entered room 134 and we were allowed there by Superior Court Order, signed by Judge Douglass Wright, to listen to tape recordings. Present at this hearing were the following: State's Attorney Thomas Wall; also State Policemen: Lieutenant Fuessenich, Officers Rebillard, Pennington and Holden. Approximately five minutes after we were in the room, one of the officers remarked that the door to their room and lock had been tampered with. One of them showed us then, half-jokingly, a disturbed and detached portion ostensibly of the door and/or lock thereto. The hearing of the tapes then transpired until approximately 10:55 P.M. We were then invited to leave by the State's Attorney, Thomas Wall. Feeling that perhaps this business of a tampered lock might be a device employed by the State Police to embarrass or harm the undersigned Attorneys and their client, Solberg, and his cause, we reported this immediately to the night auditor on duty at the Howard Johnson Motor Lodge, Stratford, Conn."

The next day Mr. Shew said, "John came out of there scared. I had to stop him from calling the Bridgeport Police and giving a statement to them. He was afraid of what these people would do. It was a fear born of the tapes—listening for hours to what they did—because of the pressure they exerted on Harry. The boy just didn't have a chance."

"I'm shocked," McKeon said. "This is like burning witches. There are five more tapes. I don't think we need them for *Miranda*. The first two are enough."

21

"Lieutenant, by virtue of your position as commanding officer . . . at Canaan, were you in charge of this investigation on June 15, 1965?"

"Yes, sir."

With this as foundation, Mr. Wall continued, through Fuessenich, to fill in the details of the crime. Much of a retrial is repetitious (how could it be otherwise?) and for old hands this was a slow morning. Seventeen photographs introduced with long waits while, as before, Fuessenich acted as guide and interpreter, pointing out details.

One studies the Judge. He is at ease on the bench, sits quite still, is a careful listener. Remembering his competence during the voir dire, one sees now a firmness in the mouth and chin—and humor, too, to maintain a sense of proportion, although on the bench he rarely smiles. One looks at the Jury—attentive and sober, shocked at these bloody details they must examine and absorb. Fuessenich is articulate and precise as he describes the events, the articles, the condition of Dorothy's body, the appearance of her clothing. He makes a good impression. His manner on the stand invites confidence.

Mr. Wall is calm today, although all the nervous mannerisms are evident. He rocks on his heels—his sentences, delivered in a neutral monotone, are studded with "uh, uh"—his mouth narrows at an objection, his face shows a quick flush when he is angry. He seems most hostile while he is waiting. While questioning Fuessenich or handing photographs to the Jury, he is pleasant and courteous, but in the pauses, while he waits for court business to catch up with him, it is as though he remembers then all the slings and arrows of this case, and he purses his mouth until the lips become a thin half-circle turned down.

Yesterday Mr. Wall introduced the floor plan, the forks and the nail set; today, the toaster, the cord, the hammer, the rock (proper emphasis on the rock). Quite early he brought out the fact that Agnes Thompsen had lived upstairs and that a single entrance served the two households. Just after recess he offered something new—a photograph taken five days after the crime from the window in Agnes Thompsen's bedroom, looking down to the back porch. (What would this have done to the last verdict, if it had been available?) Surprisingly, Mr. Shew suggested that perhaps this might come later—it would take too much time now—and Mr. Wall remarked that he had thought Defense Counsel would probably want it and withdrew it for the present.

Fuessenich continued with testimony about the sledgehammer found in the woods, and the table fork, the bloody sponge, and the rock found beside the body. He said there were no fingerprints— only a partial palmprint found on the toaster, never identified. By noon the picture had been pretty much filled in.

"Now, you say you were in charge of this whole investigation, Lieutenant?"

"Yes, sir, up to a point."

To Mr. Wall the question had been a foundation for the lieutenant's testimony. To Mr. Shew it was a launching pad. "What point?"

"The point when it was taken over by the Detective Division in Hartford . . . the following Monday."

"And who was in charge of the Detective Division in Hartford?"

[Crisp] "Major Samuel Rome."

Mr. Shew pressed for details of the shift in command. "At the meeting at which Major Rome assumed command . . . was the Commissioner there?" He was not. "Well, was Major Rome appointed by Commissioner Mulcahy? . . . Or would he automatically take charge because of his rank, superseding you?"

"Yes," Fuessenich said, "that would be general practice."

"So that, whether he was ordered by Commissioner Mulcahy or not, he would take charge?"

"Yes, ordinarily he would." (This is not what is reported elsewhere. Rome, himself, testified that he must wait to be assigned.) The point had been made—Major Rome had been placed in the wings—and Mr. Shew moved to another subject. "Lieutenant, do you have any records of what you did that night? Do you keep a record . . . a log? Or are you quoting from memory?"

"Some of the things I am quoting from memory, sir. Some of the things . . . are noted in the log."

[Easy start] "I am trying to find out what the practice is. . . . Don't you keep a record in your barracks of your activities . . . ?"

"Yes, sir, generally speaking." (The tone is still authoritative, the words are becoming vague.)

[Quicker] "And have you such a record for that evening?"

"I have a record of some of the things that I did, I believe, yes."

[To the point] "And where is that record, Lieutenant?"

"Part of it is in the file. I may have notes from which I made that record. [Backing off] My activities that night were general in nature. And there were very few things of which I have made a written notation."

Mr. Shew: "Well, would you not make a written record of the members of your department that were there?" Not necessarily. "So that we have no records of what members of your department were at the scene that evening?" Fuessenich explained that he could find that out: the men themselves made notations of having been there. Mr. Shew [incredulous] "Do you mean you have to go through the whole State Police Force and find out from each individual whether he was there that night?"

"No, sir, not the whole State Police Force. Merely those men who were on duty that day . . . at the Canaan Barracks." (Impatient muttering at the press table. Everyone knows that he would not have to go scrounging about to each man in order to get this information.) Also, Fuessenich added, there were men present from the Detective Division. "These records are available."

Mr. Shew: "Well, don't you think we should have them, Lieutenant?"

"Well, you can have them if you wish. . . . As far as I am concerned I see no purpose in it . . . but the information is available."

For a moment Mr. Shew looked at Fuessenich. Then he asked him to have that information for him on Tuesday, and Fuessenich said he would do so.

The Cross-Examination was turning out to be far less routine than Direct Examination. Mr. Shew asked now for another piece of information. "Lieutenant, did you ascertain that night who was the last person to see the deceased alive?"

[Efficient] "We believed at the time that we had, yes, sir." Who did he believe that person was? [Restrained smile] "Christa."

Mr. Shew [patient] "And next to Christa, who did your investigation disclose was the last person to see the deceased?"

"I can't say beyond that point, sir."

"Oh, Lieutenant! You mean you left that place that night without knowing who, outside of Christa, was the last person to see the deceased?"

[Flat] "I'm speaking from my own information, sir."

"Well, you had charge of this." Yes. "And before you left, didn't you find out?"

"Yes, sir, we believed we knew. However, I can't be certain of that." (Fuessenich very much of a purist now about what he knows of his own knowledge.) Then a partial answer. "As I remember . . . Christa had had a child playing with her during the day."

"And who was the child playing with her that day?"

"I'm not positive whether we knew this that night or whether we found that out the following day. This is why I hesitated to say definitely."

"Your records must show that."

"Yes, sir, they would."

(*Everyone* knows that Mr. Shew has learned that someone interviewed Randy Stadler. In this case there are no secrets anymore.)

Mr. Shew: "Well, wouldn't you normally think it would be important to interview the last outside person that saw the deceased?" Yes, sir. "And . . . to do it as quickly as possible?" Yes, sir. [Sharper] "So you probably did, did you not?"

"This may have been done. I cannot tell you offhand without checking the record."

"What excuse would you have for not doing it?"

"There would be no excuse. There might be a good reason . . .

[A wide swing from the point] The person might not be available."

Mr. Shew [edged] "Do you know *now* whether that person was interviewed that evening?"

[Stolid] "I cannot tell without checking the records."

Mr. Shew [quite sharp] "You are coming in here and testifying that you are not able to tell of your own knowledge whether that was done. Do you want to go on record as stating that, Lieutenant?"

Still Fuessenich held that he could not say without checking the records, and Mr. Shew reminded him that he was to produce those records on Tuesday. "And will they then give me the information I am trying to elicit from you, do you think?" Yes, sir. "Will they show who, if anybody, interviewed that person?" Yes, sir. "And will they have the information that you derived from that person?" Yes, sir.

(The exchange does not sit well. It should not be necessary to wrench out information that was gained while in a position of public trust. The officer was not at the scene in his own self-interest. His responses should not be guided by self-interest now. He was there and he is here by reason of a public trust.)

Did the police, Mr. Shew asked, make a floor plan of the second floor of the house, as well as the first floor? Fuessenich said they did not. "We felt it was not necessary."

"You thought it was not necessary! You do know who lived upstairs, Lieutenant?" The subject introduced, Mr. Shew asked what investigation was made of Agnes Thompsen that night and, hurdling a few objections, he brought out—just before the luncheon recess—that she had been a patient in a mental hospital and was returned to the hospital that night.

After lunch it turned out that Fuessenich had found some information about the interview of Randy Stadler. The officer was Detective Lester Redican of the Detective Division.

Mr. Shew: "And what conversation did he have with this boy?"

Objection. "This is entirely hearsay," Mr. Wall protested. "It's a three-year-old child. I can't see the relevancy. There was nothing brought out on Direct relating to it."

The Judge: "If it's hearsay, I must sustain the objection."

Fuessenich had a report in hand and Mr. Shew asked to see it. Objection. Mr. Wall hurried forward. "There was no examination in connection with it. It is not in exhibit."

Mr. Shew: "I will examine it, Mr. Wall. [Firmly] *You* stand over there."

Mr. Wall [testy] "I think we could save time, Your Honor. This has nothing to do with the case at all."

Mr. Shew [lashing back] "*Save what time?* [Sharp turn] Lieutenant, what have you got in your possession right now?"

"Object to that, Your Honor. It's immaterial what the lieutenant has in his possession."

Mr. Shew: "Maybe it isn't. Let's find out."

The Judge directed Fuessenich to answer the question. Mr. Wall plowed over to the jury box and back to center court. Fuessenich said, "I have a list of State's personnel—"

Mr. Shew: "Mr. Wall, I would be very happy if you sat in your chair."

Mr. Wall [sudden switch] "May he answer the question, Your Honor."

Again Fuessenich was directed to answer and now, for the first time, we heard the complete list of State personnel who were in the Thompsen home that night: Fuessenich, Soliani (the first man to arrive), Rebillard, Pennington, Redican, Ragazzi, Captain O'Brien, Yuknat (the CSBI man), Sergeants Riley and Chapman (the photographers), Policewoman Butler, Salafia and Detective Jacobs (who accompanied Agnes back to the hospital), and a few new names, Lieutenant Donald Paige, Troopers John Bonolo, and Donald Simmons (all of the Detective Division).

Back to the interview of Randy Stadler. (Mr. Wall still pacing, pacing. Once he is on his feet he seems to find it impossible to stand still.) The record does not reveal the place or the hour, but it does indicate that Redican interviewed Randy that evening. Mr. Shew asked whether anyone was with Redican at the time. And we were off and running again.

Objection: Hearsay. "If Detective Redican is wanted as a witness he is available." Again the question: Was anybody with Redican? Again objection. "The best evidence is Redican, and he is ready to testify at any time."

Mr. Shew: "Well, Mr. Wall, there may be somebody else who is able to testify. I am trying to find out. I believe I am entitled to it. I don't know what you are covering up."

[Bridling] "I object to any statement that the State is covering up anything. The State is very happy to have all the witnesses in."

The Judge asked Fuessenich whether Detective Redican had another police officer with him when he questioned Randy Stadler. And at last the names. Trooper John Bonolo and Captain O'Brien were with Redican.

(The press table: "Shew is a changed man! He's really giving it back this time.)

Mr. Shew: "Did you go upstairs to Agnes Thompsen's apartment that evening?"

Fuessenich went up the following morning. To say who accompanied him, he would have to consult the record. Mr. Shew digressed to ask where all these records were at the present time.

"All the records are in the State's Attorney's file." Then: ". . . All the records of the Canaan investigation are in Mr. Wall's file. . . . There may be some records from the Detective Division . . . in Hartford."

Concerning his actions in Agnes Thompsen's apartment, Fuessenich testified that he supervised a search there the following day.

Mr. Shew: "Did you find anything that you thought might be important?"

"There were a number of things which at that time were questionable. They would be considered important at that time." And what were those things? "Again without looking at the record, I cannot tell you offhand what they were." (This in effect is asking Fuessenich the important items taken to the laboratory from Agnes Thompsen's apartment, and Fuessenich cannot think of a thing! There is not one of us who attended the first trial who could not rattle off quite a list.)

Mr. Shew [light sarcasm] "Well, perhaps I can help you remember. Did you take the traps off anything up there?" Yes, sir. "Well, now, Lieutenant, you remembered that without any prompting, didn't you?"

"No, sir, it had slipped my mind. This happened later in the afternoon and it had slipped my mind."

[Plainly disbelieving] "In the first trial, that was quite a bit in issue, was it not, in your presence?" Yes. "And it slipped your mind?" Yes, sir.

A long doubting look at Fuessenich. Then: "Did you find a bloody towel up there?"

Mr. Wall: "I object to this. It doesn't have any relevancy to this case at all that I can see."

Mr. Shew: "Well, I will try to show you, Mr. Wall, if you can't see it."

"It is not part of the Direct Examination."

"This whole investigation was part of it, Your Honor."

Mr. Wall [snap] "If it is considered part of the Defendant's case, he will have an opportunity to put the evidence on at a later time."

Mr. Shew [coming right back] "If Your Honor please, I prefer to try my own case in my own way."

The Judge ruled that the question was proper.

Mr. Wall: "I object to it on the further ground that he is talking about a bloody towel. There is no such thing as a bloody towel. That is just waving a flag."

Mr. Shew: "I am not asking *you* to testify, Mr. Wall. If there isn't one, he can say so."

The Judge questioned Mr. Shew, and Mr. Shew replied that it was mentioned in the first trial.

Mr. Wall [positive] "There was no such thing as a bloody towel mentioned in the first trial, Your Honor."

The Judge: "If this is just a shot in the dark I must sustain the objection."

Mr. Shew: "It certainly is not a shot in the dark!" (*Everyone* knows that Mr. Shew is after the blood-spotted dishcloth but has mistakenly called it a towel.) Further questions of Fuessenich did nothing to straighten out the error. "Was there a towel found in Agnes Thompsen's apartment?" Several. "One was given to Dr. Stolman, was it not?" Not to the lieutenant's knowledge.

"All right—describe the towels found in Agnes's apartment."

Fuessenich [innocent tone] "They were a normal type of towel that would be found in anyone's house. There was nothing unusual about these towels."

"Did you examine the stairs going up to Agnes Thompsen's apartment?" He did. Nothing unusual about them, either, that Fuessenich could remember. Mr. Shew elicited the information that Agnes Thompsen said she had sanded the stairs that afternoon. Now Mr. McKeon had supplied the correct information about the dishcloth, and Mr. Shew asked, "Lieutenant, do you recall a white dishcloth with yellow stripes which was found near the sink in Agnes Thompsen's apartment with spots on it that proved to be human blood?"

"Yes, sir, I do."

"Well, when I asked you if you found anything unusual up there, you didn't feel a dishcloth with blood on it was unusual?"

[Smoothly] "This was not shown to be blood until it went to the laboratory."

[Hard] "You knew there was blood on it at the time you were testifying just now?" Yes, sir. [Ringing] "It did go to the laboratory. It was found to have blood on it. You did not think that was unusual?" No, sir.

(It sounds lame.)

"Lieutenant, did you get a report on what they found in the traps?"

Mr. Wall [cutting in] "Your Honor, we intend to have Dr. Stolman here. He is under subpoena. If Counsel wishes to shorten up the case, we would be very happy to have Dr. Stolman come down and give his full testimony relating to this."

Mr. Shew [*This subject* still infuriates him] "You didn't before I got this in, Mr. Wall."

"He was under my subpoena and ready to come."

"He didn't come. Please sit down, Mr. Wall. I want to try this case my own way."

"I think it is courteous for me to stand when addressing the Court."

Again Mr. Shew asked what was found in the traps.

Fuessenich: "There were minute traces of blood found in the traps."

(Shades of the other trial! Dr. Stolman had used the term "minute trace of blood" once—with reference to an admittedly unimportant object, the icepick—and Mr. Wall then had applied the description to everything, which had precipitated quite an argument.)

Mr. Shew: "Human blood, Lieutenant?"

"Animal blood."

"Animal blood!"

Fuessenich: "May I explain that? It could be human or animal. They couldn't tell what. But it was of that type."

[Sharp] "Then when you said it was *animal blood*, you didn't mean that, did you?"

"No, I meant that it was of that type. It couldn't be identified further."

(This is wrong! In the last trial Dr. Stolman testified that the blood in the traps was *human blood*, but that he was not able to determine the *blood type*. Report #2301.)

Mr. Shew: "Do you know what kind of blood was on the yellow and white dishcloth?"

Fuessenich [again] "It was the human-animal type."

(Dr. Stolman's testimony: Human blood, unable to type. Report #2321.)

Mr. Shew: "What kind of blood was found on the floor of the house?"

Fuessenich: "That was human blood."

It had been agreed in Chambers that Court would adjourn today around midafternoon, and now, having reached a possible stopping point, Mr. Shew said he would not object to adjournment at this time, but he requested that Fuessenich remain on the stand after the Jury was excused.

When the Jury had gone, Mr. McKeon addressed Lieutenant Fuessenich. "You have a document there which contains an interview of the last known witness to see the victim alive outside the immediate family. Is that true?"

Mr. Wall objected to questioning by Mr. McKeon on the ground that Mr. Shew had been the one to conduct the Cross-Examination. Mr. Shew made the request instead. He asked that Redican's report of the interview of Randy Stadler be impounded.

Mr. Wall: "Impounded! If they wanted to see it, they could have asked me, and I would have been very happy to have them see it. There is no question about it. If they want to look at it now, they can look at it." (In view of the effort it took to get even the name of the officer, this falls rather flat.) "There has never been any question about anything of this sort where Counsel wants to look at something. They are entitled to look at it. If they wish to take a look at it, they can."

Judge Wright ordered the document marked for identification.

Mr. Shew: "Mr. Wall has stated that he has no objection to our reading it, Your Honor."

Mr. Wall: "I think it has no part in the case here now."

The Judge: "As I understand it, over the weekend, you want me to seize this exhibit?"

Mr. Wall: "Your Honor, if he merely asked me for it, I would be very happy to have him have it. In fact, he may take it for the weekend. . . . And he could have had it by merely asking me."

Mr. Shew: "I didn't know it was there, Mr. Wall."

Commenting that it was just as well to have it marked, the Judge handed the report to Mr. Shew. "You are loaned that for the weekend."

Still the day was not over. Mr. McKeon wished to bring another matter before the Court. With Fuessenich about to be excused, Judge Wright took a moment to clarify which records he was to produce on Tuesday.

"I want him to bring everything that is now available to him," Mr. Shew said. "Also the records that were sent back to Hartford after the other trial. I have subpoenaed them by others. But if the lieutenant brings them, we can be sure they are here."

The Judge inquired whether Fuessenich had not said that the Hartford records were under another control, and Fuessenich replied that he could get them. Remembering the first trial one cannot believe that this is the end of *this matter*, but for now Fuessenich was excused.

"Your Honor, this is in connection with a subpoena directed to Lieutenant Fuessenich to produce seven tapes," Mr. McKeon began. Mr. Wall, pacing, quickly turned. "The tapes have been marked for identification. Now last evening—"

Mr. Wall [whipping forward] "May I see the subpoena, please? I haven't even seen that."

Mr. McKeon: "Well, Your Honor, this is a matter of record—"

Mr. Wall [a challenge from Mr. McKeon always triggers his temper] "There should be a subpoena here in Court, Your Honor. If there is some talk about a subpoena, there should be one here in Court. . . . I have never seen any such thing, and nothing has been presented to the Court concerning such a subpoena. May I see the subpoena, Your Honor?"

Four days had produced an immunity to these attacks, and Mr. McKeon held his ground. "We listened to two of those tapes last night," he said. "The remainder of the tapes, even though they are Court's Exhibits, are still in the custody of the State Police." Now the effects of the broken door disk! "There is a chance that those tapes can be purloined by interests inimical to the Defendant. . . . The State's Attorney reported that the lock to the door of the room where those tapes were last night had been tampered with."

(In the back row the Canaan men doubled over with laughter.)

Mr. McKeon asked the Court to impound the tapes and place them in the Court safe. "Frankly, Your Honor, I intend to press before this Court the *Miranda versus Arizona* case. [Reading from the decision] 'A heavy burden rests on the State to demonstrate that the Defendant knowingly and intelligently waived his privilege against self-incrimination and his right to retain counsel.' The best possible evidence on that is contained in those tapes. . . . The State Police in this case are antagonistic to the interests of the Defendant. . . . It is very much like putting the fox to guard the chicken coop for them to have those tapes now. I urgently request that they be impounded."

Mr. Wall [ignoring all this] "Your Honor, first I would like to see the subpoena that this attorney says was served. . . . I have never seen the subpoena, Your Honor. The subpoena has never been served on Lieutenant Fuessenich. May I see it, sir?"

(It has been fairly obvious that the subpoena was served. Fuessenich stated that he tried to contact Defense Counsel to ask when he was wanted.)

The Judge: "Let's cut across all this preliminary argument to the fact that we already have marked seven tapes. Where are they now?"

Mr. Wall: "They are in the possession of Lieutenant Fuessenich, Your Honor. [Then off on another byway] I might say that . . . the statement is absolutely untrue by Counsel relating to any attempt at a break."

The Judge: "I don't believe for a second that there was an attempt to alter these tapes. But I am just asking you, Mr. Wall, why not give them to the Clerk over the weekend?"

Mr. Wall [put-upon tone] "I haven't listened to them myself, Your Honor!"

(*This* is a surprise! A boy is standing trial for first-degree murder for the second time—he is facing a possible death sentence—the case has become a statewide cause célèbre—the police are split asunder—there are rumors of intrigue in high places—and the State's Attorney who brought the case and prosecuted it—*twice*—has not yet listened to the tapes!)

Now Mr. Wall pursued another argument. "It's necessary for us to show proper custody of them. . . . As a matter of fact, Lieutenant Fuessenich hasn't let them out of his possession at any time. . . ."

The Judge: "If the Clerk has them, that's his responsibility."

Mr. Wall: "If they are passed out to anyone other than Lieutenant Fuessenich, we have lost the chain on proper custody that we have to prove in Court."

The Judge: "If they are deposited with the Court, I will grant you they will be considered properly in custody."

Mr. Wall: "I don't say that anything is improper. But when there is a misrepresentation to the Court . . . about the lock being tampered with—May I state, Your Honor, what happened relating to that? There was a little lever that tells whether you want the maid—or want not to be disturbed—and that fell off. . . . And as Counsel were leaving last night, Attorney McKeon said, 'Let's stop at the office and report the door being jimmied before we are accused of it.' That is exactly what he said. The door was not jimmied."

Judge Wright [pained] "Gentlemen, this is so ridiculous. To avoid anybody accusing anybody of anything, let's give the tapes to the Clerk. . . ."

Mr. Wall [contemptuous] "I am not afraid of any accusations—these ridiculous types of accusations."

The Judge: "I am asking you this question: Why not give the Clerk the tapes for the weekend?"

"I would be very happy to give them to him!" Mr. Wall said. While Fuessenich went to get the tapes, Mr. Wall walked away and stood jingling coins in his pocket, then returned to the bench. "Your Honor, while we are waiting, I would like to say that during the time that we were listening to these tapes, there were rude remarks made by Counsel for the Defense. One of them said, 'Don't change those tapes.'"

Judge Wright [one suspects he has more than an inkling now of what to expect in this trial] "If you want me to allocate a Court Officer to be there next time, I will do so."

The next listening session was scheduled for Tuesday evening at 7:30. Mr. Scofield offered to go, saying that he lived in Stratford. The offer was accepted, and Court adjourned until Tuesday morning.

22

A late start—forty minutes late. Always a reason to suspect that a storm was blowing up in Chambers.

The press had wangled itself a room—a very good large room (the library and office of the district judge who was sitting elsewhere this session)—and, to everyone's delight, it was right next to Judge Wright's Chambers. Through the heavy door between the rooms one could never catch the actual words but when the shouting became hearty enough the sound came through, promising an interesting court day.

"They're arguing about the Hartford *Courant*," someone speculated.

"They're arguing about the tapes. There's another listening session tonight—with Scofield as referee."

"Just headlines for the Hartford *Courant*."

"They're arguing about something else altogether. There are vast untapped areas that they can argue about."

Whether or not it had been discussed in Chambers, the day in Court began with one of the vast untapped areas. "Your Honor," Mr. Shew said before the Jury was brought in, "I have Major Rome under subpoena—"

(Mr. Wall front and center.)

"I called him yesterday," Mr. Shew said, "and told him that I would like him here at the end of the week. He said that I would have to get a Court Order if he was to appear here for anything more than to just testify." Rome's orders, issued by Commissioner

Mulcahy, were that he was to come into court, testify, and leave. "That is unsatisfactory to me. There are exhibits here that I have to go over with him. I would like a Court Order permitting Major Rome to come here on Thursday of this week and stay here when I deem it necessary."

The Judge turned to Mr. Wall for comment.

"Your Honor, I haven't talked to the Commissioner about this—" Quickly Mr. Wall assumed a censorious tone. "But it arises from a definite abuse in the last trial. It seems that Major Rome came down to assist in choosing the Jury, under their subpoena, and was here with five men for about—I would say, ten days with five men, assisting the Defendant here. Undoubtedly it was this abuse which gave rise to any such ruling." (At the press table, quick glances at the Canaan men who have hardly missed an hour of either trial.) Mr. Wall grew more caustic. "I am sure that Major Rome *has a great stake in this case*—and that he is cooperating with the Defense in every way *because of a personal stake that he has,* and I'm sure that they would have no difficulty in reaching him on a weekend or any other time. . . . I see no reason why he is different from any other witness who is subpoenaed. . . . He should be here to testify, and any further order of the Court would just overemphasize the man's position."

Immediately Mr. Shew denied the charge that Major Rome had assisted in the selection of the last Jury. "That is an absolute misstatement! . . . Major Rome was there off and on. . . . The State Police that I subpoenaed were there and I had subpoenaed him. [To the present problem] Now Mr. Wall states that he is available weekends. . . . I would be very glad to talk with him weekends, but this, under his present orders, *he* is not supposed to do without a Court Order. This is my understanding."

Mr. Wall [innocently] "Certainly nothing that the State has ever done would keep Counsel from interviewing any witness. . . . [Firing another volley] This man's testimony was absolutely—not even—I doubt if there was even any relevancy in it. [Now a lateral shot at the enemy press] Although it was highly touted *by the staff of the Defense here* that his testimony was important. It was, as Your Honor can observe, insignificant so far as having any relevancy. It was just window dressing, that the Defense is attempting to obtain at the present time by having his presence here."

The Judge, bypassing this rehash of old animosities, turned to the legal aspects of the problem. "What power does the Court have to compel a citizen to remain in attendance except for the purpose of testifying?"

Mr. Shew: "He is perfectly willing to come and I think that Commissioner Mulcahy is willing to have him come. [Pointedly] I have my reasons as to why this prohibition has taken place—but I don't *know*—" In his subpoena, he asked Major Rome to appear here with his records. Now the records were all here in Court—or should be. "The records should be available to Major Rome the same as they are available to the four or five officers who have been in *constant attendance here* during the picking of the jurors and everything else. Major Rome should not be handicapped in his testimony by not having his records available."

Mr. Wall was quick to point out that it was the *Defense* who had asked Fuessenich to bring the Hartford file to Court. "The State was perfectly satisfied to have it remain in Hartford until it was required." (This is a rather fuzzy area. One suspects that whatever the State considers pertinent was transferred long ago to the Canaan file. At the press table: "They had Redican's report here last Friday. He's in the Detective Division.")

Now Mr. Shew said that he had never been able to get straight what Canaan had and what Hartford had and that apparently Canaan had a great deal more. "Major Rome was placed in charge of this case at a very early date, and all those documents which are now in Mr. Wall's possession should be made available to him. If he can only step in here and testify and walk out, we cannot do justice to the testimony that's available from Major Rome."

Judge Wright looked puzzled. "I was under the impression that you had agreed that Major Rome would not be here except for the purpose of testifying."

Mr. Shew [astonished] "We had agreed to that!"

"That's my impression. Was I wrong in that?"

Mr. Shew: "That's the first time I've heard of that!"

Mr. Wall [hedging] "I couldn't say definitely, Your Honor, that that was the case. . . . But I do say this—that any reports that were made by Major Rome—any reports signed by him and submitted by him—we will certainly make available to the Defense—[crisp] so that they may discuss them with Major Rome at their leisure."

Putting the issue temporarily on the shelf, the Judge instructed

Mr. Shew to bring him a copy of the subpoena. The Jury was brought in and Lieutenant Fuessenich resumed the stand.

•   •   •

On Friday there had been little testimony that we had not heard before. Today with an old Exhibit—one of the photographs—Mr. Wall went off on a new tack that absorbed most of two strange and puzzling days. The focus was State's Exhibit J—a photograph of the kitchen showing footprints in the blood at the entrance to the dining room. "Will you describe the footprints as you observed them on that day?"

Photograph in hand, Fuessenich said that it showed one full footprint and several heelprints in the blood. "Blood outlines the edge of the shoe. On the full print the blood is drawn away from the toe. It's scraped—away from the footprint."

Now Mr. Wall began an attempt to qualify Fuessenich as an expert in several areas so that he could interpret the photographs and give his own conclusions about this evidence. A review of Fuessenich's credentials. Nineteen and a half years with the State Police, spent in investigation. Also he has taken an extension course for four years at Northeastern University in criminal investigation, and photography courses at the Kodak and the Leitz companies. "By reason of your training and experience, Lieutenant, are you particularly able to interpret photographs with relation to what they represent and what interpretation can be obtained from them?"

"I believe so, sir."

When he ran into an objection to interpretation of a photograph, Mr. Wall changed emphasis. "Will you then describe what you yourself *observed* relating to this footprint?"

Fuessenich: "Close examination of this footprint showed that the blood at the toe had been drawn away from the print and was very thin and had dried. The thicker blood forming the outline of the footprint had not dried as much as the thin portion had."

Now the question: "From your observation of it, do you have a conclusion as to *when* this footprint was made on the floor?"

Objection! Argument. And a battle began that lasted more than two hours—and broke out sporadically for the rest of the day—over whether Fuessenich was qualified in any special way to deduce the hour at which a bloody footprint had been made.

The Judge asked whether Mr. Shew wished to cross-examine on

his qualifications, and Mr. Shew certainly did. "Will you tell us," he began, "what qualifies you to make a statement as to when a footprint was made?"

Fuessenich [authoritative] "My experience in investigating crime . . . in seeing blood at the scene of a crime . . . in knowing how long it takes blood to dry . . . in recognizing at the scene of a crime, evidence such as this evidence."

Mr. Shew [easy tone] "How long does it take blood to dry, Lieutenant?" It varies. "How long did it take the blood to dry here?"

"It varied. Some dried soon. Some was still wet six or eight hours afterwards. Some was still moist twenty-four hours after this."

[Quietly] "And do you know whether there was any urine in this blood?" No, sir. "Would that make a difference?" Fuessenich answered by repeating the question and then said that it probably would, in the blood as a whole; not, in his opinion, between one portion and another. Mr. Shew continued to poke at this hole. "If there was urine in some portion of the blood and not in the other, it would make a difference, would it not?" Mr. Wall suggested that the examination be confined to the witness's qualifications. Mr. Shew shot back, "I am trying to do that, Your Honor, and I choose to do it in my own way."

The Judge ruled that it was all germane to how long this patch would take to dry, and Mr. Shew, reiterating that Fuessenich did not know the contents of the blood, said, "Then you are not in a position to make any estimate as to time, are you?"

"All I am saying, sir, is that in my opinion, part of this blood dried faster than other parts." (The original question asked for his opinion on when this footprint was made.)

"Do you mean that where it was thin it dried faster than where it was heavier?" Yes—that was it. [Challenging] "But you are not in a position to state any *particular time* when the footprint was made, are you?" No, sir. Mr. Shew repeated his objection to Mr. Wall's question.

Judge Wright asked, "Can you tell from your experience, Lieutenant, how long it takes blood to dry?"

"No, sir, I can't say that it would take a certain number of hours for blood to dry on any occasion or under any circumstances."

The Judge excused the Jury while he heard the lieutenant's answer to the original question.

Fuessenich: "In my opinion, that print was made soon after the blood was placed on the floor."

The Judge: "How would you arrive at that conclusion?"

Fuessenich: "This print was made by blood adhering to the sole of a shoe." (Fuessenich believes that somebody stepped in blood and then moved to a clean spot where the blood ran off the shoe onto the floor.) "The blood around the outside of the print is quite heavy. The blood on the toe which had been dragged away was thinned out so that it dried faster than the blood around the outside of the print, which at the time I first saw this was still moist." (It does not really answer the question. At the press table: "What is this all about? What are they getting at?" One is beginning to wonder.)

With the Jury out Mr. Shew resumed questioning. "Lieutenant, when is the first time you came up with this theory?" Fuessenich replied that it was before the Coroner's Inquest. "Did you testify to this in the Coroner's Inquest?" He did not attend the Coroner's Inquest. He did discuss it with the Coroner—and with Mr. Wall.

The lieutenant realized, did he not, that with this physical violence a person would be likely to urinate? Fuessenich replied that he had examined the victim's clothing and had seen no evidence of urine. Mr. Shew: "It would have occurred long before you appeared on the scene?"

"Probably five hours, six hours."

Mr. Shew [quickly] "Seven hours—something like that." (Significance here beyond blood drying.) The lieutenant believed it still would have been evident on the clothing.

The Judge interrupted to pose, without realizing it, a sensitive question. "Is there some area of agreement between Counsel as to when she died?"

Mr. Shew: "I think there is a great area of disagreement."

"You have been cross-examining about some five to seven hours before as being a point of death. Is that agreed upon or not?"

[Quick] "Not so far as the Defense is concerned. It certainly is not."

Going back to the lieutenant's answer that the footprint was made soon after the blood was placed on the floor, the Judge asked, "What do you mean by soon?"

"I mean within a period of perhaps not more than an hour—but certainly less than six or seven hours."

Mr. Shew stood aside while the Judge questioned Fuessenich. Then he moved in with another barrage aimed at the lieutenant's qualifications as an expert. (This attempt to so qualify him appears to have struck an indignant chord.) Could the lieutenant name other investigations in which he had used this skill and knowledge? He could not. Could he name a case in which he had attempted to judge the lapse in time between blood being deposited and a print being made in it? He could not. Could he name courses that he took that would have given him this knowledge? A course in accident investigation at Northeastern University. Had he read a book on the subject? He named one. When did he read it? Around 1963.

"As a matter of fact you have never attempted to testify to anything such as this before, have you?"

[Crisp] "No, sir. I have never attempted to testify to this."

Having gained this admission, Mr. Shew drove on, bringing out that Fuessenich did not give this testimony at the other trial and that Trooper Yuknat, not Fuessenich, had investigated the footprints. He read aloud from Yuknat's testimony at the first trial, stating that Arnfin's shoes and the footprints were similar in size, shape, and location of nail holes. If Arnfin made these footprints, obviously they were not made at the time Fuessenich had concluded they were made. Fuessenich replied that Yuknat did not say the prints were made by Arnfin's shoes—only that they were similar.

Mr. Shew turned to the Judge ". . . I feel that I've demonstrated that he isn't qualified. He allowed a man under him to testify at an official hearing and make a different statement. . . . He hasn't indicated that he has had any experience other than to read a book. He hasn't had any other situations similar to this—he hasn't testified to any matters like this before."

Again Judge Wright had a few questions. "In your courses at Northeastern, did you have anything on blood coagulation . . . on how long it takes to coagulate blood?"

"I don't believe we went into how long it takes . . . except that many factors must be considered . . . to determine when blood was left."

The Judge: "Well, how can you, from your experience or education, come to the statement that no more than one hour had elapsed . . . ?"

"This is my opinion from seeing the blood on the floor and seeing blood in the stages of drying. . . . The thicker blood takes longer to dry. The thinner blood dries more rapidly. I was at the scene about an hour after Arnfin Thompsen . . . would have made the track, had he made it, and I do not believe that his shoe would have picked up this blood and deposited it on the floor and had it dried—absolutely dried around the toe. It would have been sticky around the edge."

The Judge: "Well, have you seen other footprints—or hand-prints—that you can pinpoint as to time?"

"I have investigated breaking and enterings where perpetrators cut themselves and left blood at the scene. I have investigated homicides where blood was left, and knowing the time this took place, I've had experience seeing how that blood dried in a known period of time."

The Judge asked if there were further questions.

Mr. Shew: "I'd like to spend a lot of time with this man because I think it's absolutely outrageous that he should pose now to have such qualifications."

Mr. Wall: "Your Honor, I move that remark be stricken from the record. It's absolutely uncalled for."

The Judge suggested that "surprised" might be a better word and declared the morning recess. It was already a few minutes past noon. Almost an entire morning had been given to this matter of the footprints and it still was not finished.

•   •   •

The Press Room

"Shew is a changed man." (At least the tenth time *this* has been said.)

"He has a case this time. Last time he was groping in the dark."

"He's convinced now that Harry didn't do it. And he has McKeon. No one can try a murder case without help."

"Last time he felt that the police held back an awful lot. This time he's going to get it out of them. He'll show no mercy."

"He hasn't shown any to Fuessenich."

"Do you think the tapes had anything to do with that?" (After hearing the first tapes, Mr. Shew had said, "Fuessenich was the toughest. He began in a very crisp, confident manner. Then he picked up the beat—like picking up the pace in rowing from thirty-four to forty. He was relentless." Mr. Shew has picked up the beat today.)

• • •

After recess—the Jury still absent—Mr. Shew began again. ". . . If the temperature in the house had increased by twenty degrees, what difference would that have made in the time of coagulation of this blood?" I don't feel qualified to answer that question. "Humidity affects coagulation of blood. What was the humidity on this day?" I don't know. "Are you assuming that there was no water in this blood?" I am assuming that if there was water in the blood, it would be in all the blood—all over the floor. "How does temperature affect coagulation of blood?" It would affect it. I don't feel that I'm qualified to tell you how. "You don't feel qualified . . . and yet you baldly make a statement about the time within which it took to coagulate blood?"

"I believe I can give an opinion based on all the things that appeared at the scene."

"Well, one of the things at the scene was the temperature of the day. . . . What was the temperature?" It was a warm June day. . . . I cannot give the temperature. ". . . And you made that diagnosis without knowing the humidity or the temperature? . . . Actually, you are not qualified as an expert to testify the length of time it takes blood to coagulate, are you?"

"No, sir."

Coming up to lunch another piece of information. Fuessenich said that there were spots of blood on the floor in that area. "Some of those spots are within the shoeprint itself, made after the print was made."

(One is still groping for the significance of all this. If Fuessenich is saying that Harry walked in the blood within an hour after the murder, this proves nothing. No one denies that he was there. But if he is saying that this footprint was made by the murderer as he moved the body toward the dining room, then this is very hard to buy. The body was dragged. The toe of the footprint is *toward* the dining room. Would it not have been awkward and most unusual for the murderer to walk front first, dragging a body by reaching down and back behind himself? The natural way would be to face the body and back out through the room. And if the dragger preceded the body, would not the dragged torso have disturbed the footprints far more than just a scuffed toeline? Is it not more likely that the footprints were made later? Could not the scraped toeline have been the result of a slip in the blood—or an involuntary start when the person realized he had stepped in heavy blood? And the spots of blood the result of an effort automatically to shake the blood off the shoe? Although the stronger evidence seems to indicate that the footprints were Arnfin's, even if they were Harry's they do not make him the murderer.)

"Actually," Mr. Shew said, "all you know about these footprints is that they were made between the time of the crime and the time you got there, isn't that correct, Lieutenant?"

"Yes, sir, that's all I know."

"And you have never posed as an expert on blood before?"

"No, sir. I'm not posing as an expert on blood now." Fuessenich had remained calm and poised, but he was obviously far from happy.

Mr. Shew turned to the Judge, "If Your Honor please, this man is certainly not qualified to give the opinion he is attempting to give. We have a man's life at stake here. . . . There is absolutely no qualification as an expert on blood based on any past experience."

Now Mr. Wall said, "Your Honor, there is no claim that this witness is an expert on blood. . . . There is a claim, however, that he is an expert and a *trained observer* at the scene of the crime."

The Judge: "Well, the witness said that in his opinion the footprint was made . . . not more than one hour after the blood fell on the floor. This question of timing could be very important. . . ."

The ruling: "There is not enough qualification for this witness to testify before the Jury . . . as to the time when, in his opinion, the footprint appeared. He is a trained observer and what he observed may be told to the Jury."

Then Judge Wright's first specific instructions to the press. Repeating that the question of time might be important, he said, "I'm going to ask the press—at this time I'm asking as a gentleman's agreement—not to print what happens in the absence of the Jury. If this gentlemen's agreement is not observed, I will go on from there at a further date."

The Jury returned—for a few minutes. Mr. Wall resumed questioning about the footprint, and immediately another argument developed on the interpretation of the Judge's ruling. Mr. Wall understood only that there would be no opinion from Fuessenich as an expert on blood. This time the Jury was told to go to lunch.

Mr. Wall: "I believe that the ruling was that this witness has qualified as an expert in the investigation of crime and that he is a trained observer who could give opinions, based upon his own observation, that would . . . be of assistance to the Jury in coming to a conclusion."

The Judge: "The only thing I ruled out was an opinion as to how long the footprint had been there because he is not an expert on blood. What opinions do you want from him now?"

Mr. Wall: "As a trained observer, as a State Policeman of the length of experience which he has had in the service, his training in Northeastern University [it has the flavor of the introduction of a candidate for office], his training in other phases of police work, his own experience in the investigation of crime—all of those I feel highly qualify him to give an opinion relating to the interpretation of certain evidence which is available here and which he has already testified to."

Mr. Shew [the roles are indeed reversed from the last trial] "I've always assumed that was up to the Jury, Your Honor. Just because the witness is probably an excellent police officer certainly doesn't entitle him to draw conclusions in a murder case."

The Judge said that he would have to know more about the opinions being sought and adjourned for lunch.

·   ·   ·

To many, Mr. Wall's last argument was ironic—especially the claim that the experience of nineteen years qualified Fuessenich to give opinions that would be of assistance to the Jury in coming to a conclusion. There are memories of contumely heaped on another investigator when it was suggested that he might qualify as an expert of twenty-nine years experience and perform this service for another Jury.

·   ·   ·

After lunch, with still no agreement on that fine line between observation and inadmissible opinion, Judge Wright sent for the Jury. "Put your basis of facts and observation on the record," he said to

Mr. Wall. "When we come to the conclusions or opinions we will have the Jury excused again."

A plodding half-hour, during which Mr. Wall, picking his way through relentless objections, placed these facts before the Jury:

—The blood at the toe of the footprint was smeared forward—away from the print itself—in the direction of the dining room.

—There were lines in the blood in the center of the kitchen floor, going in the same direction—toward the dining room.

—There were blood spots in the area of the footprint and spots within the footprint itself.

—The toe of the victim's right shoe was scuffed.

—The blood on the body was mostly in the front—no substantial amount of blood in back.

Mr. Wall asked Fuessenich for the conclusion he reached from these facts, and Mr. Shew let this answer come in without objection. Fuessenich said, ". . . The body had been dragged from the kitchen to the porch, head first and face down . . . with the feet last."

(If a body were face down, it would be even more difficult to get a hold on it by reaching back and proceeding face forward through a room. It would be almost impossible!)

Mr. Wall asked, "Do you have an opinion as to which event preceded the other—the making of the spots or the footprint?"

Objection to the opinion. Sustained. The spots speak for themselves. Mr. Wall tried again. "Do you have an opinion on what came first—the footprint or the lines in the footprint?" Objection. Sustained.

Mr. Wall [a slight nod of his head] "Thank you, Your Honor. I have no further questions of this witness."

Is it over? One hopes so.

Mr. Shew began again. It has been a tedious day and still it goes on. "Lieutenant, while you were observing things around this area, did you notice any dishes?"

"Yes, sir. There were dishes in the sink."

"Had they been washed or were they dirty dishes?" The lieutenant does not know. "They were *in* the sink?" Yes, sir. "Did it occur to you that it might be important whether or not they were dirty?" At that time it did not.

"But it did occur to you to notice these spots?"

"Yes, sir."

"Why did you keep it a secret all this time?"

Objection. Sustained.

In the front row, Tobey and Solveig listen with a resigned attitude of just waiting. Sharon is busy. During lunch a reporter talked with her, learned that she is taking down the testimony of this trial in shorthand. Why? To be occupied while she suffers here? Does it give her a sense of purpose? Is it a record for Harry? Or for their child to read one day—a document of proof of her father's innocence? Sharon has brought pictures of the baby to Court—is eager to show them. She is three months old now—a round, happy-looking baby. "She had two teeth at two months." Then, "How will I tell her about this someday?"

At the Defense table Harry sits erect, paying attention. He is neatly dressed every day in a suit and shirt and tie. He does not slump or lounge about. Orders from his attorney. At the start of the trial Mr. McKeon said to him, "You sit straight with your hands folded and don't laugh—*whatever* happens." Harry is following orders to a T. Although no one seems to notice him very much.

At about three o'clock Arnfin and his brother Ted came into Court and sat in the back row. Ted is shorter and heavier than Arnfin—a rough-complexioned man with heavy eyeglasses and a bulldog face. Arnfin is pale—black hair back from a peaked forehead, thin nose, black eyes. He wears a harassed look, as though always on the edge of a sigh.

The tedious day dragged on. Fuessenich said that he observed these spots at about eight o'clock that night. At that time they had dried out. (Two hours now for the spots to have dried if Arnfin made them. Wild thoughts on a dull afternoon: Someone ought to spill a drop of blood and leave it to dry. Who will offer a drop of blood?)

On Cross-Examination, Mr. Shew invited the opinion he had blocked on Direct: Fuessenich believed the footprint was made before the spots. Could not the spots have been there first and dried out and then been stepped on? Fuessenich believed they would have been smeared or, if dry, scratched. The photograph was examined. There *are* smears within the footprint as well as spots.

"Lieutenant, isn't it obvious that someone stepped on these blood spots within the perimeter of this footprint?" Yes, sir, I think I can explain—. Mr. Shew [cutting in sharply] "So it would appear, would it not, that these spots within that footprint were made *before* the footprint?"

"Yes, sir, the ones that are smeared were made before the footprint was made." (Again a variation from the first flat statement that the "footprint was made before the spots.") *Some spots* were smeared and came first and were stepped on. *Some spots* were not smeared and, Fuessenich believes, were made after the print. (It still does not seem to add up to very much.)

Mr. Shew suggested that the scuff mark on the toe of the victim's shoe could have been simply a worn spot already there. Fuessenich replied that there was blood on the toes of both shoes. He believed that the scuff mark was the result of dragging.

"The dishes in the sink—would you say it's a fair assumption that they had not been washed, Lieutenant?" I cannot say, sir. "Wouldn't your long training as a detective lead you to some conclusion on that?" In this instance, it did not. "You mean you hadn't had the proper training along those lines?" I am beginning to believe so, sir. "Can you tell us how many dishes there were in the sink?"

"No, I cannot. . . . My remembrance is that there was . . . a sinkful of dishes. . . . I know that there were dishes in the sink. How many and what kind, I cannot answer."

After recess (the Jury out again—they have been out almost the entire day), a long argument about what time Agnes Thompsen said she sanded the stairs. Familiar territory—we have been here before. And a familiar problem. Fuessenich has always said that he heard this information that night from other officers including Captain O'Brien. Now he said that he believed it was between 1:15 and 2:00. "I know the time varied somewhat from time to time. But it was essentially in the early afternoon between 1:00 or 1:30 and 2:00 or 2:30."

Mr. Wall handed him Captain O'Brien's report to refresh his memory and Fuessenich read it and said, "The time varied between 2:00 and 4:00."

Mr. Shew showed him the transcript of the first trial at which Fuessenich had testified that the time was between 1:00 and 3:00.

"This was an answer you gave at the last trial, Lieutenant?" Yes, sir. "When it was fresher in your mind?" Yes, sir. "Now, do you wish to change the answer you gave in the last trial?" [Stubbornly] No. "Well—in that you stated that it was sometime between 1:00 and 3:00." Yes, sir, that's as I remembered it at that time. "Now—do you wish to change that?" [Riding it out] I don't wish to change it, sir. "You don't wish to change it? Do you wish to amplify it?"

"Only to say that I cannot set a definite time. It was early in the afternoon."

Mr. Shew turned to the Judge and asked that the answer be given to the Jury when they came in. The Judge commented that he had four different answers. "Do you want all of them read to the Jury?"

Mr. Shew: "Yes, I think I do, Your Honor. It might have a bearing on his credibility—and his ability as an expert police officer."

Objection from Mr. Wall to giving hearsay answers to the Jury.

The Judge [to Fuessenich] "If the Jury were here, what would you say was the time she sanded the stairs?"

"From my own knowledge?" Yes. [Flat] "I couldn't say."

The Judge: "Who would have the knowledge on that?"

"Captain O'Brien, I believe. Or Major Rome."

The Jury returned and Mr. Wall went again to the footprints. "From your observation, were these spots underneath the smudge area or superimposed upon the smudge area?" Objection. The question calls for a conclusion. Sustained. Mr. Wall refused to give up. Again and again he rephrased: "Did you make any *observation* whether these spots were underneath . . . ? What did you see as to whether the spots were on top . . . ? Was there something you could see with the naked eye as to whether the spots were on top . . . ?"

At last the Judge permitted an answer to what he had seen with the naked eye, and Fuessenich said, "I saw these spots on top of the smudges."

Mr. Shew asked for an exception. "That calls for a conclusion on a highly debatable matter. [Sharp] And he has finally answered with his own conclusion."

At about a quarter to five Fuessenich was excused. Almost an entire day had been given to a scrap of evidence that, at the last trial, the State had been aware of and had not even bothered to mention. At least one reporter called it the first sign of weakness in the State. "They're worried. They're grabbing at straws."

·   ·   ·

Trooper Enrico Soliani, the first officer on the scene, took the stand for the final minutes of the day. A short stocky young man, nervous on the stand, Soliani, who did not testify in the first trial, told of arriving at the house, seeing the bloody kitchen, following the trail, seeing the body. He looked at photographs and said they were a fair representation of the scene. He was on the premises but he did not see the photographs taken—he was carrying out another assignment.

Mr. Shew: "Do you remember what the weather was, Officer?"

"It was a warm summer day, clear. . . . The sun was out."

(This is puzzling. Fuessenich, too, said at least twice that it was a warm summer day. Carole Stadler, in conversation, said it was a cold gray day—"I wore a jacket outside." An unimportant detail. Or is it? On a cold day the windows might have been closed. On a warm day they would probably have been open. And Carole Stadler, in her front yard until one o'clock, might have heard an argument—if there had been one—or a scream.)

The day ended except for confirming the arrangements for listening to the tapes tonight. The meeting would be in Mr. Wall's motel room again and Mr. Scofield would be there. Mr. Shew asked how long the remaining tapes—all of them—would run. The answer, from Fuessenich, "Probably eight or ten hours."

(Eight or ten hours more! After three hours last time!)

It was agreed that tonight's session would last for four hours—from seven until eleven o'clock.

23

Again a quality of *déjà vu* as Arnfin, pale, harassed-look-ing, took the stand to tell again his unhappy tale. Today he could be heard. Between answers he would dart a quick look at Mr. Wall, who stood at the far end of the jury box to encourage him to speak up. He would rub his hands together, he would sigh deeply and often—but he could be heard. The day of the murder: coffee in the morning, to work at the Carpenter Brick Company, his return home at 6:15—and then . . .

"I went upstairs to my mother's. . . . I ran across the street . . ." (The mind wanders: What happened last night with the tapes? What did they disclose about that Sunday afternoon in Hartford when Harry was taken to Headquarters for a lie-detector test and sent home four hours later?) ". . . I called Dottie's mother . . . I took a couple of shots and waited for the police. . . . I poured the shots in the kitchen, waited in the living room. . . ."

Time has not tempered the emotional reaction of the Solberg family to this man who was once their friend. Every day, although the courtroom is always nearly empty, they sit close together in the front row. This morning Tobey's head was down, his face a study in pain. Solveig clutched herself with one arm, her head high, face set, eyes down. Only Sharon looked directly at Arnfin. When Arnfin spoke of the Solbergs, his voice faded.

The pink plastic piggy bank—soiled, red-snouted symbol of hap-pier times. "I had guessed it contained twenty to twenty-five dollars." Arnfin leaned forward and touched it, pointed to the hole on top. . . . The ladder, the tools. This time Arnfin was careful to say he had not seen them that morning. . . . The sledgehammer, which had belonged to his mother. (New. We had not heard this before.) . . . The pile of stones under the porch. And one stone beside Dottie's body.

(At the press table: "What happened last night with the tapes?" "Shew said the whole thing was Riemer. No one else." "I thought Riemer only gave the lie-detector test." "The whole thing was Riemer.")

Arnfin said that his mother was taken back to the Middletown Hospital that same night and that she died there last November. He no longer seems to be quite so protective of her.

This is a trial of peaks and plateaus. The old material is over-familiar—a more-than-twice-told tale. It has lost the fascination of story, the challenge of offering new clues if one is sharp to detect them. The only challenge lies in catching slip-ups, conflicting statements, contradictions.

Just before recess Mr. Wall introduced the Letter. After recess he read it to the Jury slowly, in a strong voice, giving full weight to every phrase, spelling out the misspelled words. " 'I killed your wife . . .' " At the Defense table, Harry stared down at his hands, clasped together on the table. Tobey sat crumpled forward, his face ashen, eyes red. Solveig stared relentlessly at nothing. " '. . . I'll kill the baby someday soon. I'll kill the baby, too, and my wife.' "

Mr. Wall: ". . . You stated that you walked into the kitchen at least twice to go to the telephone . . . and you also walked through to the dining room. . . . Now, on any of these occasions . . . did you walk in the blood?"

Arnfin: "You had to walk in it to get through. You couldn't avoid it."

[Monotone] "And what portion did you walk in?"

[Ready reply] "Along the edges."

(The press table, slight stir. "*That's* different from last time!" "Are we *still* on those footprints?")

Mr. Wall: "Did you walk in any of the large pools of blood?"

Arnfin [without expression] "No."

"Are you *certain* of that?"

"Yes."

Mr. Wall produced the photograph that was pawed over interminably yesterday. "Are those footprints your footprints?"

[Pointing, voice fading] "These could be. I walked along the edge of the cabinet."

At Mr. Wall's request Arnfin attempted to describe the course he followed about the kitchen. Considerable time spent on this; considerable confusion. The Judge [cutting to the core of the problem] "Well, the question really is—did you or did you not step into the blood?"

"I had to step in the blood."

"But not the pools of blood?"

Arnfin: "Not in the pools, no."

Now a bit of thunder stolen from the Defense: the fact that Arnfin was "keeping company" with his present wife, Jean, while Dorothy was still alive—followed immediately by the mitigating news that he and Jean now had a new baby, a three-week-old daughter. (On the whole Arnfin's manner is better this time. The Jury does not seem unsympathetic.)

Then another attack on the Defense—the matter of the economics paper. "Had Harry Solberg ever . . . come to you relating to his studies?"

"Yes." (Answer unheard—repeated.) And when was that—with reference to June of 1965? "It was the winter—the winter of 1964–65 probably was the last time." Approximately how many times did this happen? "Oh, four or five probably."

[Deliberate tone] "And about the time of June 15, 1965, did you have any contact with him relating to any economics paper . . . was there any conversation along that line at all?"

"No."

"Do you know of any reason that the Defendant, Solberg, might have had to come to your house on June 15, 1965?"

"No."

The Solbergs were more controlled now—Tobey had straightened up, Solveig had relaxed somewhat. Still neither looked at Arnfin.

"They *can't* look at him," Sharon said to a reporter during recess. "They feel he has let them down. Tobey said, 'That's what you get when you try to help someone.'"

Sharon herself is a changed personality. In Litchfield she was withdrawn, overwhelmed, wretched and pregnant. This time she is warm, outgoing, serene. Today she has brought her wedding picture to show to the reporter. As she pours out her feelings about these past ten months, one comes to understand that this young girl is accepting and enduring this nightmare supported by a remarkable faith. "My parents are not Christians—they haven't given themselves to God," she said. (By this she means in the strict sense of Low-Church Lutheranism.) "This doesn't bother me. If God wants them, He will reach them.

"I was a Believer before I started to go with Harry." She speaks of her faith in much the same tone as she speaks of her child. "After Harry was taken away I stopped believing—I became very bitter. I know now that the hand of the Lord is in this. I don't know what the Lord's purpose is, but it wasn't fulfilled in October and that's why Harry didn't come home. [Absolute conviction] He'll come home—but he won't come until the Lord's purpose is fulfilled.

"I was very bitter. I stopped believing in the Lord. I didn't want anything to do with Him. I lost faith and Harry was unhappy. He never stopped believing. He never lost faith." (Is it possible that here is the explanation sought by so many during the first trial when one heard at least once a day that Harry did not seem to be worried, that he was the most relaxed defendant anyone had ever seen?)

"At Thanksgiving I didn't eat a bite of turkey. I said I didn't have anything to be thankful for. Then my faith came back. I opened my Bible one day—I don't know why, because I didn't believe, anymore—and I saw so many messages that the Lord was sending me. Now I have a verse all my own. From Psalms. 'I left thinking that You had shut Your eyes upon me. But You cared anyway. Even though I turned my back on You, You didn't turn on me.' And First Corinthians says, The Lord isn't going to tempt you over and above what you can take.

"The Hand of the Lord is in so many things. I was down to my last dollar, and a check for fifty dollars came from the church. That wasn't gone and another came for twenty-five dollars—from some girls at a college in Ohio. A girl from East Hartland goes there. . . . All decisions have been made for us. Even the lawyer. A friend got a message from God and said, 'He's the only one. Hold onto that

lawyer.' . . . We were going to get married the next June. The
Lord was in that, too. We got married in January instead. So we
were together before Harry was taken away. . . . When I found I
was pregnant I was hysterical—I couldn't support the baby. I
couldn't get a ride to Pratt-Whitney. Nobody would give me a ride.
Nobody would give me a job. My father-in-law gave me a car to use
and I cracked it up. The Lord didn't want me to work—I was trying
to decide for myself and the Lord didn't want me to. I've witnessed
at churches—my church and other churches, too—on the way the
Lord showed himself to me. There are church groups all over that
are praying for us. With all the people praying, it has to be all right.
God has to answer them."

A pause and then, with truly no doubts about the outcome of this
trial, "I want a large family. I have five sisters and a brother. Harry
and I both want a large family. . . . I was upset about some things
they said about Harry in the last trial. They made him seem like
some kind of a kook. They didn't make it clear that he didn't do
things like dancing because it was against his religion." She looked
down the corridor at Tobey and Solveig. "They've aged," she said.
"A year ago they looked in their thirties. Now they look in their
fifties."

Sharon still looks like a child.

It was nearly lunchtime when Mr. Shew began his Cross-Examination. He had learned that Arnfin had arrived in Bridgeport yesterday morning and had been in town all day. (In the courtroom we
did not see him until three o'clock when he came in with his
brother.) "What members of the State Police Force did you talk
with yesterday around here?"

[Offhand] "Oh, whoever was here."

"Will you point out the ones you talked with?"

"Mr. Wall, Lieutenant Fuessenich . . . Rebillard . . . Pennington."

Now it turned out that he had spoken to them in their private
room several times yesterday—before Court, before lunch, after
Court—and again at nine thirty this morning.

Did they have any photographs in the room? "Yes, I think they
did. Yes. Yes." If I showed them to you, do you think you could
remember them? "No, because I didn't look at them." What did you

talk about this morning? "We were reading the newspaper. [Pause] And I was asked a few questions." What questions were you asked? [Vague] "I don't remember specifically." Were you questioned concerning the footprints on the floor? "Yes, I think so. Yes." You think you were. You *know* you were, don't you? [Hedging] "It might have been this morning—or yesterday."

"Were you questioned concerning the places you walked?"

"No, they asked me if I had stepped in any large pools of blood."

"And you told them what?"

"I told them I didn't."

Mr. Shew picked up a transcript of the Coroner's Hearing. "Now, of course, this is quite some time after June 15, 1965. . . . Would you think that your memory was better in July, 1965, than it was last night or this morning?"

Arnfin [fading] "It probably was. I don't know."

Clearly Mr. Shew was just beginning his examination on this point and it was already past one o'clock. The Judge interrupted to call the luncheon recess.

•   •   •

At lunch Mr. Shew and Mr. McKeon gave us a brief glimpse into the interrogation in Hartford that Sunday afternoon.

Mr. Shew: "It was a lot more than a lie-detector test. Riemer would give Harry the tests and then he'd just keep right on questioning him."

"The *tests?* More than one?" (At the first trial Fuessenich testified that Harry took one test on Sunday and one on Monday.)

Mr. Shew: "On Sunday they gave him three distinct lie-detector tests, together with elaborate preparation."

Mr. McKeon: "The polygraph was nothing but a pretext for interrogation. [Going back to the beginning] They got to Hartford and the parents and his wife were there. Harry's crying—the mother is hysterical. Fuessenich explained the thing to them. He said [reassuring tone] 'Harry's a good boy. We realize this.' They didn't know the whole thing was being taped. Fuessenich went out and they began to talk—trying to keep their voices down so the police wouldn't hear them. Then Fuessenich came back and they signed the consent form."

(Where would they have found the temerity to refuse to sign it?

Even after Harry was arrested, these people were afraid to telephone Mr. Shew at his office.)

Mr. Shew: "Riemer was as much an interrogator as the others. He
kept telling Harry that he was his *friend*—he wanted to help him.
[Snort] They were doing the whole darn business just for Harry!"

Mr. McKeon: "After he'd given him a test and questioned him,
Riemer said 'I have to call my wife—' And he went out. I had this
mental image of Harry bound up in all this paraphernalia—straps
and air cups—and there he was all alone—and all of a sudden he
said, over and over, 'I did not kill Dorothy Thompsen—I did not kill
Dorothy Thompsen.' "

"John thinks he was looking at the polygraph."

"It made your flesh crawl," McKeon said. "I felt like screaming,
'Shut up, you fool!' "

How much of this indignation is the result of involvement? No
one in this case is detached anymore. Curiosity is boiling over. Will
we hear these tapes in Court? Mr. Shew said, "At one point Rebillard said to me, 'You think these are rough. You should hear the
tapes Sam Rome took of Agnes Thompsen.' " Will we hear *those*
tapes?

After lunch Mr. Shew resumed his Cross-Examination. "Did you
talk about your testimony with any State Police officers this noon?"
Arnfin did. "Did you talk about the footprints this noon?" Yes.

(This is disturbing. The impression is growing of a last-ditch fight
to drag in a red herring—that no one considered worth mentioning
at the first trial—and make it stick. One studies the Jury. How do
they react to this? Are they put off by these efforts of the State to
discuss this testimony with the witness? Or will they think that
these footprints must be important—the State has harped on them
for two days—with all that smoke there must be a fire. Their faces
tell us nothing. This Jury reveals less than the other.)

Taking up the transcript of the Coroner's Hearing, Mr. Shew
asked again whether Arnfin's memory about that night would not
have been clearer in July, 1965. And Arnfin again [low voice]
"Probably."

"How many trips did you make across the kitchen floor that night
before any of the officers came?"

"Probably five or six."

"And how many trips did you make from the kitchen to the dining room?"

"Just one that I remember."

"And you were naturally upset at this time?"

"Yes."

Now Mr. Shew showed Arnfin the transcript of his testimony at the Inquest and waited while he read it. Mr. Wall paced in front of the jury box, stopped and jingled coins at a rapid rate—the sign of mounting tension. Arnfin looked up from the page. Mr. Shew: "Did you state at that time [reading] 'Well, I stepped in something here. I had to get a glass out of the cupboard.' Do you remember stating that?" Yes.

Mr. Shew continued to read from the transcript:

> (The witness pointed to a spot of blood to the left of the sink.)
> Q. And you know you stepped in there when you got your drink?
> A. Yes. And the bottle of whiskey was in this side of the refriger-
> ator. And so I went back there this way and over here. (The witness
> traces the course fairly close to footprints in the foreground of the
> photograph and says he took that course to the refrigerator.) At that
> point I didn't notice the smear marks.

[Looking up] "What did you mean by that, Mr. Thompsen, if you said that? What smear marks didn't you notice?"

Arnfin: "Apparently he must have pointed to something on an exhibit."

[Handing him the photograph] "Could those have been the smear marks?" Could be, yes. "And at that time you stated you didn't notice whether you made them or not?" Yes. "And *at this time*, you would be unable to tell us whether those were your marks or whether they were there before you arrived home?" I couldn't tell, no. "And you could have made them yourself?" It's possible.

The Judge had a few questions. Above all Judge Wright appears consistently to want to get the facts and get them straight. "Were the same smear marks on the photograph at the Coroner's Hearing that you now find on this photograph?" I believe so. "Now, what do you say about those smear marks? Are those yours or someone else's?"

"I don't know."

"Could they have been yours?"

"They could have been."

"They could have been. All right . . . I think that is clear."

Mr. Shew turned to the matter of Arnfin's relationship with his present wife before Dorothy's death—and drew increasingly angry objections from Mr. Wall. Suddenly everyone's nerves seemed to be very much on edge.

Mr. Shew: "Did her mother know of this affair?"

Mr. Wall: "I object to anything about this affair. There has never been anything mentioned about this affair."

A quick retort from Mr. Shew, and the Judge said, "Please talk to me and not to each other. You object to the word 'affair'?"

Mr. Wall: "I do, Your Honor."

Mr. Shew: "I don't insist on it. I will call it anything he wants. Have you a better name, Mr. Wall?"

Mr. Wall [bridling] "If His Honor asks me any question, I would be happy to answer it."

Mr. Shew: "Perhaps you would, Your Honor, because he objects to any terminology of this situation."

The Judge: "What word would you like to use, Mr. Wall?"

Mr. Wall: "I would not like to use any word, Your Honor. I don't know what he is driving at when he is talking about an affair."

Mr. Shew: "That's very easily understandable."

The Judge [cutting this off] "Let's call it 'friendship.'"

Very angry, Mr. Wall took his seat, and Mr. Shew resumed questioning about the "friendship." Mr. Wall tilted back his chair and gazed at the ceiling. When he sat up he faced the Jury, not Mr. Shew.

Mr. Shew: "Now, Mr. Thompsen, you stated that you came home at six fifteen."

"Dottie wanted me home at quarter after six for supper."

"Did you have your supper at any specified time normally?" Not really, no. "And what time did you have your breakfast?"

"As soon as I got up, I had toast and coffee . . . at seven o'clock."

(At this moment the courtroom is about evenly divided between those who know what Mr. Shew is building up to and those who do not. The jurors do not know, and they listen impassively to this account of the daily routine. The Judge probably does not know. Mr. Wall and the State Police do know. The press knows. And one suspects that Arnfin has been briefed.)

Mr. Shew: "And were you satisfied with the way your wife took care of Christa? Was she a good mother?"

"Yes."

"Do you know when she gave her her noon meal?"

"Right at twelve o'clock. [Pause] Maybe a little before."

[Very sharp] "About a *quarter to twelve,* isn't that what the routine was, Mr. Thompsen?"

[Backing off] "It might have been a quarter of, yes."

Again to the Coroner's Hearing. "If you testified in July, 1965, that that was the normal routine, that's a pretty safe statement, is it not? . . . That she fed Christa right at a *quarter of twelve.*"

"Yes."

"And they would have lunch together?" Yes. "And that was standard routine in your house?" Arnfin cannot buck it: Yes. [Emphatic] "Your wife and Christa had lunch at quarter to twelve?" Yes.

Mr. Shew paused to let the time sink in. By now everyone understands that this is important. "And then would Christa have a nap?"

"Quarter to one."

"Quarter to one? And would your wife get her to bed promptly at that time?" Yes. "And you haven't any reason to believe that the routine of eating at a quarter to twelve was changed the day of this tragedy?" No. "And it would be a fair assumption that she and Christa had lunch at quarter to twelve on that date?"

"Yes."

A half-turn toward the Defense table and then back to the witness. [Casual] "By the way, Arnfin, what size shoe do you wear?"

"Eight and a half."

(The prints were similar to Arnfin's shoes in size and shape. Mr. Shew already knows that Harry wears size ten.)

Mr. Shew's final questions before recess were about Arnfin's mother. First her physical condition—that a few weeks before that June day she had dug the earth for the garden in the front yard. Mr. Shew suggested that she had used a pickaxe. Arnfin didn't know whether she had or not, but he confirmed that she had done all the work herself. Then to the nature of her mental disorder—that she was obsessed with fighting the devil, that she had once cut her leg with a knife to let the devil out. Not unnaturally, Arnfin shrank from these details, and as Mr. Shew pressed him, wrenching them out, one sensed a strange chemistry beginning to work. In this court-room, reactions are harder to appraise—there is no full body of spectators among whom one can wander to take soundings—but one sensed that sympathy was building for Arnfin—the feeling that this man had had just too much.

Then another new piece of information picked up between trials —the fact that Arnfin, riding in his brother's car the day after the murder, was in the area where the piggy bank was found. Arnfin: "We were around there once after we saw the minister—whether that was the next day or not, I don't know. It could have been. . . . We stopped at the church. . . . We drove around the block— whether we took the first left or the second left, I couldn't tell you." (No one has asked the purpose of the visit to the minister. Dorothy was not buried from this church. The funeral service was held at the church in New Hartford.)

On this vague note, the afternoon recess was called. During the recess June Shew, who was in Court today, commented that she, too, felt Bill was alienating the Jury by hitting so hard at Arnfin. This Jury, she sensed, felt sorry for him.

After recess Mr. McKeon again brought up the matter of the restrictions placed on Major Rome by Commissioner Mulcahy. Producing Major Rome's subpoena, he said, "If an intermediary such as the Commissioner of the State Police thwarts our right . . . the Court is empowered to issue an order commanding his appearance here—" The request that followed—that the Judge *order* Rome's presence in Court for the rest of the trial—had all the expected effect on Mr. Wall—and more.

He began with contempt—Major Rome was no different from any other witness. He moved on to accusation. "I might say, Your Honor, that there was a *definite abuse* of a subpoena in the last trial in a claim that this witness—*so-called witness*—should be in attendance at all times, even *every day* . . . while the Jury was being chosen. His photograph was taken . . . and he would have his portrait put on the front page of the paper. . . . But so far as providing any real testimony at all, this was nil. . . . This request can only be an attempt to repeat the abuse that took place in the first trial."

Mr. Shew [quickly and very angry] "Your Honor, I wish to correct the false statements—and they are *actually false statements* —that Mr. Wall has just made. . . ." In the last trial, Mr. Shew said, Judge MacDonald had ruled that if Mr. Wall had the members of the Canaan Barracks in constant attendance, Major Rome was entitled to be there, too. [Impatient gesture] "Mr. Wall has that whole gang in the back of the room. They have been here constantly, even to help pick the jurors. . . . I don't know if there is anyone left in Canaan. . . ."

Mr. Shew turned to the more serious matter. There were many exhibits that Mr. Wall did not want in evidence, he charged—exhibits which the Defense felt were absolutely necessary, exhibits which they had to dig out by trial and error because they didn't even know what to ask for. [Indignant] "Major Rome is the only one we have to help us get some of these police records. Mr. Wall says that everything is here—we can have what we want. But *what* can we have? *We don't know what is there!*"

(Mr. Wall, tilting back his chair, smiling—one wonders at what.)

"This trial depends on getting records that are in the possession of Mr. Wall," Mr. Shew said. "*A man's life* is at stake. Mr. Wall wants him to go to the electric chair, he says. Major Rome can help us. There is not *another person here* that will give them to us."

Now Mr. Wall swung down his chair and sprang to his feet. He was already speaking, sharply, as he rounded the table. "I think there should be some evidence, Your Honor, that Major Rome knows something about this case! Major Rome has in the file no report that he has ever submitted whatsoever. There isn't a report that I have seen in the file that has *ever* been submitted by Major Rome in connection with this case! [Rising voice] He . . . said on the witness stand the last time that he hadn't even read any reports about the case at all—and that he *purposely stayed away* from reading reports. *He so stated when he was on the stand.*"

(These accusations are distortions of the record. Rome testified in the last trial that he had studied the house and the grounds, talked with the men involved to get the facts. "I was briefed by, I think, each person who had anything important to do with it. I spent considerable time going through the house, studying the pictures and the grounds, making every effort to get all the facts that were available at that time. I went to the Connecticut Valley Hospital and had a talk with Agnes Thompsen. The facts that I had learned from *reports* and *investigation* convinced me that I should interrogate this individual.") But apparently Mr. Wall had not finished. He agreed that Counsel had a right to talk to Major Rome. "And I am sure that there isn't anyone more enthusiastic in the case for the Defense— really for his *own purposes*, not to help the *Defense* any. [Scoffing] His *motives* are not to help the Defense. [Sharp] *This Defendant is a pawn in the hands of Major Rome.*"

"If Major Rome knows nothing about the case," Mr. Shew shot back, "I don't know why Mr. Wall broke his neck to keep his evidence out in the other trial."

The Judge stayed with the question of law—whether the Court had the power to force a State Police officer to be in Court, possibly for three or four weeks, when his department head did not want him there. "I can't find any law anywhere that gives me that power."

"Well, if there is no ruling on it," Mr. Shew said, "I will instruct him to be here tomorrow. If he doesn't come, I will subpoena Commissioner Mulcahy and we will find out why."

(The press table: The Commissioner will not be pleased at that.) Mr. McKeon rejoined the battle with a legal argument that if Major Rome was not allowed to be here, the accused was being deprived of his constitutional right to obtain witnesses in his favor. The three attorneys stood in mid-court confronting each other with blazing hostility.

Judge Wright called Fuessenich to the stand in an effort to turn some light on the facts. Fuessenich testified that he had picked up the Detective Division file and that it consisted of some duplicates of reports in Mr. Wall's file, plus some work cards—small reports made out by officers as they completed assignments. (It sounds like next to nothing—which brings us back to Mr. Shew's earlier question: What ended up in the Canaan file, and what remained in the Hartford file?)

The Judge: "Did Major Rome or his *immediate underlings* prepare a separate file in this case?"

Fuessenich: "No, sir, this is the complete file."

"Was there a separate investigation running at different angles to your investigation?"

"Not after December 31, 1965."

Then Mr. Shew's turn—with an effort to turn the light on the fact that Rome directed this investigation. Again we heard the rather murky explanation that Major Rome was never actually removed— but that on December 31, 1965, when the piggy bank was found, Captain O'Brien told Lieutenant Fuessenich to "go ahead and pursue the investigation."

Mr. Shew: "Captain O'Brien is under Major Rome in rank?"

Fuessenich: "Under him but in a different division."

(Stringing together our information about these shifting sands it comes to this: Although Fuessenich claims to have been in charge, several officers have testified that on the night of the murder and during that first week they carried out orders issued by O'Brien. After the first week, Commissioner Mulcahy ordered Rome to take command of the investigation. Then on December 31, Captain O'Brien ordered Fuessenich to pursue the investigation. Are we asked to believe that a captain, on his own initiative, can direct a lieutenant to supersede a major without so much as a word to the major, and without approval from the Commissioner?)

Next, Mr. Wall—with an attempt to put out the light altogether by proving that the Major never had much to do with the case, anyway.

"Lieutenant, are you acquainted with the State Police file in connection with the investigation of the death of Mrs. Thompsen? . . . And have you gone through it very carefully?"

"Yes, sir."

"Is there any report *anywhere* that has *ever* been made by Major Rome?"

"I haven't seen any, sir."

"Not *any*—at any time?"

"No, sir."

Mr. Shew: "Well, Lieutenant, you are not trying to give the Court the impression that you were anxious to dig out exhibits for Mr. McKeon and myself, are you?"

"Sir, you asked me to bring things to Court. I brought them to Court."

"We also have to know what exhibits there are."

"Yes, sir."

"And how do you expect us to get them?"

"You merely ask for them, sir. We will be glad to go through the files." Always back to the same catch.

"If we don't know what it is, we can't ask for it!" Mr. Shew swung to the Judge. "Major Rome does know. We are satisfied that he can find them for us!"

The Judge regarded Fuessenich and then Mr. Shew and then said he would reserve his decision until after he had questioned Major Rome. "If you wish to call him tomorrow, we will have him heard in the absence of the Jury as to what he knows about the case and what his instructions are from the Commissioner."

Mr. Wall hurried forward. "May I ask one question? [To Fuessenich] Are there any records that indicate that Major Rome made *any investigation of his own* pertaining to the circumstances surrounding the death of Dorothy Thompsen? Are there any in the file?"

[Innocent] "I haven't seen them, sir. I have been through the file."

"And there are *none?*"

"No, sir, I haven't seen any."

(Then what has become of them? Yesterday the Judge asked who would have information on Agnes Thompsen's statement about sanding the stairs, and Fuessenich replied, "Captain O'Brien or Major Rome." How did he know this? And it was Rome, not Fuessenich, who testified at the first Coroner's Inquest. The Coroner would have had a report. Where is *that?* Judge Wright was careful to phrase his question, "Major Rome or his immediate *underlings.*" And at the other trial, while Ragazzi was reading the first interview of Agnes Thompsen, Mr. Wall appeared to be following on his own copy. Where is *that* report? And Mr. Wall said of a later interview, "If Your Honor listened to what happened on July 16 . . . there is lying, deceit . . ." Where is *that* report? And during the last trial Major Rome, on the stand, said to Mr. Wall, "*You had my reports* in your possession . . . !" And Mr. Wall did not deny it. Where are *those* reports?)

We are flirting again with the problem of disclosure, and there are chilling questions here that go beyond this case. What actually happens to police reports? How much can they be manipulated? Can reports be removed from a file—while their custodians swear that they do not exist? Does justice depend exclusively on the word of officers of the State, with no other guarantees that all information gained remains intact and that all relevant information is revealed? And who is the judge of relevancy?

The day was almost over when Mr. Wall began Redirect Examination of Arnfin. He brought out that Arnfin was questioned on the night of the murder for nearly five hours by Rebillard and again on Sunday for about two hours by Rebillard and Fuessenich. Also on Monday for about four hours. "And who did the questioning on Monday?"

"I don't remember the name."

Mr. Wall: "You don't remember the name?"

Arnfin [tossed off] "About five minutes with Major Rome—after."

"About *five minutes* with Major Rome?"

(It is two minutes to five. We will go overtime to save Arnfin the trouble of returning tomorrow.)

"During the last recess, did you look at certain photographs of the kitchen with reference to the sink area?" Yes. "And what did you observe about the dishes?"

"They were in a strainer. . . . There was a strainer full of dishes." (In one of the photographs there is a draining rack beside the sink with plates in it. Yesterday Fuessenich testified that dishes were *in* the sink: "There was a sinkful of dishes.")

Mr. Wall: "Knowing your wife's routine, do you know whether or not those dishes had been washed?"

"If they were in the strainer, they were washed."

"Now what was your wife's routine as to the time of her having her lunch?"

"It was quarter to twelve."

Mr. Wall asked what came next in her routine, and now we heard the reason for this schedule which, according to everyone who knew Dorothy, never varied. There were three television soap operas (*Love of Life, Search for Tomorrow, Guiding Light*) that Dorothy watched faithfully between twelve and one o'clock, and she planned the midday meal around them. She would prepare lunch so that she could eat it while she watched. "The first program was a half-hour,"

Arnfin said. "Then there would be two fifteen-minute programs, and
she would put the baby to bed between those two fifteen-minute
programs."

"And what approximately was the time?"

"Quarter to one."

[Slowly] "What was next on her routine?"

"She would do the housework while the baby slept."

[Patient] "How about the dishes?"

"She would do that during the commercials. Quarter after twelve.
Twelve twenty."

[Again; building] "And what time did she put the baby to bed?"

"Quarter to one."

"And was there a time in your wife's routine when she did the
ironing?"

Arnfin [smoothly] "She usually started about 1:30 on that."

Mr. Wall [strong] "1:30."

"Yes."

Triumphant, Mr. Wall turned away. (And this would bring it
right back to Harry. One shirt partly ironed—and Harry seen going
into the house at 1:30!)

(Press table: "Does any woman iron *every day*—to establish a
daily schedule?" "The program ended at one o'clock. The dishes
were washed—the baby was in bed. She didn't phone her mother.
What did she do between 1:00 and 1:30?")

After the Jury was dismissed, Mr. Wall asked to make a statement.

"Your Honor, I would like to move that Your Honor reconsider
the matter of bringing Mr. Rome here tomorrow. I feel that it would
be a protracted and unfortunate diversion of the trial. It would be a
waste of time. . . . [Pacing; droning] Your Honor might well refer
to what happened in the last trial when Major Rome was brought
down . . .[very supercilious] or at least he came to the Court
voluntarily, and requested an opportunity to appear. I think that the
man's propensity for getting in the limelight is well known. And I
think that *he does not represent the type at the present time of
justice that we like to think we have in this country!*"

(Controlled shock at the press table.)

"I feel it would be most unfortunate to bring the man down here
as a witness. I have never heard of it happening really in any other

case. It would divert us entirely from the trial. It would be highly prejudicial to the trial, and it would not be in the ends of justice. I feel very, very strongly about this, Your Honor. I feel that it is something that could serve no useful purpose, and that it could do a great deal of harm."

Mr. McKeon stepped in with another reason for summoning Rome to Court. "On the opening day of this trial," he said, "a reckless assertion was made in Chambers by Mr. Wall that I, McKeon, was in this case through a conspiracy of the Hartford *Courant* and Major Rome. He then reduced that to writing and handed it out to all Counsel. Mr. Shew and I have discussed it. We don't know whether it is a complaint of some kind. But I will demonstrate to the Court tomorrow that I have never even exchanged a greeting with Major Rome on any occasion."

Abruptly the Judge cut through to the heart of the matter. "Tomorrow, if Major Rome appears—I am not ordering him to appear—but if you bring him here tomorrow, I will hear him for one purpose. That is to see . . . whether or not he has access to certain records that could help the Defense. . . . After I am satisfied on that point, I will either tell him to remain or tell him to go. I will not go into all this other extraneous stuff tomorrow."

Mr. Wall [sharp] "Your Honor will *find* yourself in this extraneous stuff with a man like *Rome* coming down."

The Judge [calmly] "It will not be allowed. I will be asking him questions for one purpose only."

Mr. Wall [bursting out, boiling] "Your Honor, I shall say *not one word* tomorrow while this man is here, no matter what he says. I shall stay *absolutely mute* and say *nothing* while he is here. I will make an argument afterwards, and that's all. But I shall not crossexamine the man. I believe that it's highly prejudicial to have him here. I believe that it is improper to have him here. There is no precedent for it in any way. I shall stand completely mute while he is here testifying. [Flinging out another warning] And I hope that Your Honor can do what Your Honor believes he can do."

The Judge [undisturbed] "The Court has certain powers which the Court will enforce."

Court adjourned at 5:10.

24

This morning the witnesses were here to establish that Harry wrote the Letter. Mr. Slattery of Pratt-Whitney identified the job application; Detective Keller identified the handwriting sample deliberately obtained just prior to Harry's arrest. Again one marks time during these replays. Mr. Wall dragged out his questions in the same slow monotone. But this morning his speech was more than normally studded with "uhs" ("What was your—uh—first opportunity—uh—to become acquainted with him?"), and a chain of compulsive gestures betrayed his edged nerves. He ran his hand over his mouth and then his tongue across his lips. He paced about. He jingled coins. He took off his glasses and put them in his pocket and took them out again immediately and put them on. Rome was not here yet, and no one had said whether he was coming.

Now a departure from the pattern of the last trial. After the samples of Harry's handwriting had been introduced, Mr. Shew asked for five minutes for a conference. "We might be able to shorten this trial considerably."

The Judge: "If there is anything you can do to save time it will be gratefully received." (Everyone is aware that the State's case is in its fourth day and still has a long way to go. Witnesses drift in and wait and return the next day as progress bogs down in arguments.)

(The press: "Maybe he's going to plead to manslaughter." No one really believes it. "It's eleven o'clock. Rome isn't here.")

After ten minutes, Court reconvened, and Mr. McKeon stepped forward and said that he and Mr. Shew would make a judicial admission that the Letter was written by Harry Solberg. "We have had a conference with Mr. and Mrs. Solberg and with the Defendant's wife . . . and this is done with his knowledge and consent. . . . We submit that this dispenses with the need for proof of a handwriting expert."

The Judge accepted with alacrity. "Thank you, sir. Bring back the Jury."

Mr. Wall [sharply] "Your Honor, might I have something to say about that?" The sheriff stopped at the jury room door. Mr. Wall assumed a deeply censorious tone. "I am surprised that Counsel would make such an admission—particularly in view of the claim in the past of this man's loss of memory, his psychiatric difficulties. [Righteous] The *State* has an interest in doing justice here to this Defendant, even though Counsel are not interested in doing justice for him!"

Mr. McKeon: "I think that remark is out of order, Your Honor."

Mr. Wall [crisp] "The State has a duty to prove its case in connection with this. Any judicial admission would be absolutely out of order. It is the intention of the State to proceed, Your Honor."

The Judge looked puzzled. "I don't follow you, Mr. Wall. Defense Counsel has conceded that the letter was written by the Defendant. What more can you show?"

"Your Honor, the Defendant . . . has a claim here of a lack of memory. I won't go into what has happened in the past, but . . . the history of the past is such as to indicate that any judicial admission could not be relied upon at another time and that a real danger to the verdict would be encountered if the State did not proceed with its evidence. [Reproving again] Now, if they wish to make a judicial admission I have no objection to their doing it. However, in view of . . . this Defendant's claims in the past, I believe that it would be *improper* on the part of the attorneys to do so. And certainly I feel that the State has to go ahead with this testimony. [Getting in another dig] It will take a *very short time* as compared with motions that have been made by Counsel that seem to be aborted, except for *headlines*." Wheeling about, Mr. Wall walked to his table.

The Judge [still puzzled] "Well, I am not familiar with the first trial. . . . Are you telling me that some claim of insanity might arise?"

Mr. Wall repeated that there had been a claim of loss of memory. "And we don't know whether his loss of memory involved this particular document. . . . This is a vital piece of evidence. I think that in a capital case . . . it would be a terrible thing for the State not to put on its proof . . . [accusing] despite any attempts by Counsel to make judicial admissions where there could be a change in ten minutes on the part of the accused."

Mr. Shew: "If Your Honor please—Mr. Wall's solicitude for the Defendant is touching. In the first trial I didn't make any offer. But I never claimed in summation or argument that Harry did not write the letter. I never claimed it then and I don't claim it now."

The Judge: "Well, I can't direct the State's strategy. . . . If Mr. Wall will not accept your concession, I guess I have no power over that."

Mr. Wall: "I don't say I don't accept it. . . . I merely say that I wish to go ahead with proof despite it."

The Judge [pointedly] "Of course I am mindful . . . that Judge MacDonald, after the first trial, wrote out suggestions which might shorten the trial to one week. We are nowhere near that type of operation, are we?"

Mr. Wall was far too upset to stand still. While the Judge spoke he paced over to the jury box, jingling coins in his pocket. Now he turned quickly. "Not because of the State, Your Honor. I think that the *motions* have taken a large part of the time [jingle, jingle], and they are matters that have very little, if any, reference to the trial."

(To date the motions have been to produce the tapes and deposit them with the Court and to order Rome's appearance.)

Mr. McKeon reentered the argument. He would like to submit authority on the nature of a judicial admission. "I notice Mr. Wall never cites authority for his propositions, just flamboyant arguments. I am prepared to offer the legal theory behind a judicial admission . . ."

Mr. Wall's face darkened. With each speech, acrimony was increasing, and this clash, touched off by an offer to concede a point, left experienced observers incredulous. The Judge cut in: "Well, I cannot tell Mr. Wall what to do. [To Mr. McKeon] Do you still want the concession made in front of the Jury?"

Mr. McKeon: "The reason for the judicial admission was to

dispose of the need for this expert, to shorten the trial, and to minimize the effect of this witness, Liberi."

Mr. Wall: "We had Liberi here for two days."

Mr. McKeon: "What difference does that make?"

Mr. Shew: "I told him he could go home when he first came here."

Mr. Wall: "I don't know why Counsel don't speak to Counsel rather than to witnesses to inform them of their plans. [Mr. Wall swings quickly from an accusing to a righteous tone and just as quickly back again] I think there is a real duty on the part of the State in fairness to the Defendant, Your Honor—it isn't necessarily a question of solicitude for the Defendant as a person, but solicitude for *justice*—that the case be *proved*—[accusing again] rather than to rely on what might prove to be a *temporary admission*."

Mr. McKeon [patience gone] "Well, if Mr. Wall would study his books, he would realize that a judicial admission is binding for all time, Your Honor. I am wondering where he gets his theories."

Mr. Wall [lashing back] "I know of no rule of law, Your Honor, which would not allow the young man to repudiate the judicial admission and say that he didn't write the letter. There has already been a statement by him on record that he didn't write it." He stormed over to the jury box and leaned against it, head back, eyes to the heavens.

(The only such statement that one can recollect is testimony that, on that Sunday morning in Canaan, when Harry was first accused of writing the Letter, he denied it—hardly comparable to a judicial admission in Court.)

While the Judge consulted a reference book, Mr. McKeon and Mr. Shew resumed their seats. Mr. Wall remained standing beside the jury box, fingering a fistful of coins he had taken from his pocket. The Judge read (*Connecticut Evidence*, Holden and Daly), " 'It is true that in the trial of capital offenses, the Court . . . should exercise care and discretion in respect to admissions made by the accused or by his Counsel in open Court, and that every conviction should be supported by some evidence produced in Court.' " He looked up. "So perhaps Mr. Wall is correct that, to be overcareful, we should go on with the evidence."

"In that case the judicial admission is withdrawn," Mr. McKeon said, "and I would ask Your Honor, inasmuch as this pertains to evidence, that it not be publicized."

Mr. Wall: "*I* have no objection as far as publication is concerned." The Judge asked the press to observe the gentlemen's agreement.

Mr. Wall [a new accusation] "Only I understand the gentlemen's agreement so far hasn't been observed. I notice there was a great deal that happened in the absence of the Jury yesterday that was headlined in a paper . . . that appeared to be of an inflammatory nature."

The Judge, a monument of patience, replied that his request of the press was not to print any *evidence* excluded from the Jury's consideration. He had not seen any violation. If shown one, he would deal with it.

Mr. Wall [bristling] "Might I say, Your Honor, I must have misinterpreted Your Honor's ruling. . . . It was my understanding that it referred to *anything* that happened in the absence of the Jury. I stand corrected." He sat down and swung about to face the jury box.

The Judge said that he believed his power extended only to evidence. "Other matters, I am afraid, are not within my province to keep out of the press, unless you can show me authority to that effect."

Mr. Wall [a new head of steam] "Well, you know *I* am the one who doesn't read a book, Your Honor. I have to get my law from my head. And actually the books in the library are in the possession of the other side. I have no books available to me here." (Here is a new grievance. The press is in the library—and the Defense, lacking its own room, has joined them—but the door is open and anyone can enter. However, now that Mr. Wall had trained on his favorite target, no one believed that he would stop short and he did not.) "It is my belief that prejudicial matters, particularly that occur in the absence of the Jury, particularly the type of happening of yesterday—for the *purpose* of *stirring up a headline*—is to me most objectionable. And I respectfully request that Your Honor include in his ruling the matter of publicizing these *created incidents.*"

The Judge [he retains complete equanimity] "Any response, gentlemen?"

Mr. Shew: "Your Honor's attitude is perfectly satisfactory as far as the Defense is concerned. . . . I have no interest in what the press says. Mr. Wall has a tremendous interest in it . . . and I refuse to discuss the matter with him. I don't think it is my business to."

Mr. Wall: "My remarks are addressed entirely to Your Honor and not to Counsel."

Mr. Shew: "I was addressing that to His Honor in reply to his request for our attitude."

The Judge repeated his ruling, closed the discussion, and ordered the Jury back.

It had been a strange and bitter clash—aggravated, one suspected, by the fact that Rome was not yet here, had not said he would *not* be here, could turn up any minute—and it left its mark. Very aggressively, Mr. Wall's voice rang out, "Mr. Anthony Liberi, Your Honor."

He began the routine questions in a soft voice, obviously straining for control, his speech studded with two or three "uhs" in a row. "And—uh-uh-uh—during that period of time, how many—uh-uh—documents have you examined,—uh-uh—Mr. Liberi?"

Through no fault of Mr. Liberi this was fairly tedious testimony, inevitably the same as before. (The eye wanders about the room. In the back row, Detective Holden sits impassively, Rebillard's face is a mask, Fuessenich is listening with a hand cupped to his ear.) Joe Crowley went out to telephone his story to the Hartford *Times*—an afternoon paper. Somewhat calmer, Mr. Wall offered the pertinent exhibits to Mr. Liberi—Harry's known handwriting samples and the Letter. Mr. Liberi began to explain the points of similarity. The day dragged on.

A few minutes later, Mr. McKeon glanced around at the press table, turned quickly to Mr. Shew. "It's empty!"

Mr. Shew smiled. "Sam's here."

Fate follows him. He and his driver, Trooper Rasmussen, had interrupted their trip to Bridgeport to chase a getaway car from a bank holdup. Now Joe Crowley had returned from the telephone with word that he was here, and one by one the reporters left the courtroom. There was a better story outside.

At 12:30 Judge Wright dismissed the Jury for lunch and sent for Major Rome. Then Mr. Wall asked to make a statement and that

Major Rome be out of the room while he was speaking, and Major Rome stepped out again.

In a very long statement, Mr. Wall offered a severe indictment of what he considered to be the entire combined enemy forces—the two Defense attorneys, Demeusy and the Hartford *Courant,* and, of course, the Major.

"This motion has been highly publicized in the papers, with a headline that 'Wall Wants to Keep Rome from Testifying.'" (The Hartford *Courant* headline this morning: "Judge to Query Rome Before He Takes Stand: Prosecution Seeks to Block Testimony.") "That's the farthest thing from my mind. I would welcome Major Rome's speaking on any relevant part of this case. . . . And there isn't any question but that he has been available to the Defense. . . . There has never been any prohibition. . . . *This is only an attempt, Your Honor, to publicize the Defense.*"

Most agitated, circling a wide area, Mr. Wall repeated the charge that he had made the first day in Chambers and which he had since included in a written statement. Both Defense Counsel had admitted in Chambers, he said, that it was Demeusy who had approached McKeon to come into the case. "The man who made the approach is the newspaperman who is stirring up this type of motion in order that he might put it in *headlines* that 'Wall Is Suppressing Evidence.' This union between newspaper and Counsel is an *unholy one.* And I only refer to *one* newspaperman . . . I refer to Mr. Demeusy of the Hartford *Courant.*"

Now Mr. Wall stopped and faced the Judge. "I told Your Honor that, if Your Honor had Rome testify, I was going to *stand mute.* And I *shall* stand mute. I shall say nothing if he is allowed to testify and spiel ideas which are totally unsupported by the facts. I feel very, very strongly that it is most prejudicial and that it is most improper to have the man brought here. I also say, Your Honor, that the fact that Mr. Rome is here today is absolute proof that if Counsel wanted him for something other than window dressing, they were able to get him. . . . Your Honor did not order him here—it was only on order from Defense Counsel that he is here. . . . This is a *red herring,* Your Honor, *dragged through the courtroom* merely for the purpose of badgering the State's Attorney, as has been done by Mr. Demeusy and his paper."

Having touched all bases, Mr. Wall began to circle them again.

"There was a headline in the paper . . . I will be very happy to have everyone testify so that justice may be done. But justice would only be *thwarted* by allowing this man to get up here and make a speech. . . . The fact that he is here today is positive proof. . . . And I see no reason for Your Honor taking any action whatsoever after this *positive proof*. The motion of the Defendant is not well taken." Mr. Wall strode to his seat.

Mr. Shew's patience with these charges was about gone. "Your Honor, if Mr. Wall had been courteous enough to come into Chambers when he was invited, he would realize that he is now talking through his hat, as usual." He went on to say that this whole thing seemed so ridiculous that he hesitated to waste the Court's time, but he felt that both he and Mr. McKeon had been insulted by Mr. Wall and that he should reply. Up until last July, he said, he and Mr. McKeon had had adjoining offices and he had discussed the case with him many times. "Actually the Defense needs help in this case and always has. Mr. Wall has Officer Pennington. He has his own private detective, County Detective Samuel Holden. And he has available all the resources of the Canaan Barracks, who really seem to be making a career of this case. . . .

"When I found out that Mr. McKeon was willing, as a public-spirited attorney, without any hope of substantial remuneration, to assist me, I jumped at the chance. . . . Now I am willing to take an oath, Your Honor—that Major Rome knew nothing about this. . . ." Mr. Shew's statement was turning out to be as long as Mr. Wall's. With rising indignation he said that Mr. Wall had openly insulted Mr. McKeon and himself as well as Major Rome, in his statements yesterday that the Defense was a pawn of Major Rome and that Mr. McKeon was in this matter for some devious reason. ". . . As for the publicity on the trial, if Mr. Wall would not make these—what I feel are stupid—statements, he wouldn't get himself boxed in the way he does as far as the press is concerned."

For a moment Judge Wright sat perfectly still—his fine-featured face betraying no reaction to either of these very long, impassioned speeches. "Well, we seem to get into all kinds of extraneous channels, gentlemen," he commented. He asked the sheriff to bring in Major Rome.

Mr. Wall: "I still state, Your Honor, that I shall make no further statements. I intend to stand mute except to enter objections to the questions as they arise." He resumed his seat, tight-lipped, eyes turned to the ceiling.

Major Rome walked briskly to the stand and was sworn.

Judge Wright: "Major Rome, first I would like to ask you—what records or documents do you have under your control?"

Major Rome: "At this moment?"

"Yes."

"None."

"And where are all the records as far as you know?"

"They are in the possession and custody of the Canaan Barracks or the State's Attorney's office."

The Judge: "The Defense has claimed that your presence is vital to their preparation of the Defense. And so I must ask you in what way your presence would be so important?"

"Your Honor, I was in charge of the investigation from a week after the crime was committed until sometime in December of 1965. I obtained a confession that was verified and corroborated from another individual. [Businesslike] My twenty-nine or thirty years of experience led me to believe that another individual committed this crime. That individual is not in this courtroom."

The Defense, the Judge said, had claimed that his presence was necessary to steer them toward Exhibits that might be in State Police hands. Rome replied that he believed he could be helpful. The Judge inquired about his orders.

Rome: "Commissioner Mulcahy has instructed me—until otherwise ordered or instructed by Your Honor—to appear here only to testify."

The Judge turned to the attorneys. "If anybody has questions along these limited lines—*and I mean limited lines*—you may ask them."

Mr. Shew: "We will stand on Major Rome's statement."

Judge Wright returned to his original problem. "Last night I tried to find some law that would allow me to accede to your motion, Mr. Shew—but I can't find any such law."

Mr. Shew: "Your Honor, it is the duty of the State to seek the *truth*—not necessarily to get a conviction. . . . There is a *world* of evidence in this matter. And we don't know what is there. For example, in the first trial Mr. Wall ended his case without introducing any of Dr. Stolman's reports." He paused. "Am I correct in that, Mr. Wall?"

"I have agreed to stand mute, Your Honor. I am saying nothing."

"And I had to dig them out," Mr. Shew continued. "I had no means of knowing what was there. Your Honor, we are still faced with that situation. Sure, the evidence is *here*. But it is only available to us when we know about it. . . . There was a tremendous amount of evidence, in my opinion, that Mr. Wall should have brought out in the other trial, which was only brought out through digging and digging and digging. . . . If an outstanding member of the State Police feels that a man on trial for his life is innocent, he should be available to the Defense." Now Mr. Shew voiced publicly what had been his private opinion for a long time. "We have this prohibition merely because Mr. Wall has yelled his head off—and gotten into fights. I have been personal witness to all of it—and I unequivocally state that it is Mr. Wall's fault. I think Mr. Wall has provoked those fights himself—to keep Major Rome out of the case. If Major Rome is willing to be here, there should be no prohibition on his being available to us."

Mr. Wall sat with his chair tilted back, ignoring the accusation. The Judge asked Mr. Scofield for a volume of cases, saying, while he waited, "I am still groping for my authority to order what you want me to order, Mr. Shew."

"I think if Your Honor indicated that Major Rome's presence was in the interest of justice, Commissioner Mulcahy would have no objection. I think he is trying to avoid situations such as Mr. Wall has created. All of this bitterness falls on Mr. Wall's shoulders."

When Mr. Scofield returned, Judge Wright opened to a case (*State versus Guilfoyle*) which stated that "the testimony of every available witness tending to aid in ascertaining the truth [should] be laid before the trial court, irrespective of whether it be consistent with the contentions of the prosecution. It is especially . . . necessary where the circumstances . . . are attended by great excitement and confusion." Judge Wright looked up. "In other words, in a criminal case, particularly one of homicide and much excitement, our Supreme Court feels that all sides of the question should be exposed." The Judge had found a reasonable basis for his decision.

He asked the press not to print opinions (meaning Rome's) about guilt or innocence until those opinions came out before the Jury. He turned to Major Rome. "Major, I request you to ask your superior that you be available to the Defense for such help as you can give them. I don't order this because I don't think I have the power to order it. But I think I should, in all fairness to both sides, request that you do assist—as best you can—the Defense."

•   •   •

The afternoon session passed with intermittent clashes. As Mr. Liberi completed his testimony Mr. McKeon brought out that Rebillard had given him Harry's school card in August, 1965, and that, although Mr. Liberi had asked for further samples of Harry's handwriting, he heard nothing more for seven months.

By the afternoon recess we had heard Mr. Richards, the jeweler, and encountered the same confusion as before about whether Harry made a $25 down payment on the ring on June 17. Mr. Richards began by saying that he did not—"He didn't pay anything that day. He didn't get the ring that day. I think he paid the $25 at a later time when he got the ring."

Mr. Wall produced the same sales slip as in the first trial and also a file card, which was new. Referring to the sales slip, Mr. Richards said, "It says right here—'Diamond ring set plus tax. $71.10.' And then $25 is subtracted. . . . This $25 was probably written in later. The slip was made out—he paid nothing. . . . He didn't get the ring at this time because the color and size had to be changed. . . . When he paid the $25 we filled it in. . . . The date should have been there but it isn't. . . . If we had known it was such an important thing, we'd certainly have put it down but we didn't at that time."

The Judge reviewed the testimony: that Harry made the arrangements on the seventeenth, made the first payment of $25 at some later date. Mr. Richards agreed that that was correct. The Judge said that it was perfectly clear.

And so it was. But from here on, it was all downhill into confusion. Mr. Wall referred to the file card, "which definitely shows a $25 payment was made on 6–17–65. That is shown and that's the date shown, all in typing on the card."

The Judge asked for Mr. Richards' comment on that, and now Mr. Richards, in a bind, said, "That's what it says. It must have been paid then at that time. I didn't say that it *wasn't*. I said it *could* have been paid." (No hint of this until now!)

(As nearly as one could make out, this card was a typewritten record of time payments, copied from sales slips and receipts. If no date for the $25 payment was entered on the sales slip it could not have been picked up when the card was prepared.)

Mr. McKeon asked whether Mr. Richards had turned over any other papers to the police, and Mr. Richards said that he had. Now Mr. Wall handed over more of Mr. Richards' records, including a carbon copy of the sales slip which, Mr. Richards testified, Harry took home to have his father or mother sign because he was under twenty-one.

Mr. McKeon: "And the carbon copy, which was naturally executed at the same time, contains *no record of payment?*"

"That's right."

After recess more than another hour to Mrs. Clark, whose grandchild stumbled on the piggy bank. Again not much gained—really the only pertinent testimony from Mrs. Clark was that she was a witness to its discovery at the location, which she identified. But there were increasingly bitter exchanges between Counsel, tempers rising as the day wore on, with accusations flying and insults no longer veiled or restrained. When Mrs. Clark was excused it was the end of the day and the end of the week. Little had been accomplished and nerves were very raw.

The attorneys remained after the Jury left to confirm arrangements to hear the last of the tapes the following day—this time in the court building, again with Mr. Scofield present.

Then suddenly there was a final sharp clash. With the matter of the tapes settled, Mr. Wall asked to be excused, saying that he was late for a dinner he had promised to attend in Torrington.

Mr. Shew came forward quickly. "I have just one short request. Mr. McKeon and I are very anxious to confer with Major Rome. And we would like to avail ourselves of Mr. Wall's kind agreement to provide us with any information in his possession." Now Mr. Shew asked for the loan of the Detective Division and the Canaan Barracks "bindover files"—two separate files, although they may have been combined—which contained statements and reports of the officers who had participated in the investigation. Obviously Mr. Shew knew exactly what to ask for now. "They can be distinguished in a reddish brown notebook. And there may be some notebooks of investigators. . . . We would like those also."

A flushed face and round angry blue eyes revealed Mr. Wall's reaction, but he maintained a tight control. "Might this motion be heard Tuesday morning, Your Honor?"

The Judge turned to Mr. Shew. "In the absence of agreement, Mr. Shew, I can't order this," he said. "Our law says very clearly that a prosecutor's file is sacrosanct except for certain exceptional circumstances. Do you agree to this, Mr. Wall, or not?"

[Crisp] "I do, Your Honor."

[Surprised] "You do agree to show your files?"

"*No.* I agree that it is sacrosanct."

The Judge: "Oh—earlier you indicated you might show to the Defense anything they wanted."

[Cold] "That's true."

"Now are you withdrawing that?"

"Oh, I'm withdrawing. I'm certainly not agreeing to turning over my file to them! Am I going to be without a file?"

Mr. Shew: "We would have it back by Tuesday, Mr. Wall."

Mr. Wall [emphatic] "No. Your Honor, this has never happened in the history of trial of cases. [Impatient] May this be heard Tuesday morning, Your Honor? It's a ridiculous motion. I have been preparing to go to this dinner in Torrington for a long time. This has been a long day for me."

The Judge: "Well, unless the prosecutor agrees, Mr. Shew, it will have to take a lot of argument on Tuesday morning."

Mr. Shew protested that they had wanted to work with Major Rome over the weekend. "This is not Mr. Wall's file—his own file. It is a matter of the records."

Mr. Wall [very cold] "Might we have argument on Tuesday?"

The Judge [ending it] "Well, unless Mr. Wall agrees, as he is apparently not going to do now, we will have to take some other time to explore this."

Court adjourned until Tuesday morning. As Mr. Wall hurried out, Demeusy muttered, "He's got a hot date for a dinner. Harry has a hot date with the electric chair."

25

Tuesday, January 24

On Tuesday morning it was Mr. Wall who brought it up. "There was a matter on Thursday afternoon, Your Honor . . . I asked Your Honor's indulgence to put it over until this morning, and I have no objection to taking it up now."

Mr. Shew started to say that during the day, probably, the Jury would have to be excused. Then, reading the protest on Mr. Wall's face, he said, "I am perfectly willing to press it at this time, Your Honor."

Mr. Wall [edgy already] "I know that Counsel has *another motive* for bringing it up at a later time, Your Honor. I shan't go into it at the moment, but it is quite obvious. If the matter is going to come up, it should come up at the present time."

Mr. Shew [annoyed] "Mr. Wall has the unique faculty, Your Honor, of telling what's in my mind. . . . I am glad to take it up at this time."

Clearly the weekend has healed no wounds, but then the wounds have not been free of irritation. On Friday the attorneys listened to the last of the tapes. (Already Mr. McKeon has private questions. He is convinced that something is wrong. "The tapes on the 14th in Hartford end at a little past 8:30 and Harry is giving the first story—that he walked in and followed the trail of blood. Then the next thing—boom—it's midnight and they're in Canaan and he's confessing.") And before Court this morning, through the door to Chambers, we heard the sounds of a heated argument.

Mr. Shew repeated his request for a copy of the bindover file. "I understand that it comes in duplicate. I assume that Mr. Wall has

one copy—but there is another. . . . Major Rome has nothing in
his possession now. . . . Now obviously, even in a traffic case, an
officer has to refer to notes. I am not asking for Mr. Wall's file. I
think there are complete duplicates right in this courtroom—or in
the hands of the Canaan Barracks. They contain the reports of all
the officers that worked on this investigation."

Mr. Shew cited examples to illustrate the need for disclosure of
the whole file:

First he mentioned Detective Redican's report (involving the
interview of Randy Stadler). He reminded the Judge that he had
learned of its existence during Fuessenich's testimony and had then
requested and received a copy. "The police *have these reports*. . . .
Just this first document is tremendously important. . . ."

Second, "Lieutenant Fuessenich did not even bother to mention
the taking of the traps in Agnes Thompsen's apartment. . . ."

Third, "And . . . in the other trial, Mr. Wall ended his case
without putting in Dr. Stolman's exhibits. Your Honor will see when
these Exhibits come in how important they are to the truth in this
matter."

(Throughout this attack, Mr. Wall tilted back his chair, disdain-
ing to notice, and looked at the ceiling.)

"We *need* these reports," Mr. Shew pleaded. "We are *entitled* to
them. We're not taking undue advantage of anybody. We are only
trying to bring out the *truth*, and the only way we can do it is to get
the reports now in the possession of the Canaan Barracks. . . . Just
this first one [holding up Redican's report] that we nabbed here is
fantastically important. Until we got hold of it the other day, so far
as we knew, no such report existed. Mr. Wall has said, 'Sure, I'll
produce anything they want.' Now he changes his mind about that.
Well, we want the duplicate copy of the bindover files. If we don't
have it, we don't know what is there. And we are entitled to know."

The Judge turned to Mr. Wall, who swung out of his chair and
came around the table. "Counsel used a word which I think is quite
appropriate, relating to what happened to a paper which is—may I
see it please?—Court's Exhibit 8. He used the word, 'nabbed.' He
didn't *nab* it, Your Honor. It was given to him voluntarily . . . for
the weekend. And the State hasn't seen it for eleven days. It was
nabbed all right. And it's been retained and kept."

The Judge: "Gentlemen, shall we keep personalities out of this and get down to the law? The law is that a prosecutor's file is sacrosanct. It is completely privileged from production by the opposing side unless the State's Attorney wishes to produce it. [To Mr. Wall] Do you or do you not wish to produce it?"

Mr. Wall: "You mean the whole file? My whole file!"

The Judge: "Whatever they want. You can refuse and I will uphold you."

Mr. Wall: "Your Honor, I would like to cite the case of *State versus Zimnaruk* . . . which reechoes what Your Honor has stated. Certainly in view of what has happened to the one Exhibit that I did turn over to Counsel, I see no obligation on the part of the State. [Brusque] The State does not wish to hand over anything to the Defendant at the present time. . . . I feel that the Defense has abused what the State has done by keeping the one paper . . . for a period of eleven days without returning it." Flushed with resentment, Mr. Wall wheeled about and took his seat.

Quite contrite, Mr. Shew hastened to admit his error. "It was an oversight . . . I had forgotten it—and that's the truth. But it is here safe and sound, and I haven't even made a copy of it."

Mr. Wall to his feet again. "I might say to Your Honor that I have only one copy of my bindover file. I do not have any duplicate, by any means."

Mr. Shew: "Mr. Wall doesn't, but the State Police do."

Mr. Wall: "I know of no other bindover file in existence, Your Honor—but certainly I don't have it."

Mr. Shew [challenging] "May I have Lieutenant Fuessenich on the stand—or Mr. Pennington to find out?"

The Judge: "It is not a question of what there is. It is a question of what the State's Attorney will consent to. Our law is that his file is completely privileged—as a matter of public policy. If he refuses, I will uphold him."

Mr. Shew suggested that perhaps the reports of the investigating officers could be produced in another way. "We certainly have to have something."

Mr. Wall [crisp] "I am very happy to do it in an orderly process in the trial. . . . I feel that my attempt to hand something to Counsel certainly has been abused, Your Honor. Asking me for the whole file is *ridiculous,* and therefore any such offer would be completely improper on my part at the present time."

Mr. Shew [quick retort] "Well, I don't know that it is ridiculous to try to save a man's life, Your Honor. These statements should be available. If it is the only way, we will subpoena every single officer who investigated this case along with his statements and his notebooks. [Waxing very angry] We will probably be here for a couple of months. If Mr. Wall wants to stay here, I will."

The Judge [abruptly ending the argument] "Motion is denied."

Mr. Wall [put-upon tone] "Your Honor, may I have the paper back that has been kept by Counsel for this length of time?"

But now Judge Wright, after a moment's reflection, commented further. [Reading from the case cited, State versus Zimnaruk] "It states very clearly: 'Information disclosed to a State's Attorney for the purpose of enabling him to perform the duties of the office is privileged upon grounds of public policy, and an adverse party has no right to demand its production.' [He looked at Mr. Wall] On the other hand, this case also states that it is the duty of the State's Attorney to see that impartial justice is done—and to cooperate as best he can without injuring his case. [An oblique challenge?] So there are two opposing ideas mentioned in State versus Zimnaruk."

(The reason for this rule on the ground of "public policy" is that, in cases of organized crime, if the State revealed the names of certain witnesses and the important nature of certain testimony, the witnesses might very well be done away with before they could give that testimony in Court. And even in cases not involving organized crime, persuasion of witnesses and shading of evidence is not unheard of. The rule is a protection. And it is an injustice. In the law for everything given, something is taken away.)

Mr. Wall: "Might I say, Your Honor, in State versus Zimnaruk, it relates only to the production of any inconsistent statements. [Grave] Actually, Your Honor, I believe that I have attempted in this trial, and I shall continue to attempt, to see that justice is done. . . . And I pledge to Your Honor that I have always been conscious of that duty, and I shall continue to be conscious of that duty."

The Judge [flat] "All right, sir."

Now Mr. McKeon spoke up. "May I be heard on one point, Your Honor? Major Rome, as a witness, will have his ability to testify impaired and emasculated if he is not allowed to see the notes that he, himself, prepared and that were prepared under his direction. We ask that this file be turned over to Major Rome to enable him to testify intelligently as a witness." (Mr. Wall pacing, pacing—over to the empty jury box and back again.) Mr. McKeon continued:

"There is evidence that Major Rome was never relieved of this case. Technically, he has something almost akin to a property interest in that file. . . . To testify from unaided memory to events as complex as this—he has covered scores of cases since and before—is almost an absurdity. It is absolutely necessary that he have that file to prepare himself for being a witness." Concerning an exception, Mr. McKeon asked that it read that this denial was a violation of the accused's constitutional rights.

Mr. Wall [darting back] "Your Honor, there is no report whatsoever that has ever been made to the State's Attorney relating to *any facts whatsoever* in this case by Major Rome. There is *not one* in there. Major Rome is a red herring being dragged across the courtroom to assist the Defense in bringing about the type of result that they want. [Shrill] There is *no report* relating to any facts in this case—and I can say it categorically—ever made to the *State's Attorney* by Major Rome."

The Judge turned to Mr. Shew: "Apparently this document that you want is not in existence."

Mr. Shew: "Yes, it is, Your Honor. Major Rome had charge of this case—he attended the Coroner's Hearings—and he is still in charge. He has never been relieved. . . . The Canaan Barracks has appropriated his reports and we feel they should be made available to us."

Mr. Wall [sharp] "I might say, Your Honor, that Canaan- Barracks took whatever was in Hartford at the request of the *Defendant's Counsel*. [Jingling coins—rapidly] The Defendant's Counsel came in here and insisted that they were going *to put Lieutenant Fuessenich in jail* [!] because he didn't come down when the Jury was being chosen on a subpoena that had been served at 11:30 the night before. They insisted upon him taking every bit of the file that was in Hartford and bringing it here. And he has complied with Your Honor's request."

Mr. Shew: "That's part of the file that we want!"

With thinly veiled disgust the Judge ended the matter by ordering the sheriff to bring in the Jury, and Mr. Flagg, the water district patrolman, was called as the first witness of the day.

Each successive witness now reveals the greatest single contrast between these two trials. Last time the Defense—with no case and no weapon except Major Rome—was completely on the defensive while the State wrapped up its case in three days, with swift sharp blows. Now the situation was reversed. More and more it was the State that was on the defensive, struggling to shore up its position (there were sporadic flashes of attack, but they were only pockets of action), and the Defense was striking back with fresh ammunition and even seizing some of the State's weapons and turning them to its own purpose.

Mr. Flagg had been called by the State to give the testimony that he had seen a man get out of a "black '59 Ford two-door sedan—very shiny . . . I would say it was between 1:30 and 1:45 in the afternoon."

Mr. McKeon used Mr. Flagg's testimony to emphasize the time—an important block in building a defense around the time of death. "How precise can you be that it was after 1:30?"

Mr. Flagg: "Well, the reason it was around 1:30 is, I had left my father's house at about twenty or twenty-five after one . . . about two or three miles away." In the end the time was placed roughly between 1:15 and 1:45—pinpointed to about 1:30.

• • •

Bob and Carole Stadler are here today, and Mr. and Mrs. Burdick. Mr. Burdick wearing a suit to come to Bridgeport instead of the sweater he wore in Litchfield—a small man with a pinched face and wispy gray hair. Mrs. Burdick, a plump, placid woman—soft face, gray hair, eyeglasses—wearing a flowered print dress and a black hat. During the day she spoke to a reporter about Dorothy. "She was a good girl. She was very close to the family. She played the organ in church in New Hartford. But after the baby was born she didn't play, anymore—she was very nervous afterward. She was a good girl—it's too bad she had to die that way—" Mrs. Burdick began to weep and could not go on.

Prompted by repeated testimony that June 15 was "a warm, sunny day," Mr. McKeon has added to his file a Weather Service Report for June, 1965. The report shows no precipitation that day. It reads "Mostly cloudy, limited morning sunshine." Maximum temperature 64°, minimum temperature 53°, mean temperature 59°, 11 degrees below normal for the day. At noon the temperature was 62°. At 7:00 o'clock, when the police began to arrive, it was 61°.

•   •   •

The State called Dr. Murphy and we settled down to another repeat performance while this Jury was given the facts. During Dr. Murphy's testimony Mr. and Mrs. Burdick left the courtroom.

A thatch of gray hair, bright blue eyes behind round spectacles, jutting jaw, jowled neck, Dr. Murphy sat forward in the witness chair, reporting the condition of the body as he found it. "A mass of blood over the right eye . . . and on the left side of the face . . . comminuted fracture of the frontal temporal bone . . . eyeball collapsed. . . . I noticed that most of the blood stopped along the nipple line . . . from there down there wasn't any." (We are aware that this differs from Fuessenich's testimony that there was blood on the front of her slacks—no blood in the back.) ". . . Marks of two blows on the left side of the skull. . . . The autopsy showed all the facial bones and the nose were broken . . ."

Mr. Wall asked for, and Dr. Murphy gave, his opinion on the cause of death. "I believe that she died within a matter of minutes from multiple fractures of the skull . . . and I think the cord around the neck was put on after death." (We remember that Dr. Murphy and Dr. Opper differed on this point.)

Mr. Shew, in Cross-Examination, went directly to the autopsy report. Had Dr. Murphy seen it? He had. If it were available to him would it aid him in determining various aspects of the death? It would. Mr. Shew offered it and read it aloud to the Jury. (The language is technical. The jurors listen dutifully, but not with rapt attention.) There still has been no assurance that Dr. Opper will be here, and for the Defense the autopsy report is essential for one piece of information. If Mr. Shew can get it in through Dr. Murphy, he can let Dr. Opper stay in Maine.

When he finished reading the report, Mr. Shew said, "Doctor, is there anything in this report which would change your ideas of sequence as to what happened?"

Dr. Murphy: "No."

Mr. Shew reread the important paragraph, slowly, in a strong voice: " 'Examination of the gastrointestinal tract reveals *several ounces* of predominantly *green vegetable* content which appears to have been *very recently ingested* with *no demonstrable passage* of it into the duodenum.' [Looking up] Can you tell us what that means, Doctor?"

Dr. Murphy: "After ingestion, food is passed into the first part of the intestine—called the duodenum—which is ten or twelve inches long. . . . Lettuce, greens, salads are bulk. . . . Bulk passes into the duodenum within minutes."

Now the question: "In view of this . . . can you give an opinion as to the *length of time* that elapsed between the time the deceased ate and the time of her death?"

Mr. Wall: "Your Honor, I object to this as no part of the Direct Examination. It might very well be a part of the Defense . . ."

Mr. Shew argued that Mr. Wall had questioned about the sequence of events, which was the substance of this question. The objection was overruled. Mr. Wall remained standing. The question was read: Could Dr. Murphy give an opinion on the length of time that elapsed . . .

Mr. Wall: "Your Honor, the question calls for yes or no. May the witness be so instructed."

Dr. Murphy [short] "Yes."

Mr. Shew: "And what would that time be?"

Mr. Wall: "I object to that, Your Honor, as no part of the Direct Examination. Also it relates to what could be a variable factor."

Mr. Shew: "If Your Honor please, I would like Mr. Wall to confine his objections to the point and to stop testifying himself. . . . Apparently he is very much afraid I'll bring out an essential point."

The Judge: "Well, what is the purpose of your inquiry, Mr. Shew?"

Mr. Shew: "It's extremely important, Your Honor, with other evidence that will come up, indicating it is *impossible* for this Defendant to have committed this crime. It has already been established that the deceased ate at a certain time. We want the time of death with relation to the time she ate and—"

Explosion!

Mr. Wall [furious] "Your Honor, I move that those remarks be stricken from the record and the Jury be instructed to disregard them because *definitely there is no such evidence.* The guilt or innocence of this accused is entirely for the Jury to decide, and the remark is entirely out of order."

"He answered the question I posed to him, Mr. Wall, . . ." the Judge replied and then, in order to clear up several points, he excused the Jury.

First the difference of opinion on the cause of death. Dr. Murphy was adamant about this. "When a person is hung, the cord is way up here under the jawbone—it isn't midway. It starts off down there [indicating the lower portion of his neck]—then when the body weight pulls it, it's way up here. . . . The face is black . . . the tongue protrudes—the eyeballs protrude. In this case the eyeballs were collapsed."

The Judge: ". . . You said originally that you thought the cord was put around her neck after death . . ."

Dr. Murphy: "That's what I thought."

The Judge: "But doesn't the autopsy report indicate that the cord was a contributing factor in causing death?"

Dr. Murphy [sticking to his guns] "That's where we differ."

Then the other question. "Now, this evidence of green vegetables undigested. What does that mean to you, sir?"

Dr. Murphy leaned forward. "Well—if a person had eaten a salad or something like that—in a few minutes that would have gone into the intestinal tract—the first part of the duodenum. It goes fairly fast—it's a bulk. In a matter of minutes you'd find evidence in the first part of the small intestine—*within minutes.*"

"This green vegetable content would indicate to you how much time had elapsed since she had lunch before she died?"

"It would be a matter of minutes—five minutes."

"She died within minutes of her lunch?"

"That's right."

The Judge: "Now—how does that become important, Mr. Shew?"

Mr. Shew: "We expect to establish the time she had her lunch, Your Honor."

The Judge: "Well, Mr. Wall was saying that there is no other possible evidence on this score. [To Mr. Wall] What were you saying, sir?"

Mr. Wall [backing down a bit] "I said there *has been* no such evidence. . . . He has represented . . . that there already *has been* some evidence relating to it. [To his own complaint] And that was part of my motion that the Jury be instructed to disregard the statement . . . [sharp] that this is going to prove that his client is not guilty of any crime and also that it relates to evidence that has already been admitted. There is no such evidence, so far at any rate."

Mr. Shew: "If Your Honor please, I spent a great deal of time with Arnfin Thompsen establishing that his wife and child had a pattern—invariably—for eating at a quarter of twelve. And we expect to have plenty more evidence. I dislike having to call Dr. Murphy down again—I feel that this is proper Cross-Examination of him as a medical examiner. This is a very important matter." (Mr. Wall rocking back and forth, twisting his pen in his fingers.) "In the last trial," Mr. Shew went on, "Dr. Opper testified on this. Now Mr. Wall has questioned whether Dr. Opper will be here. [Firm] I'm going to make every effort to get the State to produce him. . . . If not, his opinion is available from the other trial."

Mr. Wall [still rocking] "The mere fact that there is some evidence of a habit of having lunch at a particular time does not mean that she did not eat just prior to her death, Your Honor. There is nothing in the evidence to show that she did not eat minutes before her death." (Some gymnastics in logic there. The evidence shows that she *did* eat minutes before her death.)

Mr. Shew: "We are not asking Dr. Murphy to fix the time of death. We expect to prove that later. We are merely asking him to fix it in relation to the time she ate. Arnfin Thompsen said her habits were invariable in eating at a quarter of twelve. Dr. Murphy is a medical examiner. He has the autopsy report, which has been admitted in evidence. He has been qualified as an expert. He has stated the sequence. I am asking for his opinion as to how much time elapsed between the ingestion of this food and her death."

Mr. Wall: "My objection is it's certainly no part of the Direct . . . if we are talking about *that*."

Mr. Shew: "That's what we're talking about."

Mr. Wall [quick switch] "I would like to press my motion that this *inflammatory statement* . . . along the lines of 'We're going to prove our Defendant not guilty by this testimony' is entirely out of place, improper—and that the Jury should be instructed that it is improper . . . and *that* is what I consider to be one of the matters under discussion here. I move that Your Honor so instruct the Jury, that any such statements are to be disregarded and that they are to depend entirely on the evidence rather than on these claims of Counsel."

The Judge [ignoring the diversion] "Well, I am satisfied that there is a proper claim by the Defense with relation to the luncheon hour and how soon thereafter she died." The only question was whether it must wait for the case for the Defense. It was not part of the Direct Examination. "Is the pathologist who prepared the autopsy report going to be present at the trial?"

Another flurry. Mr. Wall replied that he hoped Dr. Opper would be here, that he had made several phone calls to him and that Dr. Opper was having difficulty getting away. Mr. Shew asked to say something about *that. He* had telephoned Dr. Opper, and Dr. Opper had informed him that County Detective Holden told him he would not be needed. "I told him he *would* be needed," Mr. Shew said.

Mr. Wall [crisp] "I have told him he is needed, Your Honor. [A quick word with Holden] Holden says he never said it."

The Judge, getting back on the track, repeated that he thought this was a matter of Defense. "The only problem, Mr. Wall, is bringing back Dr. Murphy, a busy man, from Simsbury at a later date. Are you still pressing your objection?"

Mr. Wall: "As to this matter only, Your Honor."

(This is the matter he will have to come back for.)

Judge Wright [another try] "Well, I have ruled that this is a proper matter for the Defense . . . and that they may bring back Dr. Murphy later to go into the question of the green vegetables and how long after luncheon she died. My only comment, which is not a legal comment, is—I hate to see Dr. Murphy, a busy practitioner, dragged down here again."

Mr. Wall: "Your Honor has expressed it, 'How long after *lunch,*' which is the claim of the Defendant. I certainly would object to talk of how long after *lunch.* . . . At a proper time I would not object to 'How long after *eating,*' . . . but I feel that we would be getting very far afield with this witness and that the Defense may wish to call him again later on other matters. So I wish to press my objection because I feel that if Counsel wishes to have him as a witness, it should come in at the proper time."

Mr. Shew admitted that he might have to recall Dr. Murphy, and the Judge said, "Very well. Since he is coming back anyway, I'll sustain the objection."

Mr. Wall [back to his own axe] "Your Honor, as to my motion that the Jury be warned about the statement made by Counsel— that it is improper . . . to make claims that this proves his Defendant not guilty . . . might the Jury be so informed, that that was improper? I'd like to have the stenographer read just what was said."

Mr. Shew: "Your Honor, I answered your question as carefully as I could. . . . This 'inflammation' that Mr. Wall speaks about seems to have pervaded the courtroom and everything else in connection with the trial."

The Judge replied that he saw no impropriety—it was only premature, a Defense matter to be developed later. When the Jury returned he told them exactly that, that it was "a very proper line of inquiry," but that it was premature and was to be reserved for the case for the Defense. For this reason, he would ask them to disregard any statement by Counsel concerning the vegetables in the stomach. The matter might come out later. [To the witness] "Doctor, you'll come back again, won't you?"

Dr. Murphy [spirited] "I'll come back if he asks me to, sure."

•   •   •

After lunch Bob Stadler again and the familiar story of running across the street with Arnfin, coming—totally unprepared—upon the body in the back yard, returning to the front hall where Arnfin told him that he had found Christa. Mr. Wall asked what happened then. And suddenly something was different!

Bob Stadler: "From there we went into the living room . . . and Arnfin told me he needed a drink . . . and we went back down a hallway into the kitchen. *And I told him not to touch anything or walk into the kitchen. So he reached around and got the bottle and I believe a glass.* And he came back to the living room with me. And he sat down and poured himself a drink."

(This is new! Is it possible that we are in for still more on those footprints? Even Arnfin testified that he walked into the kitchen and walked around in it, had to go across the room for a glass. Arnfin said that he poured the drink in the kitchen. Bob Stadler's testimony in the last trial: "Arnfin . . . was standing right by the stairs . . .

he was just standing there. He told me he wanted a drink—a shot—
and that is when he went towards the kitchen." Q. "And you observed him taking a drink then, did you?" A. "Well, he took the
bottle and came back in the living room and I told him to go and sit
down in the living room.")

The more than thrice-told tale continued. Bob Stadler covered the
body and returned to the house. Arnfin went into the kitchen to
make a telephone call. Soliani arrived, picked up the telephone with
his hand, hastily dropped it and took out his handkerchief, telephoned the barracks, ordered everyone out of the house. (It is all
very slow. The questions are droning, the answers are mostly an old
story. Outdoors the temperature has soared to 55°—a January heat
wave. Inside, the courtroom is warm.) Mr. Wall directed Bob's
testimony to the time he first entered the house, and Bob told of
how Agnes Thompsen appeared at the top of the stairs and said, "Is
she dead yet?"

On Cross-Examination Mr. Shew emphasized that Bob had been
away for only three to five minutes while he ran around to the back
yard and returned to the front hall.

"As far as you know, Christa might have been upstairs all the
time. Isn't that correct?" Could very well be, yes. "He had only
those three to five minutes to take her out of the bedroom and get
her upstairs and get downstairs again, did he not?" Yes.

"You don't know of your own knowledge what time Arnfin
Thompsen came home that night, do you? You didn't notice him
arrive?"

"No, I didn't."

Concerning Agnes Thompsen: "Do you remember how her hair
was done up at this time?" It wasn't done up. "It wasn't in
curlers?" No.

Mr. Shew: "Now, going back—you came into the house . . . and
you went into the living room. Did you sit down at that time?"

Bob: "Well, that is when Arnfin told me he wanted a drink."

"And was he within your sight when he went out to get a drink?"

"I went with him. . . . You go down the hallway and step into
the kitchen—and the cabinet was on that same wall. . . . Then he
went back into the living room."

"Do you remember him getting the glass?"

"I don't remember him picking up a glass, but he had one."

"So that he did get a glass somewhere. . . . And you don't remember just where he picked it up?" No. "And how long after that before Soliani came?" Ten or fifteen minutes. "And in the meantime Arnfin went into the kitchen to use the telephone again?" Yes. "And that time you didn't accompany him, did you?" No. "And he was out of your sight?" Yes. "And by that time, he had had how many drinks, if you remember?" At least two. "Were they little ones or good-sized ones?" Regular shot glass. "And do you know how long he was out in the kitchen?" I have no idea. . . . It wasn't too long.

"Now, I think you said when Trooper Soliani came, he grabbed the telephone. . . . How did he reach the telephone?" He walked down the hallway to it. "Did he make any effort to avoid the blood on the floor?" That I don't know. "But he grabbed the telephone that had blood on it?" Yes. "With his bare hand?" Yes. "And then said, 'I shouldn't be doing this,' and put the telephone down and took a handkerchief. Is that right?" Yes.

(This had been patiently and skillfully done. No one can still have an impression that fastidious care was exercised to avoid making footprints in the blood.)

Mr. Shew moved on. Soliani ordered everyone out of the house and went upstairs for Agnes and Christa. "Do you recall any remarks that Mrs. Thompsen made at this time?"

Later, Bob said, he heard her make some remarks. "When one of the State Policemen asked her if she had seen or heard anything, she said first she heard two loud thumps, and then she had seen a big green car in the driveway and that it might have been her boyfriend. . . . She didn't say Dorothy—she just said, 'her boyfriend.'"

Bob Stadler had been on the stand for almost an hour when Mr. Shew brought up the police interview of his son, Randy. According to Bob, he, himself, put the questions to Randy. (This differs from the version given jointly, out of court, by his brother, Paul, and his grandmother, Mrs. Mann, who said that a police officer asked the questions in their presence.) Bob said that one of the officers was John Bonolo, that he did not know the names of the other two. He said, "We went in and my son was in the kitchen. And I asked him a few questions because he had been over there that morning."

"And what were those questions?"

Objection! Hearsay.

To those who know about this, it has been disturbing that a police officer had heard from Randy that Agnes Thompsen had been downstairs that day and that the first trial had ended without this information going to the Jury. Now in the second trial the battle was on to give it to this Jury.

Mr. Wall: "There certainly is no guarantee of trustworthiness of a child of that tender years . . ."

Mr. Shew: "I think it's very trustworthy! It was made in the presence of the State Police. [Angry] Here again we are trying to get at the truth, which Mr. Wall is again objecting to, as usual. . . . I have no objection to finding out *whatever* is the truth in this case. . . . That is what we are here for. And that is what I am trying to do."

Mr. Wall: "The impression, of course, Your Honor, is that I am not at all interested in the truth."

Mr. Shew [flinging it out] "That is certainly a statement of fact!"

Mr. Wall: "I think this is getting to be a broken record. . . . I think the Jury might become impressed with the fact that I am just dedicated to suppressing the truth."

Mr. Shew: "Perhaps they will, Mr. Wall."

(Throughout this exchange several jurors smiled openly. Why? What are they thinking? What do they say during those long periods when they are banished to the jury room?) Now, once again, they were sent marching so that the Judge might hear arguments. Quarter past three on a sleepy afternoon that was beginning to wake up.

Mr. Shew asked that Mr. McKeon be allowed to present the arguments for the Defense. "We have anticipated that Mr. Wall would try to keep certain information from coming before the Jury. . . . Mr. McKeon has researched the point." Now a bit of nitpicking as Mr. Wall said this was irregular but that he did not object. However he would "expect that Counsel would ask permission of the Court." Mr. Shew replied that he had done so.

Judge Wright: "To do what? What are we talking about now—to talk about what Randy said or to have this argument of law?"

Mr. Wall: "The argument of law by Mr. McKeon. I do not object."

The Judge: "Mr. McKeon, I will hear you." Mr. McKeon wished to lay a foundation first and then cite cases.

Mr. Wall: "I object to any questioning of the witness by this Counsel. I thought he was going to make an argument."

The Judge [to Mr. McKeon] "You have a couple of basic questions you want to ask . . . ? Go ahead."

Mr. Wall: "May I object, Your Honor, to the questioning by other counsel?"

Judge Wright: "You may object, and I will overrule your objection."

Back on the track, Mr. McKeon inquired about the hour at which Randy was questioned. "Was it about nine o'clock, sir?"

Bob Stadler: "I don't remember the time."

"Was it within a few hours of the time you discovered this body?" It was. "And had you had an opportunity to talk to the boy before the questioning?" No. "In other words, he couldn't have received suggestions from you as to something he uttered at that time?" No.

The Judge [pushing it along] "Well, apart from the law of the matter—let's hear what Randy would have said. . . . I will see whether it is germane."

Bob Stadler described the conversation. "I asked Randy who was at the house and he said Christa, her mother and her grandmother. I asked him if there was anybody else there and he said no. I asked him if he had seen a man or anybody else around the house, and he said no."

Mr. McKeon: "Did the State Policeman ask questions of the child?"

"No, I think I asked Randy the questions myself."

"Was the question repeated, to which he then replied, 'I told you there was no man there'?"

"He did say, 'I told you before there was nobody there.' "

"So he was questioned more than once as to who was there when he left the house?"

"Yes, by myself."

"Did he say anything about Christa being changed by the mother?"

"No, he didn't."

"Did he say that the elder Mrs. Thompsen was at the ironing board?"

"No, he did not say that, either."

(This is puzzling. Neither Paul nor Mrs. Mann had spoken of Bob doing the questioning or even being there. Mrs. Mann had reported that Randy, reluctant to give an embarrassing answer, had whispered it to her. Would he not have turned to his father if he had been there? Would he have been embarrassed at all at this question put to him by his own father? Is it possible that there were *two separate* interviews of Randy that night?)

Now a long legal argument from Mr. McKeon (on the res gestae rule) that these were spontaneous statements on Randy's part and were, therefore, admissible—that the boy had no opportunity or motive to fabricate—no contact with his father after the body was found, before he was questioned. "It is a child responding quite ingenuously and candidly to questions by a group of adults—within a few hours of the event of the discovery of the body."

Mr. Wall countered that these were not spontaneous statements. This was an interview—many hours later—and was hearsay. This point went to Mr. Wall. The killing occurred in the early afternoon—the questioning was at about nine in the evening. The Judge: "The res gestae rule requires an utterance made within seconds or minutes from the time of the occurrence. Objection sustained." This Jury will not hear Randy's information, either.

After the afternoon recess, Mr. McKeon stated that he wished to offer a motion and that, to save time, perhaps he might do it now before the Jury came into Court. The Judge acquiesced.

Mr. Wall [instantly] "It will wait until *tomorrow morning.*"

Allowed to proceed, Mr. McKeon returned to the matter of the files, on which, he acknowledged, there had already been a ruling. "But [citing a case] to protect the record I would ask that the document in question—namely, the bindover files—be marked for identification."

The Judge: "Well, are there such files?"

The subject has become a powder keg. Mr. Wall [most upset] "There certainly is a bindover file. I have a file, Your Honor. It is *my* file and it's the *only one in existence.* I know of no other in existence. It has been furnished to me by the State Police and it is *my file.*"

The Judge [undisturbed] "Well, to test my ruling, I suppose we have to mark it. Is it right here now?"

Mr. Wall [beside himself] "I don't know whether it's here, Your Honor. I don't believe that it does have to be marked. Do I have something to say about it?"

The Judge: "Speak up, sir."

Another three-way argument on whether any such file should be marked and then whether it existed at all. Mr. Wall argued that the case cited related only to *evidence* and that it was outrageous to think that any such thing could be offered in evidence. The Judge pointed out that, even if Mr. Wall was right that this was an outrageous, ridiculous request, still an aggrieved party could not appeal unless there was some marking. Mr. McKeon argued that the efficiency of a witness was impaired because he was unable to see his own records and that he could not go before the Supreme Court with that claim unless the records were marked for identification. The Judge asked where the records were. Mr. McKeon asked to call Lieutenant Fuessenich in order to find out.

Mr. Wall: "This proceeding is highly irregular, Your Honor. . . . I'm not even sure of just what they have in mind. There is a full bindover file that was furnished to me and there is another file that was—well, I won't go into that."

The Judge: "Well, I will mark them and give them right back to you."

Mr. Wall [caustic] "Might this be done in an orderly procedure, Your Honor? There is a witness on the stand—and the only apparent purpose in this at this time of day is to get a *headline* for the *Courant* tomorrow. . . ."

The Judge repeated that if they could produce these records he would have them marked and return them. Mr. Wall said that there should be someone on the stand to present them.

Mr. McKeon: "I will have a witness in short order, Your Honor."

Judge Wright: "Well, I am telling you now, while I'll allow you to mark them you won't see them."

Now Mr. McKeon went even further. Citing another case in which such a document was marked, he said, "To preserve it properly for the Supreme Court, the Court took custody of it and kept it under seal and I think that procedure should be followed here." (Full credit to Mr. McKeon for audacity!)

The Judge: "This is the prosecutor's file, Mr. McKeon. These are his working papers."

"I submit the bindover file is not, Your Honor."

The Judge: "Do you know where they are, Mr. Wall?"

Mr. Wall: "I know where *my file* is. . . . I think that if the Court wants to order me to do something along these lines, Your Honor, that they should be offered through a witness. We have a witness on the stand and there is interruption of the orderly proceedings here for another obvious purpose."

The Judge ordered that they continue with Bob Stadler in order to finish with him tonight and then, if time remained, go into this question.

A few minutes more and Bob Stadler was excused and another witness called, Mrs. Asa Burdick. She had been in Court all day, and her testimony was not expected to be lengthy.

Weeping openly, Dorothy's mother took the stand and told, in a nearly inaudible whisper, of the daily telephone calls from Dorothy. "At eight twenty, ten twenty, and ten of four." On June 15 she had received the first two calls. The third one never came.

At this point Mrs. Burdick appeared to swoon in the chair. Asa Burdick rushed forward with pills, the sheriff with a glass of water. Mr. Wall asked whether she would prefer to testify another day, and Mrs. Burdick shook her head. "I'd rather testify today and get it over with." According to Mrs. Burdick, Arnfin called her at ten minutes after six.

Mr. Wall: "Were you very close to your daughter, Dorothy?" Yes, very close. "And did you know of her schedule. . . . Did she have a special time for doing things?" Yes, she did—yes. "And do you know whether she adhered to this—whether she did what she ordinarily did?"

[Blurting out] "Well, she used to feed the baby a quarter of—"

[Hastily interrupting] "Well, I'll ask you that. Do you know what time she started to feed the baby?"

"Yes, a quarter of twelve."

(Answers before questions!)

"And did she have a time when she ordinarily ate her own lunch?"

"Ten of twelve."

"And what was next on her schedule?"

[Rushing on] "Well, Dorothy would put Christa to bed a quarter after one." (Arnfin testified that it was at a quarter *to* one, between the two fifteen-minute television programs.)

"And was there anything she did between the time that she had lunch and the time she put Christa to bed?"

"Well, she used to do her dishes."

[Encouraging] "Yes—"

[Blurting out again] "And then half-past one she would do her ironing."

"And half-past one she would do her ironing?"

"Yes."

"Do you know what she ironed at half-past one?"

"Well, she used to iron Arnfin's shirts."

"Arnfin's shirts?"

"Yes, and I wasn't too well. I used to take a nap after that."

"Would it be possible to tell what time it was by seeing what ironing was being done?"

"No, I wouldn't know. . . . She used to do the ironing. That's about all I know." Mrs. Burdick is hard of hearing and was becoming quite distraught. To the question whether it was necessary to awaken Christa from her nap, she replied that Dorothy wanted to put her to bed early at night. To a question about the television programs, she replied that one of them was *Portia Faces Life* and that Dottie used to watch it every day. (The listed shows for the hour from 12:00 to 1:00 are *Love of Life, Search for Tomorrow,* and *Guiding Light.*)

"Do you know what time that was?"

"Well, I don't know. I don't remember."

"Was there any other that you recall?"

"No."

In Cross-Examination Mr. McKeon emphasized that Dottie always ate lunch at ten minutes of twelve every day.

"I stayed up there with her one time for six months, and she always had the same schedule," Mrs. Burdick said.

Mrs. Burdick telephoned Dottie several times that afternoon, letting the telephone ring at least five times on each occasion. Had

Agnes Thompsen ever answered the telephone when Mrs. Burdick called Dorothy before that day?

"Well, she used to but Dorothy told her not to because she might fall down and get hurt."

"But she could hear the phone from upstairs?"

"Yes, she could. Yes."

At the press table, sympathetic but troubled eyes followed Mrs. Burdick to her seat. One can understand her distress but is nevertheless troubled by answers rushing out before questions and by the fact that Mrs. Burdick remembered little except what was pertinent to this case. Lunch at 11:45—the baby to bed at 1:15— ironing at 1:30—Arnfin's shirts first. Every day?

Mr. Wall: "I have several witnesses here who will probably be very angry with me for not calling them . . . but that would not give the opportunity to have this motion processed."

It was late now and the Judge suggested that it would be better to start with the next witness in the morning. He dismissed the Jury in order to hear argument, and they filed out of the courtroom.

Mr. Wall: "I could finish with Carole Stadler by five o'clock, but I know that Counsel wants this at this time. I know why it's important."

Mr. McKeon: "Your Honor, if the Court is impressed with the claims of the State's Attorney that we are doing this for headlines, we will do it at such time as the State's Attorney would have it done."

The Judge: "Well, this is all somewhat ridiculous, is it not? I will mark certain files if you produce them, and I will return them to the State's Attorney."

Mr. Wall: "I object to any such procedure at this time, Your Honor, because Your Honor has already made a ruling. This was all done this morning and it was obvious this morning. There was an attempt not to have it this morning and to have it this afternoon. Now there is not any oversight on their part. It's merely a postponement until this time for the *obvious purpose*, Your Honor."

Mr. McKeon: "Your Honor, at two o'clock I asked to go into this and to put a witness on."

Mr. Wall: "The *deadline of the other papers* was over at that time."

Mr. McKeon called Lieutenant Fuessenich.

"Lieutenant, in connection with this case, is there that which is known as a 'bindover file'?"

"I believe there is, sir."

Mr. Wall: "I object to the question, Your Honor. I object to any questioning relating to the evidence that the State has in this case."

The Judge: "If it gets into that question, I will sustain you. This is just preliminary. Overruled."

Mr. McKeon: "And do you know where that file is now?"

[Simultaneous] $\begin{cases} \text{"No."} \\ \text{"I object."} \end{cases}$

The Judge: "Overruled."

Mr. McKeon: "Have you seen it within the past two weeks?"

"No, sir, I don't believe I have ever seen it. . . . May I explain? . . . The bindover file that I am referring to is a collection of reports assembled by the Special Service Division in headquarters and sent to the State's Attorney."

"Does it contain reports of the Hartford Division?"

Mr. Wall: "Objected to, Your Honor, as to what is in the file that goes to the State's Attorney, Your Honor. I see no relevancy to it at all."

Mr. McKeon [abrupt] "I will do this through another witness at another time, in Chambers or in secrecy, whatever Mr. Wall suggests, just so long as I have it on the record."

The Judge: "The contents of any file is solely within the province of the State's Attorney. The location of the file, however, is important at this time. Where are these files, Lieutenant?"

"I don't know, sir. I don't think I have ever seen them."

Mr. McKeon [swinging to the Judge] "It is obvious that I can't identify through this witness. At another time I will introduce Major Rome to identify the files."

The Judge: "Where are they? Do you know?"

Mr. McKeon: "I don't want to make a statement for fear of misrepresenting."

Abruptly making up his mind, the Judge indicated Mr. Wall's files. "Let's mark these files and I'll give them back to you."

"Pardon!"

"Why don't we mark these files and I'll give them back to you?"

Again Mr. Wall protested that this was irregular. "I can hand

Your Honor certain things. There is a bindover file that has been furnished to the State's Attorney . . . but to produce anything at this stage to Counsel or even for marking, Your Honor, is highly irregular. It has no relevance to the proceedings. There is no possible right to Counsel to be asking for it."

The Judge: "Well, I think you are right but I have got to have a record made for an appeal. Why don't you give me the files and we'll mark them. We'll give them right back to you."

"Your Honor, there are two—there are two different things here and—as a matter of fact, there are errors in some of them that are embarrassing—and I see no reason why. They don't relate to the merits of the case in any way."

The Judge: "Well, they are going to stay in your custody, Mr. Wall. I won't see them. No one will see them."

"I'll be glad to have Your Honor see them."

"I don't want them. All I want to do is mark them to make a record."

Still Mr. Wall resisted. This concerned proceedings outside the hearing of the Jury. "Your Honor has already made a ruling and now they come back . . . and ask to have something marked. I feel that it's entirely irregular. If Your Honor orders me, I shall comply with alacrity, but I want Your Honor to realize that this case has been punctuated every afternoon by a motion that has no merit whatsoever—and it has no purpose except what I have stated to Your Honor previously and what is undoubtedly obvious to Your Honor. Now, if Your Honor asks me to produce a bindover file I shall hand it to Your Honor right this minute."

Judge Wright: "I request you and order you to give it to the Clerk for marking and he will return it to you immediately."

The file—in a reddish brown cover—was produced at last. It was marked. It was returned.

The Judge: "The record may show that the file has been returned promptly to the State's Attorney, not having been seen by anybody."*

* In the next session of the legislature this policy was changed by an act which leaves it to the discretion of the judge to order the State to permit the Defense to inspect and copy relevant information.

26

The Judge: "Any preliminary matters before the Jury is summoned?"

Mr. Wall: "Never at ten o'clock, Your Honor."

The Judge: "Pardon?"

Mr. Wall: "*Never* at ten o'clock."

(Mr. Wall looks tired. He has dark circles under his eyes.)

At 10:30 the Jury came into court. With Rebillard on the stand, Mr. Wall introduced documents to show that a black '59 Ford had been registered to Thorbjorn Solberg. Familiar terrain. We know from the last trial that Rebillard and Pennington went to the Solberg house three days after the murder because of this car.

Mr. Wall: "What was the occasion of your going there?"

Objection. Mr. McKeon asked to hear the answer in the absence of the Jury. "That question is so broad there is no way I can anticipate what will come out."

10:41. The Jury filed out.

Coins in his hand betraying his frayed nerves, Mr. Wall protested. "Your Honor, I feel it is highly unfair for Defense Counsel to ask to have the answers in the absence of the Jury to determine whether he likes them or not. . . . The question should stand on its own. Either it is admissible or it is not."

The Judge: "The question is proper but the answer might be rambling and improper."

Mr. Wall: "I still say, Your Honor, that to accede to Counsel's request . . . is highly prejudicial to the State's case."

The Judge: "Well, aren't we going to bend over backwards in a capital case on every possible point?"

Mr. Wall [a formal nod] "Yes, Your Honor."

Rebillard's answer was that they went to the house to check on the car.

10:48. The Jury returned.

Rebillard testified that he and Pennington glanced at the car that day and then went on to the house. Harry Solberg, his mother, his brother, and possibly a sister were at home.

Mr. Wall: "Did you have a conversation with the Defendant, Harry Solberg?" They did. "Please relate your conversation. . . ."

Objection!

11:00. The Jury out.

The pattern for the day was becoming clear. Because these were statements actually made by Harry Solberg, Mr. McKeon intended to take every precaution that nothing inadmissible came before the Jury. The Judge, perceiving it, too, said, "Before we go any further, gentlemen, it was Judge MacDonald's hope . . . that many of these excursions and delays could be surmounted by agreement. Is that impossible?"

Mr. Shew spoke up. "If Your Honor please, originally I offered to agree to, I think, practically all the suggestions and Mr. Wall said, 'Nothing doing.' I think I am quoting correctly. Now I feel that we have to go on."

The Judge did not press the point.

Mr. McKeon stated his objection to the question. "He is asking for the substance of a conversation between the officer and the Defendant. Supposing he said, 'Harry admitted to me that he killed Dorothy Thompsen.' How do I know that he is not going to say that?"

The Judge: "Well, did he testify to that at the first trial?"

Mr. McKeon: "Your Honor, there are things between the first trial and the second trial that contain a great many surprises."

Rebillard reported the conversation, which was the account that Harry gave them of his movements on the day of the murder. He said that he came home on the school bus, ate lunch, went to Hayes' Store and to the lawn mower shop and then to the Zimmer house in North Granby to work with his father.

Mr. McKeon said, "Prior to your talking to him, did you give him any indication as to his right to silence?"

Miranda was upon us.

Mr. McKeon: "What they are obviously accomplishing here is to set out a story from the accused's own mouth and then knock it down. . . . It is setting up a device whereby witnesses come in at the State's behest and contradict what is contained in this statement. A great deal of time in *Miranda* was spent on exculpatory statements extracted from the suspect."

The Judge turned to Mr. Wall, who was leaning against the empty jury box, and Mr. Wall moved toward the bench. "Your Honor, first I would like to answer what Mr. Shew said about my attitude toward Judge MacDonald's suggestions. Mr. Shew quoted me as saying, 'Nothing doing,' and I must say that I never said, 'Nothing doing.'" Justifying his position, Mr. Wall touched on all the points we have heard before. "This is a capital case . . . the grave possibility of the Defendant changing his mind at a later time . . . I feel that it is my duty to go ahead with the matter, Your Honor, and I never said, 'Nothing doing.'"

(Mr. Wall began the day with raw nerves and nothing has happened to ease the condition.)

He turned to the present objection, arguing that at that time there was no focus on the Defendant. "These questions were addressed to the accused . . . in the presence of his mother, in the presence of his brother, and were part of a general inquiry into the crime. [Sharp] The *Miranda* case has no application whatsoever, to this particular matter—*nor at any time.*"

The Judge asked a few questions to determine whether there had been any restrictions placed on Harry's freedom of action on that date. [To Rebillard] "Give us the surrounding atmosphere of your questioning of this young man. Who was there? Did you flash a badge on him? Did you make him sit down . . . or stand in one spot? Was he free to come and go? Did you pose any words of stern import?"

Rebillard said, "It was just a general conversation in which his mother took part."

The Judge allowed the question.

11:15. The Jury returned.

Mr. Wall: "Was there anything else that you observed relating to Harry Solberg during this interview?"

Objection. Mr. McKeon: "I have no way of knowing what he observed and what is meant by the word 'observation' to this officer. It could include the senses, Your Honor, *all* the senses."

11:25. The Judge declared the morning recess—after which he would hear arguments.

12:05. With the Jury absent, Rebillard gave his "observations" of Harry Solberg during that interview. "He was barefoot, rocking back and forth, appeared fidgety—nervous."

Mr. McKeon: "Object to 'fidgety and nervous,' Your Honor. The purpose is to show an awareness of guilt. And this man had never met Solberg before. There is no standard of comparison. . . . It is a conclusion."

Mr. Wall cited an authority which stated that a lay witness's opinion is admissible as to a person's apparent physical condition. The Judge supplied another case that was concerned with whether a person appeared to be excited or nervous. The objection was overruled.

12:14. The Jury in.

Rebillard testified that on June 23 (a week after the murder) he and Pennington went to Sharon's house, where they also spoke to Harry. Mr. Wall asked for this conversation.

Objection.

12:20. The Jury out.

This conversation related to whether Harry had visited Sharon on the afternoon of the murder. Rebillard said, "Sharon said he had been over about 2:00 P.M. Harry said he hadn't been there. Then he changed his mind and said he thought it was about five."

12:24. The Jury in. The question asked again. The answer—almost the same. And yet just a bit different. Now Rebillard said, "Sharon stated that he had been there about 2:00 P.M. *in his black Ford.* Harry at first stated he hadn't been there. *Then he changed that, too.* He thought he had been there at approximately 5:00 P.M. on the afternoon of June 15."

(Here is food for thought. Harry was seen at the Thompsen house at about 1:30. Was there time for him to be admitted, chat with Dottie, get into an argument intense enough to trigger off this crime—stab her with one fork, then with another fork, find the sledgehammer and use it, get the toaster, tie the cord around her neck, drag her out to the porch, pound in the nail set, tie the cord around it, drop the body over the side, go down to the back yard and heave the rock, climb up the ladder, wash part of the porch floor, throw the bloody dress into the dryer, steal the bank, rush out to his car, open the trunk and toss in the bank, stop to wipe off some of the blood, go home, change into clean clothes, and arrive at Sharon's house at about 2:00?)

Mr. Wall: "Was there further conversation . . . that day?"

Mr. McKeon asked for representation that this matter came up in the previous trial so he would not have to object.

Mr. Wall [flatly] "I have no knowledge of it, Your Honor, whether it did or didn't."

The Judge: "Well, we can save time, Mr. Wall, if you can tell us."

Mr. Wall: "I don't know, Your Honor."

Mr. McKeon: "If there is an intimation by the State's Attorney as to the purpose of it, perhaps that would suffice."

Mr. Wall [quite indignant] "I can't tell him what his answer is! This is a witness. I don't tell witnesses what to say. They come in and say what they learned and what they know."

12:27. The Jury out.

(Major Rome has come into Court. Nobody seems to have noticed.)

Rebillard answered the question. "It related to whether Harry had been south of his home on Route 179 [toward the Thompsen residence] on June 15 with his '59 black Ford. . . . Harry stated that he hadn't been south of his home, but he had to use 179 to go to the center of town."

12:32. The Jury in.

The date of the next interview with Harry Solberg was March 13, 1966. The Defense lawyers shifted a bit in their chairs. In the back row, Fuessenich and Holden leaned forward. The press table came to attention. The preliminaries were over. The main event was about to begin.

With a minimum of strokes, Rebillard blocked in the picture of these all-important days. Lieutenant Fuessenich and Lieutenant

Riemer had also interviewed Harry on the thirteenth. On the fourteenth, Lieutenant Riemer again. And then Fuessenich again.

Mr. Wall: "Were *all* of these interviews recorded on tape?"

[Firm] "Yes, sir."

"And did you hear all of these interviews—those in which you participated or those in which others participated?" Yes, sir. "And are these tapes presently in the custody of the Court?" Yes, sir.

[Sharper] "And have they all been heard by Counsel for the Defendant?"

"Yes, sir."

[Swinging about] "May we have the tapes?"

The sheriff went to get them. Mr. Wall flipped his glasses into his pocket and strode to his chair, his mouth in a deep scowl, appearing now to be most agitated. After a long minute he said that he could ask a few questions while they were waiting.

[To Rebillard] "How many tapes are there?"

Rebillard: "Seven, I believe."

[Easy tone] "And do they faithfully record what transpired in the conversations between the persons that you have mentioned and the accused, Harry Solberg?"

"Yes, sir."

[Still easy] "And were all of the conversations and interviews made voluntarily?"

[Absolutely simultaneous] } Mr. Shew: "Objection!"
Mr. McKeon: "Objection!"

The objections rang out in the courtroom. Even Harry appeared to start to his feet and then check himself!

Mr. McKeon: "Your Honor, that is very improper!"

The Judge: "Objection sustained."

Mr. Shew [exploding] "Mr. Wall, that certainly is one of the most dastardly things that I have ever heard in the courtroom. Your Honor, this man certainly knew better than to do that. He is not that dumb!"

The Judge: "Well, it's not that bad, Mr. Shew."

Mr. Shew: "Excuse me, Your Honor, I think it is worse than that!"

Mr. Wall [furious] "There is nothing wrong with that!"

The Judge [strong] "Objection sustained."

In the midst of the fireworks the sheriff returned with the tapes. Mr. Shew remained standing.

Mr. Wall [acid] "I offer them in evidence, Your Honor, and ask that they be read to the Jury or be played to the Jury."

Mr. McKeon [quick] "May I ask questions on admissibility, Your Honor?"

Mr. Wall: "Your Honor, may they be offered as one Exhibit? I feel that they should not be offered separately. They should be offered as a whole."

Mr. McKeon: "I object to that, Your Honor. I think it's very important that they be marked separately."

The Judge: "I think they should, too, Mr. Wall."

Mr. Wall: "I am offering them as *one Exhibit*, Your Honor. . . . They are not offered piecemeal. They are offered as a whole. They may have different numbers, but the offer is for the Exhibit as a whole—*all* of these tapes."

Time called while the tapes were marked. Mr. Shew sat down. Mr. McKeon returned to the Defense table. Mr. Wall remained on his feet—pacing, pacing behind the State's table—covering wide ground, very tense, very angry. Mr. McKeon suggested that the Jury could go to lunch—this might be a long discussion. (Can anyone doubt it?)

12:45. The Jury out.

Mr. McKeon: "Officer, is it your sworn testimony that *every conversation or interview* to your knowledge between Harry Solberg and the people you described is recorded on these tapes on the thirteenth, the fourteenth, and part of the fifteenth?"

Rebillard: "To the best of my recollection, yes, sir."

"And you listened in on all conversations, I assume?"

"Yes, sir."

(Mr. Wall striding about—all the way back to the spectator section and forward again.)

Mr. McKeon: "There was *no other interview*—other than what is recorded on those tapes?"

"No other interviews."

"Or interrogations?"

A sudden switch. "No, I couldn't say that."

Mr. McKeon gave Rebillard a hard look. "What *is* your recollection? I thought that was your testimony."

Mr. Shew stepped up to speak a quick word to Mr. McKeon, and Mr. McKeon turned to the Judge. "Your Honor, I ask that Detective Holden and Lieutenant Fuessenich be sequestered from the courtroom for this next question."

Mr. Wall said crisply that he had no objection and was sure that they wouldn't, either, and Fuessenich and Holden left the room. (The press table: "What's the difference? They'll all have lunch together.")

Mr. McKeon had found a crack and he went to work. "Were there any interviews between any members of the State Police and Harry Solberg between five minutes of nine on the evening of March 14 and 11:45 on that same evening?"

Rebillard answered with a question. "Between five minutes of nine and what time?"

Mr. Wall objected. There was nothing about this on Direct. "It's a question of admissibility of these tapes, Your Honor. Whether there was any other conversation at that particular time is immaterial at this stage. *These are all the tapes.*"

Mr. McKeon: "He said on Direct Examination that these tapes cover *all* the conversations or interviews."

Rebillard [backing to fill] "All that I heard."

"Did you hear any *other* interviews or conversations—other than what are recorded on these tapes which are now offered?"

[Impassive] "Yes, sir."

(Within minutes Rebillard has said that *every* conversation was recorded—that he listened to *all* conversations—that there was no other interview, other than what was recorded. Then, that there *were* other interrogations—that the tapes covered *all* conversations and interviews that he *heard*. And that he heard *other* conversations and interviews that were *not* on these tapes!)

Mr. McKeon: "When did they take place?"

". . . On the fourteenth. It would have been between 8:00 and 9:00, I believe—downstairs in Hartford."

"How about 9:30? Was there any conversation then between you and Lieutenant Fuessenich and Harry Solberg that was not recorded?"

"There would be some, but I am not sure of the time. . . . There was one interview shortly before we left for East Hartland with Harry."

"And to the best of your knowledge, that was not on tapes?"

"That's correct." Lieutenant Fuessenich, Sergeant Kielty, and Rebillard were present—and Harry.

Now Mr. McKeon took direct aim at what, for him, had always been the prime target in this case—*Miranda*. Going back to the first interview with Harry at the Canaan Barracks on Sunday morning, March 13, he said, "You were the first one to initiate the interrogation process?"

"Yes, sir."

"And the exact words you used—I'll quote them, stop me if I am wrong—it's on the very first reel—"

[Rather grudging] "You wrote them down, I believe, so they should be correct."

Mr. McKeon: "You said to him, 'You have a right to remain silent.' . . . And you said, 'Anything you say could be used against you.' And then you said, 'You have a right to counsel.' "

"Yes, sir."

Mr. McKeon turned to the Judge. "Your Honor, I submit under *Miranda* that none of these conversations after that time are admissible." Then, to reinforce his claim, he put another question to Rebillard. "You became aware within the first hour that this man was in great financial difficulty, did you not, Officer?"

Rebillard: "In great financial difficulty?"

"Yes. In your interrogation you learned that he was beset by numerous bills, that his house had bugs in it. 'Bugs'—the exact word. And that he was paying $60 a month rent and he was up against it financially."

A long silence while Rebillard sat thinking. [Flat] "I don't recall that exactly the way you put it."

Mr. McKeon: "I will read it to you. I will read you my notes."

[Quicker] "And you also left out part of the warning I gave him."

"Let's hear the rest."

"I asked him if he understood it. . . . I also told him that he had a right to have an attorney. And I asked him if he understood these rights. I also told him that he did not even have to talk to me."

"You said, 'You have a right to counsel.' Those are your exact words. Correct?"

"I believe so, yes."

"Did you tell him that he had the right to have an attorney present in the interrogation room? And that if he wished to make that choice, no interrogation would begin until that attorney was present?"

"No, sir, *Miranda* was not in effect then."

"You did *not* advise him, then, that before any questioning began he would be entitled to have counsel present with him in the interrogation room?"

"I advised him that he had a right to have counsel."

"Could you answer my question, sir."

Mr. Wall: "I submit he has answered it, Your Honor."

Mr. McKeon: "Did you say that he had the right to consult with an attorney before he started answering your questions?"

"I advised him he had a right to have counsel."

"Would you answer the question I put to you, sir. Did you advise him that he had the right to consult with an attorney before the interrogation started?"

"Not in those exact words, no, sir."

"The exact words you used were, 'You have a right to counsel.' . . . And did you tell him, sir, that if he could not afford counsel one would be appointed for him before the interrogation began if he so desired?"

"No, sir."

Mr. McKeon: "Your Honor, I claim all these tapes are inadmissible. . . . [Reading from *Miranda*] 'An individual held for interrogation must be clearly informed that he has the right to consult with a lawyer, and to have the lawyer with him during interrogation. . . . This warning is an absolute prerequisite to interrogation.' Further, Your Honor: 'It is necessary to inform an accused that if he cannot afford counsel, one will be appointed for him if he so desires and no interrogation will take place before the appointment.' [Looking up] Your Honor, it is clear—the record speaks for itself—that these tapes are not admissible for admissions, exculpatory statements, inculpatory statements, or what purports to be confessions."

Mr. Wall, who had been on his feet throughout this questioning, moved to center Court to answer. [Authoritative tone] "Your Honor, I have not laid a foundation under *Miranda*. I believe that I can lay a foundation for their admissibility under what the law was at that particular time."

Mr. McKeon started to reply and Mr. Wall cut him off. "May I continue my argument? I made no statements until Counsel was finished. May Counsel be asked to answer me when I get through? [Resuming] I submit, Your Honor, that I can lay a foundation for these tapes to be admitted if it becomes necessary to do so. However, I say that it is not necessary for me to comply with *Miranda* or *Escobedo* or any of the cases . . . because of actions of Counsel in opening the door to these tapes. [Taking on an accusing tone] Your Honor will recall that there was *newspaper publicity* about the tapes—that upon questioning the jurors on voir dire, the jurors had seen something about tapes in the papers." Now, circling about the courtroom, Mr. Wall brought up a day when Mr. Shew had mentioned the tapes before the Jury.

(On Friday, January 13, late in the day, upon completing an examination of Fuessenich, Mr. Shew had said that they had all been up late the night before listening to tapes and that this might be a good place to stop.) Mr. Wall [very sharp] "I objected in Chambers and said to Your Honor and to Counsel that I felt it was improper to bring the matter of the tapes into the case at this particular stage, particularly relating to whether Counsel were listening to them. . . . Quite without any warning, Mr. Shew came out and said before the Jury that we were all tired because we had been listening to the tapes the night before. *Those tapes were then brought before the Jury.* [Circling, pacing] I had made an objection in Chambers requesting Counsel not to say anything about tapes because I felt that it could become prejudicial in the case. Not because they would hurt the case of the State, Your Honor. As a matter of fact, it was somewhat for the protection of the Defendant himself. But I feel that the door has been opened and that the Jury has been told about these tapes in an unauthorized manner. [On to another complaint] There have been statements made time and again here that Wall is trying to keep testimony from the jurors, and he doesn't want the truth to be known. Such statements have been made in the presence of the Jury, Your Honor. I feel that the door has been opened to the introduction of these tapes by the conduct of the Defense in bringing them in over my objections . . . and also indicating that the State's Attorney was trying to keep things away from the Jury, including these tapes. They have opened the door . . . by their own actions, in a most improper manner, which forces me to bring in what I feel is most important testimony, which I feel the Jury should hear."

For a moment there was silence. Then, in reply, Mr. McKeon went to Mr. Wall's first statement, made several minutes ago. He pointed out that *Miranda* applies to all cases going to trial after the date of the decision, June 16, 1966. The trial in this case did not begin until September, 1966. And the second trial began this month.

Again Mr. Wall touched all bases. "My present argument is not related to *Miranda* or *Escobedo* or any of those cases, Your Honor. I feel that the Defendant has waived any such thoughts by opening the door and insisting that these tapes be brought forth, and by emphasizing them before the Jury. I feel, the door having been opened by them, that these other considerations and objections have been cast aside by them deliberately. That these are therefore admissible for that reason alone."

It was five minutes past one. Without a word of comment Judge Wright called the luncheon recess.

At the press table Demeusy said, "This trial is going to end this afternoon."

After lunch, with hardly a missed beat, the argument resumed.

Mr. Shew wished to answer Mr. Wall's charges of impropriety in having mentioned the tapes. "I explained it so that the Jury would understand. I used almost the identical words suggested in Chambers by Your Honor. I merely wish to call that to Your Honor's attention."

Mr. Wall: "Your Honor, it was definitely stated in Chambers by me, and the impropriety of mentioning that was pointed out to Mr. Shew. I agree that there had been some conversation between Counsel and Your Honor relating to it. However, it was definitely pointed out how improper it was. . . . I feel that the door has been opened—no matter by what means or by whose authority . . . for these tapes to be admitted."

Mr. Shew: "If Your Honor please, most of Mr. Wall's argument is beneath notice and is childish. . . . Mr. Wall interpreted the statements that way. Your Honor did not and Your Honor is presiding in this Court. . . . As for it being improper, those are characterizations that Mr. Wall made—they were not agreed to by anyone else, other than in his own mind. . . . The rest of his argument is childish and beneath notice, Your Honor."

Mr. Wall [loftily] "I would like to inquire, Your Honor, whether Counsel is withdrawing his charges of my talking through my hat and he now feels it's merely childish?"

Mr. Shew: "That's right."

The Judge [not about to sit for this] "What's before me now?"

Mr. McKeon: "I object, Your Honor, to the admissibility of these tapes."

Mr. Wall: "I claim them, Your Honor. . . . The door has been opened. . . . They have been talked about before the Jury intentionally by Counsel."

The Judge: "I'm not concerned with that aspect, Mr. Wall. . . . A fundamental constitutional right protected under the *Miranda* ruling certainly could not be waived by Counsel by some injudicious remark—if he made one." He turned to Rebillard, who was still on the stand. "Officer, at the time these seven tapes were taken, was Mr. Solberg under arrest?"

Rebillard: "He was under arrest after the fifth or sixth tape. I'm not exactly sure on that, Your Honor."

Now Judge Wright undertook to learn the facts of the Two Days. "Where did he spend the night of March 13? . . . Did he go home under custody or at his own free will? . . . At what time did the arrest take place? . . . Before that time of arrest had his freedom been infringed in any way?"

"You mean had he asked to go? Or had we detained him by force?"

"Or any other way. By moral force, even."

"Moral force?"

"Yes. How did he happen to come to Police Headquarters for the taking of these tapes?"

Again the story of how Rebillard picked Harry up in front of his house that Sunday morning and took him to the Canaan Barracks. "I . . . told him he was not under arrest." The Judge inquired whether, that evening, Rebillard took him home again, and Rebillard replied that he went home from Hartford—with his parents or his wife.

The Judge turned to Counsel. "My inquiry, gentlemen, at this juncture is whether or not during the taking of these tapes, Harry Solberg was under custodial interrogation. You may inquire along those lines if you wish to."

Mr. McKeon forward at once. "Officer, at the time you were aware of the fact from Mr. Liberi—and you were reasonably convinced—that he was the author of the letter . . . were you not?"

"Yes, sir."

"And your investigation with regard to the murderer of Dorothy Thompsen had focused on him at that point?"

Rebillard: "It had focused on him in this sense—that he was the author of this letter and we wanted to find out why."

Again Mr. McKeon read from *Miranda:* " 'By custodial interrogation we mean questioning initiated by law enforcement officers after a person has been taken into custody or otherwise deprived of his freedom of action in any significant way.' . . . [Looking up] I submit that the mere fact that the police sought in an emasculated way to advise him as to his rights indicates a police attitude that he was an accused at that point. Investigation had focused entirely on him. . . . [Strong] Your Honor, this is a boy who had not achieved majority. It had taken him six years to complete high school. . . . He had an IQ below average. . . . His parents were misled and he was held incommunicado for approximately three to four hours in that Canaan Barracks. The parents were told that he was being held on some matter totally unrelated to any murder. . . . Your Honor, I submit that this is exactly what the Supreme Court contemplated in its terms 'custodial interrogation' or 'being deprived of his freedom of action in any significant way.' Therefore, none of these tapes should be admitted. *Further* [waxing warm] I have Lieutenant Riemer on subpoena. I will show that the so-called lie-detector examination was nothing but a device to commence and to carry out an almost vicious interrogation lasting for six hours." Mr. McKeon looked around to see whether Riemer was in Court. "If I may, Your Honor, I would like to get that before the Court now—relative to the lie-detector examination."

The Judge turned to Mr. Wall for his response.

Mr. Wall pointed out first that Rebillard's answer was that the investigation had focused on the accused *only* for having written the Letter. This was a general inquiry. The police had learned that this man had written the Letter. They certainly had a right to find out what he knew. "The attention of the police was focused upon him . . . only as a witness, Your Honor." Since the luncheon recess Mr. Wall had been speaking in a very soft, restrained voice. "Counsel is again indulging in the use of a word which has no place in the proceedings at all—the word 'vicious.' Your Honor, we all listened to these tapes. . . . The only conclusion that one could reach from them was that the man was treated just as gently under the circumstances and as courteously as you would expect a member of your own family to be treated."

The Judge restated his own position. "The one question remaining in my mind as to admissibility of these tapes is whether or not at the time . . . Harry Solberg was under custodial interrogation or whether his freedom of action had been infringed in any significant way. Any evidence you want to give me on either side, I'll listen to."

Mr. Wall turned to Rebillard again. "Mr. Rebillard, were you at any time on March 13 in uniform?" No, sir. "Did you on March 13 indicate to Solberg that you had any authority to keep him in custody?" No, sir. "Did you indicate at any time that you intended to keep him in custody?" No, sir. "Did he go with you voluntarily?"

[Crisp, without expression] "Yes, he came voluntarily."

Mr. Wall [very slow] "And was there ever any question throughout that day, the thirteenth, of his ever expressing any wish to be other than where he was?"

Rebillard [casual] "He may at one point have indicated he wanted to go home or something of that nature."

"Do you recall any discussion of that?"

"I don't recall the discussion, no. . . . He mentioned something about he wanted to see his father, and I asked him if he wanted his father to come down and see him or his pastor or something like that and he said no, he didn't want them to come down."

[Hushed voice] ". . . Was any restraint placed upon him . . . that day?"

"No, I saw no restraint put on him as such."

"And was he deprived at any time on the thirteenth of his freedom of action?"

"No, sir."

Going now to the matter of the lie-detector test, Mr. Wall brought out that Harry had discussed it first with his parents, who spoke to Fuessenich as well, and "made the decision" to take the polygraph test. Mr. Wall introduced the polygraph form signed by Harry and by his parents. "Did he sign this freely and of his own accord?"

"Yes, sir."

Concerning the polygraph form, Mr. McKeon asked exactly what it was that the parents agreed to. "What was told to them? . . . They agreed that Harry should submit to a lie-detector examination and nothing else. Isn't that true, sir?"

Rebillard: "No. He was *asked and urged* by his parents to take this test to show whether . . . he was involved in any way other than writing this letter—to get at the truth of the matter."

Mr. McKeon claimed now that the polygraph form was not admissible—that *it* contained an inadequate warning of rights.

Mr. Wall [still hushed] "Your Honor, it's the claim of the State that at this particular stage, this was entirely voluntary . . . [louder] that this was not custodial interrogation and that *no warning whatsoever was necessary,* Your Honor, in view of the fact that this was *not custodial interrogation.*"

The Judge [to the heart of the matter] "Wholly apart from these points about warning, how can any lie-detector test become a part of this trial? Our courts have never recognized the validity of a polygraph examination."

Mr. Wall: "Your Honor, I am not trying to introduce the results of the test. I am merely trying to introduce the actual interrogation that took place in connection with it. Our Supreme Court has not disapproved of the use of a lie-detector test which came along shortly before a confession. . . . There is no intent to bring in any decision of the lie-detector test. The tapes are offered solely for the answers to questions. . . . [Citing a case] That was considered proper in *State versus Traub.* . . . [Yielding a bit] I agree that anything on these tapes that indicates what the *decision* was on the polygraph test might be eliminated."

The Judge [businesslike] "Again I ask you, sir, what bearing does an agreement to take a lie-detector test have upon these tapes?"

Mr. Wall: "It shows, Your Honor, the consensual nature of what happened—the fact of there being no custodial interrogation. It indicates that this was entirely agreed upon after a consultation with his father and his mother. It shows that he remained there without restraint. . . . He had a choice as to whether he would go home or stay there, and there was no restriction on his freedom of action. There was no compulsion whatsoever and this written document fortifies that conclusion—that this was not a custodial interrogation."

Mr. McKeon: "Your Honor, if Mr. Wall wants to put in just the responses to the lie-detector questions, there is no objection on our part. But that is surrounded—it's *submerged*, it's *drowned*—in a complete interrogation. . . . The lie-detector test was nothing but a device, almost a fraud, to keep this boy there and wear him out. . . . He went home in fear and indicated he didn't sleep that night. The next day when he returned he said, 'I wasn't going to go to work today but I was so scared you'd be over to pick me up that I went.' He came back in fear, ostensibly to assist in a lie-detector examination, and then there was more relentless questioning from 5:00 until 8:30, during which time something like an inculpatory statement was elicited from him. I submit, Your Honor, that Lieutenant Riemer in that examination *did not let up* on that boy—asking him 'Why? Why? Why?' almost two hundred times—under the pretext of a lie-detector examination. If I'm misrepresenting, Lieutenant Riemer is right here in the courtroom to deny it. I'd be happy to put him on the witness stand."

Mr. Wall [the hush replaced by a tone of deep condemnation] "Your Honor, these statements made by Counsel are reckless and untrue. He is attempting to testify. . . . There is no such evidence before this Court. . . . It's highly improper to state at this time anything that is not in evidence."

The Judge: "Well—for the first time I'm getting a glimmering, Mr. Wall. This was not so much an interrogation as it was a lie-detector test—these seven tapes. Is that correct?"

Mr. Wall: "There were two lie-detector tests, Your Honor. And there were other interviews by policemen. . . ."

The Judge pointed out that in the case cited by Mr. Wall, the lie-detector test did not rule out the subsequent confession but did not, itself, come into evidence.

Mr. Wall: "And I didn't intend to have it."

The Judge: "But you are offering these tapes now."

Mr. Wall: "Well, really I offered them originally for another reason. . . . It may be that any portions of them . . . where *results* are indicated, might be deleted. [Rocking, twisting a pencil between his fingers] But in the administering of a lie-detector test there are certain discussions—certain questions and answers—and these would be material, even though they were part of the lie-detector test, and would be admissible apart from any results. . . . So that I concede the possibility of certain portions not being admissible . . . where results were being shown. But as far as the questions and answers are concerned, I don't agree with what Counsel has said about the evidence. [The pencil into one pocket, a fistful of coins out of another] I can say without any question that on numerous occasions Lieutenant Riemer stated to the accused that the last thing he wanted him to do was to confess to something he didn't do. And when they talk about wearing down the Defendant who was being questioned, this was the third lie-detector test that Lieutenant Riemer had given that day. *He* would have been worn down, Your Honor, to some extent, so there was no wearing down process and no indication of such, and I think we can bring that out. But right now we are talking about the admissibility of this present document, and I submit, Your Honor, that it is part of the totality of circumstances showing the voluntariness of the act of the accused in entering this discussion or in taking this lie-detector test."

Silence.

The Judge undertook another effort to clear up the only real question, which was whether this was custodial interrogation. "At one point, Detective, you said he wanted to go home, is that correct?"

Rebillard: "He wanted to see his father."

What happened then? "I told him I would call his father and have him come down or his pastor." How soon did his father arrive? "Well this was while we were at Canaan . . . when I had first started." Again: How soon did his father arrive? "Well, his father went to Hartford and we went to Hartford to meet him."

"Oh, you met the father in Hartford?" The Judge was still confused—for the very good reason that the presentation had been
reluctant, sparse, and confusing. "Didn't you tell us a moment ago
that at one point on the thirteenth Harry Solberg said he wanted to
go home?"

"I don't recall if he said he wanted to go home or if he wanted to
talk to his father."

[Squarely on the table] "Did he *ever* say he wanted to go home?"

[No ducking it] "Yes, I believe he did."

What did Rebillard do at this point? "I asked him why." What did
he say? "He said he wanted time to think." Then what happened? "I
told him, 'I'll have your father come down.'"

"Did you refuse him the right to go home?"

"Not as such, no. He didn't press the point. If he had stood up
and said, 'I'm going home,' he would have gone home. That's all
there was to it. He went home that night about 8:30."

The Judge asked Rebillard to examine the tapes, which were
marked, and identify those included in the lie-detector test. Then,
pushing things along, he said, "Well, now, can we agree on this,
gentlemen? At a certain time, somewhere on the fifth or sixth tape,
Harry Solberg was placed under arrest. Do you agree, Mr. Wall,
that at that point the *Miranda* rule was not satisfied and those tapes
must go out?"

"No, Your Honor, I do not!"

"Why not?"

"Because I believe that *Miranda* was satisfied. We haven't come
to the evidence on that yet. . . . This evidence related to what was
said on the thirteenth—at a time when the State contends no warning was necessary because of the lack of any detention. There was,
at a time after the arrest, a warning of the accused of his rights
which did satisfy *Miranda* and that will be testified to. It relates to
the stenographic report taken by the Court Reporter on the fourteenth."

"Your Honor, that's a misrepresentation!" Mr. McKeon's voice
rang out. "The language before Stenographer Roberts is the identical language used by Rebillard."

The Judge: "Where is this evidence, Mr. Wall?"

"It is one of the Exhibits from the previous trial." Mr. Wall handed the Judge the transcript of the "confession," and the Judge asked him to point out the warning.

"It is on page one, Your Honor."

The Judge read page one. "Well—the same three warnings were given but there are other warnings that *Miranda* requires."

Mr. Wall [holding on] "We intend to have evidence that there was no other one required under those circumstances, Your Honor."

The Judge [reasonably] "Well, sometime on the fourteenth of March, Harry Solberg was placed under arrest. . . . Now certainly after that he is under custodial interrogation, is he not?" Correct. "And, therefore, the three old requirements are not enough."

Mr. Wall [still in there] "Well, I believe that this is sufficient in connection with other evidence which we intend to produce."

"Well, where is it? I'm trying to find this other evidence."

"Through another witness. [Quick look at Rebillard, who was still on the stand] I could, perhaps, through this witness."

The Judge: "Well, go ahead and offer the evidence."

Then—a precaution, perhaps, against wandering down further byways—Judge Wright reviewed the three additional warnings required under *Miranda*. "That if the man cannot afford a lawyer, the State will provide a lawyer for him. That the interrogated party has the right to terminate the questioning at any time. He should be told this. And, finally, the State must prove that he knowledgeably, with full knowledge and acquiescence and understanding, waived his right to remain silent. So now there are six requirements that must be satisfied. You have satisfied only three of them so far."

Total silence in the courtroom. The issue was on the table.

The reporters at the press table sat motionless, their pencils poised. In the back row Holden looked sober and Fuessenich seemed deeply worried as he leaned forward, a hand cupped to his ear. The Solberg family looked bewildered, left behind; they knew this was important—were not sure how or why. Harry, hands folded, quiet. Mr. Wall moving back and forth, back and forth—as though searching every inch of ground for another round of ammunition to carry on this battle that seemed to have exhausted him and turned against him.

"Your Honor, as to the matter of affording a lawyer, that's the evidence that I intend to bring out," he said, "*Miranda* says that this

THE SECOND TRIAL   481

isn't necessary if the questioner has knowledge of the fact that the man does not need counsel and does not need to have one hired for him. That is the case and it was so found in the previous trial—that that was the situation. And knowledgeably waived his right to remain silent is set forth on the first page here of Exhibit RR [indicating the "confession" transcript] where there was a response made by the accused to the question in which he indicated—[a brief flash of spirit] when such a *well-worded and understandable notice* to him was given, he acquiesced and said yes."

The Judge: "That's only the third requirement—the old-fashioned requirement—the right to remain silent."

"Well, there is also the right to an attorney there, Your Honor."

"That's one of the original three requirements also, but there are three new requirements."

Mr. Wall: "But Your Honor . . . [circling, searching]. Actually, my interpretation of *Miranda* is that the offer to have a lawyer appointed for the man is only on the basis where it is definitely required—or on the basis that the questioner has no knowledge of the man's ability to hire a lawyer on his own. *Miranda* so states."

Now the Judge read directly from *Miranda* the fourth requirement: ". . . 'It is necessary to warn him not only that he has a right to consult with an attorney but also that if he is indigent, a lawyer will be appointed to represent him. Without this additional warning the . . . right to consult with counsel would often be understood as meaning only that he can consult with a lawyer if he has one or has the funds to obtain one. The warning of a right to counsel would be hollow if not couched in terms that would convey to the indigent— the person most often subjected to interrogation, the knowledge that he, too, has the right to have counsel present.' So your warning in this statement is only the old-fashioned third warning."

Still Mr. Wall held on. The passage referred to an *indigent*. "And the evidence will show that this man was no indigent—that he was employed in one of the best-paying factories in the State. The excerpt relates to a person . . . who would require the obtaining of a lawyer for him as an indigent, but we intend to have evidence here that will show that he was certainly no indigent, that he was well employed here. *Miranda* [a quick, impatient gesture], somewhere in the long pages of it—"

The Judge said that he would give him time to find the reference and called the afternoon recess. We had not seen the Jury all afternoon.

The recess began at 3:29.

In the press room, Mr. Shew, Mr. McKeon, Major Rome, June Shew, who was in Court this afternoon, and the full complement of reporters stood about in small groups talking in low voices, smoking, predicting. Nobody went downstairs for coffee. A sense of crisis was in the air.

At a little before four o'clock, Mr. Shew and Mr. McKeon were summoned to Chambers. Someone reported that Mr. Wall had entered Chambers several minutes earlier.

"Something is up. Something is cooking."

"This trial is ending."

"I don't know. One thing about Tom Wall—he's not a quitter."

"It's not quitting. Without the confession there's no case. He can't proceed."

Voices in the next room—indistinctly heard. Major Rome, over against a window, quiet, noncommittal—looking as though he knows this is not just another idle argument. Some still say that his career hangs on this trial. Some still say he is through, no matter what the outcome. Some still say this was one of the goals—accomplished however it goes.

Suddenly, like the first twist in winding a spring, the report came. "Shew and McKeon just went down the corridor. They're talking to the family." The press room door left open—reporters leaning into the corridor to keep watch. Mr. Shew came back, walking quickly, Mr. McKeon a step behind. A brief flash of Mr. Wall and the Judge as the door to Chambers closed.

The press moved out to the corridor. Another twist—like winding a top. The door to Chambers opened and Mr. Shew strode out again, moving very quickly, Mr. McKeon just behind. Past the reporters, past witnesses, past Mrs. Shew—no word spoken. Through the courtroom and down the other corridor again to the room where the family waited. Major Rome remained in the press room, revealing no emotion. People milling about the corridor. The spring twisted tighter. Mr. Shew and Mr. McKeon were back. The door to Chambers cracked open and closed. Outside it was growing dark. The lights of Bridgeport had come on. Once more out. And once more back.

The recess continued for an hour and a half.

At 4:55, Court was called to order.

Rebillard, still the witness, returned to the stand. Holden and Fuessenich came in and sat in the back row, looking glum and worried; Major Rome across the aisle—no word, no glance exchanged between them. Mr. Wall smiled a humorless smile.

The top began to spin.

Mr. Wall withdrew the offer of the tapes and offered, instead, the transcript of the confession. Mr. McKeon objected to the confession on the basis of *Miranda*. The Judge examined the document.

He said, ". . . In view of all the evidence . . . I must rule that this Exhibit does not satisfy the *Miranda* rules and therefore the Court cannot accept this offer. It is inadmissible."

The State's case had come to an end.

5:00. Mr. Wall requested a short recess to confer with Defense Counsel.

A brief word exchanged, and Mr. Shew and Mr. McKeon left the courtroom, returned less than three minutes later. A quick nod between Counsel.

In the first row Sharon sat with a white Bible open in her lap, her lips moving.

At 5:05, the State offered a substituted charge based on the Letter. "In view of Your Honor's ruling relating to the confession," Mr. Wall said, "I ask permission to file a substituted information . . . charging the Defendant with malicious threatening under the blackmail statute."

At the press table, Joe Crowley dropped his pencil and burst out, in a low voice, "Chrissake—that's exactly what Sam Rome said they should do a year and a half ago when the letter came in."

(Rome had used the term "breach of the peace"—not "blackmail.")

At 5:06, Harry Solberg was put to plea. Pale, trembling, he stood before the bench, his attorneys beside him. The Clerk intoned, "To the information charging you with malicious threatening, how do you plead—guilty or not guilty?"

The first word ever uttered in Court by Harry Solberg was almost inaudible: "Guilty."

Judge Wright said, "Before the plea is accepted, Mr. Solberg, I must ask you a few questions. How old are you?"

"I'm twenty-one."

The Judge: "This statute under which you are now charged has a possible penalty of up to ten years in prison or a fine of not more than five thousand dollars or both. Do you understand that possibility, sir?"

"Yes, sir, I do."

(His mother sobbing openly, his wife's lips moving over her Bible.)

The Judge: "Are you doing this freely and voluntarily?"

[Voice breaking] "Yes, sir, I am."

"And have you any understanding about promises being made to you?"

[Choked] "Nobody made any promises."

Judge Wright: "All right, sir. The plea is accepted. You may sit down."

Deathly white, eyes brimming, Harry Solberg returned to his seat. Racking sobs wrenched from him and his entire body began to shake. He reached for a glass of water—could not take it—drew back his hand and let it lie on the table, shaking so that he seemed on the verge of a convulsion.

The State nolled the charge of first degree murder.

The Court business went on, the top spinning itself out. Harry would spend the night in the Bridgeport jail and would be returned to Litchfield tomorrow. Bond was set at $5,000. Sentencing would take place in Litchfield next Friday, February 3.

It was over.

Smiling Mr. Wall shook hands with Tobey and Solveig Solberg. Then ten months and ten days after Harry's arrest, these bewildered people gathered themselves together to leave the courtroom for the last time—Tobey dazed, Solveig in a fresh burst of tears, Sharon clutching her white Bible, murmuring over and over again, "Praise the Lord. Praise the Lord."

• • •

In the press room, Major Rome telephoned State Police Headquarters. "This is Major Rome. Tell the Commissioner that the State's Attorney just nolled the case."

Through the receiver a stunned, rising voice: "What!"

"You heard me." He hung up. In this trial it was his first and last display of emotion.

On the way out, Joe Crowley cornered him for a brief interview. Now Major Rome, who had never wavered in his conviction that Solberg was innocent, made no mention of his own investigation or of a corroborated confession from another person. He said that the Defense had proved that Solberg could not have committed the crime. He emphasized that the autopsy had showed that Dorothy Thompsen died within minutes after she ate lunch and that she always ate lunch at 11:45—that a neighbor's child had come home that day at 11:45 because the Thompsens were about to eat lunch— and that a car resembling Solberg's was not placed at the house until 1:30.

He said, "These facts should be placed clearly before the public. The man hasn't been found Not Guilty. The public should know that he is innocent of this murder. Otherwise people will say that he got off on a technicality and that a murderer is walking the streets."

Another reporter asked a question and he looked at him sharply. "If you analyze this case, it was a series of coincidental happenings. The man wrote the letter. He was placed at the scene—he went there and he didn't report it. This would make any ordinary policeman suspicious. They had a right to check him out very thoroughly. But this case should never have gone to court." Then, to another, "Don't ask me to say anything disparaging about the police. I've given my life to building respect for the Connecticut State Police. If you undermine confidence in the police, what's left?"

Out on the sidewalk, where it was already dark, he snapped on his hat and walked off to his car. After that he was silenced. He has not commented publicly on the case again.

•   •   •

The next day Tobey Solberg, putting up his home and the cottage as collateral, produced bond, and Harry Solberg went home to his family for eight days.

On February 3, in Litchfield, he was sentenced by Judge Wright to not less than a year and a day and not more than ten years in State's Prison. He served a little more than eight months of the sentence and was paroled, with credit for exceptional good behavior, in October.

Many people who followed the case in the press still believe he is guilty.

PART FIVE

THE REST OF THE STORY

27

Two trials had been held—and the troublesome questions were still unanswered. What did Agnes Thompsen say to Major Rome at the Connecticut Valley Hospital? Was there anything to it? And, over the course of the Two Days, what happened to Harry?

The public, no longer searching, commented, "What good is the confession of an insane woman?" (To which Rome's answer from the start had been: "Even from an insane mind you can get details that can be corroborated. She can't dream these things up. No matter what inducement you offer, she cannot tell you what she doesn't know.")

And about Harry, the public said, "He must be guilty. Why would he confess?"

After the sentencing on February 3, in a conversation with Mr. Wall and Judge Wright, I asked Mr. Wall if I might hear the tapes of the police interrogations of both suspects. Now that it was all over, he agreed readily to make them available. For three days during the week of February 13, I listened to the tapes in the library of Mr. Wall's law office in Torrington.

Here is what the public never heard.

◆

Major Rome's Interrogation of Agnes Thompsen— August 5, 1965

The tapes did not cover the entire interview, Mr. Wall stated, but they were all he had. The transcript of the Coroner's Hearing indicates that the preliminary questioning was not included.

(In Litchfield, a reporter: "What if you told her what to say first?" Rome: "This was done in front of a roomful of witnesses—five police officers, two doctors and a nurse. Every conversation was monitored. If I were feeding it to her, she might say, 'You told me to say that.' With all those witness Wall would have put someone on the stand. He'd have showed the world that I told her what to say.")

Throughout the interrogation, an ebb and flow in the clarity of Agnes Thompsen's mind is apparent in changes in her voice. When her mind is clear, she sounds alert and aware. When her mind wanders, when she is guessing or giving a nonsense answer, her voice sounds vague and mechanical. We learned the circumstances surrounding this interview during the first trial. The persuasion and the inducements are all there. The policewoman, Valerie Hageman, is present as "Jean." She calls Agnes, "Ma," and engages in earnest pleading, along with Major Rome, for her to tell them what happened.

At the start Agnes denies everything. "I didn't do it . . . There was a car outside . . . I heard two big bangs." Then, suddenly the first break: "Ya, I guess I did it then," followed by a denial, a partial admission, another denial. Finally, again, "I did it then."

Rome mentions a hammer first. "What kind of hammer did you hit her with?" Agnes is evasive. Rome: "How big was the hammer? What kind of hammer?"

Agnes: "It was a *sledgehammer* . . ." How big was the handle? "Not too big." Several times Rome asks what she did with the hammer when she got through and Agnes says each time that she does not know.

Rome [with Valerie Hageman lying on the floor] "Show me where you hit Dorothy with the hammer."

Agnes is vague at first. Then, "Over here on the head."

"How many times?"

"*Twice*, I guess." Show me how you held the hammer—with one hand or two hands. "Maybe it was with *two*."

Then her mind appears to wander. What did she do to Dorothy's pants? She thinks she took them off. Did she hit Dorothy in the nose? She says maybe she did. (At these times, throughout the interview, Rome reproves her, cautions her not to guess.)

A hint that she is coming back. Rome: "What was tied around her neck?"

Agnes: "An iron *cord*." She says she wound it around Dorothy's neck eight times—then three times.

"What was the cord attached to?"

[Suddenly clear] "Wasn't it a *toaster?*"

Rome: "What did you do with her then?"

Agnes: *"I dragged her outside."*

[To see if she will be misled] "Where outside? Downstairs?"

Agnes: "No. *Out on the porch.*" How was her body when you were dragging her out? "Oh, her body was dead." Was her face up or down? "The face was up." [Again misleading] Was the face down? "No, the face wasn't down."

(During her lucid moments, Agnes does not agree readily, does not take suggestion. She seems very sure of what she wants to say.)

The interview has settled down to a conversational mood. Rome's tone is one of curiosity, suggesting to her that he would like to hear this story. Agnes is soft-spoken, except when she is upset—appears to be interested, too.

Rome: "How did she die?"

Agnes: "With a hammer."

"And what else did you hit her with?"

"Mmm—let me think. There was a *fork.*"

"Where did you hit her with the fork?"

Agnes: "I hit her in the *throat.*" How many times? "Just once."

He accepts the answer with no suggestion that it is incorrect, asks what she hit her with next. Agnes becomes vague and Rome, leading her, mentions the meat fork, asking only whether she remembers it, stopping short of any other information about it. For another moment Agnes is dull, mechanical—says maybe she hit her on the head with the roast fork. Then she sharpens up and supplies the correct information, pointing to a place *high on the back.* She does not accept a misleading suggestion that it might have been low on the back.

Rome: "She fell to the floor. Where did her head fall?"

Agnes: "Near the kitchen counter."

(The thickest blood was near the counter next to the sink.)

Rome [curious tone] "Tell me where you threw the hammer."

Agnes: "Maybe outside." *Where* outside? . . . Did you go out on the porch? . . . Don't say maybe. Where did you throw it? "Down below."

[A choice] "How far from the house? Or did you throw it right down?"

Agnes: *"So far as I had strength."*

Did it hit anything? [Misleading] Did it hit the barn? "There's no barn." Which way did you throw it? "Straight out." Rome does not suggest that this is incorrect.

Rome [setting the scene] "This is the house . . . you're standing on the porch. Where was Dorothy's body now?"

Agnes: *"Down there . . . off the porch."*

He asks whether she is right-handed or left-handed. She is right-handed.

Rome: "Now, which way did you throw it? [Equal choices] This way to the left? Or this way to your right?"

Agnes: "Oh, I threw it *to the right.*"

(The hammer was found in the woods to the right.)

Consistently Agnes denies all knowledge of the piggy bank. "That I can't remember. I didn't take the bank . . . somebody must have stolen it . . . if I could tell you, I would."

Rome: "There was blood on the telephone." (The first mention of this detail.) "When you hit Dorothy here in the throat . . . with the fork, what did she do?"

At first Agnes does not pick up the suggestion, gropes to remember. Then: "Maybe she went to the telephone. . . . I don't know whether she called or not." (Her answers are fading. One feels that he is losing her again.) What did she do while Dorothy was phoning? "I hit her with a sledgehammer."

Rome: "Was she lying down or was she standing up when you hit her with the sledgehammer?"

Agnes [stronger, aware] *"She was lying down."*

She follows this with information that Dorothy was lying *face up,* and that she hit her on the *cheek* and on the *forehead.* Rome attempts to mislead her by suggesting other places. She rejects the suggestions. She says that she tied the cord around a *nail.* Efforts to have her describe it more specifically are unsuccessful. At this point he takes a break to get her some milk. There is idle conversation during this break.

The interview is resumed.

Rome: "What was Dorothy doing when you walked downstairs?"

Agnes: "She was *ironing*." What was she ironing? "*A shirt . . .
Arnfin's . . . White . . .*"

Rome [as though to a child] "Tell me—what started the argument?"

Agnes [suddenly out with it—hurt and resentful] "Because
Christa couldn't stay upstairs." [Quoting Dorothy's words] "'Because it's hard for me to get her down,' she said. I said I would help
her get her down. She said she had to take her down by might.
. . ."

Rome [sympathetic] "What else was in the argument?"

Agnes: "Nothing else. I got mad."

[Patient] "You got mad. O.K. And then what did you do?"

"I hit her."

Again Rome reconstructs the scene. "Dorothy is at the ironing
board. And you come in and go over and start talking. Then what
did you do?"

"I said, 'I want Christa.' . . . And she said, 'It's hard for me to
take her down. So I can't let her go upstairs.' . . . And then I hit
her."

What did you hit her with first? "With a fork . . . in the neck."
How many times—twenty-five times? "No—a couple of times."
Then what did Dorothy do? "She was going to call—her mother,
I suppose." Was she bleeding at the time? "Yes, I guess she was."

Rome: "Now—she's at the telephone. Then what did you do?"

Agnes says that she hit her with the sledgehammer. The question
is repeated, and she says that it was with the *fork* and indicates
where she struck her—*very high in the right shoulder—a couple of
times in the back.*

Another break for milk. Light banter. "Did you ever milk a cow,
Agnes? . . . Did you ever milk a bull? . . . Am I kidding you,
Agnes?"

Agnes says that she wore a dress that day with some pink in it, that
she washed the dress in her kitchen sink, but does not remember the
water becoming bloody. To wash the porch, she used cloths and
carried water from Dorothy's sink in a metal pail, does not remember what she did with the cloths afterward.

Rome [conversational tone] "When Dorothy's body fell—this is
the porch, this is the way you're facing—did you throw it off or roll
it off?"

Agnes: "Roll it off."

"And which way was the head—to the right or to the left?"

Agnes: "To the right." (Correct.)

Leading up now to the stone, Major Rome asks if Agnes went down to take another look at Dottie, but Agnes, rather shocked, denies it. He chides her, again as though she were a child. "Agnes, you want to tell the truth. Did you go downstairs? There was a big stone there. Remember the big stone?" (Rome has mentioned the stone first, again leading, again stopping short of any information about it.) Agnes agrees now that she does remember it.

Rome: "What did you do with the big stone?"

Agnes [promptly] "Oh—maybe I hit her with it." (These "maybes" are a speech habit with her. She does not seem to be in doubt.)

Rome [asking Valerie Hageman to lie down on the floor] "Where did you hit her with it? Now I don't want any guesses here. Where did you hit her?" Agnes's answer is inaudible. Rome [even tone] "Did you hit her at all? Did you or didn't you hit her?"

Agnes [promptly] "I hit her."

Rome: "How big a stone? Show me how big."

Agnes: "Kinda big."

"Show me something." He points out several items which are handy—a can, a cup, a box—giving her an unweighted choice. She rejects the box as too big, indicates the can as closest to the size. Rome describes the can as four inches in diameter and about four or five inches high.

"And where did you hit her?"

At first Agnes indicates the area of the chest. Rome [quiet, inquiring tone] "Did you hit her in the nose?" No. "You hit her in the chest?" Ya. "Did Dorothy have a big bosom?" No. "Did you hit her in the breast or [offering other alternatives] here—or here? Take this can and show me just how you did it."

Now Agnes indicates an area which he describes for the tape: "You're hitting just below the breast. . . . Was the stone a white one or a black one? Was it a house brick? Was it rough or smooth?"

Agnes: "Rough."

[To see if she will be misled] "Did you hit her on the side here? Did you hit her on the side? Or did you hit her right directly on the—"

Agnes [interrupting, positive] "Right here—ya."

Rome describes it for the tape: Just above the navel.

Valerie Hageman [backing him up] "That's *exactly the part.* Yes. Here is the navel."

Rome [rechecking] "You show me where the navel was when you hit her."

Agnes [clear] "Right here."

Again he describes it for the tape: Just above the navel. [Again rechecking] "You didn't hit her in the breast?" No. "You hit her just below the breast?"

"Yes."

"Right smack in the belly?"

"Yes."

Agnes gives the information that there was a *lot of blood* on the floor, most of it *close to the counter.* (Correct.)

"Did you break the fork?" No. "Did you damage the fork at all?"

Agnes: "That could be . . . I *bended* it."

But on the piggy bank Agnes holds her ground. "This is the one thing I cannot tell you for I don't know . . . I haven't the slightest idea . . ."

She says that Dorothy put Christa to sleep at *quarter to one.* A few minutes ago, discussing Christa, she said that she had wet and had had a bowel movement and that she changed her, and that she had her upstairs and returned her to her crib at about four o'clock.

Rome: "Did Christa wake up when Dorothy hollered?"

Agnes: "She didn't holler." Why didn't she scream? "I don't know why. I guess I hit her so hard." Which blow? "On the head." Which side of the head? "The *forehead.*" Which hammer? "The *sledge-hammer.*"

Rome: "Why did you tie the cord around her neck?"

Agnes: "Maybe to stop her breathing . . . she was still breathing a little bit."

[Curious] "Why didn't you leave her? What did you have in mind when you dragged her out to the porch?"

Agnes: "I was foolish. I should have left her in the kitchen." Was she heavy to drag? [With a sigh, as though remembering] "Yes, she was very heavy."

On the bank, Agnes is adamant. "That's stolen. . . . There was a person there. He took it. That person is going to come someday . . . I haven't the slightest *idea* about that." She can describe the bank: "Pink—Big."

Rome: "How would you get the money out?"

Agnes: "You have to cut out a piece." How much money was in it? "That nobody knows . . . I haven't the slightest *idea* about that bank . . . so if you want me to stay in the hospital for that I'll have to stay . . ."

Rome: "When you tied a rope around Dorothy's neck, why did you do that?"

Agnes: "Maybe it was to stop her breathing."

[Quiet] "And you tied it around something and rolled her off the porch . . . Why?"

Agnes [quick recognition] "Oh! Oh! Maybe it was so that *people would think she had hanged herself.*"

She washed the porch, she says, to wipe up the blood.

Then Agnes says that she cannot talk anymore and Rome says, "All right," and the interview is over.

28

The Interrogation of Harry Solberg

Included in the text of the *Miranda* decision is a discussion, with quotations from certain police manuals, on the "most effective psychological stratagems to employ during interrogations." These are not official police manuals, but they are said to be widely used. In the interrogation of Harry Solberg there are striking parallels between psychological stratagems used by his interrogators and those described in this decision.

These are some of the suggestions, taken from those police manuals, as described by the Chief Justice in *Miranda:*

1. *Privacy.* " 'The principal psychological factor contributing to a successful interrogation is . . . being alone with the person under investigation'* . . . in a room of [the investigator's] choice. . . . 'In his own home [the subject] may be confident, indignant . . . more keenly aware of his own rights. . . . His family . . . are nearby, lending moral support. . . . In his own office, the investigator possesses all the advantages. The atmosphere suggests the invincibility of the forces of the law.' "†

2. *Certainty of guilt.* The investigator should "display . . . confidence in the suspect's guilt . . . and an interest [only] in confirming certain details. . . . Explanations to the contrary are dismissed and discouraged. . . . The interrogator should [discuss] the *reasons why* the subject committed the act, rather than . . . asking whether he did it. . . ."

* Inbau and Reid, *Criminal Interrogation and Confessions* (1962).
† O'Hara, *Fundamentals of Criminal Investigation* (1959).

3. *"Minimize the moral seriousness* of the offense. . . . The subject should be offered legal excuses for his actions." (Probably the victim used "abusive language," or the act was self-defense.)

4. "The interrogator should possess *patience and perseverance.* . . . He must [leave] the subject no prospect of surcease. . . . He must overwhelm [him] with his inexorable will to obtain the truth."

5. "In the event that the subject wishes to speak to a relative or an attorney, 'the interrogator should [suggest that] the subject first tell [him] the truth rather than get anyone else involved. . . . He may add: Joe, I'm only looking for the truth and if you're telling the truth, that's it.' "*

•   •   •

And here is what happened to Harry on March 13, 14, 15, 1966. (According to the testimony, Harry was picked up at about 9:30 on Sunday morning, March 13, and taken to the Canaan Barracks, where the interrogation began at about 10:45. All Canaan references are based on a 10:45 starting time.)

The first interrogator is Rebillard. He speaks in the same soft, detached voice that we heard in Court. "Well–uh–we're not going to beat around the bush. We're not going to hurt ya. And–uh–before we talk to anybody we always advise them of their rights. [Offhand] You know what I mean? In other words you don't have to say anything–you don't have to make any statements. You don't have to write any statements. You don't have to sign any statements. And–uh–you're entitled to counsel. Well . . . you understand what I mean?"

Harry sounds bewildered. "Yeah."

Rebillard goes directly to the Letter. ". . . What we want to know is why you wrote that nasty letter to Arnie Thompsen?"

Harry [surprised] "Hmm! [mumbles] I didn't write it."

Low-key sparring as Rebillard convinces Harry that he knows that he wrote the Letter. They have some of his school papers; they have compared the handwriting. "You wrote it, Harry. The question is *why* did you write it?" A long silence. "*Why,* Harry?"

[Worried, nervous] "I don't know why. [Braver] I can't say I wrote it. That's all."

* Inbau and Reid, *op. cit.*

The first strokes to suggest invincibility. Rebillard tells Harry that the police have also found out that he was caught once cheating on an English examination. Harry admits that readily. And, Rebillard says, they took the Letter to a handwriting expert. Rebillard has been keeping score of what he says are Harry's true and false answers—an oblique suggestion that he already has all the facts—and now, with assurance, he comments that Harry has told him about eleven lies. "Are you ashamed to tell me why you wrote the letter, Harry?"

"I didn't write the letter. [Then, anxiously] Do you think I had something to do with the—with the accident, too?"

[Soft] "It's possible. . . . I think you wrote the letter because you were afraid. . . . You were real scared the day I tried to talk to you."

"All I could think of was the *car*. Boy, I was even thinking of putting my car in back of the garage . . . I was scared. I'm scared now."

10:57. After about twelve minutes Harry gives up on the Letter (in the first trial, Fuessenich testified that he held out for about an hour; in six months, recollection can become inexact) and comes out with the reason: "'Cause I was scared of the car. [Long silence] I—I—That's all I can think of . . . I'm *scared*."

"Tell me now why you wrote the letter, Harry."

[Quietly] "I wrote it to divert suspicion. From off my car . . . because they were looking for a black Ford." What did you do with the black Ford that day if you wanted to divert suspicion away from it, Harry? [Plaintively] "I don't know—I can't remember." (Harry does not seem to find this strange.) "All I know is I was—in school—[trailing off] I don't know. I went to work with my father, I guess."

[Dismissing that] "That's not too good a story, Harry."

"Yes, because I had the same kind of car they were looking for! [Then, more spirited] I gave you my fingerprints. . . . Why didn't you come sooner?"

A hint of official strategy. "We had lots of reasons . . ." Rebillard attempts to discuss the Letter—Where did he write it? Where did he mail it? What did it say?—but Harry says that he does not remember. Instead Harry attempts to reason: "*Why*—why would I want to hurt them? . . . *No reason* . . . There *is* no reason. I didn't have nothing to do with that. Arnfin and I—we worked together. And she even brought us apples and pears—from her father's farm."

"You still haven't told me why you wrote the letter. . . . *Why, Harry?* Cause you're afraid we'll find out you did something bad?"

"No. No. Cause I didn't—do nothing wrong with that. I've got a wife now—and a child coming . . . I've got a lot more than that car. . . . I wouldn't hurt her. I wouldn't hurt nobody."

He cannot remember where he was with the car that day, tries to patch together the story. "I went to work with my father—" Rebillard tells him that he has checked that story and it is not true.

11:15 (half-hour). "Harry, why did you have to write this letter?"

"I was scared because of the car. . . . I had no other reason." Yes, you did. [Sigh] "Like what? Like I killed her? No—no, that's not right." Rebillard [soft, sure] Yes, it is. [Whisper] "No, that's not the truth."

Rebillard is patient, soft-spoken, persistent. "Harry, *why* did you write that letter? . . . *Why* were you scared of the car?"

Harry bursts into tears. "Because I've seen people get pinched for no reason at all. . . . Fellow got pinched because he had the same kind of car in a speed trap. I didn't have nothing to do with it so I was scared."

Now comes the first suggestion that Harry take a lie-detector test, and Harry backs away from it. "Not right—not right today."

"Harry, why did you want to divert suspicion away from your car? . . . You can talk to me . . . I'm only interested in the truth."

11:20. Rebillard: "Do you think Agnes did it?"

"I don't see how she could. [Protective] She's too small."

[Soft] "But you're not small." Rebillard suggests that Harry might have had an argument with Dottie. "Why did you stop there that day?"

"I was nowhere around there that day."

"Will you go to Hartford and take a lie-detector test and tell me that?"

"No, I can't. You got to give me a chance to think."

"Are you covering up for someone . . . is that why you wrote the letter?"

Tearfully Harry bursts out with a more detailed explanation. ". . . My mother wouldn't let me take the car out of the yard. . . . My mother was on my back all the time . . . 'cause I wasn't any good in school—I know that's not her fault. . . . My father came home and told us what somebody had done. I didn't think nothing of it. I just went to bed. Then I heard it—or my mother told me—that they were looking for a black '59 Ford—and the way she *looks* at you. . . . She said she didn't know what she'd do if someone came and started to ask questions. So I couldn't quite think of anything else—so that's why I wrote the letter . . ."

11:30. Harry: "I didn't have no *reason—at all.*" Maybe you did it without a reason. "*Why?* Why should I do it without a reason?" Maybe you just stopped there—and you had a fight or something. "No. [Then, picking this up] About *what?*" I don't know. [Quick] "Yeah, me neither!" Were you in love with her, Harry? [Dully] "In love with her? Eleven years older than I was?"

"Tell me the truth . . . where did you go that day in the black car? . . . Why did you write the letter? . . . Did she catch you taking the piggy bank and you were so afraid you killed her? . . . Or did you take it afterward?"

"I didn't take it at all."

11:33. A third time: "Harry, let's go and take a lie-detector right now."

"I want to talk to my father first. [Shaky whisper] I'm *scared. I don't know what to do.*"

Again Harry says that he gave his fingerprints willingly—he had nothing to be afraid of. Rebillard, a fourth time, suggests a lie-detector test. Again Harry says, "I want to talk to my father first . . . I just want to talk to him."

Harry's replies are slowing down. Then suddenly he mentions the Bible, and Rebillard encourages him to talk about it. Harry: "There's nothing in it in itself . . . the Bible is only a means of communication between two people. . . ."

Rebillard [quiet] "Thou shalt not kill."

"That's right. Nobody can live by the commandments but I try." Did you kill? [Calm] "No, I didn't." Did you help someone kill? "No, I didn't. But I stole." [Soft] What did you steal, Harry? "I stole from my mother once."

This reminds Harry of his financial woes—bills from the wedding —monthly bills—and his mother is always asking about them. And their apartment. "It's a dirty place. We painted the kitchen and polished the floors. There's still bugs in there and I hate it."

Rebillard hears him out, then gets back on the track. He tells Harry that he has told the truth four or five times but he has told a great many lies. "Is there something in the Bible about that, too?"

"Yeah. [Pause] In the Bible it says, 'If you're delinquent in one commandment, you're delinquent in all.'"

(What can he mean? Does he feel guilty of all sins because of minor sins?)

11:45 (one hour). "Harry, I know you were down there that day."

"You couldn't know 'cause I wasn't down there."

Softly, persuasively, Rebillard tells Harry that he can understand. He has five children of his own . . . Everyone does wrong at one time or another . . . He had to kill a man once—in self-defense . . . Things like that can happen at the most unexpected times.

12:00. Harry: "No, I never would have hurt her. I wouldn't hurt nobody. There's no sense in hurting people."

Rebillard: "Sometimes it just happens."

Harry [firm] "No, it doesn't just happen."

"Sometimes it's just fate."

[Firmer] "I don't think so."

Rebillard: "Why did the Lord let her get killed like that, Harry?"

[Soft] "Why does the Lord let anyone get hurt? Because everybody has their designated time to depart." Then that was her time? Harry [unquestioning] "That must have been her time . . . and He knew from the beginning that that was going to happen. He knew before she was born . . . I'm quoting from the Bible. I'm not saying that it was right for somebody to kill her. [A deep sigh] What are you going to do with me now?" We just want to talk to you, Harry. [Tired] "I can't talk anymore now . . . I want to call my wife."

"How did the piggy bank get two and a half miles from the house, Harry. . . . Did you have the piggy bank in your car? . . . You did have that piggy bank in your car. . . . What did you do with the money that was in there, Harry?"

"I didn't touch no money."

"Why did you write the letter saying, 'I killed your wife—'?"

12:10 (one and a half hours). Rebillard shows Harry a copy of the Letter, tells him to read it out loud. Harry replies that he cannot. "I'm too shaky—I can just about see it." Rebillard reads him the first few lines: Why did you write that, Harry?

Harry sounds sick. "I don't know. [Whimper] Do you think I killed her?"

[Soft, confident] "Yes, I do."

[Whisper] "No!" Silence. "You gonna book me now? I—I just gotta call my wife. I gotta see her for a couple of minutes—"

"No, we want to talk. We'll have her come down here. We'll have anyone come down that you want." He offers him dinner and Harry refuses. Silence. Deep troubled sighs.

Harry: "No! I can't say that I killed her because I didn't . . . Why? Why? . . . There's no *reason*. I couldn't touch her."

"Someone did, Harry . . . and someone wrote a letter because they were afraid they were going to get caught. . . . That person was you, Harry."

"Yeah, I know I did. But—that's not killing her."

Very long silences now, broken only by heavy sighs.

"Did you hit her with anything? . . . Did you stab her with anything? . . . You said in the letter that you stabbed her. It was true, Harry. She was stabbed."

Harry: "I know it. 'Cause it was written in the paper—and it was on the radio. And my mother gets all the latest—"

"All I want is the truth, Harry. You have to tell someone. . . . You can tell God."

"I've told Him everything. I've always told Him—"

Rebillard asks where Harry got the twenty-five dollars for the ring, and Harry says he was saving for a motorcycle and then he met Sharon.

•   •   •

At about 12:20, after an hour and thirty-five minutes, Fuessenich takes over. Where Rebillard was patient and soft-spoken, his manner is crisp and businesslike. (Both Fuessenich and Rebillard testified that Fuessenich interrogated Harry for about half to three quarters of an hour. The tapes of his interrogation run for about an hour and a half. Again recollection has suffered with time.)

Harry [plaintive] "Could I ask a question?" Sure. "Am I going to be permitted to go home and see my wife or am I going to have to stay here in jail?"

Fuessenich [tosses it off] "You're not in jail."

"Oh, aren't I? I honestly don't know . . . I'd like to talk to someone—"

Fuessenich cuts in and gets down to business, quickly minimizing the seriousness of the situation. "You know how the Coroner has— uh—given his finding. We just want to clear up what happened— pick up the loose ends. . . . Now that's why I turned to you."

For the first quarter-hour Fuessenich, too, dwells on the Letter. Harry remembers only the first few lines, which Rebillard read to him—that he killed her, worked with her in the bank, borrowed a car. "I just don't remember anything more. Can I have a glass of water?"

Fuessenich [side-stepping that] "Yeah—we'll get you a glass of water. Now—I'm trying to pin this down, Harry, so there won't be any doubt in anyone's mind that you are telling us the truth—"

12:40. Without warning, Fuessenich drops the next blow. "Now— why would your car be seen down by Arnfin's house on that afternoon?"

Harry [plaintive] "Did it have to be my car?"

[Certain] "Yes . . . it has been identified as your car. We *know* it was your car. Now if there's a reason why . . ."

Harry: "I wasn't down that way. I was working with my father that afternoon. [Groping] It seems like I was someplace else that afternoon, but I can't remember where." Then how does he remember that he worked with his father? "Because I just do. *Little pieces that I remember.*"

Suddenly he remembers a new detail. [Excited] "Wait a minute! . . . The plumbing supply—I helped them unload that big truck." He hastens to describe it. He cannot remember the firm's name but knows its location. "They should have records."

Fuessenich returns to the car, suggesting that his father might have been working in that area. In that case, Harry agrees, his car could have been down there.

Fuessenich: "All right . . . there's no doubt in your mind or my mind that your car was in front of Arnfin Thompsen's house that day."

[Quickly] "I can't say that."

[Hard] "No, *we* can say that—because we *know* . . . and *you know* it was there, too."

[Holding on] "I'm not trying to argue but I can't agree with you . . . 'cause I can't remember being down that way that day."

12:50. Fuessenich takes a new tack. "Now, Harry, when you wrote this letter, this began to be an awful load on your mind, didn't it? . . . Now that we know, that's a big load off your mind, isn't it?"

[Unconvinced] "Yeah—I don't have to worry about it, anymore. [Wary] You're bringing up something else now, huh?" What? "About—the rest of it. . . . The other fellow . . . thought—that I went through with everything." Went through with what? "Well, the murder and everything. [Falters] But I wasn't—"

Fuessenich cuts in, very authoritative. "Harry . . . when these things are cleared up, it's going to be a relief to you. . . . Now—we know other things, too. You wouldn't be here unless we had quite a bit of evidence. . . . [Picking up the beat] Now, you had a reason for writing the letter. You had a reason for having your car there in front of the house—"

Harry: "But I didn't have my car there in front of the house. [Distressed whisper] *I want to talk to somebody.*"

"We have people who can identify it. . . . Harry, do you know where your car is now?" No, I traded it in. "Yes, but do you know where it is *now*?" No. "It's in our garage. [Hard] Now we're *not kidding.*"

While Harry copes with this fact, Fuessenich strides on. "Now—we know that there is a *reason* for everything that's happened. . . . Now—*I am certain*—that there is more to this than meets the eye. Now it is my understanding that Dottie was something of a flirt—"

Harry [puzzled] "A flirt?"

Fuessenich elaborates. Perhaps Dottie brought this on herself . . . "Somewhere somebody was—invited in—perhaps egged on a little bit—perhaps flirted with—and one thing led to another—and this thing happened."

(*Is this the seed—planted here—of Harry's second story, which prompted the State to call this a sex slaying!*)

"You are the only person who can tell us exactly what happened. Right?"

"Yeah, but I wasn't down there." Again he asks what the reason could be.

"No reason. You are a good boy. You're big and husky and good-looking. You've got a lot to go for. But—you can't keep running."

[Bewildered] "I'm not running. I haven't felt—"

"*You have been running.* You have been wondering when they're going to find out about the letter . . . when they're going to find out about the car. . . . And your home life isn't what it should be. Because other people are concerned. . . . They didn't want to show it, but they *did* show it. . . . Now, if there was a reason . . . if this was a case of self-defense . . . *We know the facts*—but we want to know the reason. . . . We're going to get the facts some-time. . . . Tell us your side of the story. . . . Don't think for one minute that the truth is not going to come out. . . ."

"Do you remember anything distinctive about your black '59 Ford? . . . Well, maybe you never noticed it. . . . [Mysterious] I can't tell you now. . . ."

This is something that really bothers Harry, and he wants to straighten it out. [Puzzled] "Is it a dent? . . . Or the broken glass in the back? 'Cause I can show you that maybe that's wrong—" Fuessenich will say only that it was something conspicuous and that the person who saw the car there said that undoubtedly this was the car.

1:00. Harry: "I gotta have something to drink. I'm just plain dizzy. Please—just a glass of water."

"All right, I'll get you a glass of water and I'll be right back. Now while I'm gone, think about your family. Think about your wife."

Harry: "Am I going to have to stay here?"

[Offhand] "Let's skip it now."

[Insisting] "No. I gotta know if I'm gonna be here for good. I gotta call my wife. I can't let her sit home like that." Fuessenich says that he promised to let her know if Harry was to be delayed. There is a long silence. Harry still doesn't have the water and it seems to have been forgotten.

"All right now, Harry. Tell us the truth . . . you can't say that you know nothing about this case."

"All I know is what I've been told because I had nothin' to do with it." You can't say that truthfully. "Oh, yes, I can." [Quick] You cannot. "Yes, I can." [Hard] You cannot. "Yes!"

"*No!* You cannot say that truthfully. You have been worried about this. Your family has been gravely concerned . . . your mother and your father and your wife. . . . We *know* you were there. We want your side of the story. Why were you there? If you can give us an explanation—"

"I can't say I was down there because I wasn't . . ." You *were* there. "I *couldn't* have been there." You've *got* to be there [Puzzled] "Why did I go there?"

Another groping effort to reconstruct the day that he can't remember, and Fuessenich says, "Harry, you can't account for your time. There's no sense in trying to." Harry protests that it was all too long ago to remember. Fuessenich [hard] "You'll *never* forget this. You'll have dreams about this. As much as you'd like to, you can't forget it. . . . We have records to show that you were not on the job. . . . Your girl says you were with her."

"All afternoon! [Absolute astonishment] Ah, come on! All afternoon! . . . At night I was with her, 'cause that's when I had permission—"

From the start Fuessenich has been the hard-driving man of authority, and has achieved no tangible results. But Harry has revealed his deep attachment to his family, and Fuessenich returns to this point. "How do you feel your parents are going to take this? . . . Are they going to believe you any more than I believe you?"

Harry [worried] "It's going to be hard."

"You bet it's going to be hard! . . . Do you think you can live with these people, having them suspect that you haven't told the whole truth? . . . Your wife, I'm sure, suspects something. . . . Do you think they're going to believe you? . . . Would you believe someone if they told you that story?" A final push. "Would you like to prove one way or the other to them?"

Harry [instantly wary] "I'd like to talk to them first."

[Quick, insistent] "Answer this question. Would you like to prove to them definitely whether you are withholding any information?"

"I want to talk to them first."

[Offhand] "All right. We'll let you talk to them first. . . . But why don't you want to prove to them that you are telling the truth? . . . Why should there be any question? . . . What are you waiting for?"

[Tearful] "I'm waiting—just to *think*. This morning I got up an'—"

"I gave you the opportunity of proving to your family and your wife that you are telling the truth and you say no!" I want to talk to them. [Excited] "Why do you want to talk to them? You want to tell them the truth, don't you?" [Calm] Yes, I want to tell them the truth. "All right . . . why don't you want to tell me the truth right now?" I am telling you the truth right now. "You *haven't* been telling me the truth. [He calms down] Harry, for your own good—for your family's good, let's have the truth right now."

"I had nothing to do with anything that happened down there. Nothing."

[Fast] "Do you want to prove that?" [Whisper] How? . . . Not the way the other fellow suggested—lie detector. "You don't want that?"

[Weary] "I'm mixed up. I don't know what I'm talking about half the time here."

Now Fuessenich offers to let him talk to his parents, and Harry asks, miserably, "Does it have to be down here?" Where would you suggest? *"Home."* Why? [Anguished] "Because that's home. Just because it's home."

"Very often home is not the right place to do this." Fuessenich suggests that they telephone his family to meet them in Hartford. Then another push for a quick test: "We can't say that you've got to do this. . . . You'll know what the questions are going to be. If you don't want to answer these questions, you just say so. . . . Other people have taken a polygraph test in connection with this case . . . and afterwards they were very happy that they had because it proved they were telling the truth. . . . Now, do you think you want to prove that you are telling us the truth?"

But Harry holds tight—he wants to see his family. "I gotta talk to them. Give me a little time. Just ten minutes. I'm all mixed up. I just want to be left alone with them and talk. . . . If I haven't tried anything in nine months, I'm not going to. . . . I got a wife and a kid on the way."

The tape ends as Fuessenich is leading Harry out to call his parents. His interrogation lasted an hour and twenty-five minutes. The time is about 1:45.

•   •   •

Then, we were told, they had something to eat and drove to Hartford, where Harry's family met them. The tape of this meeting begins at about 3:40, with Fuessenich explaining to the family that Harry wrote the Letter and that they would like him to take the polygraph examination. "This is an opportunity to let us know if he is not withholding any information whatsoever and I think that, in fairness to him—in fairness to his wife and his parents, that this is what he should do. . . . Harry was very cooperative—and he's a good boy, we all realize this."

Mrs. Solberg is crying bitterly. "Harry! *Why?* I can't understand it." Sharon, the most controlled, says they would like to talk to him alone. With his mother weeping convulsively, Harry begins to cry, too, gasping out his explanation. "You were afraid. . . . You didn't want me to take the car. . . . I had to do something to keep them away from you."

"Harry, is it my fault then?"

[Weeping] "No, it isn't your fault."

Harry has emerged considerably confused from the morning interrogation, and now he urges his family to try to remember details to corroborate the statements that they told him were untrue. Can his father find out about the plumbing supply truck? And about the lawn mower? And about working at Zimmer's? And did Sharon say they were together that whole afternoon? Sharon: "No!"

Then the worst: "And they have my car in the garage! [Urgent whisper] And he said that's the car that was down there!" An excited conference and Harry's voice rises above the others. "But you don't understand. *They're going to pin it on me!*" More than anything, the claim that there were marks on his car bothers Harry because he can't believe it. (And, of course, there were not. Mr. Flagg observed only that it was shiny.) "Remember when I backed into a pole? They said there was a dent in the back. . . . And remember when you pushed me and we broke the back light? Was that *after* that happened?" Yes, these things happened after the murder.

When Fuessenich returns, the family attempts to confirm Harry's statements, but Fuessenich concentrates on the test, emphasizing that this is to prove that Harry has no more information. "In justice to you—in justice to Harry himself—now is the time to show us. . . . Then everyone can go home and relax. . . . This is a grand opportunity for the whole thing to be finished—right here and now."

Harry: "Do I have a choice? Can I be made to take that test?"

"No, you cannot be made to take that test. . . . We are giving you this opportunity to prove that you have no further information. . . ."

Mr. Solberg is succumbing. "You have nothing to hide, Harry. . . . If you have something you've got to tell them—"

Fuessenich urges that Harry "owes it to his family to let them know that he is clean. . . ." If he has further information it will bother him the rest of his life and it will bother his family. "I think your parents and your wife would want you to do this."

And so, halfheartedly, Harry agrees. The decision is made.

Mrs. Solberg: "Will this take long?"

Fuessenich: "It may take half to three quarters of an hour."

•   •   •

Harry's session with Lieutenant Riemer, who administers the polygraph examination, begins at about 4:00. Warm, friendly, informal, Riemer begins by taking down routine information—name, age, education—and then skillfully slips into interrogation. (This is a pattern throughout two sessions with Riemer. With the same ease he moves from the polygraph tests to interrogation as though it were only idle conversation.) Harry warms up to Riemer quickly, as Riemer communicates concerned interest in him. [Puzzled] "Did you deny at first that you sent that letter? . . . Why?"

"I was scared."

[Sympathetic] "Well, naturally you were scared. Harry, if you weren't scared, I'd think there was something wrong with you."

There are a limited number of points to be explored in this case—the Letter, Harry's relationship with Dorothy, the piggy bank—and all the questions were asked many times this morning. Riemer asks them all again.

After about twenty minutes he begins to go over the test questions with Harry and tells him the first question: "The day that Dorothy Thompsen was killed, were you at that house at all?" Then he slips over into interrogation. [Friendly] "You see, I'm going over them now. . . . Now if you *were* there, then I want to know about it. . . . I want you to be perfectly honest with me because I'm going to be perfectly honest with you."

Harry: "I agreed to this and I'm going to be honest with you."

[Soft, easy] "Now if I ask you, 'Did you kill Dorothy Thompsen?' —would you have any problem answering that one?" I would say no. [Easy] "O.K. Is that the truth? . . . Because lots of people say this is a lie detector. Actually, it's a truth detector. . . . Do you know who did this down there?" No, I don't. "Do you suspect anyone?"

Harry volunteers that when Agnes Thompsen was accused he didn't feel it was possible. "I used to cut lawns for her. She didn't seem like the kind. [Affectionate, fatherly] She was *small—*"

The next question: "Did you remove the piggy bank from the Thompsen home?" This leads to interrogation about the bank (Harry cannot describe it), about Harry's allowance, about the ring.

Questions about how well he knew Dorothy: Did he ever have a date with her? . . . "No sir, I haven't been out with another girl than the one I have here. . . . There was one—and only one—for me."

The Letter again. Harry says that he read the details in the Hartford *Courant.* "So—I went right along with it. . . . And the way the talk goes around, you pick up other pieces. . . . I can't tell you, though . . . I don't remember anything in that letter."

Riemer appears to believe him implicitly. "Mmm. You didn't read the letter today?"

"I read the first few lines and then I couldn't read any more. He was going to read it to me and he only read the first few lines, too—"

Again the explanation that he wrote the Letter to divert suspicion. Now they wander far afield of the test, discussing Harry's predicament, and Riemer, assuming the role of concerned friend and counselor, delivers a long spellbinding monologue in an attempt to elicit a confession before giving the polygraph test. [Soft voice] "I'm sure that even without the letter eventually they would have asked you to take a test. . . . They never close one of these murder cases, you know. And eventually the person gets caught. Maybe the police don't catch him—maybe his own conscience catches up with him . . . [Compassionate] If a person made a mistake and lost his head—*we can understand this*—it's a little different than a guy who sticks up a bank and shoots people down in cold blood. [Explaining] You see, there's what we call a *crime of passion*. A person loses his head. Now if this is what happened, we could *understand* it, Harry, *believe* me . . . [Paternal] So just talking frankly to you— if you did this thing, better you clear it up, you see? Because eventually you'll be caught anyway. And it certainly would look a lot better for *everyone* concerned, if you were the man who did it—and made a mistake—and didn't know how to get out of it, to tell your side of the story—with no one telling you what to say. Better for all concerned, Harry—believe me."

Harry is silent—spellbound. Then, softly, "I wish I could—but I can't say I did that."

Riemer approves at once. "Harry, I wouldn't want you or anyone else to tell me that they did something when they didn't do it." Then a shift. "But I say this to you. For your own salvation, Harry— if you are involved, better you tell about it. It's going to hurt to start talking, but it's going to hurt to live all these years and look back. You're going to have children—you'll look at these children and you will think about this. It'll never escape you. And if something happened down there that day—and bingo!—better you get the thing out. [Evangelical] And then start your life over again from this day on. Be reborn again—on this day." A pause while the spell deepens. Riemer continues in the same soft sympathetic voice. "From this day on, you will think, 'Why didn't I get it cleared up?' . . . You're a good clean-living boy, Harry. You're not like a guy who'll stick up a bank and shoot 'em down. . . . Over there with Dorothy, that wasn't a premeditated crime. I know it wasn't."

Harry [dazed] "I—I told them everything I could think of."

"Yeah, but if you were involved—for your own *salvation* . . . You have to live with yourself, Harry. [Very sympathetic] I've talked to people here who've been involved in murder—and I have a real compassion for some of these people because they become involved and don't know how to get out of it. If they could only relive that moment again—and correct that little mistake they made. [Instructing him] The *big mistake* that a person makes, Harry, is *not admitting* to what he did. That's the mistake. Because the other part [dismissing the murder] is an error in judgment—but this is *cool, calculated* thought. Before, you did something in haste— bingo, it's done. But *now*—to sit there and say, *no—no*—[Shifting into high gear] And to think of all these people trusting in you— and believing in you. And what are you doing? You're *denying* their trust. . . . If you did this, Harry, and you think that, by saying it, you'll hurt them—no! You'll hurt them more by not telling the truth. [Pause; then, soft] My mother and father are both dead, but I wish to God that I could tell them the things I do wrong *yet*. What a comfort it is to talk to your parents."

Harry is mesmerized. "That's why I wanted to talk to them before."

"They want to know the truth, Harry. And even though you did this, they'll trust you and stick by you. This is what you're afraid of. . . . Your parents want you to take this test. . . . But, Harry, if you did this to Dorothy, you tell me about it right here and you call your Dad and say, 'Look, Pa, I don't want to take this test—I want to tell you.'"

[Waking up] "No, I want to take the test."

Riemer's voice is soft, almost caressing. "Harry, I want you to be sure before we go any farther. I want to give you the golden oppor- tunity—to show them that you're the boy, Harry, that they wanted to bring up and be their boy, Harry. Not somebody who had to be caught with a polygraph examination. [Sorrowful] They're always going to ask, '*Why wouldn't our boy trust us?* Why does he have to go through scientific devices? Doesn't he believe we'll stand by him?' [Pause] You only have your parents once in this life, Harry— and once they're gone you'll never have them back. There's nobody who can take their place."

Long silence. Harry [sobbing] "I—still have to say I didn't touch her."

"Harry, you have a wife who trusts you. You have a mother and father who trust you. [Soft, persuasive] Harry—I know what to do."

Harry [bewildered] "No-oo. I can't say I did it."

5:00. An hour has passed. Riemer has reviewed the polygraph questions and has asked other questions, too, and Harry has said that he heard the piggy bank was found by some hunters on Bushy Hill Road, that he doesn't know how the bank was opened. He has attempted to discuss the marks on his car. He still has not taken the test. Now Riemer goes out of the room, saying that he must telephone his wife, and Harry is left alone. Silence—broken only by deep sighs. Then, sitting there in the silent room, all alone, Harry begins to speak. [Soft whisper] "I didn't kill Dorothy Thompsen. No. I didn't kill her. [Softer] I didn't kill Dorothy Thompsen. I didn't kill her. Why don't they believe me? [Hushed] What does it mean?"

Riemer returns and at last Harry is given the first test. Between each important question there is a routine question—where was he born, where does he live, what is he wearing—with long pauses between each question.

The test:

—Last June 15, were you in the Thompsen house? "No."

—Last June 15, did you do anything to harm Dorothy Thompsen? "No."

—Did you ever hurt anyone physically? "Well, I might have, but not that way."

—Last June 15, did you remove a piggy bank from the Thompsen house? "No."

—Besides what we're talking about, did you tell any other serious lies? "Some."

—Are you withholding any information about Dorothy Thompsen's death? "Not that I can recall."

When the test is over, Riemer reminds Harry that he was supposed to answer only yes or no. "The first test was just to get you used to sitting here. . . . From here on it will count." He discusses the test and then goes out of the room again and again Harry is alone. In the silence we hear only the deep troubled sighs. (Are these the periods of respite to which Rebillard testified in the first trial: "He was left alone for five-minute periods—perhaps three times.")

5:30. The second test. The same questions. Then a third test—the same questions in a different order. After the third test Riemer lets Harry know that he didn't do too well. "Harry, there's a couple of spots here—" Mumbling, Harry asks what's wrong. "Well, there's a couple of questions here where you certainly take off . . . Harry, I want you to tell me the whole story. You haven't told me the truth. . . ."

5:45. Now the tests are finished and the serious interrogation begins. What happened on June 15? What was between you and Dorothy? Was she attracted to you—or wanted you?

Harry: "Ah-h, that's ridiculous."

"No, I've heard a lot of stories in here, believe me. . . . After a while, it's no longer, were you or did you? . . . The next step is *why?*"

And Harry is back where he was with Fuessenich.

Silence—a deep sigh—and he whimpers, "No, I didn't do nothin'! . . . I wasn't down that house that day . . . I didn't even see her that day . . . I didn't—I didn't have no *reason* to hurt her. No reason in the world."

"Harry—why these things happen *I* don't know. Was there something between the two of you—something that caused an argument?"

"There was nothing between us—and there were no arguments between us. I didn't even know the girl that well . . ."

"Harry—this *says* you're involved. . . . When I ask if you were at the house you certainly respond to that question. . . . Only two people know exactly what happened, Harry. She's dead. And the other person." And that *has* to be me? "You know if it's you."

Now Riemer, too, has taken a position of certainty. "That letter is certainly somebody trying to cover up what they did. . . . You lost your head, Harry. And I can understand it. . . . I want you to know I'm still your friend. . . . *You* have to live with what you've done. I don't. [Then, underscoring his certainty] I *know*, Harry.

Once that polygraph records what's going on in the inner man—in his soul—then I *know*."

"No, I—I don't want to argue—but I wasn't down that house."

[Bearing down] "Then what reason did you have to write that letter? You *had* to write that letter, Harry. I've studied psychiatry. You *had* to tell someone what you did . . . so you could cleanse your soul. That's why you wrote that letter." No—no, that's not right. "Certainly it is, Harry. I *know*. When people do things they *have* to talk to someone. I *know* this. . . . [Soft] I feel sorry for you, Harry."

Hope has died. Harry: "What happens now?"

"What happens depends on you, Harry. . . . You don't think these fellows in Canaan are going to stop this investigation?"

"No. I know they're not . . ."

6:00. "Well, may God forgive you, Harry."

Harry [simply] "I've known the Lord a good many years. I haven't felt guilty at anything like that. I know that letter was wrong, but the rest of it—I just—never felt wrong because I didn't do it."

[Showing him the polygraph] "You showed me there that you felt wrong. Every time I asked you that question, 'Are you withholding information?' I get a response. This is a recording of *you*, Harry."

Then, suddenly, a few minutes later, there is new hope. Harry says that he is all mixed up inside, and Riemer asks if he would be willing to come back another day for another test. Harry is astonished. "Would you trust me that much?"

"Certainly . . . I have great trust in you, Harry."

Harry asks eagerly if he can come back the next afternoon. "I don't want to hide nothing. . . . Do you trust me to go home?" I trust you. "Oh, I'll go home. I've got a wife and a kid coming. . . . We've been looking forward to that for many years." It is agreed that Harry will come back tomorrow after work.

Then: "Harry, I wish you'd be really honest with me. [Pause] It won't turn out any differently tomorrow. . . . There's no sense in prolonging it." When Harry is not persuaded, Riemer leaves again, and when he returns, he asks for a sample of Harry's hair. "Just so we can complete your part of the investigation. Just to be sure that you're completely clean." Harry agrees, signs a paper that he gave it voluntarily. The time is 6:23.

And still they remain, discussing arrangements for tomorrow. "But if I come up with the same thing I have here, Harry . . ."

Harry [worried] "Yeah, I know—"

"I'm really extending myself today. I'm doing this for you, Harry. Normally, I wouldn't even bother. . . . A lot depends on you, Harry—your wife, your unborn child . . ." A long silence. Worried, Harry asks what will happen if tomorrow it is the same. "They *will* prove the same if you are involved. . . . I didn't even ask you if you killed Dorothy Thompsen. I asked if you hurt her. . . . I don't think the person went there with the idea of killing this girl. He went there for another reason and then something happened. Harry, I would like to know what happened." Silence. Hope is dying again as Riemer picks up the interrogation and Harry's answers are inaudible. "Harry, a man comes in here and puts his hands out and says, 'Please help me.' My hand is out to you, Harry. I can understand."

There are only long silences now, and as Riemer gets no answers he continues. The time stretches on.

"A change comes over a person when he gets that lump out of *here*. [Soft, solicitous] They say, 'Bob, thanks for listening to me. I just didn't know where to start or who to tell.' It's like learning to walk. You have to take the first step. The first step is *why?*"

Harry: "I wish I could tell you that I did do it and then the reason why. But I can't. There's no reason why I should have done it."

"Harry—if I could answer *why* people do things, I could write a book. We don't know, y'see. [Shifting without a ripple] And how many people have I had say, 'If I could *only relive* that moment again.' But you can't. It's like a bad dream. But this isn't a dream, Harry. This happened. . . . I don't like to see people in your position—especially young people, who have a whole lifetime ahead of them. But I wouldn't envy you—having to live this whole lifetime carrying this weight around with you—Harry—"

"If I could only think straight . . . [Soft] What do you want me to say?"

"Harry, I want you to know—no matter how this turns out I'm

still your friend. Remember that. You can always call on me and I'll be your friend."

Long silence.

6:45. Riemer has reassured Harry again that he trusts him to return tomorrow. "I trust you . . . I believe you." [Then, spinning magic again] "*Why? Why* did that happen?" Silence. "Tell me *why*, Harry. I have to hear this from you—not from somebody else . . . I believe in going direct to the source. The source is you and I want you to tell me *why*." Silence [Soft] "You *want* to tell me, Harry. . . . Get it off your chest, Harry. . . . It's lying there like a big lump of dough right in your stomach. I want to relieve that feeling. I want you to tell me *why*." Silence. "Harry—tell me *why*. And then we won't talk about it if you don't want to, but just tell me *why*." Silence. "Just tell me *why* it happened, Harry. I won't ask you a lot of questions. I just want to know *why*."

Harry struggles against the spell. "I don't know. I wasn't down there."

"Well, Harry, when I say to you *why*, it's because I believe you were there. I want to know *why* did it happen."

"Are you asking me why was I down there or why did I kill her?"

"Why did you kill her, Harry—?"

"I wasn't down there. I had no reason."

"Harry—didn't I say whoever killed her had no reason when he walked in—?"

Harry: "You still have to have some kind of a motive. Right?"

Riemer pauses a moment. "There's such a thing as temporary insanity. But we have to know *why* did it happen, Harry. A person goes—[snap]—like that—momentarily . . ."

Here the tape ends abruptly. Harry's lawyers were told that there was approximately another five minutes of interrogation that night.

◆

Harry went home with his family and the next day after work he returned to Hartford Headquarters.

The interrogation begins at about 5:00 with a replay of yesterday. Riemer: "If you weren't there, Harry, I don't want you to tell me

THE REST OF THE STORY

you were. . . . If you weren't there, no one in the world can ever say you were. Remember that." Then, "If there's anything that you haven't told us, this is what I want to talk to you about now." He offers Harry food and Harry refuses. He reviews the polygraph questions—the same ones as yesterday. Then, as yesterday, the test is forgotten in favor of interrogation with questions again about the Letter, the ring, Harry's savings account, and whether he went to the Thompsen house that day.

After about fifteen minutes there is a new twist. "Harry, if you just stopped by there and saw this—the end results of this—and then you took off . . . this is what I want to know."

Now a fleeting hint of the memory lapse. Riemer says that surely if Harry saw her—and saw the state the house was in—he would remember that and, very weakly, Harry replies, "Yeah—" Riemer: *Wouldn't you?* Harry [vague, uncertain] "Oh-h—yeah."

A few minutes later the first polygraph test—the same questions as yesterday—and then Riemer interprets the results to show Harry that he is lying. The interrogation begins again. "What do you know about that death, Harry, that we haven't talked about? . . . About you and Dorothy—were you ever close? . . . Did you ever kiss her?"

"*Never!* . . ." Harry says that he was never alone with Dottie—nor with Arnfin, either, except for one time when he got hurt. Asked what happened, he replies, "Gee, that's a funny question because I can't answer it! I fell two flights down the chimney. And I was knocked out. The only thing I remember is coming to and him pushing me up the ladder. Otherwise I didn't know a thing that was going on—where I was—" (Is it possible that Harry suffered brain damage in this fall? Would this account for his mental confusion and his extremely bad memory about ordinary events?)

Another plodding half-hour. Harry tries to talk about that most troublesome enigma, the markings on his car. Then he is given a different lie-detector test, this time about the piggy bank. The questions: "On June 15, did you take the piggy bank from the kitchen counter? From the kitchen table? From the hearth of the fireplace? From the bedroom dresser in Dorothy's room? From the dresser in Christa's room?" To each question Harry answers no. The test is repeated twice.

Then, in the same conversational tone Riemer slips into interrogation about the piggy bank: Harry, do you know how the piggy bank was opened? [Long pause] "Hmmph! Seems to me I was told that!" Through the top? Through the side? Through the bottom? [Another long pause] "I don't know. I'm just thinking. They probably put the money through the top—or the side . . . and there's usually something on the bottom to open it up. That's the way with my bank, anyhow." Do you know whether it was made of metal, china—? "No, I don't know." Whether they smashed it with a hammer, or pried it open with a screwdriver or cut it with a knife? "I don't know. [Weary] How much longer will this take here?"

Again, as yesterday, Riemer goes out of the room, ostensibly to make a telephone call. It is about 6:00. And Harry is alone again—silent, heaving deep sighs. Then, as before, all alone, he speaks—very softly. "I didn't touch her. [Despair] Why me? *Why me?* [Anguish] Goddammit!"

At this point apparently the tape recorder was switched to a slower speed. Played back at the regular speed (3¾) the voices are garbled. It is difficult to calculate how much time is lost. When the tape becomes clear again, Harry's attitude has undergone a change! The first words are Riemer's. ". . . I told you last night. The man who puts his hand out gets help. This is like coming into the world again. You have to be reborn."

And Harry's reply! "If I told you I did do it, it's not because I did. I couldn't say that. The only reason I'd say I was guilty was because maybe then I'd get off in a little while."

(This is the first time we have heard the word "guilty," the first reference that we have heard to the possibility of serving time in prison.)

Riemer: "I want you to tell me exactly what you did in that house . . . Did you black out?" Then, "You'd be willing to admit it and take a chance on getting time? That'd be very foolish, Harry."

"I love my wife."

"Then you owe it to her to tell the truth."

[Crying out] "Then the truth would send me up for life! If I said I didn't do it and the evidence is against me, then there it is."

"Harry, if you didn't do it, I want you to promise me—never admit it."

"I can't say that. That's what my wife said last night. I can't say that. Supposing this says I did it and I insisted I didn't do it!"

"Harry, if you didn't do it, they'll never prove you did."

"Why not!"

A corner has been turned.

For two days interrogators have impressed Harry with the overwhelming scientific evidence against him. Now comes another blow. "Harry, there was a hair in her hand. If it's not yours, that's it—you're clear. But it's not hers, it's not Arnfin's, it's not Agnes's, it's not Christa's. . . . That hair has gone to Washington. If it's your hair, that's it. . . . Harry, was it your hair?"

"I don't see how . . . [Puzzled] There's no way it can be mine."

"They have a big machine in Washington. The FBI has it. If it's yours, that's just another link. Then later if you say, 'Well, I did it and here's why,' they'll say, 'He only told because we had him—not because he's sorry.' I think you are sorry, Harry."

"About the letter, yes."

"This is the time for you to tell me the whole story, Harry. . . . You can be caught through scientific evidence. . . . We won't know about the hair for a week or two. . . ."

Harry: "I want to call my wife and tell her what's happening. . . . I don't care what I go through but—"

Riemer continues on his own course. "If you were the judge or the prosecutor, and a man did something and it bothered him so much he wanted to tell about it—wouldn't you feel compassion?" Would it make any difference? "You think of the logical conclusion. . . . The person who admits what he did or the person who got caught through scientific evidence? . . ."

"We all have to face the final judgment day, Harry." I can't say I did it because I didn't. "Harry, when you meet your Maker, will you be able to stand up and say you didn't do it?"

Harry [quietly] "Yes . . . We prayed last night. All four of us. And in my heart I felt me and Somebody Else had close communication. And I asked for forgiveness about the letter. But I had nothing to do with Dorothy Thompsen's dying."

Riemer: "If I said they wouldn't put you in prison for life, would that make a difference, Harry?"

Harry cries out, "I don't know how my family would be taken care of!"

Today Riemer is touching all the same sensitive areas—scientific proof, religious retribution, and Harry's obligation to his family—but with added intensity. "Whatever else you tell me, you still have to back it up."

"I can't back it up. I don't know what happened."

"Then maybe scientific evidence will back it up. . . . Harry, if the hair is the same, that's it. We have the hair and we have a sample of yours, which you gave me *voluntarily* yesterday. . . . Is there any reason your hair would be there?"

[Mumbling] "Just if she pulled it out."

"Now I'm not fooling, Harry, when I say we've got yours and it'll be back. . . . It takes time but the truth will out. . . . [Sadly] I spent a lot of time with you, Harry. I wanted to help you. I wanted to listen to your story. . . . When the time comes they'll say, 'Was this man given an opportunity to confess?' "

[Miserable] "I want to tell you—just for the sake of my people being all right."

[Comforting] "Your people'll be all right, Harry. . . . They are the ones who have a right to know. They're the ones bearing a cross. [Soft, sorrowful] Your mother bore you, carried you, took care of you all these years. Now you're letting her down. You let her down first last June 15. Don't let her down again on March 14, Harry."

Harry [sobbing] "I didn't touch her! I didn't!"

"You owe it to your family, Harry. You're going to put them through a lot of bother. A man's family wants to believe him. Harry, it's more of a wrongdoing to mislead a trusting family. They have such trust in you. And you lie to them . . . That's the tragedy, Harry. [Deep sorrow] The family. The trust they've put in you. To betray that trust is worse than the actual crime. . . . Think about it."

"I've *been* thinking—all last night. [Long silence; sobbing] I wasn't going to work today. I wanted to think some more. But I figured you'd be after me."

"Well, the hair is going to be the clincher. There's nothing we can do to change that. If that hair isn't yours, that puts you away from the place. If it is yours, Harry, nothing in the world can save you."

Harry: "Let's go downstairs and find out what happens. I can't sit here no longer."

Again Riemer suggests that Harry didn't intend to hurt her: "When they hurt you first, you have to defend yourself."

Harry: "No-oo! Not that way!"

"Somebody grabs you by the hair."

[Shocked] "That's pretty hard to swallow. Something like that could come out because someone pulled your hair!"

"You have two choices, Harry. Either you went there and an argument broke out . . . or you went there and said this is what's going to happen. . . . The hair will be the clinching factor, Harry."

And Harry still protests. "I didn't argue with her. I wasn't there. I didn't touch her . . . I'm *positive.*"

Once more Harry says that if he said he did it, it would only be for the sake of his wife and his expected child—so that he might get a small sentence, and again Riemer tells him that that would be foolish. But Harry is very low. "But then, if I keep insisting that I didn't, like I am now, and all this here—"

Riemer is quick to underscore the feeling of hopelessness: There was a car there—and a blond fellow got out of it. And there was the hair in her hand. And the piggy bank was found close to Harry's house. And he wrote the Letter. All those things are facts. "The scientific evidence tripped you up on the letter and the scientific evidence will have to trip you up on the rest of it."

7:00 [two hours]. "I've wasted a lot of time with you, Harry. . . . I always thought Norwegians were men. I've had other Norwegians in here. They all said, 'When I do something wrong, *I* pay.' *You're* making your family pay, Harry."

A long silence. Harry murmurs that he is dizzy again, and Riemer offers him a sandwich, but Harry wants only to call his wife. Riemer goes back to the hair. "If it's your hair, they're not going to care *why* then. They'll say, 'He was in the house . . . his hair is *in her hand.* How did it get there? [Bearing down] He *killed* her—that's how. She was struggling for her very life.' . . . Later you'll be trying to soften the blow. Well, they're not going to be in a buying mood."

Harry [plaintive] "I don't understand. You told me that if I wasn't involved there was only one way to get out—tell the truth."

"If you're not involved, don't ever say you were, Harry. [Then, injured] I've spent a lot of time with you, Harry. I think I deserve to hear the truth. I don't want to read it tomorrow in the papers. I deserve to hear it."

Long, long silences. Riemer is moving from one tactic to another. He shows the polygraph results again. "Are you going to let poor Agnes Thompsen take the brunt of this?" (Very long silence. Deep sighs and heavy sobbing.) "Harry, you *know* I've got the truth."

Harry protests that it must show something else. "Not the truth about me doing that . . . because I didn't do it."

Back to the hair—and now there is a transition from question to certainty about it. "The next time I talk to you, maybe the question will be: How did your hair get in her hand? . . . Harry—how did your hair get into her hand?" Silence. "How *did* your hair get into her hand? *How*, Harry?"

[Bewildered] "There's no answer. How could it be?"

"If it isn't yours, you can say, 'You see, I told you it wasn't.' But if it *is*, how will you explain it?"

"I can't!"

[Whip-fast] "You betcha you can't. How you gonna explain that one?"

[Holding on] "What if I don't—have to explain it?"

"If you don't, that will certainly put you away from there at the time of death. [Then the switch] There should be no doubt, Harry. *I* don't have to explain. It's not mine. Lieutenant Fuessenich don't have to explain. It's not his. Fred Rebillard don't have to explain. It's not his. But how about Harry?"

[Holding tight] "I'm puzzled . . . it can't be because I hurt her."

"Then why are you afraid it will be your hair in her hand?"

"I'm sure it *can't* be."

"You're *denying* it's your hair?"

"It *can't* be."

[Hard] "O.K. So when the lab report says, 'That's Harry Solberg's hair,' I'm just to presume that you're a killer. A *killer*. Not just a person who got involved in an argument, but a killer."

Harry [begging] "Let's go across the hall—"

"Your car was at the house. The piggy bank was found near your house. *Your hair was in her hand.* These are the facts."

Harry: "I want to call my wife."

It is nearly 8:00 when Riemer returns to the suggestion first made nearly three hours ago. "If you walked in and saw her and now you're afraid to tell us. . . . There she was and you saw her and thought, 'Let me out of here—' and ran. Is this what happened? 'Get out fast before they think it's you . . . Boy, I'd better write a letter.' Is that what happened?"

Harry still denies it.

Eight o'clock has come and gone and now only Riemer is speaking, in long monologues. When he stops there is silence. Or a quick whisper: "I didn't kill her."

"Well, then, what happened, Harry?" Silence. "I want to believe you, but what happened?" Silence. "Harry, are you telling *me* nothing happened? [Wounded] I spent *hours* with you—of my own time. Yesterday was my day off. I came in here. And tonight I'm staying here again . . . because I wanted to help you. But you get just this close to letting me help you, Harry, and then you shy away. [Soft, persuasive] Tell me what happened, Harry."

"N-nothing happened."

"You're denying me, Harry. You denied a friend. . . . Tell me the way you would tell your father—your confessor—your priest—minister—" Now the silences are very long. Riemer continues [soft, hypnotic] "Harry—tell me, Harry. In your own words. What happened? Just get started and it'll fall like water over a waterfall. And how much better you'll feel—just to talk with somebody you can trust!"

Then suddenly, as though hypnotized, Harry speaks. "We had an economics report due at school—"

Quietly the first part of the story, that we were to hear in Court months later, comes out. Harry's subject was marketing and he had asked Arnfin for information and Arnfin never called him.

"So that day on the way home from the lawn mower I stopped in. . . . The door was open . . . and I knocked . . . and the baby was crying, so I walked in an'—" He falters. Riemer prompts him to continue. [Distressed] "Then I saw blood on the kitchen floor—" He stops, remains mute, drawing very deep breaths. Riemer urges him to continue. Silence. Then [dazed; deep, distressed breathing] "Well—then I seen that it led into the living room and out on the porch—" The words are dragging, coming hard. "And I seen her on the ground. She was still alive. I went to pick her up. She was too full of fight."

"Then what happened?"

"Oh, I ran. [Whisper] I ran."

Quickly Riemer asks about the bank.

[Dazed whisper] "No, I didn't touch the bank. I didn't touch the bank."

"What happened—if she was too full of fight?"

[Same] "I just ran . . . I tried to pick her up." Riemer presses him: Where was she when you tried to pick her up? "Outside." Did you do anything to her? [Whisper] "No." Where did you go? [Faint, bewildered] "I don't know." Did you ever tell anyone about that, Harry? Harry's answer is a whisper, inaudible.

"Harry, you've got to tell someone the truth."

Suddenly the spell is broken. Sobs burst from Harry and his voice goes to a wail. *"It's not going to go over! It's not going to go over!"*

Riemer attempts to quiet him.

"No, I can't sit down no more—not no more. [Wailing] I just don't want to hurt my mother."

Deep guttural sobs rise to another frustrated wail. "It all sounds so *corny!*"

"No, it isn't corny, Harry."

The words rush out. "I was even going to head down to Granby. Because I knew an officer—State Police—" The sobs increase and the words are lost.

Riemer tries to stay with the story. "You walked into the house— and what was the first thing you saw?"

"I walked in through the hall. And I kept asking if there was anybody home and the baby was crying—" The story of the report repeated—he handed in another report, anyway. Riemer holds fast to the story: She was alive when she was out there on the ground? "She was still fightin'." Well, who was she fighting? What did she say? [Hushed; dazed] "She didn't say nothing. She didn't even look at me." Did you touch the toaster? "I don't remember whether there was a toaster or not."

Riemer [not unkindly] "Harry, she was pretty well beat-up . . .

and stabbed and hung off that thing. I'm sure they thought she was dead when she was on the ground."

Harry repeats in a dazed whisper, "She was fighting."

A full five-minute silence.

Riemer wants to get this story down on paper—and here is the "first statement" that Mr. Shew stumbled on in the first trial. It takes Harry about ten minutes to write the one paragraph. Riemer tells him to write that the statement is voluntary. The time is 8:27 P.M.

It is done. Riemer: "Is this the truth now, Harry? Because I'm probably going to have to give you another test. Have you told me the whole truth?"

Harry [dully] "There's parts I don't remember." Like what? "I don't remember what the house looked like. I don't remember where I was or what I did. After that I—[pause] I know I didn't hurt her or anything."

"Harry—look. If you *did* hurt her, at the beginning, I told you I understood. Y'understand?"

"No, I don't."

"Now, Harry, is this the whole story?"

[Whisper] "Yes."

(*Could* Harry Solberg, unschooled, unsophisticated, who took six years to get through high-school, possibly have dreamed up this classic case of traumatic amnesia?)

With the statement behind him, Riemer gives it another try: Harry, I've talked to you like a brother. . . . What actually happened? How did she get stabbed? "I don't know. I just seen her there." Did you stab her? [Mumbling; tired] "No—no, I didn't stab her . . . there was no reason . . . but I just—I just had to run—out of there."

"Well, you say she was full of fight—on the ground outside. The doctor said she was dead. . . . So if she was full of fight, it was before she was on the ground."

[Dully] "She was on the ground."

He does not remember what clothes he was wearing—he must have changed out of his school clothes because he was going for the lawn mower. A mumbled effort to repeat that story, and Riemer gives up for now, tells Harry he will see if the men from Canaan are here. In a whimper Harry asks, "Can I go home?" Riemer, impersonal now, explains that all he does is the polygraph work.

Then [curious] "Harry, you knew that I knew yesterday. Why did you come back today?"

[Simply] "Because you trusted me."

"That's right. And you trusted me. [Picking up the beat again] Was I kidding you yesterday, Harry? No. And I'm not kidding you today. And I won't be kidding you the next time I ask you questions about this. . . . Now there's more to the story yet, isn't there?"

[Mumbling] "Probably. I can't remember. I didn't hurt her though."

Long silence.

[Warning] "Don't forget the hair . . ."

Then Harry is alone again. And again, first there is a long silence. Then Harry's voice comes in an agonized whisper. "*I need help . . . I need help.*" Hope is dead. "*Always love me, Sharon.*"

This is the end of taped interrogation in Hartford. On the final Court day, Rebillard testified that there was more interrogation which was not taped, before they left for Canaan. Fuessenich testified that Harry was placed under arrest that night in Hartford at about 9:30.

•   •   •

They left Hartford and stopped at the Solberg home where Harry spoke to his wife and to his parents. On the next tape they are back in Canaan. The time appears to be somewhere between 11:30 and 11:45. (This interrogation lasts for approximately one-half hour and appears to go immediately into the "confession" interrogation, which began at 12:13 A.M., Tuesday, March 15.) Fuessenich is the interrogator. Sam Holden is present. And a completely different story is coming from Harry!

Fuessenich's manner is the same—crisp and authoritative. "All right. Now, you're going to tell me some more. Tell me what happened."

Harry sounds hopeless and very tired. His voice is soft, his tone is dull as he describes parking his car and going to the front door. ". . . And she let me in . . ." (!)

"Who let you in?"

"Dottie."

Fuessenich does not reveal the slightest reaction to this extremely significant alteration in Harry's story—not a pause, not a flicker of change in the inflection of his voice. One has a strong impression that he has heard it before. In a completely matter-of-fact tone he continues with a most prosaic question: Was anyone else there? This time Harry says that he does not remember hearing the baby. "And then what happened after she let you in?"

Harry [deep sigh] "Things must have snapped. I don't know. I don't remember what happened."

For a few minutes Harry's story is the story of the first statement. In very brief replies to question after question he says that the next thing he remembers is climbing up the ladder. From the porch he just went out and went home. He does not remember the route he took through the house to the front door. "I can't say positive. Either through the kitchen or the living room. I can't say."

"What happened while you were going through the living room or the dining room or whatever you went through?"

[Dull, mechanical] "I guess I took the piggy bank."

Now he has information about the bank. Here are his answers, eked out a word at a time. Fuessenich begins by asking the approximate size. "Uh—big." How big? "Maybe a foot and a half long . . . eight inches, nine inches tall . . . plastic . . . pink . . . about sixteen dollars in change . . ." Then, mechanically, he recites a longer speech: "After I got home the piggy bank was still in the car and it wasn't till the day after that I disposed of the bank." (Is *dispose* a word that Harry would use spontaneously?) He says that he threw it out through the car window, on the passenger side, in Granby.

How did you get the money out of the bank? [Quick whisper] "I cut the top." With what? "Either a knife or scissors. I don't remember." Did you slit the bank? "No—just cut a loop, I guess." How big? "Oh, I don't know—I don't remember."

"Now—what happened after Dottie let you in?"

[Whisper] "I don't remember."

Harry repeats again—he never wavers on this—that the reason he went to the house was the economics paper. Asked when he talked to Arnfin, he says, "I hadn't talked to him. He was supposed to call me 'cause he was working late every night." (This was *before* Arnfin's personal life came out at the trial.) "His wife was going to give me the information."

Concerning the Letter. "I don't remember that whole letter, neither. Just—" He recites again the few details that Rebillard read to him. "I won't deny anything that *was* in the letter, but—"

Fuessenich asks: Do you remember describing anything that happened *in* the house? "No, I don't." Anything that happened *outside* the house? "No, I can't remember." Do you remember describing about taking Dottie from the house to the outside? "No, I don't remember what I wrote in there."

[Stern] "Harry—"

[Weary] "I'm not fooling around. You—you guys got it straight —" (When did he hear their version?)

"We've got it straight but we want to make sure that you remember."

"Yeah, but I *don't* remember."

[Impatient anger] "You *do* remember. You remembered afterwards—enough to write the letter. . . . This is important—that we find out from you exactly what happened and the reason why it happened."

"Yes, but I don't *know* the reason why. . . . Why did the rest happen?"

Again Fuessenich suggests that there was something more than friendship between him and Dottie, and Harry denies it. "You've got everything else. Why should I try to hide that now . . . ?"

The interrogation proceeds at an even, unemotional pace. It is interesting primarily for the information Harry gives—for the first time, after two days—and for the way he qualifies his statements. Fuessenich attempts to get corroborating details about the crime, asking many of the same questions that Rome asked Agnes Thompsen six months ago. Harry's most frequently repeated words are still, "I don't know—I don't remember." And, "I must have done that but I don't remember. . . . I know because I read it in the papers. . . . You just told me."

Fuessenich brings up the hammer. "What happened to the hammer?"

Harry: "What hammer?—Oh! The sledgehammer? [In bits and pieces] I threw it in the woods . . . in the back of the house . . . just a regular sledgehammer." He does not remember how long the handle was or whether he had to use two hands. It was on the porch . . . he does not know where he picked it up—or when—or how far he threw it.

Did you give it a hard heave or did you toss it off the porch? [Soft] "I threw it. [Long pause] I threw it." Was it quite a distance away or close to the porch? "I don't know. I just threw it." In which direction? "Just back."

Fuessenich brings up the *fork:* "How about the fork? Where'd that come from?"

[Puzzled; soft] "What fork?" [He seems to be struggling to remember; still puzzled, weak] "What fork is that?" Either. Any forks. Where'd they come from? [No answer. Talking to himself, as though trying to help himself remember the answer] "*What fork?*"

Then he remembers. "Oh—nn—nn—the meat fork. . . . It was laying on the counter." (This is beginning to sound like an effort to get through a poorly learned school lesson.)

Fuessenich asks which counter, gets no answer, attempts to lead him by asking if there was a sink in that kitchen and whether there was a counter near it. Harry replies that of course there was a sink and that, if there's a sink, there's a counter. It does not seem to jog his memory. Fuessenich: "Do you remember any more about the meat fork?"

"No, I'll tell you—I was in the house—[faltering] I just remember going in the house. [Hesitates] And—and I remember climbing up the ladder." (Nothing here about Dorothy opening the door.)

Fuessenich mentions the *toaster.* Harry does not remember it. "I remember a lot about it after I read it in the papers, but that's all I remembered."

Do you remember anything about a *cord?* "She was strangled with a cord, but I don't remember from that. I just remember something about it, that's all."

The Letter again. He remembers writing the Letter.

"Do you remember anything about *another fork?*"

"I only remember parts of it. [Sigh] A couple of days after I didn't remember anything until I started to read it—and then it started to come back to me." (Months before Dr. Von Salzen's testimony!)

Fuessenich: "Do you remember anything about a *stone?*"

"Just that I wrote it in the letter . . . that I hit her with a stone." What kind? [Whisper] "I don't remember." A big stone or a little stone? "Easy enough to pick up, I guess." Did it take one hand or two hands? "I don't remember. It must have been heavy . . . I wanted to do a job . . . Hit her in the head."

Do you remember using the *hammer?* "I know there was one. I don't remember doing anything with it." Do you remember about *wrapping a cord about anything* out there? "No, I don't remember what happened to the cord." What was the cord on? [Perplexed] "You just told me a toaster." What did you use the cord for? "I guess I must have strangled her." In what manner? "The papers said it looked like—somebody made it—tried to make it look like a suicide. . . . I don't remember. I just don't remember what happened."

The piggy bank. Where did he find it? "I don't remember that, neither, but I know I took it." Harry tries to reason out the answer as though he would get a better grade for coming up with something. He can only remember being in the kitchen and the living room. "I must have been—on the way out—the living room is about the shortest way I can think of . . . When I was upstairs in the other room, he said he thought it was on the hearth by the fireplace. [Pause.] I guess that's where I must have gotten it."

The effort at corroborating details does not improve. Harry does not remember what Dottie was wearing, does not remember any conversation with her. He guesses the time as "the later part of the afternoon"; then figures out, by going through the whole story of the school bus, the plumbing truck, and the lawn mower, that it was about two o'clock.

How long were you there? [Sigh] "I don't remember that, either. It went so fast. It was like a dream." How did he get down to the ground? "If the ladder was there I must have climbed down." He doesn't remember whether Dottie was alive at that time. "I don't remember getting down. I remember climbing up the ladder."

And here the interrogation ends as Fuessenich says he will call in a stenographer to get this down. A final word of advice to Harry. "Harry . . . if you get it all off your chest, you can relax and say, 'Look, I've told them everything I know—' "

Mournfully Harry says, "It doesn't work. I've tried it but it doesn't work."

.   .   .

And that is the path—over two days—that led to the "confession." The "confession"-interrogation (page 143), it turns out, is nothing more than a repeat of the immediately preceding dress rehearsal. Nothing new is added. The impression from the tapes is quite different from the one created by the vigorous reading Mr. Roberts gave in Court. Harry's tone is dull and mechanical, bewildered, very slow at times. There are long pauses and heavy sighs.

Especially noticeable is this passage:

"Why are you here, Harry?"

His answer is a whispered monotone. "Because I am accused of killing Dottie Thompsen."

"Did you?"

[Sigh; silence. Weak] "Do I have to answer that right now?"

"Don't you want to answer it right now?"

"No. [Fast, frightened] I killed her. That's what you want."

"Is that the truth?"

[Long silence] "That's my *answer*."

"Is that the truth?"

[Long silence] "That's my *answer*."

"Is that the truth?"

[Dull] "I can only give you my answer."

"What is your answer?"

[Blurts out] "I killed her."

Throughout the confession, although he is ready to say anything, Harry repeats that he remembers nothing—that everything he knows is what he read in the papers or was told by the police during the interrogations.

.   .   .

But there is more!

When the tapes were played by order of the Court for Harry's attorneys, they ended with the confession. Out of curiosity, after listening to the confession, I turned over the tape—and discovered that there was still another interrogation! Mr. Shew and Mr. Mc-Keon had no hint of this—were astonished to learn that it took place. This interrogation lasts about three quarters of an hour. The location seems to be Harry's jail cell.

There is a new interrogator, unidentified, with a rather hard, harsh voice. Harry sounds exhausted. "I can't think anymore tonight. Maybe in the morning I'll remember more. I just can't think anymore."

Nevertheless the interrogation begins, and the interrogator inquires about his relationship with Dottie. "Did you ever have intercourse with Dottie?"

[Indignant] "Never! I never had intercourse with anyone except my wife—and not with her until we were married."

"Did the thought ever occur to you that you'd like to have Dottie?" (This is not a subtle man.) Wearily Harry denies it. The interrogator stays with it. "Did she ever make a pass at you? Did you ever make one at her?" Getting nowhere, he is already losing patience. "Goddammit! You just don't do things like this without a reason, Harry. This isn't something you do every day of the week. Then why?"

"I can't answer that. [Weary] There's nothing to hide anymore. . . . I can't remember what happened."

You don't remember what happened in the kitchen? There was evidence of a very violent struggle. *Why?* [Harry is at the edge of tears] "I don't know why. There's no reason to hold back now. I don't know what happened in that place the whole time. I don't remember."

"How the hell could you *forget* it?"

More questions: Did she say something to make you mad? Did she call you any names? Did she abuse you? Did you call *her* any names? Harry's answer remains the same: I can't remember. "You know you did it but you don't know why?"

"That's right. And I don't remember *how* I did it—"

[Interrupting; overbearing] "You *told* how you did it."

"I know what I used, but I can't remember doing it."

A stream of questions about details of the crime. Harry thinks the first thing he used was the meat fork . . . doesn't remember where he jabbed her . . . says they told him there was a toaster cord . . . [Plaintively] "There's no sense in hiding nothing no more now. I can't remember."

[Hard] "Harry, I think you've remembered this for the past nine months—day and night." Long, long silence. "That's as vivid in your mind as the nose on your face. . . . Man, you've got a conscience . . . and it's been bothering you, hasn't it?" No answer.

(This interrogation has been going on for twenty minutes.)

"You'll *never* erase that. You know when you'll erase that? When they lay you out on the table. Your conscience isn't going to give you a moment's peace. And you better believe it."

Even in the face of this verbal assault—and tired as he is—Harry does not supply any more information. Then Rebillard comes in and the first interrogator leaves. Rebillard's manner is still the same— soft-spoken, patient, detached. At his first question, Harry succumbs suddenly to tears. ". . . Just the part where I killed her, but I can't remember why I did it or how I did it—"

Rebillard: "How do you know you killed her, Harry?"

"Because all the evidence says I did! I don't remember doing it!"

"Harry, is the reason you went there so terrible that you're afraid to tell anyone?"

"No. [Harry's words are beginning to run together] I can't tell you any more tonight, I'm too tired. Please. [Whisper] I can't no more tonight." Harry—we put our trust in you. "And I put my trust in you—and *I told you what you wanted*. [A minute later] I can't take it anymore. I'm too tired." Just another five minutes, Harry. "Tomorrow's another day. You can drill me all day again then. I can't talk anymore tonight." Harry—. "*No*." Harry—. "*No*. I can't talk anymore tonight."

A vulnerable spot: Is it something involving your wife? Is that why you're holding back on us?

Harry snaps back. "*What?* [Sharper] Something involving my wife. *What do you mean by that?* [Demanding] I want to *know*. *Involving what?* . . . She had *nothing to do* with what happened."

Harry, would you remember a loud scream?

"A loud scream? No. I'm not going to answer no more tonight . . . I'm tired and I gotta get some sleep." Harry—aren't you ashamed to tell me—[Bursting out] "You can say that again. I'm ashamed of everything that's happened. . . . I'm not going to answer any more questions tonight. . . . I'm tired and I want to think." Did she scream when you stabbed her? "She *must* have."

Did you hear her? "I can't remember. I must have heard her if she screamed. But I can't remember. . . . What's the *difference?* If I could remember, why shouldn't I tell you? . . . I've told you everything else in the last two hours. . . . [Pleading] Let me talk to you in the morning. I can't *think* no more now. . . . Let me get some sleep, huh?"

"Do you think you'll remember better in the morning, Harry?"

"I can't promise you that, neither. If I promise, I'll keep it. And I can't. 'Cause I don't know."

"Was she facing you? . . . Do you remember the look on her face? . . . You *do* know, Harry. . . . Five minutes, Harry . . . and you can clear your soul of everything. . . . We put an awful lot of faith in you, Harry, and you're letting us down on the most important part."

Harry [suddenly] "I appreciate you taking me to see my wife, too. *I told you that I'd tell you everything else before I went. . . .* I know I killed her. *Everything's against me. The letter. The polygraph test. The car.* But I can't remember what went on in the house."

"If I showed you a picture would you remember?"

"I don't know. Maybe in the morning. But I can't promise I can tell you what happened in that house. Because I can't remember. If that's gonna make you sit down again, you'll have to, because I can't promise that I can tell you."

Rebillard gives up. He tells Harry to take off his coat, asks if he has his Bible, says he will talk to him in the morning.

In the morning the Public Defender told Harry to say no more— and the interrogation of Harry Solberg ended.